## Praise for *Master of the Game*

"It's fair to say [Bruck] has come to know Ross better than he knew himself. . . . Such a man is the groundsoil of a great book . . delicious."
—*The Washington Post*

"Nothing short of dazzling"                    —*Chicago Tribune*

"*Master of the Game* [is] truly must reading, literally indispensable for investors and all who care about what people are made of, and what society has become."                    —*Barron's*

"Fast-paced . . a fine book about a man exceptional in his reach, his extravagance and his deceit."                    —*Hartford Courant*

"Bruck artfully reconstructs Mr. Ross's rise . . . *Master of the Game* is at its most compelling when [she] explores the way Ross lived his life, conducted his personal affairs, and catapulted himself into the big leagues."
—*The Wall Street Journal*

"What makes *Master of the Game* so compelling is the skill with which Bruck captures the tension between Ross's magnetism and his enormous moral flaws, without reducing him to either "    —*Elle*

"Bruck honors her obligation to the truth and to readers, however painful that sometimes may be."                    —*Esquire*

"[The] revealing portrait of Ross—alternately attractive and (mostly) repellent—makes this book fascinating."                    —*San Francisco Chronicle*

"By the time you finish reading Connie Bruck's book . . . you're ready for a nice long shower. . . . Are there any good guys in this intermittently juicy tale?"                    —*Newsweek*

PENGUIN BOOKS

MASTER OF THE GAME

Connie Bruck is also the author of *The Predators' Ball*. She is a staff writer for *The New Yorker*. Her articles have also appeared in *The Atlantic*, *The American Lawyer*, *The Washington Post*, and *The New York Times*. She has received numerous awards, including a 1991 National Magazine Award. She lives in New York City.

# MASTER OF THE GAME

Steve Ross
and the
Creation of
Time Warner

# CONNIE BRUCK

PENGUIN BOOKS

PENGUIN BOOKS
Published by the Penguin Group
Penguin Books USA Inc , 375 Hudson Street, New York, New York 10014, U S A
Penguin Books Ltd, 27 Wrights Lane, London W8 5TZ, England
Penguin Books Australia Ltd, Ringwood, Victoria, Australia
Penguin Books Canada Ltd, 10 Alcorn Avenue, Toronto, Ontario, Canada M4V 3B2
Penguin Books (N Z ) Ltd, 182–190 Wairau Road, Auckland 10, New Zealand

Penguin Books Ltd, Registered Offices: Harmondsworth, Middlesex, England

First published in the United States of America by Simon & Schuster, 1994
Reprinted by arrangement with Simon & Schuster
Published in Penguin Books 1995

THE LIBRARY OF CONGRESS HAS CATALOGUED THE HARDCOVER AS FOLLOWS:
Bruck, Connie
Master of the game: Steve Ross and the creation of Time Warner/Connie Bruck
p   cm
Includes index
ISBN 0-671-72574-2 (hc )
ISBN 0 14 02 4454 9 (pbk )
1 Ross, Steve, 1927–1992   2 Mass media—United States—Biography
3 Time Warner, Inc   I Title
P92 5R67M37   1994
302 23´4´092—dc20   [B]   93–48609

Printed in the United States of America
Set in ITC Garamond Light
Designed by Levavi & Levavi
Photo research by Natalie Goldstein

for my mother,
Edith Bruck

# Prologue

Steve Ross would have loved his funeral, his friends and family later agreed. Its planning, however, had provoked the usual dissension. His grown children, Mark Ross and Toni Ross, wanted to have a private family ceremony, and a memorial service later for that other "family" of thousands: all the friends Ross had made in his years of building Warner Communications Inc. which was now Time Warner, Inc.; his current associates at that mammoth company; the Hollywood celebrities whom he'd cultivated; and more. But Ross's wife, Courtney, had insisted that they hold a private ceremony for a select group of several hundred, including the celebrities, some of whom she wanted to ask to eulogize Ross, and some to perform. "It's what Steve would want," she is said to have told Mark Ross.

"But Steve isn't going to be there," Ross reportedly rejoined.

Courtney Ross, however, had had her way. And she, the producer of a couple of documentary films, had thrown herself into planning this event with a producer's zeal. Ross had died in the early hours of Sunday, December 20, 1992, in Los Angeles, where he had gone, after a year's agonizing battle against prostate cancer, to undergo radical surgery. It had been a kind of Hail Mary play, to halt the cancer; and, after further weeks of suffering, it had failed. Courtney Ross returned from Los Angeles to New

York, and set the funeral for Wednesday morning, at the Guild Hall, in East Hampton.

The auditorium of Guild Hall was too austere, she decided; she preferred the Guild's art gallery. The pictures were taken down, and in the next two days the space was completely renovated: the room was repainted; a carpet was run up the center aisle; a stage was built; the lighting was adjusted. On the back wall, facing the room, Courtney Ross hung a huge, brilliantly colored Willem de Kooning painting—one of her husband's favorites.

The funeral was scheduled to begin at 11:00 A.M.; by 10:30, the small drive in front of Guild Hall was choked with limousines. Since it was two days before Christmas, many people had been away on holiday; Guy Salvadore, who had started working for Ross in the Kinney days, and after Kinney's acquisition of Warner-Seven Arts had become "head of transportation"—overseeing the company's growing fleet of limousines, helicopters, and planes—had been working furiously for the past several days, flying people in from all over the country. Ross's bodyguard, Tony Battisti, who had been at his side perpetually for over ten years, stood at the door, surveying each person who entered. The cold was too bitter to stand outside, so people pressed into the vestibule area to wait.

It was not an altogether congenial group to be in such close quarters. In the days immediately preceding Ross's death, Gerald Levin, Ross's co-CEO, had carried out a restructuring of the board of directors, forcing off several of the strongest Ross loyalists. Although Levin had not known Ross was dying, he *had* known that Ross was weakened and incommunicado —and he had seized the moment.

"The family viewed it as an assault on Steve," asserted one close to them, "and Courtney did not want to invite Levin to the funeral. But Arthur [Liman] persuaded her that she should, because otherwise it would be a cause célèbre and would create even more dissension." (She had held fast, however, on the issue of inviting J. Richard Munro, the former chairman of Time Inc. and current director of Time Warner, who had been Levin's agent—and a particularly combative one—in this maneuver. Although the rest of the board was invited, Munro was not.)

Crowded into this uncomfortably small space, therefore, were Levin, on the one hand, and those he had so recently deposed, and their allies, on the other. Martin Payson, WCI's long-time general counsel, and, more recently, the vice-chairman of Time Warner, who had been ejected from the board and, in the ensuing battle, resigned not only from the board but the company—his home of twenty-two years—stared straight ahead, stony-faced. Not far away was Arthur Liman, who for more than twenty years had been Ross's lawyer, close friend, booster, and protector—and who within the past week, attempting to protect him to the last, had engaged in a furious scene with Levin.

If, knowing Ross's history, one had tried to guess who from the past would be present on this day and who would not, one would surely have been surprised to see, standing on the periphery of the crowd, Herbert Siegel, the chairman and president of Chris-Craft Industries, who was a veteran of a different corporate battle—the most protracted and bitter one Ross had ever waged. Siegel had been called and told that Courtney Ross wanted him to come, but the antipathy that he and Ross had felt for each other was so well known that many seemed taken aback to find him there. Not surprisingly, Jay Emmett, who had pled guilty in the Westchester Premier Theatre scandal in 1981—and who was the closest friend Ross ever had—was not invited. Nor was it surprising, all things considered, that Solomon Weiss, the WCI assistant treasurer who had refused to cooperate with the government and had been convicted in the same scandal, *was* there.

There were Steven Spielberg and his wife, Kate Capshaw; Chevy Chase; Lisa and Dustin Hoffman; Quincy Jones and Nastassja Kinski; Paul Simon; Barbra Streisand; and Anouk Aimée. Ross had made the stars his intimate circle in the last decade, but there were some here who still recalled his former life. Caesar Kimmel, who had run Kinney Parking—and was now the manager of a gambling casino in Moscow—had first met Ross in the late fifties, when Ross was working for his father-in-law, Edward Rosenthal, at the Riverside funeral home. (Ross's daughter, Toni, would smile when she mentioned how her father's occupation was described on her birth certificate: "undertaker.") The investment banker Felix Rohatyn always liked to tell people that he and Ross had made their first deal on the backstairs of the Campbell funeral home (owned by Riverside), while a funeral was being conducted inside.

Now, waiting for this funeral to begin, Rohatyn was commiserating with Albert Sarnoff, Ross's former brother-in-law, who had thrown in his lot with Ross when Ross was taking Kinney Service Corporation public, in 1962. Rohatyn, in a philosophic and somewhat morose frame of mind, was commenting that it was "what the Greeks call fate" that Ross should have been allowed to engineer his consummate design, the Time-Warner merger—thus bringing into being the world's largest media and entertainment company—but had then been denied the time he needed to try to make it work.

"Although it may have been undoable," continued Rohatyn, who had had a hand in that merger. "As I get older, I am struck more and more at how, in these things, it is the intangibles that matter most—personality, culture, ego."

Did Ross, perhaps, after effecting the merger, come to think that—that it was, in the end, "undoable"? Both Rohatyn and Sarnoff exclaimed that that was impossible. "Steve would *never* have thought that," Sarnoff declared. "He was the eternal optimist."

"But now," Rohatyn concluded, "it's like Schubert's 'Unfinished Symphony.'"

With that, the doors opened, and everyone filed in.

As a pianist played—and a cameraman filmed—Ross's nine-year-old daughter, Nicole, and several of her schoolmates placed flowers in a large vase that had stood, empty, near Ross's casket. The casket itself lay beneath a mountain of lavender Sterling Silver roses, Steve Ross's favorite. ("I never saw a casket with so many roses on it—that was fitting," Ross's long-time lawyer and friend, Milton (Mickey) Rudin, would comment later.)

The service began with a reading from the Bible by someone many in the audience took to be a rabbi but who was, in fact, Gershon Kekst, a public relations executive who had worked for Ross for years and who had been a close friend. Steve Ross had not been an observant Jew. Courtney Ross, therefore, had asked a Ross associate helping her with the logistics of the funeral arrangements whether it was required that there be a rabbi; and having been told that it was not, she had given the role to Kekst, who is religious. Although Kekst delivered a traditional prayer, the fact that a PR man was officiating did suggest, fairly or not, that this was a heavily managed event, bent on creating and burnishing a specific image.

The procession of speakers confirmed that impression. Ross's life had been his business and, over decades, his closest comrades those who worked with him; but the only business associate to address the group was Arthur Liman. Reading from notes, Liman spoke about Ross in much the same way he always had—emotional, admiring, adoring. "I rail, as you do, that I cannot speak to him just once more," he said, his voice quavering. "What is this magical quality that Steve had that drew us to him and has generated such emotion on our part?

"Steve was a giant of a man—giant in his accomplishments, giant in his vision, giant in his capacity for love, giant in his loyalty and concern toward others, giant in his energy, whether in business, on the tennis court, or on the dance floor, giant in his philanthropy and giant in his generosity of spirit. He gave more to every friendship than he took.

He made all of us feel important and good. . . . He considered nothing impossible. He inspired us to perform beyond the limits of our abilities and made us better than we were. . . . There was a personal side to every relationship with Steve. It was never all business. He derived his authority from his relationships, not his position."

In closing, Liman said: "I cannot imagine him at rest. I only hope, therefore, that you Dear God have plenty of yellow pads and pencils, for if you do and can understand his math, Steve will show you how to make heaven a better place, as he did every institution he touched." Finally, gazing toward the casket, Liman concluded: "Steve ended all of his letters with the words 'much love.' With that understated emotion, on behalf of all of us I bid you goodbye, dearest friend."

Liman was followed, mainly, by the stars, and a few members of Ross's family. Quincy Jones spoke, in a sort of rambling way, often addressing Ross directly ("On a dance floor, you could really kill it!") and recalling times they had enjoyed together—like a Valentine's Day dinner at the Box Tree restaurant in New York ("and, ironically, Nastassja is expecting our baby this Valentine's Day").

Then Steven Spielberg, who had been one of the people closest to Ross in the last decade, went to the lectern. "For the last couple of days, I feel cold, I can't keep warm, I feel like there's a draft through my heart— and I know that Steve is up there, trying to figure out a way to plug up the holes.

". . . The day I first met him, he was on the phone, yelling at New York City. It had to be bigger, more ambitious, more colorful, *bigger*. I said to myself, well, that's a typical CEO. He builds empires. And then I realized he was talking about the 1981 annual brochure—he was like an art director! He had style, wit, pizzazz, he was creative . . . being in his life was like being in a world that spun a lot faster than it is."

Beverly Sills followed Spielberg. "I can't mourn Steve, I have to celebrate him," she began. "The first time I met Steve was when I came to ask for money for my bankrupt opera company. Steve didn't know anything about opera, but Carmen [Ferragano, his long-time aide] said he should see me, and she said, 'She's called 'Bubbles.' '"

She knew that Ross thought big, Sills continued, so she came up with some complicated proposition about how Warner Brothers could film the opera and there could be a PBS tie-in—and he said, "Bubbles, I never heard a more cockamamie idea in my life. Why don't you just ask me for the money?" After further talk, Ross said that he would give the more expensive package that she had proposed—if she would join the board of Warner Communications. And that was how their relationship of the last decade began. "He was like an opera singer," she continued. "He was larger-than-life; he knew how to make grand entrances; he knew he didn't have to yell at the top of his lungs all night to keep an audience's attention; he was always on a diet; and he knew how to share curtain calls.

"He had infinite grace," she added. "Whether you were talking to him in the boardroom or around your dining-room table, you had his total attention. He had this knack of making you feel that you were the only one in the room.

"We used to bring out the Brooklyn in each other," Sills concluded. "We never said goodbye. It was always, 'I'll see ya, Bubbles!'—'See ya, Steve!' Today is no exception."

The singers' performances were interspersed through the program. At one point Valerie Simpson and James Ingram sang "I'll Never Love This Way Again"; later, they sang "How Do You Keep the Music Playing?" Paul Simon sang "Bridge Over Troubled Water."

The family speakers, for their part, were brief; Toni Ross said just a few words, and Steve Ross's sister, Connie Landis, read a poem. So did Courtney Ross's sister, Lindsay Lonberg—who (to the surprise of many in the audience who knew Ross as a decidedly non-literary sort of person) prefaced her reading of a poem she said had been written by Ralph Waldo Emerson by saying that it was one that Ross "always carried with him, in his briefcase."

Barbra Streisand, who is said to dread live performances, and who on the trip east on the Time Warner plane had told Terry Semel, Warner Bros. president, that she could *not* sing at the funeral, did. Saying that she had loved Ross as though he were her father, she sang "Papa Can You Hear Me?"

Mark Ross, who had been, in effect, the master of ceremonies, introducing each speaker, went last. To many, his presence was the most poignant. He resembled Ross a great deal, and some of his mannerisms —especially a slightly awkward wave of his hand, a kind of extravagant gesturing—were so suggestive of his father that it startled. But many in the audience knew (and those who didn't were about to discover) that Steve Ross's relationship with his children, and his son in particular, had been troubled, and that however much the stars may have thought of him as a "father," it had not, in reality, been his best role.

Ross noted, ruefully, that he had helped to decide the order of the speakers, and yet had allowed himself to follow Streisand—something, he knew, that his father, who planned such things with great care, would have advised against. "I can hear my father saying, 'Never follow Barbra!' "

After the laughter, Ross said, "I struggled to find my place in the ceremony today, as I struggled to find my place in my father's life. . . . It was hard to have a father who shared his self with so many people, and who considered so many people a part of his family.

" . . . I realize part of your legacy to me is your love for other people," he said, gazing at the casket strewn with roses, "but many times I just wanted you all for myself."

A chill rain was falling as the funeral cortege wended its way through East Hampton. It passed by Nick & Toni's, the restaurant owned and run by Toni Ross and her husband—a huge banner, draped across the front, read: "GOODBY, STEVE, WE LOVE YOU"—and continued into the area known as the Springs.

Courtney Ross had asked Edward Bleier, an executive at Time Warner who had worked for Ross for many years, to investigate which cemetery might be appropriate. He had told her there was a Jewish cemetery, brand new, next to a synagogue; or there was the Green River Cemetery, often referred to as "the artists' cemetery," where Elaine de Kooning, Jackson Pollock, and the art critic Harold Rosenberg are buried. Courtney Ross chose the artists' cemetery.

As the mourners left their cars, Nicole and her friends were handing out single long-stemmed roses from flower baskets to each person, to be placed on the casket. The gravesite was on a hillside, from which few other graves could be seen. The night before, more than a dozen pine trees had been planted around it, as well as blooming azaleas. Someone announced that the family wanted everyone to know that in the Oriental culture, rain at an interment is considered auspicious. Gershon Kekst said the mourner's kaddish in Hebrew.

Chairs for the family and special guests had been placed in rows alongside the grave, under a canopy. Mark Ross—who at one point turned to the cameraman and angrily ordered him to stop filming—was seated next to his mother, Carol Maslow, Ross's first wife and the daughter of Edward Rosenthal of Riverside. Streisand was seated behind them. Suddenly, she poked Maslow from behind. "Who are you?" she asked.

Maslow—who had met Streisand on several occasions—said, "I'm Mark's mother."

"Oh," said Streisand. "I thought you looked familiar."

"Yes," Maslow replied, with a withering look, "I thought you did, too."

A line formed, in which everyone waited their turn to step to the casket and lay down their flower. Like so much that had gone before, it was a moment carefully orchestrated and highly theatrical yet also quite moving: an inescapably personal gesture of farewell. Few in the group came through it dry-eyed.

While this procession continued, Toni Ross at one point drew the attention of her mother to the brilliant pink azaleas that ringed the grave. There were azalea bushes, just like these, in the Rosses' garden at their estate on Georgica Pond, in East Hampton, and Ross—who had recently become more of a fancier of fine gardens—*loved* them. A man who, over the course of his extraordinary lifetime, had grown accustomed to being able to obtain whatever it was that had materiality and pleased him, Ross had chafed at the brief bloom of his azaleas. He had insisted that he wanted to find azaleas that would bloom longer. He wanted, even, to find azaleas that would bloom in winter. To Ross, as Liman had said, nothing was impossible.

"See?" Toni Ross said to her mother, and pointed to the azaleas, blooming furiously on this sleet gray December day. "There they are."

From the start, Ross prided himself on his shareholders' meetings. Over the years, he would become more polished, but even in the early days of Kinney Service he came to these events like a natural: showcasing his depth of knowledge about the company, his numerical nimbleness, his salesmanship so consummate that it seemed more about the art of romance than about selling. As he did with other business tasks, Ross made his preparation for these meetings into a game; he challenged his associates to find a question that would stump him, as though he were about to appear on one of his favorite television quiz shows. He had a strategy for these meetings ("You never play a shareholders' meeting to win, you play to tie") as, it often seemed, he did for everything in life. And once he was on the podium, taking questions from the audience like so many lobbed balls, he seemed to want them to go on forever. "To make him stop answering questions," recalled the company's long-time secretary, Allan Ecker, "you'd have to turn out the lights."

Despite his prowess, however, in later years Ross liked to recount how he had gotten into trouble in one of those early meetings. "We were in the parking business then, and a woman asked why we didn't have a garage at a particular location in Brooklyn," Ross told me. "I gave some response, and she said, 'You're making fun of me because I'm from

Brooklyn.' And I said, 'No, no, I'm not doing that at all. I wouldn't do that. I'm from Brooklyn, too.'

"Well, after the meeting, my mother came up to me. 'Steven.' (She only calls me that when she's angry.) 'Do you know how many years we've been trying to live down that we came from Brooklyn, and now you've come right out and said it, in front of all these people!' "

Ross's mother, Sadie, was a diminutive woman with an invincible penchant for elegance, apparently imprinted in her early childhood. Her father, Benjamin Smith, had owned a construction company, and according to family lore had participated in the building of such famed sites as Ebbetts Field and the Flatiron Building. He would ultimately lose everything in the 1929 stock market crash; but Sadie, who was born in 1899, enjoyed the height of his fortunes, with an upbringing notable for its ease and style, in a four-story Brooklyn brownstone fully staffed with servants. After high school, she had attended the Parsons School of Design in Manhattan; and then, at nineteen, she had eloped (her father considered her too young to marry) with a young man named Max Rechnitz.

Rechnitz's father had also worked in the construction business, though his family was not as affluent as Sadie's. He began working as a builder, too, and became quite successful; by the time their daughter Connie was born in 1922, they were living a solidly middle-class existence; and when Steven was born, five years later, it was appreciably better. They had moved to a three-story house on Brooklyn's East 21st Street, in a well-to-do neighborhood; they had maids, and a chauffeur, and gala parties. Five-year-old Connie would creep in her nightgown to watch from her hiding spot at the top of the circular staircase, entranced at the sight of the women, especially, resplendent in costumes with feathers and tiaras, dancing the Charleston.

With the crash, however, Rechnitz's building business came to a halt overnight. He prevailed upon his wife, Sadie, to surrender all his gifts of jewelry so that he could sell them and thus pay his workers two weeks' wages, as severance—something she did, but would always say later that she regretted. They then moved to a small house in the Clinton Road area that Rechnitz's father had built, where they could live rent-free—and stayed there for a couple of very hard, threadbare years. Rechnitz was unable to find work for about a year. It was around this time that he changed his name to Ross, telling his children that it would make life easier for them in school, since people were always misspelling and mispronouncing "Rechnitz"; he also thought, more importantly, that the removal of his German-Jewish surname might make it easier for him to find work. Eventually, he got a job as an oil-burner salesman and they moved to a rather dreary apartment building on Newkirk Avenue, in

Brooklyn's Flatbush section, where they would remain for roughly ten years. Steve was then about four years old; virtually all his memories of childhood would center there.

It was a tough neighborhood—a mix of blacks and Irish and Jews—and as he got older, Steve learned, as he would later say, "the importance of picking your fights, in order to be able to walk the streets." He would later recall it, too, as an existence so sparse that there was sometimes not enough to eat. His mother, however, clung to the niceties. She drilled her children in fine manners. When company came, she still did her best to set the kind of table for which in their circle of friends she had been renowned: each place was set with a fingerbowl, and she would measure the distance from the edge of the table to the bottom of the flatware. She was so fastidious that in drinking from a cup, she always held it in her left hand so that, in case it had not been perfectly washed, her lips would be less likely to touch the place where another's had been. "My mother," Ross would say years later, "was a class act."

In school, at P.S. 152, he was most conspicuous as a mischiefmaker; his other grades sometimes varied, though they were generally good, but "Conduct" was virtually always a C. His mother was called to school so often that, as she would often complain, she spent as much time with Steve's teachers as he did. While school seemed to bore him, making money did not. It was not that he was working to help support a desperately impoverished family; both he and his sister were given modest allowances, and Connie got along on hers without working. But, from the time he was eight years old, he loved the idea of it—sometimes, it seemed, even more the idea than the thing itself, since he would often return home having lost half his earnings through the holes in his pockets.

When the nightly weather report on the radio predicted snow, he would set his alarm for 4:00 A.M., so that he had several hours before school to shovel the driveways of the large houses that lined Glenwood Boulevard a few blocks away. He constructed a cart with roller skates and a plank of wood, so that he could carry groceries home from the supermarket for older women. He delivered dry cleaning. He hawked magazines. Once, his mother and sister emerged from the Newkirk Avenue subway station to see ten-year-old Steve, ink from the magazine covers smudged all over his face, his cap askew, knickers that were up far above one knee, calling: "*Get* your *Cosmopolitan, get* your *Saturday Evening Post!*" His mother was mortified—what if the neighbors saw him, looking such a mess? But his father, hearing about it, revelled in the image of his young son, the go-getter.

"My father trained me," Ross recalled. "He was a heavy smoker. So I used to take money I'd made shining shoes and buy a carton of cigarettes for fifty cents a pack, then sell them to my father on a per-pack basis. I'd make a nickel profit—and movies were a nickel!" Movies at the neighborhood Loews, he added, were his "escape."

Max Ross seemed to have become resigned to the fact that he would never regain the standard of living that had briefly been his in the late twenties, and he enjoyed simple pleasures—taking his children on a weekend to the Automat; or to Coney Island, where they would change into bathing suits in the car; or to Prospect Park to watch a baseball game, then stopping at Dubin's for a loaf of rye bread so pungent that it would always be half-eaten by the time they brought it home to Sadie. She, however, never became resigned to what she saw as their fall from grace. As Connie would say later, "My father saw things as they were. Mother saw things as she wanted them to be."

Sadie Ross's hope of regaining the life lost to her was pinned on her son; he was, said Connie, her parents' "pride and joy." Connie adored her younger brother but probably could not help feeling overshadowed by him—her mother, especially, was fixated on him and on what he might become. The whole family agreed that there was something special about him that went beyond his handsome face and winsome charm. When Steve was in his teens, Sadie's brother, Al Smith, used to declare, "Mark my words: this young man's name is going to be in *Fortune* magazine one day." And Steve himself believed that his destiny lay somewhere far beyond Newkirk Avenue. His bedroom was always messy and once, when he was about ten, his mother scolded him, saying, "How in the world are you going to manage things when you're an adult if you live in such disorder? You will have to learn to handle details even if they are distasteful to you."

"Don't worry, Mom," her son replied, with a grin. "I'll have other people to handle the details."

In 1942, Connie, nineteen, married, and her father went to work in the plumbing supply business for her in-laws. Sadie and Max Ross were finally able to move to Manhattan, as Sadie had been longing to do, and Steve obtained a scholarship to a private school, Columbia Grammar. Most of his classmates were from wealthy families; his best friend, Judson Richheimer, for example, whose father was in the jewelry business and who was thought by some in the class to be its wealthiest member, lived in a palatial apartment on Park Avenue. (The Richheimers, too, however, had Brooklyn roots; they had been part of the Rechnitzes' social circle in the gilded period in the late twenties.)

Because he was a scholarship student, Ross was given the job of taking the younger children to Central Park each day; and the school's coach, noting his way with the children, asked him to be a counselor-in-training at a summer camp in Maine, Camp Kohut. Ross was given a bunk of five-year-olds. For Ross's young charges, he made all of life a game: they didn't *walk* to the mess hall, they got there by playing. In order to come out of their bunk, they had to guess in which hand Ross was holding a coin (he was already practiced at sleight-of-hand); whoever guessed right was allowed to descend one step, and whoever got to the bottom of the steps first won.

One of Ross's campers, a difficult little boy who cried a great deal, was named Henry Jaglom. His parents seemed always to be travelling and missed the visiting days. That summer and the next (Ross again was Henry's counselor), when visiting days arrived, Henry would always guess the right hand and make it first to the bottom—and then, while his bunkmates were with their parents, he would set out for extended nature walks with Ross.

About thirty years later, introduced to Ross in a restaurant, Jaglom thought they were meeting for the first time. But Ross, upon hearing Jaglom's name, declared with a broad grin, "You were the one who gave me this gray hair"—and then recounted to Jaglom how his lucky streak had been arranged. Jaglom later said that he "felt something welling up in me as he told me what he had done. It was so extraordinarily kind. I remembered the feeling of soaring down those steps. I'm sure that that was the first taste of winning I ever had."

In Ross's senior year at Columbia, a new student named John Heckler entered the class. He felt ostracized by his classmates; they all had their friends, and no one even bothered to talk to him for days—except for Ross. Heckler thought Ross seemed like a really "good guy"—tall, good-looking, with an easy charm.

At Columbia Grammar, Ross distinguished himself most on the playing field; he played varsity in football, basketball, and baseball. Nothing really sparked him in his academic subjects; even math, in which he excelled, did not inspire him to further study. As Ross would say, he always did well in math "without ever having to crack a book."

After graduating from Columbia in 1945, Ross—with his friend Judd Richheimer—enlisted in the Navy; they were bunkmates for part of their stint. When they were discharged in 1947, they both enrolled at a junior college in upstate New York named Paul Smith, which was just opening that year. (Ross would claim, later, that he had received football scholarships to both Duke University and the University of Wisconsin but fell in love, instead, with Paul Smith.) Here, too, Ross performed extraordinarily in math; in order to achieve a score of 100 in an advanced math course titled "Combinations and Permutations," one had to score 100 in every test and answer the two bonus questions on the final exam. He did.

But at Paul Smith, the two friends mainly enjoyed themselves. They shared a '41 Chevy. They skied. Ross played football, broke his arm, and had to have a metal plate put in it—which came in handy in fights, Richheimer would later say. They played pranks on each other. (Knowing Richheimer was likely to come in drunk one night, Ross replaced all the lightbulbs in the room with camera flashbulbs, so that when Richheimer flicked the switch, they would all pop. Richheimer, in turn—knowing that Ross always threw himself down on his cot after classes—put dynamite caps underneath his mattress.) The school was small—there were only two hundred in their class—and, by Richheimer's recollection, they ran it. Richheimer began to think that Ross was compulsive about winning—whether it was a game of cards for a penny a point or a school election —and that Ross could, essentially, have whatever he wanted, at least in this tiny universe. Their class consisted of 187 men (all veterans) and 13 women; at the end of the first winter, 12 of the women were engaged or married, and the other one was dating Ross.

When the two graduated after two years, Richheimer went to Lehigh to finish his college education and Ross went to work at a sports slacks company, H. Lissner Trousers. It was located in a loft building in Manhattan's garment district; the office, showroom, cutting room, and shipping office were all on one floor, and Ross worked in all of them. Sent to a convention in place of a more senior salesman who was ill, he sold so well that he was given New Jersey as his territory; he then travelled every day, selling slacks to stores throughout the state.

Ross renewed his friendship with John Heckler, who was also working in the garment district. The two played gin rummy on Friday nights, and with their winnings, usually $40 or $50 each (Ross was an outstanding player), they would double-date on Saturday nights. Their favorite movie —they saw it as many as twenty times—was *Gunga Din.* Ardent Giants fans, they went to games every Sunday: Heckler's parents had seats, first at the Polo Grounds and later at Yankee Stadium. Heckler and Ross would gaze at the Giants owners striding up and down along the sidelines, and they would swear to each other that someday they would own the Giants and they would walk up and down, just like that, wearing cleats and vicuna coats.

By 1950, Ross's father was gravely ill with lung cancer (he had first been stricken in 1945 and had spent six months in the hospital then), and Heckler would often join Ross in the evenings at Lenox Hill Hospital.

Heckler was particularly fond of the tall, silver-haired Max Ross, whom he found gentle and easygoing. Steve's drive, Heckler had long thought, came much more from his mother, who seemed to chafe at the bounds of her life and to have been disappointed in her mild husband's failure to overcome them. Whatever slight security they had achieved had been eaten up now by Max Ross's years of illness. Connie Ross would say later that the economic reversals in her mother's life—mainly that first, traumatic one—"made my mother money-crazy. She never felt there would be enough, no matter how much there was."

Ross's father died on May 14, 1950. About one year later, Sadie Ross married Sam Kellner, a widower who had lived across from them on East 21st Street in Brooklyn, and who owned a plumbing business in Manhattan. He, too, would experience economic hardship, deepening Sadie's fixation on such failure—and, perhaps, her son's as well.

In the summer of 1953, Ross, twenty-six, met eighteen-year-old Carol Rosenthal, whose father, Edward Rosenthal, ran a funeral business, largely family-owned, of which the most prominent chapel at that time was the Riverside, in Manhattan. Doris Rosenthal, Carol's stepmother (she had married Carol's father when Carol and her sister Ellen were babies, after their mother had died), met Ross when he brought Carol home after their first date. "Now, that is my idea of a man!" she told Carol.

"When he walked into the apartment, my parents flipped," Carol Rosenthal said. "They thought he was so handsome, so charming. He knew exactly what to say. He was proper. He was dressed just right, with perfect manners."

Ross began to court Carol quite avidly—and, it sometimes seemed, the entire Rosenthal household as well. Upon arriving at their apartment at 101 Central Park West, he would promptly make a beeline for the kitchen to greet Naomi, their long-time housekeeper; she soon became utterly devoted to him. By this time, he had left H. Lissner Trousers and was working for his uncle, Al Smith, in a company called Farragut, which made girls' high-style bathing suits. He gave Carol's younger brother, Peter, and all his classmates a tour of the Farragut plant. Ross also introduced Peter to the world of cards—bridge, blackjack, card tricks—and showed him shortcuts in his trigonometry homework. He would bring the latest bathing-suit styles so that Carol's youngest sister, Patricia, then eight years old, could "model" them; she would don them and pose in the family's living room, and Ross would take pictures of her which he claimed he would show to buyers.

"He was just so charming to everyone that people were whispering, 'Watch out, he's after her money,'" Carol's older sister, Ellen, recalled.

When Carol and Steve announced that they wanted to marry, about six months after they had met (Richheimer's father provided her diamond engagement ring), the Rosenthals did have reservations, though not because they were suspicious of Steve's motivations. Carol was just a freshman at Connecticut College—where they had hoped she would remain for four years—and had gone out with very few men. Doris Rosenthal tried to persuade Ross to wait, arguing that because of the difference in Carol's and his ages and experiences, Carol had everything to lose by an early marriage, and he, everything to gain. But Ross was all ardor.

His mother, Sadie Kellner, was well pleased with the match. "Sadie was a very pretty, vain, rather shallow woman," Doris Rosenthal told me. "It was very important to her that you come from the right side of the tracks. I guess Steve had gone out with a lot of girls, and she was relieved that he had ended up with someone like Carol."

They were married in June 1954, in an outdoor ceremony at the Rosenthals' country home in Greenburgh, New York. There were about one hundred guests (according to one family friend, Rosenthal would later attempt to deduct it as a business expense—when challenged by the IRS, he would argue that all the guests were potential customers). As a wedding present, the Rosenthals gave the newlyweds a four-week honeymoon in Europe.

When they returned, they moved into an apartment at 241 Central Park West, about twelve blocks north of Carol's parents. Ross continued to work at Farragut and Carol took classes at Finch. They lived on a tight budget, eating hot dogs so that they could see an extra movie. Despite his constraints, however, Ross set a certain tone. When he visited the Rosenthals, he was always handing out large tips to the doormen and elevatormen. At Christmastime, he borrowed $100 from the bank in order to buy his new in-laws Christmas presents.

After he and Carol had been married for nearly two years, he told her parents that he was unhappy in his job. Carol's brother, Peter, would later say that he thought the reason was that Ross had been promised by his uncle, Al Smith, that he would make him a partner, and he had not. But what Ross said to his wife and to the Rosenthals—and what he would always say years later, when describing this period of his life—was that he was made miserable by the sight of the poorly paid seamstresses.

Now, Rosenthal told Ross that he was sorry he was unhappy in his job, but that all he could offer him was the funeral business. As Ross would later tell me, Rosenthal did "a little selling job. I said, 'I'm getting out of the business I'm in because it depresses me, and now I go into the funeral business?' But Eddie said that now I would be helping people, and that while they make money at it they don't gouge—they're making the money because they're making sure everything is going well at a difficult time."

Doris Rosenthal said later they were surprised that Ross agreed. "We didn't think he would be interested in the funeral business. I mean, who would? He said he didn't want to go to embalming school, but that was fine with us. He was so great with people. We wanted him on the floor."

Ross threw himself into his new vocation. He was tutored in his role as funeral director by Marc Iglesias, who had been at the Riverside chapel for a number of years, and who now became Ross's close friend; they both lived at 241 Central Park West, and would walk to Riverside together each morning. Their wives became best friends, as well, and the couples made a perpetual foursome. Ross's Friday-night gin rummy games, with Heckler and other cronies, were now held at Riverside, occasionally in a room with occupied caskets. Often, Ross worked round the clock, taking the middle-of-the-night calls that had been Rosenthal's burden before.

It was difficult for him because, as Carol later pointed out, he always had trouble dealing with others' pain; but here (perhaps because he was so clearly not its cause) he became the master of solicitude. Certainly, his keen sensitivity to others (not to mention his ability to move them, chess-like, according to his own design) had taken root much earlier. But in later years, Ross would always maintain that he "learned about people in the funeral business. It's a service business. You service people in an emotional time—you learn about their needs, their feelings.

"You have to watch every word you say," Ross would add. "If you say to people who are grieving, 'Can I help you?' they will say, 'No one can help me.' So I would say, 'Can I be of service to you?' "

Edward Rosenthal's grandfather had started the business in 1897 with the establishment of Riverside Memorial Chapel; it had then been expanded by his son, Charles, and subsequently, by Charles's two sons, Edward and Morton. Carl Grossberg and Mac Passerman, relatives of the Rosenthals, were their partners. It was, moreover, a family business in style as well as substance. Edward Rosenthal had a file of 3x5 cards on which he kept the names of the family members of every employee. He frequently studied them, using them as drill cards—and was always asking after workers' wives and children by name. Every year, on May 6—Charles Rosenthal's birthday—there was a dance, held at a hotel; all employees, from funeral directors to hearse drivers, and their families were invited. The band would always play "Down by the Riverside." "We all dreaded that evening," Doris Rosenthal said later, "but Steve loved it. He was such a great dancer. He was always the life of the party.

"And he was a wonderful funeral director. The families loved him.

Everyone loved him. My father-in-law, who was in his eighties by then, adored him."

From the outset in his new business life, Ross remembered his friends. One member of his Friday-night gin rummy group, Joe Lehman, had a small printing business. Upon joining the funeral chapels, Ross promised Lehman that he would have the funeral account within six months; six months later—to the day—he did. And several years later, Ross would hire Judd Richheimer, and his brother Michael as well.

Ross's game plan for himself was less clear. As the son-in-law who had married into an affluent family and then joined the family business, he had to be circumspect. Moreover, Edward Rosenthal had instituted a strict rule, that family members had to start at the very bottom of the company and earn their way up. Ross had proven himself quickly; not only was he performing his prescribed duties superbly but he had, upon his entry, contributed what proved to be a lucrative idea: the limousines used for funerals during the day could be rented out at night. Nonetheless, after about two years in the business Ross had only limited say in its management. And he was chafing at what seemed to him the constricted, small-time mentality of the people in charge, who, as he would say later, "used to walk back at night to turn out the lights and save money."

In the spring of 1958, Joseph Albritton, an entrepreneur from Cut 'n Shoot, Texas, who would later own the *Washington Star*, contacted Ross. He had just bought the Pierce Company, a funeral and insurance business located in California, and he wanted to sell the funeral portion. Ross flew to California; they negotiated and reached what Albritton called "an understanding," in which Albritton would finance Ross's purchase of the funeral company. "But then the Rosenthals said, 'You can't take our daughter and move out to California—we'll turn the business over to you, and you can expand it here,'" Albritton recalled. "I said to him, 'Steve, you can't beat a deal like that—it's a family business, you've got a stake in it, and they're turning it over to you.'

"I was willing to back him, because I saw him as a comer and a winner, par excellence," Albritton continued. "He would never put a foot wrong. He may appear to be charming, which he is, and he may appear to be relaxed, which he is—but if you think the brain is not working, you're wrong. He has what I would call a relaxed intensity."

It was only later, after Albritton decided to keep the funeral business, that he realized what a favorable deal Ross had struck for himself in their negotiations. He called Ross and jokingly chided him, "My tax man tells me it's a great cash-flow business. Why didn't you tell me what a gold mine it is?"

In early 1958, when Ross's main duties were still in the chapel, a young man named Abraham Silverstein approached Edward Rosenthal about starting a small car rental operation, and Rosenthal agreed. By early 1959, however, Rosenthal decided that the business, Abbey Rent-A-Car, which was making no money, should be shut down; he offered to make Silverstein a funeral director. Silverstein asked for a little time. He would find a way, he told Rosenthal, to expand the business. He decided to call someone whom he knew from a prior deal—Caesar Kimmel, of the Kinney System—and propose that Kinney lend its name and some space at its parking lots to a car rental operation. Kimmel agreed to a meeting at the Kinney office in Newark, New Jersey. Rosenthal told Silverstein that Ross should attend, too.

Ross walked into Kimmel's office and immediately spotted a framed photograph on the wall of one of Kimmel's racehorses, taken just after it had won a big race. As anyone who knew Kimmel was well aware, he was extremely proud of his horses. Ross laughed, and said, "Morty Rosenthal owned the number-two horse in that race!" What would later become vintage Ross was already in place: always coming to a meeting well prepared, which for him meant researching not only all angles of the business deal but also the personality of the principal, and trying at the outset to strike a personal chord—surprisingly personal, if possible, one that might set the other person slightly offbalance, albeit in a pleasant way. ("You're going to see Joe Albritton? Walk in, and say, 'How's Cut 'n Shoot?' " Ross would urge me. "That'll really get him!")

The meeting went well. Ross pointed out that for a rental car business to succeed against established companies like Hertz and Avis, it needed something that would give it an edge. Why didn't they offer free parking (in Kinney's lots) with a rented car? Ross argued that since they were only renting cars in Manhattan (not at the airports), the vast majority of their customers would be renting cars in order to leave the city—and thus would never avail themselves of the parking. Still, there would be the psychological edge. Within two weeks, the deal was done. Kinney received 25 percent of the stock of a rental car company, in return for which it made available its sixty-odd locations (where cars could be rented and, theoretically, parked) and lent its name.

The first ad for Kinney Rent-A-Car read: "3 ways to park for free in New York," under enlarged photos of three license plates: "MD 16712," "DPL 1371," and "KINNEY." The plan was so successful that the rental car business bought new cars, which in turn took up more spaces in Kinney lots. The parking business began to suffer, and Kinney's principals were unhappy inasmuch as they owned 100 percent of Kinney Parking but only

25 percent of the rental car business. The solution, Ross proposed, was to combine the businesses—and he knew the best way to do that.

Ross had been dreaming of taking the company public for some time. It was a notion that found favor with the Rosenthals and their partners, also, since some of them were older and beginning to think about estate problems; this would enable them to cash out some of their shares. Ross had approached investment bankers at Bear, Stearns & Co. with the idea in early 1960. As Silverstein later recalled, "They said, forget it—you can't sell death to the public. And in any event, you really don't want to show the profits you're making on funerals—all that money off people's misery."

Now, however, a combination of these two companies would be especially happy—inasmuch as it would enable each of them to do together what they could not have done apart. Thanks to Kinney, the company going public would be not just a funeral business but also a parking and rental car business, and since the earnings would not have to be broken out for the separate companies, the funeral business's profits—which were monumentally greater than Kinney's—would not be discernible. And thanks to Riverside, which would dominate the corporate entity on the board and in management, Kinney would be able to escape the kind of scrutiny that it never could have withstood had it attempted to go public alone.

It had from Kinney's inception been unclear to the public who the owners of the company were. The company had been incorporated in 1945. In 1948, after Kinney had been awarded leases on the two biggest parking lots in Newark and the question of Kinney's ownership arose, Sigmund ("Jigger") Dornbusch first denied that he had any interest in Kinney. Several days later, Dornbusch claimed that he was Kinney's sole owner. "There is nothing peculiar or shady about this whole transaction," Dornbusch told the *Newark Evening News.* " . . . It's true I used dummies as incorporators of Kinney Corp. but that was for the reasons I have given [believing that the current lessees would demand higher prices for their equipment if they knew his identity]. I think they are good reasons. I have nothing to hide."

Dornbusch had had a varied career. In the twenties, he had been a bootlegger, a bail bondsman, and a stockbroker. In the thirties, he had gone into the fuel-oil business, starting a number of companies (Dornoil Products, Liberty Fuel, Climate Control Products, Inc.). By 1948, when Cities Service acquired Dornoil Products, it owned a fleet of trucks and controlled a chain of more than one hundred gasoline stations in northern New Jersey.

The person who had started Kinney, however, and who was a hidden partner of Dornbusch's, was Emanuel ("Alabam") Kimmel. Kimmel is said to have been a bootlegger; he also had been one of the first operators in the numbers rackets in Newark during the twenties and thirties, in company with New Jersey's most powerful racketeer, Abner ("Longie") Zwillman—who would be named in 1935, at the height of the Thomas Dewey prosecutions, as one of the "Big Six," the other five being Charles ("Lucky") Luciano, Benjamin ("Bugsy") Siegel, Louis ("Lepke") Buchalter, Jake ("Gurrah") Shapiro, and Meyer Lansky. Kimmel had owned several garages in Newark; Zwillman leased the garages as storage places for his bootlegged liquor, and with that income Kimmel is said to have begun to buy the lots that would eventually form the basis of Kinney. (Indeed, according to someone who knew both Kimmel and Zwillman well, Kimmel decided to buy the lots because they were ideal for the numbers business: cars could come and go without attracting suspicion.) One much-told story, perhaps apocryphal, is that Kimmel won the lot on Kinney Street in Newark—from which the company would take its name—in a crap game, after some hapless fellow who had run out of cash put it up as collateral.

Jack Bendet, who in the twenties had worked in a delicatessen on Prince Street in Newark, had known Zwillman, Kimmel, Herman ("Red") Cohen, Joseph ("Doc") Stacher, and others whose names would come up during the Kefauver Committee hearings in the early fifties, as active in one area or another of organized crime (Kimmel as a bookie). "The Third Ward [of Newark] was where everything was going on," Bendet recalled. "And, over the years, nothing went on that Zwillman didn't have to okay. All these guys had a little piece of everything they were involved in—it was all intermingled."

The numbers racket, Bendet explained, worked as a kind of small-scale lottery. "There were stores where you went if you wanted to play a number—any number, say, from 1 to 1,000. Runners picked up the numbers and brought them to the office, and then the office sent the money for the winning number to the store. They paid 600 to 1. And Manny Kimmel had the office. He was the banker."

Unlike Dornbusch and certain other bootleggers—even one as notorious as Zwillman—who subsequently, in an attempt to gain respectability, went into some legitimate businesses and allowed themselves to be visible there, Kimmel continued over the course of his life to appear to be what in fact he was: a major bookmaker and gambler, in whom the FBI maintained an active interest at least into the sixties. As an FBI document noted in 1965, "Kimmel is known to be a lifetime associate of several internationally known hoodlums. He is an admitted gambler and consorts with many well known gamblers throughout the United States." Another document described him as having "taken over the operations of the sports books at the El Rancho Vegas Hotel in Las Vegas as well as the horse race book covering all Eastern tracks." He also reportedly testified in 1954 before a federal grand jury that was investigating the income taxes of Zwillman.

That same year, Kimmel also testified in the trial of mobster Joe Adonis. In the late twenties, as Mark Stuart recounts in *Gangster #2*, some reform district attorneys were causing trouble for the New York gambling spots run by Lansky, Luciano, Frank Costello, and Adonis; so they got together with Zwillman, the don of New Jersey, and agreed that they would open up a string of roadhouses in Jersey. By the mid-forties, Ben Marden's Riviera in Fort Lee, just over the George Washington Bridge, was among the most popular. And, as reported in the *Newark Evening News*, Kimmel testified that from 1948 to 1950, he had agreed to allow limousines operated by one of Adonis's partners to park in one of the Kinney lots, on Broadway between 51st and 52nd Streets, which then transported dice players to crap games at the Riviera and other clubs in Bergen County. As one of Kimmel's associates told me, "It was a service Manny was providing for his customers."

In light of these activities and associations, it was critical that Kimmel's interest in Kinney be disguised.

When Dornbusch in 1948 had been pressed to come forward publicly so as to secure the city's award of the leases to Kinney, the company's previous incorporators (three current and former employees of his) were replaced by Dornbusch, Manuel Rosenstein, and Rosenstein's cousin, Seymour Wortzel. Manuel Rosenstein was a partner with Kimmel in a couple of lots, and borrowed money from Kimmel for his stake in Kinney; and Wortzel, a bookkeeper, was essentially standing in for Kimmel.

Manny Kimmel's eldest son, Caesar (he had changed his name from Seymour), was active in the operating of the lots. What Caesar Kimmel would say in later years was that his father had had a couple of lots which he had given him, and that he (Caesar), Dornbusch, and Rosenstein had been partners. But, as one associate of those men explained to me, "Manny always had a lot of cash—thousands and thousands of dollars. Half the time he carried it around in a shoebox. But he couldn't be out front in the company. He was 'connected.' So Caesar was his front— Manny laundered it through Caesar."

In the fall of 1961—as Ross and Caesar Kimmel were preparing to take the merged companies public—Manny Kimmel was setting out on a new foray. An MIT mathematics professor, Edward Thorp, had just gone public with his claim that he had used a computer to devise a card-counting technique that enabled him so to circumvent the odds in playing black-jack that he could be guaranteed of winning more often than losing. Kimmel promptly got in touch with the professor, and soon he was arriving at Thorp's home, in Cambridge, Massachusetts, to test his claim. In a *Life* magazine article published in March 1964, Thorp told the re-porter of his first meeting with the man whom in his book, *Beat the Dealer* (published in 1962), he described only as "Mr. X."

"I was looking out the window at about 4 o'clock," Thorp recounted,

and I saw a huge, midnight-blue Cadillac coming up our street. A ravishing blonde in a mink coat was driving it. Another ravishing blonde was sitting on the other side of the front seat. It stopped and both girls got out before I actually saw Mr. X. He was a tiny, white-haired, gnomish man in a long, dark overcoat and he'd been hidden between them. He actually intro-duced the girls as his nieces when they came in. Then he told me he hoped I'd been practicing. He sat down and began dealing me blackjack hands. We played for two hours. I seemed to satisfy him, and, when he left, he reached into one pocket of his coat, pulled out a tangled handful of jewelry and held a pearl necklace out to my wife.

Thorp grinned at the memory. "We had it appraised the first thing in the morning. It was worth $16. Mr. X believed in the incentive system. He also used to present me with a salami from time to time."

Kimmel and his close friend, Edward Hand ("Mr. Y"), then accompa-nied Thorp, whom they viewed as their secret weapon, on a trip to Nevada, covering Reno and Lake Tahoe (they didn't go to Las Vegas be-cause Kimmel was so well known there that he would quickly attract attention). They won about $100,000 in two days. During this trip in the winter of 1961, just a couple of months before Kinney Service would go public, Kimmel told Thorp that he owned a great deal of stock in Kinney Parking, and sixty-four parking lots.

Indeed, Kinney's initial prospectus, filed in February 1962, stated that Kinney "owns seven locations and leases or manages 64 other locations." There was no mention, however, of Manny Kimmel (while the origins of Riverside were described in detail with mention of Charles Rosenthal as one of the founders, the parking section had an artful lead: "The Company began use of the 'Kinney System' name in the parking business in 1945 with a lease to operate one station").

Ed Hand would later say that he believed Kimmel was boasting to a degree, inasmuch as he strongly doubted that Kimmel owned or even had interests in all sixty-four lots; he said he had in fact been told by Kimmel that he had partners (certain of the lots, for example, were leased from corporations in which Dornbusch had an interest). But Hand was certain that Kimmel had an enormous ownership stake in the lots (one which would prove very lucrative to him over the following decades) and, Hand added with a smile, he was anything but a passive proprietor.

"Manny even booked the lots—he'd mortgage them for thirty or sixty or ninety days, when he had to get cash to pay off bets," Hand recalled, noting Kimmel's voracity as a bookie. "What was he a bookie for? For everything! Vegas, football, baseball, the horses. At Saratoga, in the old days, he used to straighten out the jockeys [meaning, Hand explained, that he fixed the races]. Manny was great at talking people into betting. He could always find a sucker." In the sixties and seventies, Hand added, Kimmel was a bookie for H. L. Hunt, who "thought nothing of betting a million on a football game." According to a sports gambler who frequently used Kimmel as his bookie, Kimmel was for a time "one of the biggest—if not the biggest—in New York."

Another hidden partner in Kinney may well have been Longie Zwillman. When Kinney, represented by Dornbusch, had made a bid in 1950 to build parking lots under the West Side Highway in New York, it ultimately withdrew its bid after allegations were made that Zwillman had an interest in Kinney. By the time Kinney went public, Zwillman was dead. Found hanging in the basement of his mansion in West Orange, New Jersey, in February 1959—in what was officially deemed a suicide—Zwillman had died without leaving a will. Ralph Salerno, the former supervisor of detectives for the New York Police Department, said that Zwillman's hidden interests were believed to be handled after his death by Gerardo Catena, who had been his close associate and his partner in the New Jersey gambling ventures, and who was a top-ranking member in the Vito Genovese crime family. According to Hand, Kimmel—who "didn't trust his own mother" and had few friends—did consider Catena his friend.

Moreover, a young man named Howard Stone was dating Zwillman's daughter in 1960. At the time, Stone told a friend, Larry Dietz (who recounted this anecdote to me), that the girl's mother, Zwillman's widow, had told him that her daughter wanted to marry him, and that if they were to marry, the following assets, in which the Zwillman family owned major stakes, would eventually be his. "She listed a bunch of things, including some Las Vegas hotels, and also Kinney Parking," Dietz recalled. (Stone declined her proposal.) Through the sixties, in any event, talk of Zwillman's stake in Kinney would persist among its employees.

Outlandish as it was to imagine that a company such as Kinney could go public, it was also—once presented by Ross—an irresistible notion to the Kinney principals. Sigmund Dornbusch had died in 1956, and Kinney was being managed, day to day, by his son Howard, Caesar Kimmel, and Manny Rosenstein. While its properties and leases had value, Kinney was in a very shaky financial state; often, Howard Dornbusch, who was also managing Liberty Fuel out of the offices shared with Kinney in downtown Newark, would lend Kinney money from Liberty to meet its payrolls.

Caesar Kimmel set about preparing for the transaction. He would later say that he bought out Rosenstein's stake, in order to control two thirds of the company's stock. In fact, one associate said later that Manny Kimmel had lent Rosenstein the money for his stake. Caesar now demanded that that loan be repaid, or Rosenstein forfeit his share; and Rosenstein had to forfeit it. As for the rest of Kinney's relationships—with Manny Kimmel, and any other hidden partners, and the sixty-four lots—those would remain obscured, as ever, behind a shield of over forty dummy corporations.

(Despite the considerable pains taken to hide Manny Kimmel's interest, U.S. law enforcement was apparently not altogether deceived. One FBI document, written in early 1962, would note that "the Kinney System Parking Corporation was seeking Securities and Exchange Commission (SEC) approval for a public stock offering and that SEC was considering rejecting this application. The [Justice] Department requested a check of our indices, noting that the founder and present owner of a large share of this parking corporation is Emanuel Kimmel, better known as Manny Kimmel, Maplewood, New Jersey, engaged for many years in gambling activities in New Jersey, Florida, and Las Vegas, Nevada. We are forwarding to the Department a detailed summary of information in our files concerning Kimmel." The SEC, however, did not ultimately reject the application—presumably accepting the representations of the company's lawyers that Manny Kimmel was *not* a "present owner.")

It was agreed that Richard Seley, the trusted attorney who had been the agent for so many of Kinney's dummy corporations, was to become an officer of the newly combined company. Solomon Weiss, an accountant who had first gone to work for an accountant named Seymour Wortzel, and who, along with Wortzel, had then come in-house at Kinney, would also join Kinney Service. Over the years, Weiss would handle not only the company's but Ross's personal financial matters, and would be his single most trusted aide. Kinney Service would be employing two mainstream firms as general counsel and auditor—Paul, Weiss, Rifkind, Wharton & Garrison, and Arthur Young & Company. But with these two men, Seley and Weiss, a repository of all legal and financial information on Kinney's dealings could be transferred, intact and insulated, to the new company.

Kimmel and Dornbusch were both to join the company as vice-presidents. Only Kimmel, however, was to go on the board. This was not surprising. Not only did Kimmel (with his father) control a much larger stake in the company, but he was a personable, studiedly comic individual, with no hint of menace in his public demeanor. Dornbusch, on the other hand, was a conspicuously rough, albeit intensely dapper, type. Ross, in his most smooth-talking manner, told Dornbusch that he thought he ought not to be a director because his father had been a bootlegger. Dornbusch, a man widely known for his hair-trigger temper, retorted that Kimmel's father not only had been a bootlegger but was currently a bookie. He furthermore told Ross that if he were not made a director, he would make trouble. He left it purposely vague; experience had taught him by this time that there was no ultimatum better than that which invokes the unknown. Not long after this exchange, Dornbusch did, in fact, become a director (he was not listed as one in the initial prospectus, but by the next year he would be).

As one of the Kinney principals would say later of Ross, "He was an exuberant wheeler-dealer, a con artist—not to cheat you, but to get you to believe what he wanted you to believe. And he could talk a blind man into seeing."

Machinations in the prelude to going public were not limited to the Kinney side. The funeral business had been structured so that it was comprised of over sixty separate companies—not only one for each funeral chapel, but one for the florist, one for the hearses, and so on. "Eddie Rosenthal did that for tax reasons," Abe Silverstein later explained. "Tax laws allowed you to have a lower tax rate on your first $25,000 of earnings. So it was better to have ten corporations earning $25,000 than one earning $250,000—and paying 40 percent in taxes." And each of these, with their varying ownership stakes among the Riverside partners —like the dozens of Kinney companies—had to be valued.

"Sitting down with members of his family and cutting the deal by which all these million companies got translated into Kinney Service had to be Steve Ross's single most difficult negotiation—until he did Time Warner," John Rosenwald, a Bear, Stearns & Co. investment banker who worked on the offering, told me later.

This was unmistakably Ross's deal, as much as every deal the company would make over the next thirty-odd years would be. Nearly everyone involved was eager for the company to go public, but no one craved it quite as Ross did. And he alone had the capacity to drive it—arbitrating others' arguments over their allotted numbers of shares, placating those who worried about going public in what was a bear market and thus getting robbed of value—not only because of his persuasive powers but because he appeared to be fighting for the transaction, and not (at least in the short term) for himself. Ross, who would become president of Kinney Service, was to receive a relatively small amount of shares: 66,348, compared to chairman of the board Edward Rosenthal's 129,921, and Morton Rosenthal's 157,662. And Ross demonstrated that he believed in this new company's equity; of all the major shareholders, he sold by far the smallest percentage of his shares in the public offering: 2,000, out of his 66,348.

The largest single shareholder was Caesar Kimmel, who with 169,500 shares controlled 10.8 percent of the company's stock. Kimmel also received the largest number of options of all the executives. According to Jack Schwartz, whose auto-leasing company would be acquired by Kinney in 1962, "the reason Caesar's stake was so large was because Manny Kimmel's stock was in there, too, which couldn't be shown." Even so, the size of Kimmel's share is somewhat surprising, particularly given the financially stressed state of his company.

Under the general rubric of a diversified "service" company, an office-cleaning company (Kimmel would always like to refer to it as "the Tiffany of cleaning companies," because it cleaned Radio City Music Hall and the Time-Life Building) was also added to the mix. There was a family connection, in that it was owned in part by Lewis Sarnoff (the brother of RCA's David Sarnoff); and the Sarnoffs' nephew, Albert Sarnoff, was married to Edward Rosenthal's eldest daughter Ellen. Both Albert Sarnoff and his brother, William Sarnoff, who together had had a small razor blade company, also joined Kinney Service. Albert Sarnoff became its treasurer. He was a very careful, probative young man; he seemed rather staid to Edward Rosenthal, who in financial matters was always looking for an edge—and, in that sense, felt much more akin to his other son-in-law, Ross. "Al Sarnoff is very honorable," Rosenthal would comment later, with a wry smile. "Too honorable, if there is such a thing."

Doris Rosenthal had a favorite story that she thought perfectly captured Sarnoff. He had five suits, which he hung in a line in his closet, and after he wore one, he would replace it in the back of the line; it was a routine he never varied. When the family was preparing for his and Ellen's engagement party, Sarnoff's mother said, "Al, I hope you are planning on wearing your gray suit [his newest]." To which he replied, "If it comes up in the line, I'll wear it."

The offering—one of the few successful initial public offerings in a very bleak season on Wall Street—took place in March 1962. The stock, which was listed on the American Stock Exchange by its symbol, "KSR," was offered at $9 a share, and almost immediately began to rise.

Kinney Service had gone public, but it was still, really, the family company it had always been. The Rosenthal family, including Ross and Sarnoff, controlled 51.6 percent of the company's shares. Referring to the voting on the slate of directors that was about to take place at the first shareholders' meeting, an officer of the company quipped to an associate, "If one more person comes in who doesn't kiss Eddie Rosenthal, we're in trouble." And over the years, as the company grew larger than any of its principals except, perhaps, Ross, had imagined it would, the familial ethos would not dissipate but would grow only more marked—an anomaly, really, among companies of comparable size.

With Kinney Service's move into its offices at 10 Rockefeller Plaza in November 1962, the first stage of metamorphosis began. Taking their places in the executive suite, Kimmel moved over from the Kinney office in downtown Newark, and Ross, Rosenthal, and Marc Iglesias from the Riverside funeral chapel, where they used to have to have bodies cleared out of the "conference room" for meetings. Ross, emancipated from his role as funeral director, dedicated himself to mastering the nuances of business life. Essentially unschooled, he would eventually hone his skills so well that, as Allan Ecker, the company's secretary, would later say, he would be qualified to be a lawyer, a tax lawyer, and an accountant as well as a CEO. "He got his knowledge through interacting with people," Ecker said. "He was a serious reader of legal documents, and when he didn't understand something, he would ask. Now, he reads documents better than anybody I've ever known. That's how he learned GAAP [Generally Accepted Accounting Principles], too, and how he learned to use it so much to his advantage. He picked it up through osmosis."

Ecker and Ross used to play a game, in which Ecker would plant two typographical errors in lengthy documents for Ross to find. "He always found them—even when I put them in the boilerplate," added Ecker. Ross had never been a reader, and never would be (friends would remark on the fact that, even on vacations, they had never seen him reading a book). But once it became a game, as with the documents—find the typos, find the trick clause, outwit the other side, *win*—it fully engaged him. In later years Ross, seeming embarrassed by the fact that, as he allowed, he read little, would blame it on his having trained himself to read so slowly in the search for Ecker's plants that he was consigned forever to being a painfully slow reader. He would point with admiration to his friend, former Governor of New York Hugh Carey, who "has a great mind. He reads a book in an hour. And then, you can ask him something about it, and he'll say, 'That's on page eighty-three, in the third paragraph,' " Ross said.

In February 1962, just a month before the company went public, Riverside had contracted to purchase a location on Broadway which it intended to convert into a new funeral chapel, to take the place of its major chapel on Amsterdam Avenue. Shortly afterwards it was announced that Lincoln Center was to be constructed—just across the street from the projected Riverside chapel. As Ross would later tell the story, he instantly realized that this would be an opportunity to make money. Before long, he received a call from Governor Nelson Rockefeller, who asked if he were thinking of building a funeral chapel across from Lincoln Center. When Ross assented, Rockefeller asked if Ross had received approval from the zoning commission. Ross said he had.

"Then he said, 'Have you checked that?' and I said, 'Yes.'

"And then he said"—here Ross paused, relishing this punch line that never seemed to lose its zest for him, despite his having delivered it hundreds of times—" 'No, I mean, have you checked that *tomorrow*?' "
Rockefeller then directed Ross to enter into negotiations with Percy Uris (the land was owned by Columbia University, and Uris was in charge of its real estate).

If negotiation is in large measure the art of intuiting so well the makeup of one's foil that one can induce that person not only to grant what one wants, but to think that he or she has gotten *their* desire, Ross was not exactly a novice. He had been practicing these skills in an informal way—complaining to Rosenthal about how unhappy the sight of the seamstresses at Farragut made him, but demurring briefly about entering the funeral business; negotiating a deal with Albritton and then consenting to stay at Riverside, with the newly given power to run and expand the business. And he had led the marathon, mainly intrafamily negotiations involved in bringing the company public. But his sessions with Uris would be the first of their formal kind, and Ross would in later years look back upon them as his debut.

As Ross would recall, Rosenthal and the other principals decided that they wanted about $100,000 over their investment—so, about $250,000. "I went to see Percy Uris. He had this big office, and he was very gruff. He said, 'I understand you're interested in selling.'

"I said, 'No, no—we're interested in building a funeral chapel.' "

"He said, 'No. It will be an eyesore.'

"Eyesore, I thought. So he is *really* opposed, not just doing this to please Governor Rockefeller. So I figured I was in a good position. I said, 'We really want the chapel.'

"He offered me $278,500—a weird figure. That made me think he'd already done a whole calculation on what he was willing to pay, and then taken maybe three fourths of it. With my heart in my throat, I said, 'No, we can't take that.' "

As Ross tells it, Uris kicked him out of his office. The next day, though, he called with an offer of $333,500—which, Ross noted, was another weird figure. Ross went back several times, and by the end they agreed on $1.6 million. In his retrospective critique, Ross would comment, "He let me walk out each time with the offer on the table. After the third visit, he should have said, 'My first offer is on the table.' But every time, after he'd upped his offer, he'd say, 'Isn't that enough money?' And I would say, 'I just want to build my funeral chapel.' "

Eddie Rosenthal was mightily impressed with his clever son-in-law. A graduate of Wharton, Rosenthal considered himself astute in business matters, and he had taken the lead in the family business; but he felt that Ross, despite his lack of schooling and of exposure to the business world, had natural talents that dwarfed his own. This did not threaten but, rather, delighted Rosenthal. A confident, lively individual, given to speaking his mind—even in situations where the more conventional would refrain—Rosenthal had a habit of firing off notes to people, famous and not so famous, about subjects that had sparked his interest, or something that had moved him, or a recommendation he had. Now, he sent a handwritten note to Frank Stanton, the president of CBS.

"He was saying that he had the perfect candidate for my job," Stanton recalled. "There was a hint in it that [William] Paley ought to get out, I should move up, and Steve should succeed me. So I showed it to Paley, sort of as a joke, and he said, 'It's some crank.' But then I had Rosenthal over and I saw that he was a perfectly sincere, warm person, interested in helping his son-in-law." Ross, Stanton added, knew nothing about it; years later, he would show him the letter, to Ross's great amusement.

Rosenthal was anything but profligate; he and his family lived well but quietly, without the telltale insignia of wealth—never travelling first class, never using limousines. He was therefore quick to notice that Ross, now beginning for the first time to have some financial wherewithal, had very extravagant tastes. When Rosenthal offered to build a pool for the Ross house (which was part of the family compound in Greenburgh, New York), he had in mind a rectangular, forty-foot pool. (Even having one's own pool, in the Rosenthal milieu, was quite a luxury. As Preston [Bob]

Tisch, a good friend of Ross's in the sixties, would later remark of the Rosenthal-Ross compound, "They were the first people we knew who had their own pool and tennis courts.") Ross, however, wanted the pool to be not forty but eighty feet, and not rectangular but kidney-shaped. And so it was.

The love affair between Ross and the Rosenthals continued unabated. Ellen, Carol's sister, would later say that she had observed Ross for some time, expecting that once he and Carol were married his attentiveness to the family would diminish. But, if anything, it grew. It was Ross who always reminded Carol to send flowers to Naomi the housekeeper on Valentine's Day. It was Ross who made sure to include everyone on the family vacations—indeed, he and Carol never went alone.

A typical entourage might include family members from both Carol's and Steve's sides: Ellen (now divorced from Albert Sarnoff); Steve's mother Sadie; his sister Connie (also divorced); and all the various nieces and nephews. Often they went to the Tisches' Americana Hotel in Miami Beach. Ross always commandeered the best rooms—on the top floor, with huge wrap-around terraces big enough for shuffleboard games. When they went to Puerto Rico, where there was gambling, Ross—who had taken some card-counting lessons from Manny Kimmel and read *Beat the Dealer*—before heading for the blackjack tables would ask every person what they wanted (money for a bathing suit for Ellen, a dress for Sadie) and then return, triumphant, distributing his winnings. On these trips Ellen found him a sympathetic confidant, too, always ready to listen to her stories of her romantic problems, even offering her advice on what to wear for a date. She gradually surrendered her early skepticism and became his greatest booster, something she would remain over the years (indeed, Ellen would later claim that her father sometimes remarked that perhaps she, not Carol, should have married Steve).

The only one of the Rosenthal family who, by the mid-sixties, was growing slightly less enraptured with Ross was his wife. It was not lost upon her that they never went away alone, that in private Ross's public persona—all warmth and intensity of focus—seemed to dissipate. She told her sister, Ellen, that she had begun to wonder whether this person who appeared to connect in an emotional way with others better than anyone she'd ever known—he was the maestro of rapport—was in fact incapable of connection. Ellen would recall later that when she rhapsodized to her sister about Ross's thoughtfulness and his patience with her monologues, Carol would sometimes say rather bitterly, "Of course he has time to listen to you. He has time for everybody—everybody except me and the children."

Their daughter Toni had been born in 1957; their son Mark in 1962; and Carol found herself more and more isolated at home with the children. Ross was, mainly, either absent or abstracted. He was a fond father, and a consummate planner of family social life, organizing swimming races, for example, with the neighbors—mothers against the mothers, daughters against the daughters! But it took an event to engage him; everyday domestic life did not. Years later, Carol would recall that the best conversations they ever had were those in which he would explain, with great patience and in some detail, the financial transaction of the moment that he was undertaking at the company. Sometimes, she would ask him when he would stop working so hard, and he always gave the same answer: "When we have a million dollars in the bank." Carol came to realize that this was his way of placating her; as he well knew, she did not understand enough about finances at the time to realize that Ross would never have a million dollars just sitting in a bank account.

Unlike his wife, Ross did not exactly think of what he did at Kinney Service as work; rather, it provided him the means to define himself, and he felt utterly impelled to do it. It was giving him entree to the wider world, a monied and powerful world that he had set his sights on as a boy, in his hardscrabble years on Newkirk Avenue. He was awed by the Tisches, for example, and very eager to make a friend of Bob Tisch; Ross had met him when he directed the funeral of Tisch's father. In the early sixties, too, Ross was able to cultivate a friendship with the renowned coach of the Giants, Allie Sherman. From the time he was a teenager, football had been his fantasy (he would play pro ball, he would own the Giants); as Carol would later say, when she first met him it had been his "raison d'être." Indeed, he had told her that he had played briefly for the Cleveland Browns before breaking his arm and being forced to quit; so he had pursued this corporate life, but not without pangs of regret.

Now, through his friendship with Allie Sherman, Ross enjoyed vicariously the life that, as he said, was nearly his. He revelled in the association. He employed Giants team members, off-season, as salesmen in the Kinney rental car division. Sherman coached the intramural football games between the Kinney executives (who always lost) and the parking lot attendants (in one game, Ross had his arm re-broken by Nick Gravianno, a beefy garage manager). And when Sherman offered Ross the chance to attend a Giants' training camp one August, Ross nearly exploded with excitement. Sherman thought that Ross was acting like he'd just been given a million dollars.

In these early days of Kinney Service, Ross seemed to see opportunity beckoning like a friendly apparition, everywhere. He was never at rest.

Friends would later recall that on the rare weekend afternoon that he was not at the office or at one of the car rental locations, he would don a sportjacket before going out for a walk on Manhattan's East Side (he and his family had moved to the Imperial House). "You never know who you might meet," he would say. A young lawyer at the company would later remember setting out with Ross for a bondholders' meeting and walking down a street where there was a line of cars waiting to get into a parking lot—while a Kinney lot stood, uncrowded, further down the block. Ross bolted into the street and began waving the traffic ahead, gesturing to the Kinney lot. When his associate remonstrated that they would be late for the meeting, Ross protested that he had to get some more cars and remained transfixed for several minutes more, waving them in.

However splendid a marriage of convenience the union of the parking and funeral businesses was, it was not trouble-free. Eddie Rosenthal had spent roughly forty years inculcating the concept of "service" in his employees in the chapels, and he, for one, took seriously the pronouncement in the first annual report of Kinney Service Corporation: "Service Is Our Middle Name." Now, he set about spreading the gospel to the parking lots. Kinney System distributed thousands of questionnaires to parking customers asking how its services could be improved; and as part of the new regime, the annual report also noted, "we now clean the windshield of each car parked in a Kinney garage and provide many customers with umbrellas during inclement weather." (Indeed, in a 1966 *BusinessWeek* article about the company, Ross would be pictured in a lot, holding a large Kinney umbrella overhead.)

Just as Caesar Kimmel and Howard Dornbusch for years had hired shills, posing as customers, to go to the lots in an effort to catch attendants stealing, so Rosenthal now carried out his own checks—not for stealing but courtesy. He would park at a garage and, his identity undisclosed, observe: Were the attendants polite? Did they, in fact, clean the windshields? Or were they uncouth, and sloppy, and did they burn the rubber on the tires? After one such surveillance (where a surly attendant had threatened him with bodily harm when Rosenthal asked that his windshield be cleaned), Rosenthal summoned all the company managers to an early morning meeting and lambasted Kimmel, before the group.

At a board meeting not long after that session, Kimmel announced that he had taken Rosenthal's criticism to heart and wanted to introduce to his fellow directors a "courtesy expert" whom he had hired to help bring some refinement to the parking lot crews. The expert began his presentation, and after a few minutes of a rather odd, increasingly garbled speech, Ross gave Kimmel a knowing look (the "expert" was comedian Al Kelly, famous in the sixties for his routines of double-talk).

Rosenthal may have been displeased at Kimmel's lampooning what was to him a serious business matter, but Kimmel was nonplussed. Not only was he the largest single holder of the company's stock, but he and Ross were close companions, congenial pranksters with a shared sense of humor. Sometimes they travelled together, and Kimmel took Ross to his favorite gambling hang-outs. Once, as Kimmel would later recall, the two were in Florida, gambling at an "after-hours club," when a couple of men pulled out guns, lined all the patrons up against the wall, and ordered them to empty their wallets and remove their jewelry. "When these guys were just about four people down the line from us," Kimmel recalled, "Steve reached into his pocket and said, 'Caesar, you know that $700 I owe you? Well, here it is!' "

And Ross, if not Rosenthal, understood that courtesy was not going to become a watchword in the parking lots. "Polite? POLITE?" Kimmel said later, rolling his eyes. "C'mon, these guys were Teamsters!" Indeed, the lots, as Kimmel knew best, were a primitive world unto themselves. Ross's best friend from schooldays, Judd Richheimer, had joined the company, along with his younger brother, Michael, in the early sixties. Michael became Kimmel's closest aide, managing the parking division with him; Judd worked mainly in auto leasing but spent about a year in one of the parking garages, where he received his indoctrination from the garage foreman, whom Richheimer later referred to only as "Butchie."

"One day, a black guy came in and tried to steal a car," Richheimer recalled. "Butchie turned the air compressor on so there would be a lot of noise; then he took the guy downstairs and broke both his arms and both his legs and threw him out on the street. I had said, you know, that I could call the cops and have him arrested; but Butchie said, 'No, he'll be out in a day and he'll be back. This way, the message goes out to his friends, too.' "

Butchie's were underworld mores, and he had learned them first at home. "His father did fifteen years hard time in Sing Sing for a murder he didn't commit. But he wouldn't rat on the guy who did it. Butchie's mother was given a house, and she got money every month. When his father got out, they gave him the West Side docks as his territory, as a reward," said Richheimer.

Richheimer recalled, too, that sometimes he would accompany his brother and Kimmel, who would routinely negotiate with Teamsters officials at a midtown Italian restaurant, while other men, jackets bulging with their shoulder holsters, stood behind the Teamsters. Neither he nor his brother, he said, had felt uncomfortable in that milieu. Nor, for that matter, he claimed, had Kimmel. On the general subject of doing business with the Mafia, Richheimer said, "I'd rather make a deal with them than with regular businessmen. With regular ones, a deal just means, whose lawyer can be cuter? But with them, a deal is a deal. And if you break it, there's simple justice. But, basically, they're businessmen. That's really what they are."

Richheimer was equally matter-of-fact about the company "slush fund," which he claimed in the sixties contained at least $1 million a year, accumulated by padding employees' expense accounts (including his own) and skimming from the parking lots. "We needed that money to pay the union guys, policemen, firemen, sanitation men, inspectors, you name it."

Nor were these needs restricted to the parking lots; the funeral business, too, relied on the city permits. The policy, according to Richheimer, was companywide. "I once saw $100,000 in a brown paper bag, left on someone's desk to solve a problem," Richheimer claimed.

In the late sixties, Richheimer had become a funeral director at Riverside. "When I was at Riverside, a cop would come to see me. I'd say, 'I have to go to the bathroom.' I'd leave an envelope with the money on the urinal. Then I'd go back and say, 'That felt good. Why don't you do it, too?' That way, neither of us could wire the other."

"It's like that old saying," Richheimer concluded. "Green grease makes New York run."

## 2

Notwithstanding the rapid expansion of Kinney System parking locations in the sixties, Ross had no more interest in becoming a parking lot czar than he had had in dominating the funeral business. Each was a means to an end, ill-defined other than that it would be lucrative and it would be big. From the outset, Ross's gaze had been so fixed on that hazily roseate future that his manner of expression sometimes seemed grandiose, oddly disjunctive with the utilitarian present. The final page of Kinney Service's first annual report (devoted, of course, to the funeral, parking, and cleaning businesses) had borne the title "Beyond the Kinney Horizon," and featured a small epigraph that read, in part: "Kinney . . . knows . . . that public demands for service are destined to increase in the future beyond anyone's grandest expectations."

Ross had not yet been able to discern his specific destiny, but his modus operandi was plain: from the time Kinney Service went public, what most mesmerized him was the prospect of doing deals. It was there that he was at the top of his form, using his numerical facility to outwit, his psychological prowess to subvert—his greatest wins those in which his opposites did not even realize the way in which they'd been bettered, and so left the negotiation dumb and happy. And while it is true that he was industriously schooling himself, poring over documents and asking questions of his lawyers and accountants, what he so excelled at was far more instinctive than learned. He had to learn the language of GAAP, of course, because those were the rules of the game; but the skill with which he played, and bested those rules, was native. His acumen about personality, too, was unleavened by any reflection about his own inner life, or any propensity to articulate what he might have thought about others'; rather, what he knew about human nature seemed to spring from the viscera.

Given Ross's fascination with dealmaking, Kinney Service went public at a particularly propitious moment. It was the eve of what would be the largest wave of merger activity in American history up to that time: between 1962 and 1969, 22 percent of the companies included on the Fortune 500 list of largest manufacturing companies were acquired. And over 80 percent of these were conglomerate mergers (mergers between firms in unrelated businesses), which, of course, was precisely the form in which Kinney Service had been born. Kinney's coming mergers, like so many of these combinations, would be effected not with cash but with an exchange of stock. A company's stock price, therefore, was critical; the higher the market value of the acquiror, the cheaper the acquisition.

Kinney Service's stock price became Ross's fixation. Anything that might hurt it was taboo. Indeed, two employees would later claim that executives of one acquired company subsequently stole over $1 million from Kinney Service but were quietly let go for fear that their prosecution would hurt the stock price. Some acquisitions, too, were done in order to inflate the stock price. A commonly used method of accounting for an acquisition in the sixties was a "pooling of interests," in which the acquired company's earnings were commingled with the acquiror's; this often provided a substantial boost in the calculation of the percentage gain in earnings over the previous year. And earnings' gains, of course, generally had a happy effect on stock prices. (In 1967, the effect of Kinney Service's pooled acquisitions was to elevate its percentage gain in earnings per share from what would have been 19 percent to 34 percent; and, in 1968, from what would have been 8 percent to 16 percent.)

Alan Greenberg, a partner of Bear, Stearns & Company who would years later become its chairman and CEO, and who was an adviser to Kinney Service, joining its board in 1962, later remarked that "Steve Ross was *really* aggressive. Excuse the expression, but you've heard of the guy who would screw anything, even a windowshade? Well, Steve Ross would merge with anything, just to get bigger."

In the first year after going public, Kinney Service acquired two new car-leasing companies in Long Island, as well as two small printing companies (one of them, Candid-Golden, Inc., partly owned by Ross's friend, Joe Lehman). The following year, it acquired Terminal Cleaning Contractors, Inc., another commercial cleaning business. In 1964, it expanded its funeral business by acquiring the business of Walter B. Cooke. The next year, it continued to expand in funeral and cleaning operations, acquiring businesses in New Jersey and California.

In 1966, it made a $25 million acquisition, its largest yet: National Cleaning Contractors, Inc. With this acquisition, Kinney doubled its size, and the combined entities became the largest diversified service company in the United States. William Frankel, the chairman and CEO of National Cleaning, had stipulated that he had to be chairman of the merged company or there would be no deal; so Rosenthal stepped down to become vice-chairman and Ross remained president. Kinney Service changed its name to Kinney National Service.

In 1967, Kinney National acquired Star Circle Wall Systems, Inc., and Hudson Painting and Decorating, to be followed the next year by Panavision, Inc., Schatz Painting Company, Circle Floor Co., Inc., Circle Acoustics Corporation, the Star Carpentry Companies, and Wachtel Plumbing Company.

In the end, none of this frenetic agglomeration would be successful. It would disintegrate bit by bit. But it would have cohered long enough to serve its purpose, vaulting Ross to what he recognized, intuitively, as his ideal sphere. He had begun to gravitate in that direction in 1967, when Kinney Service acquired a talent agency, Ashley Famous—the first acquisition of Ross's career that was engendered by something other than a craving for size.

Ross was introduced to Ted Ashley by a young man named Kenneth Rosen. Ross had first met with Rosen back in 1963, when Rosen had just graduated from Middlebury College and was trying to decide whether or not to go to law school, as his parents wanted; Rosen's uncle, Louis Lefkowitz, was the New York State Attorney General. Introduced by Morton Rosenthal, Rosen had visited Ross in the Kinney Service offices at 10 Rockefeller Plaza. The first thing most people, men as well as women, generally noted about Rosen was that he was stunningly handsome; the second was his ambition—a trait so marked that it almost seemed to have achieved a physicality, so that one could see it in his gestures, hear it in the timbre of his voice. Many thought, too, that it was in disproportion to his talents.

Ross would later say that it was that quality that he had found so captivating, from the moment they met Rosen was then a twenty-two-year-old with no work experience, and Ross was the thirty-six-year-old president of a small but growing public company. "He was sitting opposite me in my office, and he kept staring at my chair," Ross recalled, "and I knew that he wanted more than anything to be there!" Whatever its source, a high-voltage current was struck between the two of them. They rapidly determined that Rosen would forgo law school (much to his parents' displeasure) and join the company as Ross's assistant.

In the summer of 1964, Ross's erstwhile potential backer, Joseph Albritton, who was a major supporter of President Lyndon Johnson, asked Ross to lend some Kinney limousines for the Democratic National Convention, which was to be held in Atlantic City; Ross dispatched them with Rosen. At the convention, Albritton introduced Rosen to a young woman from Texas named Lou, who was even more striking in appearance than Rosen; with deep blue eyes and a nimbus of flaxen hair, she could have stepped out of a Botticelli painting. Several months later, they were married. Rosen had brought his fiancée to meet Ross, before she met Rosen's parents; it was Ross who lent them money for their wedding and their honeymoon. The wedding was held at the Drake Hotel (owned by Bob Tisch, by now Ross's close friend), and Ross was best man.

Despite the intensity of his relationship with Ross—or perhaps because of it—Rosen did not stay at Kinney. He wanted to make much more money than could be justified at the company for someone of his years and experience. Also, his wife would later say that it was important to him to achieve his success independent of Ross, and that Ross understood that he could not hold his young friend too tightly. After some casting about, in September 1967 Rosen joined the Ashley Famous Agency, where he was to concentrate on finding business opportunities in areas outside the talent agency business. Almost immediately he began importuning his boss, Ted Ashley, to meet Ross.

Ashley, who had dropped out of school and begun working at sixteen, had built Ashley Famous into America's second largest talent agency, with an impressive client list that included Tennessee Williams, Arthur Miller, Burt Lancaster, Ingrid Bergman, Jane Fonda, Sean Connery, and Vanessa Redgrave. Now, though, Ashley had tired of it ("the bigger the stars, the more the demands," he would say) and he was eager for something new.

As for Ross, he had decided after Kinney's acquisition of National Cleaning that the company was now big enough that it could afford to branch out in an altogether new direction. William Sarnoff, one of the relatively few at Kinney who had had formal business school training (he had an MBA from Harvard), had done a report on what he concluded would be growth industries in the coming decades: airlines, business machines, money management, and leisure time. It was leisure time (an increasingly "hot" area in the late sixties, when economists believed—mistakenly—that Americans' leisure time would increase, perhaps eventuating in a four-day workweek) that fired Ross. He made his first foray into that territory with the $60 million acquisition of National Periodical Publications, which published *MAD* magazine but was primarily a distribution business. That deal had just been announced when Rosen began urging Ashley to meet Ross.

As Ashley would later recall, his first response was, "Is Kinney shoes or parking lots?" He then told Rosen he had no desire to affiliate with anyone in the parking business. Rosen added that they were in the funeral business. Worse, said Ashley. And the building maintenance business. "I said, 'You mean janitorial?' Forget it.

"Then, Kenny came back with it four or five times. I said no. Finally, he said, 'Look, just put it on the basis of doing me a favor. It's awkward for me not to be able to set it up with you, when he's been asking me to.'"

Ashley agreed to a half-hour meeting with Ross; it lasted for three hours, and the next day they met again and closed the deal. Ashley, who prided himself on his astute sense of people—it was that skill, he believed, that had enabled him to build his company—quickly decided that signing with Ross would provide him the means to transcend his bounds. "I felt that he would buy my talent agency, and I would be under contract to run it—but that this man clearly wouldn't be content with that." For his part in engendering this deal, Rosen received a generous finder's fee.

Kinney's $13 million acquisition of Ashley Famous was announced in November 1967. Ashley would later claim that within a few months, Ross, as expected, asked him what he really wanted to do. "Either run a television network or a movie studio," Ashley replied.

It seems implausible that the two had not communicated this design to one another earlier; indeed, according to one of their colleagues, it had been Ross's plan even before his introduction to Ashley. Considering that anti-trust laws forbid the co-ownership of a talent agency and a production company, acquiring a talent agency might seem a very odd way to choose to enter the production business—since the agency would have to be divested. But, as Ashley would later point out, "they were acquiring me and my guys. They knew *nothing* about it—they didn't have a pass to go to the movies."

In the summer of 1968, Ross and a group of his key executives—Ashley, Ashley's partner W. Spencer Harrison, William Sarnoff, and Allan Ecker, the company's outside lawyer—went to Miami to plan their next move. Ross liked to say he had chosen Miami in tropical midsummer on purpose: no one would be inclined to do anything but stay inside and work. Sarnoff, once again, had made a study, this time of all the movie companies and television networks. By the end of their session, they had selected their candidates: ABC, MGM, and Warner Bros.-Seven Arts.

Ashley knew the principals, so he set up the meetings. ABC's Leonard Goldenson and Elton Rule were cordial but, as Goldenson is said to have put it, such an alliance was "not for us." Robert O'Brien, the MGM chairman, was also polite but, at the same time, deprecating—and certainly not interested. Elliot Hyman, chairman and CEO of Warner-Seven Arts, seemed to view the Kinney contingent somewhat more seriously, at least, but he was noncommittal. And by mid-August, the reason for his evasiveness became plain when it was announced that Warner Bros.-Seven Arts would be acquired by National General Corp., the West Coast conglomerate built by one-time used-car salesman Eugene Klein.

The announcement was followed by almost immediate speculation on Wall Street, however, that the deal would never be consummated because of opposition from the U.S. Justice Department on anti-trust grounds: companies were prohibited from owning both movie production and distribution businesses and National General owned, among other businesses, a chain of movie theaters. Klein, however, was optimistic because he was willing to divest the Warner movie production business, if he had to. What he was most keen on—like all the other would-be suitors who were eagerly eying Warner-Seven Arts—was its music business. As Emanuel Gerard, a leading entertainment analyst on Wall Street whom Ross would later hire, declared to Ross when he came to see Gerard about Warner, "It's not a movie company, it's a record company!"

A. Bruce Rozet, the head of another Los Angeles conglomerate named Commonwealth United, also was intent on acquiring Warner. Commonwealth United was a marginal entity, so much a creature of the heady times—in which creative accounting was making conglomerates, with their feverish merging, look far more profitable than they were, and in which many of these mergers were being accomplished with paper that would turn out to be worthless (becoming known as "Chinese paper")—that Kinney Service looked almost staid by comparison.

Commonwealth had an assortment of insurance companies, some oil interests, and real estate; its major asset was a jukebox company named Seeburg, which it had just acquired in August 1968. The Seeburg deal had been put together by Los Angeles stockbroker and deal maven Burt Kleiner, who concocted many of the deals for the wildest of the conglomerators, and whose office on Wilshire Boulevard in Beverly Hills (appropriately close to where Michael Milken's would be, in a later, kindred decade) was referred to as "Wall Street West." Now, in the late fall of 1968, Kleiner (who was adviser to National General) told Rozet privately that he doubted the National General deal was going to go through, and that Rozet should get ready to move. One of the first things he had to do, Rozet knew, was reach an accord with Frank Sinatra.

Thanks to a maneuver by his long-time attorney and manager Milton Rudin, Frank Sinatra held veto power over any deal that Warner Bros.-Seven Arts might make. In 1963, Rudin had struck a deal for Sinatra with Jack Warner, the last of the four brothers who had started their business in 1903 with a nickelodeon called the Bijou in Newcastle, Pennsylvania. Warner and Rudin agreed to merge a Sinatra record company, Reprise, an unsuccessful division of a parent company which was being dissolved, with Warner Bros. Records, which had been started about four years earlier and done terribly, but by 1963 was just beginning to prosper. Warner would pay Sinatra $2 million, and he would then pay $500,000 for one third of the stock of Warner Reprise. ("They didn't understand the deal," Rudin would say later. "We were trading two thirds of an unsuccessful company for one third of a successful company—plus getting $1.5 million.")

Warner, however, kept putting off signing, and finally the president of Warner Bros., Benjamin Kalmenson, told Rudin, "Go see the old man. He has something on his mind."

Rudin felt a certain warmth for Warner; in this, he was unusual, since Warner was notoriously rough and vulgar, and widely disliked ("I don't have one real friend," he wrote in his autobiography). The relationship between Rudin and Warner had not started auspiciously (Rudin would always recall how, as a young lawyer come to take Warner's deposition, he had first entered the mogul's office back in 1949, and Warner had looked up from his desk and barked to his assistant, "What does this schmuck want?"), but it had improved over the years. To Rudin, Warner seemed remarkably unsophisticated about financial matters, someone who was embarrassed by and eager to hide his naivete. Once, Warner had asked Rudin's advice: he had an old building, and he was wondering what it would cost to tear it down and build a new one. Rudin had said that it would depend on his basis—what had it cost? "How do I know?" Warner had retorted. "This guy said he liked my Rolls-Royce, so I traded my Rolls-Royce for the building."

Now, Warner told Rudin what was troubling him about their deal. He was worried about Sinatra. "Frank spends too much money. What if he decides to sell his interest—and then I have a partner I don't like?"

"You can always buy it," Rudin answered.

*"Ich hab nicht kein gelt* [I have no money]," said Warner.

Then we'll give you the right of approval of the buyer."

"Okay," Warner replied.

The two began to stroll to the studio's executive dining room for lunch, and as they went, Rudin added, "Jack, wouldn't it look better if we made the approval mutual?"

"Sure," Warner said.

Thus it was that Sinatra gained the extraordinary prerogative to veto any sale of Warner Bros.' two-thirds interest in Warner Reprise. Several years went by; the record company, under the aegis of a talented young executive, Mo Ostin, flourished and grew; and then one day in November 1966, Rudin read in the newspaper that the seventy-four-year-old Warner had agreed to sell his stock for about $32 million to Seven Arts Productions, Ltd., a distributor of television films based in Toronto. Rudin did nothing; he preferred that Seven Arts be deep into the acquisition of the whole company before discovering Sinatra's trump.

Which they were—when Alan Hirschfield, a young investment banker from Allen & Co. who was taking a leave of absence from that firm to put Warner and Seven Arts together, was going through some papers and suddenly discovered, to his dismay, Sinatra's veto power. The deal they ultimately struck gave Sinatra $9 million and left him owning 20 percent of Warner Reprise—and his veto still intact.

By 1968, when the latest flock of suitors were approaching Warner Bros.-Seven Arts, each of them understood full well that Warner Reprise was the company's most valuable asset, and Sinatra a power separate and distinct from the rest of the company. Rozet began to court Rudin, as Eugene Klein had, a couple of months earlier. And after December 24—when it was announced that the Justice Department was indeed opposing the National General-Warner combination—Rozet's efforts intensified. He thought he was making some headway. Rudin, however, would later say that he never intended to do a deal with Commonwealth United; he meant it to be merely his "straw man."

On January 28, 1969, the contest Rudin was hoping for emerged Commonwealth United announced, as expected, that it would be making an exchange offer, which it valued at $400 million, to the holders of Warner Bros.-Seven Arts securities. In a surprise move, however, Kinney National Service announced a few hours later that it, too, would be making an exchange offer, one that would be competitive.

Ross was in his element. It was the biggest deal by far of his career—in magnitude, in visibility, in portent. It was, moreover, his first competitive bidding situation—and nothing, but nothing, sparked him like competition. He set up a large blackboard in the conference room at 10 Rockefeller Plaza and began charting plays, much as Allie Sherman had done at the Giants' camp.

Felix Rohatyn, an investment banker at Lazard Frères, was to contact Charles Allen of Allen & Co., who had had long relationships with both Warner Bros. and Seven Arts, and had done more to broker that marriage than anyone. Rohatyn was also to try to enlist Bernard Cornfeld, whose firm, Investors Overseas Services (IOS), owned major blocks of stock of both Commonwealth United and Warner Bros.-Seven Arts. Manny Gerard, the entertainment analyst who had told Ross that Warner was, in essence, a record company, was to investigate Commonwealth United. Ted Ashley was to rally the Hollywood players in their favor. Alan Cohen, a tax lawyer from Paul, Weiss whom Ross had relied on in previous deals, was to devise a novel security that would give them the financial wherewithal they needed to be able to do the deal. And he, Ross, would court those who, in the end, controlled the game: the two biggest shareholders of Warner Bros.-Seven Arts, and, of course, Sinatra.

Rohatyn had met with Ross and Eddie Rosenthal years earlier when they had been considering expanding their nascent rental car business by buying Avis and had sought his help. Now, Rohatyn went to see Charles Allen, who not only had long held sway over the financial dealings of both Seven Arts and Warner Brothers but was now representing Warner Bros.-Seven Arts and Commonwealth United. Rohatyn, slightly intimidated by the crusty Allen, handed him the most recent annual report of Kinney National; Allen gave it a perfunctory glance and tossed it back across the desk, saying, "This is all over—don't waste your time."

Cornfeld was more receptive. An erstwhile Socialist at Brooklyn College, he had hit a bonanza with the idea of an offshore fund. In the late 1950s he had started one called Fund of Funds, which by this time had grown into IOS—with 20,000 employees, 1 million customers in over 100 countries, and managed assets of $2.5 billion. Cornfeld was perhaps most famous for his personal style: a château in France, a stable of classic cars, and legions of girls surrounding him at all times. As John Brooks reported, John Kenneth Galbraith had once asked about IOS, "But where are the *customers'* girls?"

Perhaps Cornfeld had Galbraith's sally in mind when he met Rohatyn. "He had this big office at Park Avenue and 57th Street, "Rohatyn recalled. "There were two girls in mini-skirts and boots, wearing big purple glasses [it was the height of the Beatles craze]. He came in wearing a green Carnaby suit, and suggested I might be interested in the two girls. But I made it clear I was there for tea, and stock. I said he should throw his lot in with us rather than Commonwealth United, which I said I thought would soon go bankrupt."

Rohatyn's assertion was based on the revelations of the Kinney investigation of Commonwealth. It had been summed up by Manny Gerard (who had a propensity for one-liners), announcing excitedly: "There is no Commonwealth United!" In poring over Commonwealth's financials, Gerard had noted that nearly all of its earnings for 1968 had been booked from a transaction that took place in the last few days of the year—the purchase and virtually immediate sale, at enormous profit, of a piece of real estate in Hawaii. And, moreover, the document did not describe the property as having been sold "to an independent third party." It had been sold, they then discovered, to partners of the ubiquitous Kleiner, Bell—one of Commonwealth's advisers in this transaction.

"Someone went to Hawaii to see it—the property was described as a lava bed!" Gerard told me. "What they had essentially done, figuratively speaking, was to buy a piece of land for cash for two dollars and the next week sell it for six—payable at 1 percent over the next twenty years!"

Kinney did not keep this information to itself. It submitted the results of its investigation to a major accounting firm, which then passed it along as a series of questions to the Securities and Exchange Commission (SEC). In order to go forward with its exchange offer, Commonwealth's registration statement, filed with the SEC in the first week of February 1969, had to be cleared by the Commission. "Our strategy was, he will never get out of registration," Gerard said.

Throughout the first three weeks of February a bidding war ensued, with each company revising its offer twice. Critical to Kinney's offer was a novel security devised by Alan Cohen, who by this time had been working on structuring transactions with Ross for several years. "Steve pushed me so that I had to get a tax ruling on nearly every deal—we were always on the cutting edge," Cohen explained. "He was unschooled, but he was so clever. We had the same philosophy: if it made business sense, it should be doable. Here, he said a warrant won't work, we can't use common stock because we can't stand the dilution, but there *should* be a security that will do this. He had the greatest feeling for how problems could be solved in a tax-acceptable way of any businessman I've ever known."

With Ross's urging, Cohen had concocted a security that would be dubbed a "C" preferred stock ("C for Cohen," he liked to say). It was in reality not a preferred but a warrant, inasmuch as its value was predicated on a future stock rise; but, given the laxity of securities regulation in the late sixties, Cohen was able to dress it up so that it appeared to be what it was not. It was crucial that it pass as a preferred, not a warrant, because a warrant would have meant that the transaction could not be tax-free— and the major holders would not agree to the transaction if it were taxable. (What passed muster here, however, would be corrected "before the abuse became too rampant," as Cohen wryly put it later; by the fall of 1969, the IRS would rule that such a security was not a preferred. And by 1970, the rules on pooling would be tightened.)

With the financial legerdemain in place and the Warner board meeting to review the two competing offers just several days away, Ross set off to meet with the two biggest shareholders of Warner-Seven Arts, M. Morris Schwebel and Carroll Rosenbloom, who were in Florida aboard Schwebel's yacht.

Schwebel and Rosenbloom had been friends and co-investors for many years, first linked by their closeness to Louis ("Uncle Lou") Chesler, the notorious 300-pound, hard-drinking Canadian stock promoter, who also had ties to Meyer Lansky and assorted bookmakers and gamblers. Schwebel had been Chesler's lawyer and right-hand man for many years; Rosenbloom, who owned the Baltimore Colts, met Chesler in 1956 when a syndicate of which Chesler was part took over the General Development Corporation, where Rosenbloom was a major shareholder. The three men also invested in a company called Universal Controls, which specialized in the leasing of pari-mutuel equipment for racetracks, and in Associated Artists Productions, which was the predecessor company to Seven Arts.

Chesler was the chairman and largest stockholder of Seven Arts; its second and third largest were Schwebel and Rosenbloom. Schwebel, however, had had to resign from its board after he was convicted of securities fraud in 1961. In 1964, Seven Arts' president Elliot Hyman and others decided that the company should be listed on the American Stock Exchange—something which would be impossible as long as Chesler remained. So Chesler was bought out, the board was reorganized, and Schwebel and Rosenbloom remained as the company's largest stockholders.

Now, Ross worked his charm on the two men He had brought along a dossier on Commonwealth United which they found persuasive. Schwebel was quickly taken with Ross's talents (his appreciation of them would grow over time, as Schwebel attested in a speech at every Warner board meeting for the next twenty-four years). The bond Ross established with Rosenbloom, as the owner of a football team, was predictable; less so, the equally strong one he formed with Rosenbloom's young wife, Georgia, a former chorus girl upon whom Rosenbloom doted. Ross had heard that she took astrology so seriously that she always factored it into major decisions. As he would later tell the story, he had done some research and then scheduled this meeting for a day when (as he was able to discuss in casual conversation with her) the planets' positioning favored her husband's striking a deal.

While Ross was in Florida, finalizing his deal for the Rosenbloom and Schwebel stock, Ashley made the Kinney presentation to the Warner-Seven Arts board; Rozet made his; and the directors voted to recommend the Kinney offer.

Despite the vulnerability of Commonwealth United, which would in fact dissolve in the early seventies, it had by no means been a forgone conclusion that it would lose this fight. Commonwealth was largely a confection, but no more so than others whose acquisitions went unchallenged and were consummated in the late sixties. It was one of those periods of ecstatic derangement in the financial world when, for a brief time, everything seems possible, the miraculous becomes mundane, the outcasts are let in, the infirm walk. Commonwealth had merely sought to join the ragged procession.

After the Warner Bros.-Seven Arts board voted for Kinney, Ross's last major step was negotiating final terms with Rudin, with whom he had already had several meetings. The two deal aficionados went at it with gusto. Rudin had always considered himself facile with numbers, but he thought Ross outmatched him. Ross, for his part, thought he might have met someone trickier than he. In the midst of their negotiations, Rudin suffered a throat hemorrhage and was advised by his doctor not to speak for several days. In his sessions with Ross, therefore, he indicated that he would communicate by writing notes. Ross suspected a ploy—maybe Rudin was doing it to gain more time to think, and, thus, an edge. So he, too, wrote notes. They were both heavy smokers, and at the end of each session, Ross, abstracted, would inadvertently pocket Rudin's gold Dunhill lighter.

When they finally came to terms, Rudin handed him the lighter, saying, "There. *Now* you can keep it." Ross considered it his good-luck charm; for many years to come he kept it with him always, lighting his cigarettes, extending it to light others' before they could reach for a match, flipping it continually in his palm; it would be his trademark.

Sinatra's agreement, however, did not ensure that Ahmet Ertegun, the Turkish-born, urbane, socially pretentious president of Atlantic Records, which had been acquired by Warner Reprise in 1967 and was intensely successful, would remain with the company; his contract, in fact, was just coming up for renewal. Ertegun had indicated, moreover, that he would not stay. When Ross, accompanied by Ashley and Rohatyn (Rohaytn and Ertegun knew each other socially) went to see Ertegun, Ertegun remarked to Rohatyn in French (utterly confident that neither Ross nor Ashley would understand him) that there was no way he was going along with such a group.

"Ted had this jive talk: 'We're going to have a great marriage, we're going to make love,'" Ertegun would recall. "I thought, what the hell is he talking about?"

One of Ross's favorite anecdotes in years to come would concern an exchange that took place with Ertegun during dinner that evening at "21." As Ross would tell it, a young friend of his son's had stopped by at home the day before and, upon hearing that Kinney was going to acquire Atlantic Records, said, "The guys at Atlantic are geniuses. They're the ones who just managed to put together Stevie Winwood and the old guys from Cream in a group called Blind Faith, and they've already sold out Madison Square Garden without even cutting a record."

At dinner, Ertegun, resistant, was offering an example of how little Ross knew about the music business. "Look, I've got a new group, Blind Faith—"

"You mean the guys from the Old Cream and Stevie Winwood, and they just sold out Madison Square Garden without cutting a record?"

"Yeah, man, you've got it!" Ross would describe Ertegun as yelling excitedly, leaping to his feet—and then agreeing to clinch the deal.

Ross's version made the better story, although it did not happen quite that way. His son's friend had mentioned the group, but it was Manny Gerard (a rock fan) who had elaborated on it to Ross just the day before the dinner with Ertegun. More important, the canny Ertegun did not make the deal because he was so easily gulled. He did appreciate Ross's gambit, inasmuch as it indicated more of a willingness to relate than he had expected from this person whom he thought of, simply, as an erstwhile funeral director. But what was decisive, he would later say, was Ross's earnestly pleading, "Give us a chance," and his assurances that he would do everything in his power to keep Ertegun happy (a vow that he would keep).

However humorous Ross's telling—and slight embellishing—of this story, it also suggested the difficulty of this juncture for him. Just a few years back, it had seemed almost incredible that he was the young president of a public company, albeit one that trafficked in funerals, parking, and office cleaning. Now, he was attempting to vault so high, again, that all he had achieved before was disdained by the denizens of this new sphere; and he had to overcome an initial bias against him in men like Ashley, Ertegun, and others.

While he was nearly always able to win these people with his presentation of himself—charming, beguiling, eager, deferential—there was on at least one occasion a crack in the facade. An entertainment executive who was about to join Ross's enterprise, and had already negotiated his deal, was troubled by last-minute doubts about what it would be like to work for Ross. He went to see him, and expressed some of his nervousness; by the end of a couple of hours' conversation Ross had sweetened the deal, and the executive had agreed to it. As he was leaving Ross's office, this executive recalled, Ross remarked, "Well, now we know you're a whore. We just didn't know your price."

"It wasn't said with a smile—it was mean, and ugly," this executive continued. "But what I told myself—and what enabled me to go forward—was that he said it because he was so insecure. And, over the years, I never heard anything like that from him again."

Kinney's acquisition of Warner Bros.-Seven Arts would not close until July 1969, but the most celebratory closing took place when Ross and Sinatra signed the Sinatra deal, in mid-March 1969. After Ross and Rudin had completed their negotiations, Sinatra and Ross met for dinner, and, as Rudin later recalled, the two "hit it off right away." They wanted to close the Sinatra deal in New Jersey for tax reasons; Sinatra suggested his mother's home in Fort Lee. But he warned Ross not to let his mother see the check, or she'd grab it. Worried about her son's spending habits, Dollie Sinatra was always trying to get hold of his money so she could save it for him.

The appointed night arrived. It was appropriately festive; Sinatra's mother had cooked a wonderful Italian dinner, and the wine was flowing. Allan Ecker, Ross's lawyer, whom Sinatra kept referring to as "Counselor," noted that the family room was hung with pictures not only of Sinatra's several wives but of the numerous women who had been his girlfriends; in the eyes of the doting Dollie Sinatra, all "Frank's girls" were worthy of display. And when they signed the papers and it was time for the check to change hands, Ross first held out one—which Mrs. Sinatra quickly grabbed (it was for $1,000)—and then quietly slipped Sinatra the other.

Sinatra received a package worth $22.5 million and Rudin, for his part, a "finder's fee" of $1.5 million, to be paid out in consulting fees over the next ten years, as well as 25,000 shares of Kinney stock for $25,000 (the stock at that time was worth more than $750,000). It was the first time Sinatra ever had that kind of money; and it represented wealth of a new order for Rudin, too. Both were suitably grateful, and Ross—despite the fulsomeness of the deal—would continue to feel indebted to Sinatra.

When a shareholders' suit was filed a couple of months later, challenging Rudin's finder's fee as a waste of corporate assets, the company fought it. (Ross would later comment ruefully that all the notes he and Rudin had written had had to be produced, in discovery. He learned his lesson after that. In future litigation he would always claim he kept no notes, not even an appointment book. And he instructed his executives to avoid memo writing. At a special Kinney shareholders' meeting called to approve the deal in June 1969, one shareholder demanded to know "what services make Milton Rudin worth $1.5 million?"

"It's most difficult to take apart portions of a deal," Ross replied smoothly, having prepared for this question well in advance. "It's the sum of the parts that counts and this is one of the best deals Kinney has ever made."

Before Warner, virtually everything Ross had done had been a preface; transient; utilitarian. Alliances he had formed had been little but handholds to enable him to climb higher. Now, for the first time, he had appropriated a business that he would not just as happily discard. He would continue to climb—he could not not—but he would never leave its province. He did not need to. It offered him everything he might want: seemingly infinite vistas of business possibility; astronomical compensation; entree to a glamorous, star-studded world. And it was, moreover, a business where his instincts with people—cultivating them, catering to them, winning their favor—would be extraordinarily, even uniquely, useful. Attending to the needs of Hollywood stars was, after all, the ultimate service business. Here, the professional empathizer par excellence of Riverside Chapel ("May I be of service to you?") had found his rarefied home.

Before Ross could become fully acclimated to life at this new plateau, however, there was an enormous amount of baggage, accumulated on the long climb, that had to be shed. By mid-1970, Wall Street's infatuation with conglomerates had ended. Litton Industries, which had once sold at over $112 a share, had fallen to $20; Ling-Temco-Vought had gone from its high of about $169 to $12. Kinney's stock, too, had declined, though not precipitously; but there was no reason to believe that it, too, would not suffer for being a conglomerate in the near future.

That was the exogenous rationale; but the more salient reason to shed the other businesses was the businesses themselves. The funeral business had been extremely profitable long before Ross ever joined it, and it continued to be; it had been the steady engine that contributed most to Kinney's unbroken record of earnings growth through the sixties. But it was an embarrassment to Ross now, something he was eager to leave behind (indeed, he would be upset by a glowing article about him in the

*New York Times* in 1972, because it bore the headline: "From Caskets to Cable"). He was afraid, however, that the Rosenthals would never part with their funeral business. So he was surprised and delighted when, in late 1970, Morton Rosenthal suggested that perhaps they should sell it.

Kinney Parking had undergone enormous expansion in the sixties (Caesar Kimmel had had the political connections that had enabled Kinney to obtain desirable leases from the city), but its operations had never been extraordinarily profitable. The rental car business, which Ross in the early sixties had promoted as the company's flagship, had grown under his aegis but never made money. It had finally been quietly sold in 1968, in a meager deal that Kinney was forced to renegotiate, downward, the following year.

According to Ross's old friend Judd Richheimer, of course, the lots were skimmed by the company for its slush fund, so they would in that sense have served an important function. But they were also a prime source of the rumors of organized crime connections that had continued to plague Kinney from the start and had intensified in the late sixties. In June 1970, moreover, *Forbes* published an article about Kinney that said, in part: "Rumors have long circulated linking Kinney with the Mafia. Forbes has been unable to find a shred of solid evidence to support them, but nonetheless put the question direct to Caesar P. Kimmel, executive vice president and one of Kinney's biggest stockholders."

Kimmel was quoted issuing a spirited denial, declaring, ". . . I've lived with this over the years—the charge that we are run by the Mafia. It just isn't true. We don't wear shoulder holsters. We've never been under the influence of any underworld group."

The rumors, Kimmel continued, had originated with the investigation by the New York District Attorney's Office of a crap game being run in New Jersey in 1948–50, to which players were brought in limousines from a Kinney lot. ". . . My dad came to us with a business proposition to let limousines use our lot at night. I was so young and inexperienced."

Asked whether his father, referred to by *Forbes* as "a big gambler," had ever once had control of Kinney, Kimmel replied, "Never. My father has never had anything to do with the founding of Kinney. My dad owned a few pieces of some parking lots and he wasn't too interested in the lots, so he gave them to me and said, 'See what you can do with them.' After that my father had nothing to do with running the lots."

Kinney had sued, and *Forbes* then issued an apology to settle the suit. But Ross had been apoplectic about the article, and it could only have heightened his determination to put some distance between the parking lots and his new environment.

As for the rest of the businesses that Kinney had so frenetically acquired through the late sixties—mainly cleaning, maintenance, and construction—they seemed likely to become millstones. Laurence Tisch, whose brother Bob was Ross's friend and a Kinney director, would comment later that he had thought these acquisitions flew in the face of one of business's most basic tenets. "Nearly all the businesses Ross was buying were personal businesses—Circle Flooring, Schatz Painting," Tisch said. "As an entrepreneur, it's one thing to work for yourself, another thing for somebody else. They're going to steal for themselves, they're not going to steal for you. I thought at the time that these were terrible acquisitions. You don't buy personal businesses." (According to Alan Cohen, however, Ross had had no illusions about the intrinsic value of these acquisitions. "He did it for the [increase to earnings from the] pooling. All the conglomerates were doing it. And he acquired construction companies because he could pay a low multiple for them. Then, the pooling rules changed in 1970. Steve and I said, 'No more fun.' ")

By the end of 1971, Ross had made all these problem businesses "disappear" with a dexterity suggestive of the sleight-of-hand he had learned as a youth, and continued to practice. After long months of complex negotiations, a deal had been struck for Service Corporation International (SCI) to buy the Kinney funeral business for about $30 million. In preparation for its signing, Ross, as usual, had done his homework on the SCI principal, and had discovered that the executive was enamored of show business; so Ross arranged to hold the closing in Las Vegas, when Sinatra would be there. Shortly before their scheduled meeting, however, Ross and Alan Cohen (who had left Paul, Weiss to join Warner in 1970 as an executive vice-president and Ross's right-hand associate) were notified by their lawyers, hammering out details of the contract at SCI headquarters in Texas, that Riverside did not have clear title to a monument business that SCI considered an important feature of the deal.

As Cohen tells the story: "The SCI executive had mentioned, some time earlier, that he'd read a book about body language in negotiations, and Steve had asked me to read it. I told him what it said. So now Steve said, 'When he comes in, we'll play it cool.' He walked in. Steve sat down next to him on the sofa, and started doing card tricks. I, meanwhile, sat opposite him, with my arms folded across my chest (according to the book, that means, 'Fuck you')." The deal was signed as planned.

All the other businesses, including parking and cleaning, were spun off to a company called National Kinney Corp.—a public company with the majority of its shares owned by the new incarnation of Kinney National, which was now renamed Warner Communications Inc. (WCI). Through this maneuver, these businesses were made sufficiently distant that any problems with corruption (National Cleaning and its two chief executives would plead *nolo contendere* to criminal charges of price fixing brought in 1976, for example) would not tarnish the image of the new WCI; but, in the event they should prove profitable, they were still majority-owned.

From Ross's point of view, the spin-off achieved many purposes, not least the dispatching of Andrew (Pete) Frankel. Joe Lehman, the old friend to whom Ross had made good on his promise of delivering Riverside's printing business, noted that Ross had always pursued only those acquisitions where he was certain there would be no one capable of vying with him for control. In the case of National Cleaning, the largest deal by far until Warner, William Frankel had insisted upon being chairman of the company, but he was an older man whom Ross never considered a threat. In 1969, after the Warner acquisition, Ross stepped up from president to be co-CEO with Frankel—a shared tenure in name only; Ross was always in charge.

However, while he accepted Ross's dominance, Frankel was eager for his son Pete to ascend to a leadership role in the company when he retired. Now, that issue had been finessed. Pete Frankel went off, quite happily, to be CEO of National Kinney—and to preside over what was, as the next several years would irrefutably demonstrate, merely the detritus from Ross's launch.

The spin-off had solved other personnel problems as well, less pressing but still troublesome to Ross. The company's management ranks were naturally filled with men who had come up through the funeral, parking, and cleaning businesses. They were not exactly the confreres with whom Ross envisioned himself moving into this new world. But dismissing them would have been another matter.

It was a signal trait: Ross could almost never face people and tell them that he was firing them, or that they couldn't have the promotion or the raise they sought. His wife Carol would recall that he could never fire their household help; he would send someone from the office to lend her moral support while she did it. The only times he could do so were those rare instances when he felt challenged, and so acted in anger; he is said to have thus fired Marc Iglesias, his old friend who had taught him the funeral business, when Iglesias repeatedly attacked something Ross wanted in a meeting with others at the company. In general, however, Ross seemed to crave the adulation that came from his being the solicitous provider of service and bounty; and, conversely, to dread—to the point of avoiding at all cost—the displeasure, or dislike, that he might incur as the agent of pain.

In the late sixties, as the acquisitions swelled the company's ranks, its board members and officers had increased in number concomitantly—until, in 1969, its board had grown from ten directors to twenty-four. There were forty-one officers, among them twenty-four vice-presidents; four assistant vice-presidents; four assistant secretaries; and four assistant treasurers.

Many of these people were the beneficiaries of Ross's almost helpless bonhomie. Salim Lewis, the legendary trader who was one of the founders of Bear, Stearns, had joined the Kinney board in 1966. In 1970, when Ross was prevailed upon by Alan Cohen to impose some measure of control over the number of board members and officers, Ross agreed that Lewis's seat could better be filled by Felix Rohatyn, who had assisted in the Warner acquisition and would be an important ally in the future. On the given day, Lewis came to see Ross and spent two hours in his office. After he'd left, Cohen, aware of the plan, went into Ross's office. "Well?" he asked, expectantly.

Ross looked up, a little sheepish. "I couldn't do it," he said. "I just couldn't do it."

3

With the creation of WCI, Ross was more untrammelled than he had ever been. It was unmistakably his company now, not his in-laws'. Even Frankel, his nominal co-CEO, would die suddenly in June 1972, enabling Ross to assume the title of chairman and president. And, for the first time, he was in businesses which—in and of themselves, not as a means to an end—thrilled him.

What had so tantalized Ross about business, from the start, was certainly not day-to-day operation, with its myriad details, or even the lofty overview of management that monitored the whole; it was, rather, what hovered, indistinct, about the edges of the thing—chimerae which promised to shower gold if one could only give them substance. For Ross, nothing quite rivalled this sweet lure of a bonanza, which some pursuits (like gambling, for example) and some businesses promised more than others. Workaday businesses—like the workaday life of his father as he had been growing up—Ross had always known were not for him.

Shortly after Kinney's acquisition of Warner, the movie company bought rights to a documentary film on the Woodstock festival for about $500,000. Within a few weeks of its release in mid-1970, it was clear that the film was going to gross about $20 million, affording Warner a profit of roughly $5–$6 million. Euphoric, Ross crowed to his associates: "Where has this business been all my life?"

"Ross liked businesses with hidden oil wells, where you could get nothing or a five-fold gain. He preferred that to a business where you were likely to have steady 15 percent returns," commented Roger Smith, WCI's vice-president for investor relations in the seventies. Both the movie and record businesses appealed to him in this way; indeed, because the capital investment required was so much lower in records than in movies, the returns tended to be greater. And the transience of these products—no sooner released than they had to be followed by new creations—was also tailormade for Ross, who needed constant fresh stimuli to keep from being bored.

Publishing, on the other hand, never held a similar allure for Ross. A book might be a hit, but there were not the sudden geysers of returns that movies and records could trigger. At Warner, therefore, publishing would always be a backwater. (One publishing executive would say that in years of meetings that Ross attended, one of the few times he remembered Ross's becoming animated was when, at one session in which they were discussing paperback sales, Ross had suddenly demanded, "Why don't we charge 99 cents instead of 95 cents?")

While Ross had considered the Warner Bros. movie production company the weak sister in the deal, it turned out upon inspection to be even weaker than anticipated. In September 1969, Kinney had announced a writedown of $59,366,000—radical in size—of the asset values of all movies, including those in process and just released. *Forbes* would pan this move as another example of Hollywood financial finagling, contrived virtually to guarantee a turnaround in profit and make the new management look good; but in the end, while some of the thirty-nine movies at issue made a little more and others a little less than had been estimated, the projected total of a loss of roughly $60 million proved prescient.

Ashley Famous had been divested in the course of the Warner Bros. acquisition, and Ted Ashley, as planned, became chairman and CEO of Warner Bros. He reached an agreement with Ross at the outset. "Most companies that are run by boards are failures," Ashley said to Ross. "There is no evidence, furthermore, that you know how to read a script, or how a budget can be shaved, or which actor is better in what movie. Leave me entirely alone. Let me hire and fire anyone, make all the decisions about what to finance—and you've got a great remedy. You can always fire me."

This pact would become scriptural for Ross: he would allow all his division heads great autonomy, telling them to make their own mistakes and just not give him any surprises. Thus, he encouraged them to feel like entrepreneurs (when one of his record company executives told Ross that he was thinking of expanding into a new area of music, but wondered whether he should since he might lose about $10 million, Ross, characteristically, responded, "It's *your* company. If you don't think you can handle being ten million in a hole, don't do it—but it's *your* company!") He was as good as his word, too, never second-guessing them; in good times and bad, he would always be their biggest booster. It was a warm, magnanimous, paternal style that suited his personality perfectly—and its effect was inoculatory. In an industry beset with management turnover that took a significant toll on competitors' businesses, Warner's top executives were uniformly long-lived.

And, as was so often the case with Ross, there was another, more subtle, hidden payoff for him, as well; for in granting his executives such autonomy, his control of the company was not diminished (as some less astute leader might fear) but fortified. For these executives in a sense became captives of their freedom; it became the essential requisite of their professional lives—and it was a freedom that Ross, uniquely, granted. (Years later, when he would be challenged for control, his executives would unite against his adversary, protesting that the company could not exist without him: that he *was* the company.)

Ashley's choice for head of production at Warner Bros. amply illustrated his just-established freedom. He chose the improbable John Calley, a producer who had never worked for a major studio and was so intensely idiosyncratic that it was difficult to imagine him in any corporate setting, albeit one in Hollywood. He had, however, a shimmering intelligence, and eliciting ideas from him was as simple as turning on the tap. Moreover, he was so quirky that the talent tended to relate to him not as a bureaucratic studio head but as one of their own. Calley, in turn, called Frank Wells, a lawyer at a small Hollywood firm, Gang, Kopp & Tyre, where he and Mickey Rudin had worked together for years. Wells, a former Rhodes Scholar who was reflexively upright and steadying (a nice counterbalance to Calley), joined the team as their head of business affairs, becoming president of the studio in 1972.

The movie business had gone into a deep slough in the late sixties, not because of the economics of the business or the influence of television (as was suggested at the time), but because of a dearth of executive judgment at the studios. It was the twilight of the movie moguls' regime; in the seventies and early eighties, a new breed of executives (Barry Diller, Jeffrey Katzenberg, Michael Eisner, Robert Daly) would take their respective places. But Warner Bros. was first. Ashley, Calley, and Wells seized the moment, securing talent in pictures for the kinds of terms (relatively little money, and a not very large percentage of the gross) that within five years would be obsolete.

By 1972, their success was writ large. The studio had produced a carefully limited number of pictures (seventeen to twenty a year), at an average cost of less than $2.5 million each. With 1971 pictures that included *Summer of '42, Billy Jack, Klute, A Clockwork Orange,* and *Dirty Harry, Variety* in late 1972 would declare Warner Bros. "by any yardstick the 1971 leader, and the smash results of such 1972 releases as 'What's Up, Doc?' and 'Deliverance' indicated that the company's winning streak . . . [is continuing]."

Warner's music business was also one of the strongest in its industry in 1972. By now it comprised not only Warner Bros./Reprise Records and Atlantic Records, but also Elektra Records (bought from Jac Holzman) and Asylum Records (from David Geffen). WCI was the only company which had several different record labels that all operated with autonomy, sometimes competing against each other for an artist ("It increased the odds—Steve loved it for that reason," said Mo Ostin, the long-time and legendary chairman of Warner Bros./Reprise). There were best-selling records on the WCI labels by Aretha Franklin, Jethro Tull, the Rolling Stones, the Doors, Stephen Stills, James Taylor, Carly Simon, and others.

Once WCI had its three major labels—Warner, Elektra/Asylum, and Atlantic—Ostin believed that the company had sufficient volume to justify starting its own distribution system, much like the one used by Columbia Records, which was the industry leader at this time. "The distributors we were using were all independent businessmen with their own priorities. We had no control over them unless we were very, very hot," Ostin said later. He urged his idea on Ross, who was quickly persuaded, and, by 1971, both Warner Elektra Atlantic, or WEA Corp. (distributing domestically) and WEA International (distributing U.S. artists abroad and also developing indigenous local artists) were formed.

The virtues of controlling a product from its creation to its sale would become one of Ross's favorite maxims. As he would declare years later, "I love distribution businesses. I love to control our own destiny. If you develop a product and you have distribution, that's the name of the game."

The movie and record executives were well rewarded for their primacy in their fields. From the beginning at Warner, Ross grasped the importance of finding the best creative people and paying them so much that money could not lure them away. He instituted a system of compensation that would become a company hallmark: salaries for key executives were standard, but bonuses—at Ross's discretion—could swell compensation to an amplitude not matched at any other entertainment company. And in the early seventies, that is exactly what happened; at least a half dozen executives of the music and movie companies, including Ashley,

Ostin, and Ahmet Ertegun, were making more money than those in comparable positions elsewhere—and more money than Ross.

Around the time of the Warner acquisition, Ross had started a tireless litany, exhorting his executives to "dream." He had begun telling a story about something that his father had said—a story which many who knew Ross in the early years did not recall having heard at that time, and which is probably apocryphal, but which he did in any event incorporate to such a degree that he would repeatedly proffer it, in private exchanges with his people and in public speeches, over the coming decades.

"When I was a teenager, my father was dying—he knew he was dying, I knew he was dying—and he gave me the best advice possible. He said, there are three categories of people in this world. The first is the individual who wakes up in the morning and goes into the office and proceeds to dream. The second category is the individual who gets up in the morning, goes into the office, and proceeds to work sixteen hours a day. The third is the individual who comes into the office, dreams for about an hour, and then proceeds to do something about his dreams.

"He said, 'Go into the third category for only one reason: there's no competition.' "

By 1972, the movie and music companies were so patently successful that Ross felt free to follow his own advice; he was scanning the world from his aerie and charting new directions. Sometimes they seemed quite random, the product of his free-floating enthusiasm. WCI became a backer of Gloria Steinem's *Ms.* magazine, owning 25 percent. It started a drive-through wildlife preserve in Milford, New Jersey, called "Warner Bros. Jungle Habitat," where animals roamed free and visitors stayed in their cars. And Ross made a deal with Dr. Peter Goldmark, the former head of CBS Laboratories, to start a research and development laboratory, Goldmark Communications Corporation, majority-owned by WCI. Goldmark, the inventor of color television and the long-playing record, would work on two-way cable television, domestic satellite communications, and electronic publishing.

But nothing so compelled Ross as cable. He had asked W. Spencer Harrison, Ashley's partner in Ashley Famous, to do a study on promising areas of growth for WCI. Harrison wrote a long dissertation on cable television. At the time, cable was largely used to enhance reception, most often in rural areas; but Harrison believed that it would become an important communications medium. And if that were true, it would fit so neatly into Ross's grand scheme—among other things, it could become the distribution vehicle for the studio's movies. For Ross, the embryonic state of cable became its appeal. He was enchanted by the prospect of entering a business barely in its infancy, whose potential for growth tested the limits of even his fecund imagination.

Finally he had found an industry where his inflated manner of expression did not seem quite so incongruous, and even, occasionally, found its echo. In his letter to shareholders in the 1971 annual report, Ross quoted the Sloan Commission Report on Cable Communications: "Cable technology, in concert with other allied technologies, seems to promise a communications revolution. There have been such revolutions before. Some 500 years ago, the handwritten manuscript gave way to the printed book. . . . Some hundred years ago the first telephone wires were strung. . . . The revolution now in sight may be nothing less than either of those. It may conceivably be even more."

By the fall of 1972, WCI had become a major participant in the cable industry. It had acquired, in exchange for WCI stock, the cable television businesses of Continental Telephone Corporation, TeleVision Communications Corporation (TVC), and Cypress Communications Corporation, all now grouped in Warner Cable Corp.—its chairman and president, Alfred Stern.

Stern, who had started TVC in 1962, recalled having gotten a call from Ross, whom he had never heard of, in late 1971. Ross came to his office, and soon was saying to him, "If you could dream—give me a rough idea of how much capital your company would require in the next five years, in order to build all the systems and do everything you would want to do."

"I'd never been so bold to think that way," Stern would say later. "So I said, 'Let me think for a minute.' And I thought about the biggest number I could think of. I said, 'Fifty million.'

"He said, 'You've got it.' "

Stern was awestruck. He thought that if Ross were for real, the numbers were gargantuan. And, he would reflect later, Ross had so quickly perceived what would tempt him. It was not that Stern's company was in trouble and needed a bailout. It was not that he wanted to cash in and retire. What was irresistible to him in this extraordinarily capital-intensive business was the notion of having a treasury of such size. And what Ross had explained to him was that with the rich cash generators of records and movies, he could afford a cash-needy business, like cable.

Ross became messianic on the subject of cable. His aides counselled him that when he met with Wall Street analysts, he should restrain himself; take ten minutes on cable, thirty minutes on the other operations, they would say—then you can come back to cable, if you must. Ross would listen, nod—and then spend forty minutes on cable. "Steve would go on and on about his vision of cable, and he would be hurt, almost, that they didn't get what he was trying to tell them," one adviser recalled. "He wanted to be liked, respected, admired. He wanted to be able to *win* them to his way of thinking. He was the ultimate salesman."

This aide thought the difficulty Ross was having with the analysts had as much to do with delivery as content. "One on one, Steve was without peer at persuading you that he was your best friend and had only your interests at heart. But that charm and ability to persuade in a group session looked fraudulent. In a group of three or more, you reached for your wallet."

Vestiges of the "con artist" that one of his Kinney partners had recognized in him a decade earlier never seemed more apparent than when Ross, in the fever of excitement that this new technology generated in him, would wax eloquent about things that did not exist. A favorite of Ross's was the "frame-grabber"—a term Goldmark had used for a cable-related device not yet invented. Several Ross associates would cringe at these meetings as he veered headlong (undeterred by their warnings) into his "frame-grabber" pitch. "He was a little off the deep end," recalled a major securities analyst. "The passion was so enormous that, finally, his advisers told him not to speak at our meetings."

Largely because of WCI's entry into the cable business, its stock became very volatile. On the strength of cable's favor on Wall Street in mid-1972, it rode up to 50; but about a year and a half later it would be as low as 6. (Ross would take this opportunity to cause WCI to buy in large amounts of its stock.) One major reason for the drop was a press report in the fall of 1972—just when all WCI's major acquisitions were completed—that the White House Office of Telecommunications Policy (OTP) was likely to recommend separation of cable television system ownership and cable television programming. Critics of that policy, obviously including Ross and his lobbyists, insisted that such a move would severely stunt the growth of the industry.

In the 1972–74 period, the specter of regulation continued to shadow WCI and to depress its stock price. Ross was no stranger to the process of seeking political favor; he just was familiar with it at a different level. He had, after all, come up in the parking business, where success had depended upon dealings with the city bureaucracy, from the inspector at the lots to the political officials who determined whether Kinney's bid for a location would win. Now, instead of the $100,000 left in an envelope on a desk, or money left on a urinal, that Richheimer had described, a list of key politicians was drawn up and each of WCI's senior executives was told to whose campaign they should be contributing.

One of the more controversial of these contributions was the one—of $137,856—that Ted Ashley made to President Richard Nixon's 1972 reelection campaign. Ashley's contribution came to light when Common Cause successfully sued to have the names of contributors made public. It aroused considerable comment, both because of its size and the fact that Ashley was well known to have been a lifelong Democrat. When he was questioned in a 1973 *New York* magazine article about whether the money had in fact come from Warner's corporate funds, Ashley replied, "Oh, no, it would have been illegal to give corporate money."

In response to further questions, he said he had not paid tax on the contribution, although the law stipulates that tax must be paid on a gift of over $3,000. He said that a Nixon emissary had told him he could avoid the tax by breaking the donation into portions of under $3,000 and giving them to separate GOP county committees. His lawyer, Ashley said, handled the details. Years later, he would say to me only that he regretted the incident, inasmuch as it had been "a mistake," and he refused to discuss it further.

Charles Colson, the special assistant to the President who in the Watergate prosecutions would plead guilty to obstruction of justice, and who, it would later emerge, had been one of the principal aides in charge of collecting illicit contributions, resigned from the White House in the spring of 1973 and opened a law firm with a partner, David Shapiro. Colson would be indicted roughly six months later. But in that period of time—although it was kept very quiet at WCI, and although Colson's partner, Shapiro, later said he was shocked to learn of it—Colson was kept on the WCI payroll as a consultant *vis-à-vis* cable regulation.

Indeed, according to a former WCI executive, it was because of Colson's relationship to the company that Warner Publishing was told not to enter into contract for the publication of a manuscript that had been submitted to them by Watergate burglar James McCord in the spring of 1973. The manuscript, in which Colson was a major player, was full of revelations that would not emerge for another four to six months, in the course of the Ervin hearings. Had it been rushed into print, it would have been a publishing coup.

The person at WCI who dealt most with Colson was Alan Cohen, who was heavily involved in overseeing the cable operations. In the fall of 1972, with ominous intimations emerging from the OTP, Cohen had begun to cultivate Colson. Cohen was very sharp, as ambitious as he was bright, and in his pragmatism, at least, he and Colson (who was notorious for the poster that hung in his office: "If you've got them by the balls, their hearts and minds will follow") were not so ill-matched.

Colson had been under suspicion in the press since the Watergate break-in in the summer of 1972; he was considered so sullied that Nixon had very nearly fired him immediately after the November election, although he then decided to let him remain another few months. Nonetheless, asked later about WCI's having hired Colson the following spring, Cohen replied, "As to why we hired him, he would have been clean (he wasn't indicted until sometime later); he certainly knew the people in the White House; and he was said to be brilliant."

Cohen had less kind words for Clay Whitehead, the head of the OTP, who was advocating the separation of ownership of cable systems from ownership of programming. Whitehead, Cohen said, was "one of those eggheads, with their idealistic theories, who don't understand that you gotta make a buck."

When Whitehead's Report to the President was finally released in early 1974, it would indeed recommend that separation, but it would go unheeded by Congress. Whitehead later said that he had believed that government should promote the growth of cable as an independent medium to create the availability of more programming in the home; but that he also believed that if ownership of systems and programming were not separated, a monopoly would be created. "I viewed my main mission in life as trying to inject more competition into the communications industry," Whitehead told me.

Colson and he had frequently clashed, he added, "but not out of any principle on his part. He saw the networks and the press, generally, as biased—on the Nixon tapes, you may recall, he talks about taking Kay Graham's license away. So when it served his purpose to use cable to beat up on the broadcasters, then he was for cable at any cost."

It was easy to recall the Steve Ross he had known in the early seventies, Whitehead continued; among all the people who had beaten a path to his White House office door on this issue, Ross had been unique. WCI was the only company that had major interests in movie production *and* cable. Ross's peers in the entertainment business were concentrating on movies and television, and they viewed cable with hostility, as a potential interloper; they were therefore strongly in favor of the kind of regulation that Ross was fighting. The fact that Lew Wasserman, the long-time chairman of MCA and Hollywood patriarch, whose acumen was legendary, had decided to stay away from cable probably served to convince the rest— all but Ross—that they didn't need to be in it, either.

And among those who were Ross's allies, his fellow cable entrepreneurs, Ross was equally anomalous. "The other cable guys had time horizons of two months, *maybe* two years," Whitehead said. "They weren't interested in understanding the possibilities for programming, the technology, the economics. For them it was, more, are they going to have tailfins on the converters next year?

"Ross, alone, was trying to figure out where the industry was going—in a much more farsighted, strategic way than anyone else. No one else was trying to put it all together."

Once Kinney had acquired its Hollywood movie studio, Ross had begun to indulge his instincts for style as well as substance. It was really more a continuum than any radical shift; he had always had a yen for what he considered the best (be it the eighty-foot pool or the top floor at the Americana) and had done the most he could with what he had. Now, he was still doing just that—but with what effect! For he had under his dominion a business that seemed to ratify his predilections, one where his taste for luxury and flamboyance could be construed as having a business purpose (particularly if one had a sufficiently acquiescent board, as Ross did). And the more profitable WCI became in the seventies, the more Ross's increasingly sovereign sense of entitlement grew; its spirit captured in a small, framed epigram that he kept in his office: "More is not an illusion."

It had started slowly. Shortly after the acquisition of Warner-Seven Arts, limousines had been provided for the executives in the corporate offices, as well as the heads of the entertainment divisions. This had prompted resentment from the holdovers from Kinney Service's mundane businesses; Morton Sweig, for example, the head of the cleaning division, is said to have protested that the Warner Bros. executives were losing money (they had just posted their writedown), while his division was making money, but *they* had cars and drivers. So then he and others were given them, too.

In 1970, the company bought its first plane, a Falcon, from Gulf & Western. A year later, it purchased a Gulfstream 2, and the following year a helicopter. Guy Salvadore, who had worked in car leasing in the Kinney days, now became "head of transportation," overseeing the limousines and planes.

And by late 1970, the company had signed a lease for its new "world headquarters," the old Esso Building at 15 West 51st Street. By the time WCI moved in two and a half years later, it was the pure entertainment company; all the parking and cleaning employees had been purged and sent to National Kinney. Of that group, only Caesar Kimmel remained at WCI. He was astute enough to realize that his colleagues were heading off to a place of no promise; he had no intention of going with them; and he held enough sway (he was still a very major shareholder, officer, and director, as well as someone who was knowledgeable about the underside of the business) that Ross would not cross him. He would continue to monitor the parking business at National Kinney, but it would be run officially by Daniel Katz, who had entered the company when Kinney had acquired Katz Parking in 1970, and who had worked closely with Kimmel since then.

Now, the new building became Kimmel's project. He had negotiated its lease. He was in charge of giving out all contracts for its renovation and maintenance. And he had contrived, through his talent for finessing whatever he wanted from the city, to get the address changed to 75 Rockefeller Plaza; he would later say, modestly, that he had "gotten someone in the postal division to do it." (No other building on 51st Street bears a Rockefeller Plaza address and 51st Street is not, of course, on Rockefeller Plaza. According to a former employee of the Rockefeller Plaza Corp., officials there promised Kimmel that if the city gave permission for that address to be used, they would not oppose it; but they did so in the belief that the city never would.)

Years later, Kimmel would still keep in his office the Plexiglas-enclosed note sent him by Ross, which read:

Dear "C,"
    It's hard to put into words the feelings I have for you and the great job you did in putting this giant together—I can only say "THANK YOU"—our home is really beautiful and you did it!

While Kimmel had been charged with its day-to-day administration, Ross (who would often tell friends that he was a frustrated architect) had thrown himself into the designing of this "home" for the Warner family. He became especially friendly with a young architect who had been assigned to the project, Rafael de la Sierra, who had also worked on designing a home in Sagaponack, Long Island, for William Paley (something which impressed Ross). "He was very much into it," de la Sierra recalled. "He would go up to the building all the time and measure, and he would argue with me over an inch. He liked to play a game. He would say to me, 'I would like to make this room wider.' He already knew the answer, of how to do it, but he wanted to see if I knew it. He did that all the time, on all levels, with all kinds of subjects."

When WCI bought a house near the famed Las Brisas resort in Mexico, which Ross named "Villa Eden," de la Sierra was given the job of renovating it. Perched on the summit of a hill overlooking Acapulco Bay, the house—redesigned with a kidney-shaped pool, tennis courts, and a screening room, and redecorated by Ahmet Ertegun's wife Mica—was considered an idyllic, almost magical retreat, even by some who took the world's most luxurious resorts in stride. Once arrived, guests rarely sallied forth to neighboring Acapulco; the chef was superb, all imaginable needs were attended to, and everything was provided, gratis.

In all this, Ross had begun to paint the landscape of his dreams, bringing long-held fantasies to life. What was primarily his personal urge, however, was dressed in a public suit: an insatiable appetite for luxury (perhaps bequeathed him by Sadie Ross's own) transmuted into a philosophy of corporate management.

Alfred Stern, the head of Warner Cable, was the grandson of Julius Rosenwald, the founder of Sears, Roebuck, but something of an outsider at WCI, since most of his fellow executives, like Ross, had humbler origins. Accustomed to a more muted style, Stern felt ill at ease with WCI's corporate extravagance, although, as he would later point out, he availed himself of it nonetheless. Like other executives, he was given a car and driver (he elected to have a Mercedes instead of a Cadillac limousine, so he could use it on the weekend as well—others then followed his lead); he, too, chose his own personal decorator (Mark Hampton) for his office at 75 Rockefeller Plaza; and he, too, vacationed at Las Brisas.

One day, when Ross invited Stern to lunch at the private Hemisphere Club on the top floor of the Time-Life Building, Ross began expounding on his theory. "He said that he wanted his executives to be happy in their role at the company and happy in life in general—and that anything that the company could do to that end (for example, the house near Las Brisas and the plane) would serve the company's interest, because they would be more productive," Stern recalled.

Ross, characteristically, was sensitive to Stern's social incongruity. "It still in those days had very much the feeling of a family business, and Steve was doing everything he could to make me feel part of the family," Stern continued. "I would get called to meetings where there was really nothing I could add, but it was very flattering to be included. Ross worked endlessly, in those days, to make people feel good about themselves, and —especially—to make them feel that they were important to him, in a personal way."

Ross, still the model counselor, wanted happy campers. Sometimes, visitors to WCI were struck by the sense that they had stumbled into a time warp—many of these executives, ostensibly engaged in the serious work of running a major American company, seemed more to be regressed adolescents at play. Ross's appetite for pranks was insatiable, and his colleagues went to great lengths to turn the tables on him. (Once, when Kimmel had lost a bet to Ross, he brought a tiger up to WCI headquarters from Jungle Habitat and, having tied ten hundred-dollar bills around its neck, let it into Ross's office. Ross is said to have leapt up on his desk.) Roger Smith recalled that a few days after he had arrived at the company, Ross popped his head round his office door with what Smith would soon learn was his characteristic query: "Are you having fun?" On the five-year anniversary of his employ, Smith received a congratulatory card from Ross—one which, at first glance, he assumed had been sent by the busy CEO's secretary. But then he saw the recognizably puerile scrawl at the bottom that read: "Are you still having fun?"

Ross was deliberate about extending his personal touch into the lower levels of his organization. Robert Friedman, who had joined Warner Bros. as a mailroom assistant in 1970, recalled that he first met Ross in 1973, at the Cannes Film Festival. One of the movies Warner Bros. was showing had not been ready on time, so Friedman was assigned to bring it to Cannes. "Steve was hosting a dinner for the Warner employees at the Café Felix, and he had requested that he be seated not with the top executives but with the troops—though he, of course, wouldn't have said 'troops.' Anyway, I was low man on the totem pole, so I got seated next to Steve.

"We spent the whole evening talking about cable, which was then used mainly to get better reception. But he was talking about two-way cable, about this doctor he had hired [Peter] Goldmark—I was staggered. I mean, in the movie business, we didn't even do TV advertising then. I said to somebody when I got back, 'I think he's a little off—we didn't talk about movies, but this thing called cable.'

"He never talked down to me at all," Friedman continued. "It was more as though he were picking my brain. It was a two-way conversation. And after that, he always insisted that whenever I came to New York, I had to stop in his office."

In many ways, large and small, Ross was constructing for his employees a home so warm, enveloping, and rich in amenities—so sweetly cocoonlike—that they would rarely, if ever, be tempted to leave it. Kinney's service businesses had all been discarded, but the mentality—"May I be of service to you?"—Ross made his own. For his upper-level executives, life's little inconveniences ceased to exist. Many of them travelled almost exclusively by limousine, helicopter, and private jet (Ross, himself, almost never flew commercially except on Concorde). During the gas shortage in New York, those who did not have limousines had their cars filled so that they would never have to wait in line. The restaurant "21," located just across the street from the back entrance to the WCI headquarters, served as a kind of company canteen. According to one person who worked for years in the accounting department of WCI, "No items were checked on expense accounts. There were no controls."

When it came to compensation, perks, and novel benefits, WCI was truly a full-service company. Ross assigned Solomon Weiss, who handled all Ross's personal finances, to devise tax shelters for WCI's favored executives. As Arthur Emil, a lawyer and old friend of Ross's, said, "I remember Steve's talking to me about how the way to keep executives there was to help them get tax benefits. Because if an executive made $100,000 and it was tax-free, then that was the equivalent of making $200,000."

Oded Aboodi, a clever tax specialist who had worked on the Kinney and, now, the WCI account at Arthur Young & Co., was assisting Weiss on these tax shelters, and also worked on general investment opportunities for Ross and other WCI executives. The company invested, too, in a variety of deals, many of them venture-capital situations unrelated to the businesses of WCI (something that was unusual for a major public company). And, sometimes, WCI invested in deals in which Ross and other executives were also investing personally—which raised the issue of conflict of interest.

One instance in which these arrangements gave rise to public controversy involved two investment partnerships, the "CI Fund" and the "FI Fund" (which stood, respectively, for "California Idiots" and "Fucking Idiots"). The principle in both was the same: WCI, as the general partner, put up several million dollars, while Ross and other executives, as limited partners, put in several hundred thousand, each; WCI was entitled to all the appreciation, until its return equalled 5.5 percent; after that, Ross and his partners were entitled to roughly 90 percent. And, if the partnership were to lose money, Ross and his partners would bear the losses until their capital contribution was exhausted; after that, WCI absorbed further losses.

So, while on the downside Ross and his partners might lose their initial investment, the upside potential for them was enormous: they stood to make 91 percent of incremental income above the 5.5 percent return rate, while they only had to put up 9 percent of the capital. The company, needless to say, was the loser. Shareholder suits were filed to protest this "misappropriation and waste of the assets and resources of the Company," and after litigating for several years, WCI in 1975 settled the suits and disbanded the two funds.

To Ross, there were myriad ways for him and his favored in the company to take advantage of the corporate vehicle; some, like the perks, were obvious, but others were more subtle and imaginative. Sharing the corporate wealth with his associates in all these ways, in any event, seemed to come naturally to him. It cost him nothing personally, and it furthered his grand design, creating an environment rich in gratification. In addition to everything else, Ross made it his practice to send lavish gifts to employees, not only on special occasions but at odd moments when they least expected it. His associates considered him the personification of generosity. There seemed to be little thought within the company in these days that the till actually belonged to the shareholders. As one executive recalled, "I think of Ross as the guy who came into possession of the candy store. But he didn't try to lock it to keep others out. Instead, he called out to the rest of us, 'All you guys from Midwood, come *on!* Hersheys on me!' "

And while these benefits—many institutionalized within WCI's corporate structure—were pleasing if not addictive, what probably did as much to weld the bonds of WCI employees to Ross were his personal gestures. In 1972, Joe Smith, president of Warner Bros./Reprise, had four years to run on his contract when he was offered a job as worldwide head of Capitol Records. He asked Ross to let him out of his contract, but Ross refused. Two years later, Warner/Reprise was doing terrifically, but Smith found himself overextended financially.

Smith's woes were due in some part to the fact that he had taken loans collateralized with WCI stock, and the stock price had plunged from about $50 a share to $6 a share in little over a year. (Other WCI executives, their net worth tied largely to the stock, were also under duress, and Ross was generally sympathetic and willing to accommodate them in some fashion. David Geffen, for example, had sold Asylum Records to the company in 1972 for $2 million in cash and $5 million in paper, when the stock was at $45; six months after they made that deal, the stock was at $8. Geffen was distraught, so Ross negotiated a new deal with him: Geffen would run the combined Elektra/Asylum label, and Ross would pay him one fifth of the difference between where the stock had been when Geffen had received it and where it was currently, over a period of five years. Thus, at worst, Geffen would at the end of five years have recouped the stock's value at the time of the deal.)

Smith called Ross. "I said, 'I'm doing great, and I'm going broke.' He said he was coming out to L.A. in ten days, and I should get my financial information together. He came, and he looked it over. He saw I owed '*x*.' He said, 'I'm going to give you a bonus of two times '*x*.' Then I'm going to give you an increase in pay.' (It was five or six times what I was going to ask for.) 'And I'm going to set up a new bonus system, so you, Mo [Ostin], Ahmet [Ertegun], will all be making seven figures. And I want to dump some more stock on you.'

"In return, he wanted another year and a half on my contract—that was all. This was a real time of crisis for me—and he did *that*."

Often, as with Smith, the help Ross proffered derived from the corporate treasury, but many times it did not. Particularly as the ambit of his influence widened, Ross became the ultimate resource, the quintessential fixer—the individual whom dozens and, later, hundreds of people felt they could turn to in extremity. In 1976, Terry Semel, then the head of distribution for Warner Bros., went to the Olympics in Montreal with his date, who was a French citizen. When they tried to return, she was stopped at the border because her passport had expired. "Who else would you call?" Semel asked rhetorically. "You called Steve." After nearly two days' machinations—with varied scenarios involving private planes, a boat, a Canadian judge, a Washington lobbyist, an immigration official, and more—Semel's date, covertly, separately from him, reentered the United States.

In resolving Semel's predicament, Ross was in his element. He had always been fascinated by the exercise of power (it was why he loved to quote the line he claimed was Rockefeller's: "Have you checked *tomorrow?*"). And probably nothing pleased him more than that he, now, was able to shift those levers himself in diverse, often imaginative ways—not only in business but also to solve people's personal problems. In so doing, of course, he was reaping private pleasure and creating too a fathomless wellspring of affection and loyalty among the growing numbers of people who felt, quite simply, that he was there for them. Robert Friedman, who would eventually become Warner Bros. head of theatrical advertising and publicity, echoed the sentiment of many of his colleagues when he told me, "Steve's presence has permeated this company. A lot of people, other places, work out of fear. Here, it's never fear, never 'three strikes and I'm out.' It's almost like this overriding desire to please. Over the years I've been offered positions at other companies. But there's been this ever-present 'how do I explain it to Steve?' factor."

Whether this persona—caring, constant, generous beyond his beneficiaries' dreams, an idealized father figure—was one Ross deliberately fashioned, realizing that it would be a winning pose, is not altogether clear. Some colleagues did believe that he was so unsure of himself in his early days in the entertainment world that his exaggerated generosity sprang from a desire to be liked, and accepted.

Whatever its etiology, what is plain is that over the years it would become his reflex—his *nature,* seemingly—and it worked. His apparent psychological need (to be the provider of good news, good fortune, good food, good times) meshed, almost sublimely, with business strategy. For by engendering such unusually strong loyalty within WCI, Ross was able to protect his company from the rapid turnover that was so endemic, and destructive, in other entertainment companies. And there was a more personal premium, as well; for while Ross was a believer in sharing the corporate wealth, he would never share its power. Indeed, the system he had constructed was in many respects more feudal than corporate, and over the years Ross would use the loyalty he'd cultivated in his various fiefdoms as his armor against any challenger.

That Ross would not even share authority with a bona fide second-in-command was something Alan Cohen did not at first apprehend. After William Frankel had died in 1972, Cohen, who was an executive vice-president and was functioning as Ross's number two, had begun to agitate for the title of president. Ross had resisted, offering to create an "Office of the President" that Cohen could share with Ted Ashley; but Cohen argued that Ashley had his responsibilities at the studio, and that he deserved to hold the title alone.

After months of discussion, Cohen recalled, Ross told him, late on a Friday afternoon, " 'I've decided you're right. I'm going to make you president.' Then, on Monday, he said, 'I've changed my mind.' " Cohen understood all too well, at that point, that Ross would never tolerate a number two, and he began to think of leaving the company.

The story that Ross was fond of telling about Cohen's departure, however, was different. Ross said that Cohen had tried to enlist Felix Rohatyn and Ashley in an attempt to unseat him, and that Ashley had apprised him of it. (Cohen would later deny this. He said that Rohatyn had called him, saying that a major shareholder, Giovanni Agnelli, was unhappy with the company's management; and that while he may have suggested Rohatyn talk to Ashley, his bottom line was that he would not mount a coup against Ross. Ross and he, Cohen added, never discussed the incident.)

But in the narrative disseminated by Ross which became part of the Warner lore, Alan Cohen, effigylike, came to embody the perils of disloyalty. Not long after discovering Cohen's attempted treason, Ross said, he made a point of remarking during casual conversation with Charles Bluhdorn, the chairman and CEO of Gulf & Western, "You can take any of my guys, I won't hold it against you. But the *one* guy I can't do without is Alan Cohen." Shortly, Bluhdorn offered Cohen the job of running Madison Square Garden and Cohen accepted

After Cohen, virtually no one at the company had any illusions about becoming a real second-in-command. While Ross tended to choose as division heads strong, talented executives, to whom he then gave general autonomy, at corporate headquarters his prerequisites were different. He surrounded himself with capable executives, but not one could be viewed as his potential successor; and he maintained a benevolent autocracy. There was a great deal of hashing things out in noisy, temperamental, marathon meetings attended by Ross and his colleagues—but it was nonetheless, and unmistakably, an autocracy. One who appeared not fully to grasp the situation was the literal-minded Albert Sarnoff, the company treasurer, who after a particularly heated debate among a large group had suggested to his fellows, "Let's take a vote." To which Ross, grinning good-naturedly, quickly rejoined, "What do you think this is—a democracy?"

Amidst all the high-spirited tumult, there was one increasingly dour voice. Eddie Rosenthal was beginning to evince disapproval about what he now viewed as Ross's excesses—not so much out of concern for the public shareholders as an aversion to such flamboyance. But though he was still vice-chairman, his power base of the funeral business was gone. And his familial tie to Ross was fraying as well. Rosenthal had watched unhappily as Ross, in the late sixties, had drifted away from Carol. He had attributed it, then, to Ross's absorption in his business; once, when they had just finished the late-night negotiation of a deal which had kept Ross working around the clock for days and Ross, barely skipping a beat, began to talk obsessively about the next deal, Rosenthal pounded on the conference table, yelling, "Enough!" But he couldn't order Ross to spend more time at home.

Moreover, Ross was apparently a philanderer even under his father-in-law's eye. Carol Ross discovered he had been having an affair with his secretary at Kinney National in the late sixties (indeed, according to others, Ross had bought her a house in Queens and a fancy car), and Carol and Ross separated for a time. But after Ross had let the secretary go, they reconciled and moved from the Imperial House into Ross's first truly grand home—a duplex with a soaring entranceway—at 950 Fifth Avenue.

Not long after they had moved in, they added a screening room on a third level, and the movies that Ross had paid a nickel to see at the Brooklyn Loews and that they had watched together as a newlywed couple in the fifties became a staple of their life together. Carol's all-time favorite was *An Affair to Remember;* Ross loved that one too, as well as *Gunga Din, Miracle on 34th Street, Drums Along the Mohawk, Four Feathers, House of Rothschild,* and more. But the one he loved best of all was *It's a Wonderful Life.* With his son, Mark, Ross consumed a steady diet of John Wayne movies.

Ross's incessant recasting of himself, in ever more stylized ways, seemed only to widen the gulf between him and his wife. Carol Ross did not share his grand ambitions. She did not care about amassing great wealth. It was not that she was unsusceptible to luxury (she loved their new apartment), but rather that it was not essential to her. She was unfazed by the limousines and private jets. She did not want to consort with Hollywood stars. It is true that when Frank Sinatra was her dinner partner at the extravaganza to celebrate Kinney's acquisition of Warner Bros., which was held on the movie set of *Camelot,* she was too nervous and excited to eat (Sinatra, for his part, had absentmindedly called her "Dearie" all night because, she was convinced, he could not remember her name). But she had no desire to cultivate these people as friends. Nor did she have any desire to start lunching at Le Cirque in order to be seen more, as one WCI publicist urged her to do in the early seventies.

What she wanted was a comfortable family life, not so different from her parents'. It was what she had pictured when she'd married Ross, and she wondered, sometimes, what had become of that person. This one, whom she still idolized, was overpowering. When they were in public, she felt slight next to him, so shadowed by his enormous presence as to be almost invisible.

Ross, by contrast, seemed never to look back. He was given not to introspection but to constant, galvanizing motion, and now more than ever he had worlds to conquer. Though he may not in all cases have done it as deliberately, he was gradually shedding old ties as he had shed the Kinney businesses. Judd Richheimer, John Heckler, Joe Lehman, Abe Silverstein, Marc Iglesias—all had been close friends, but they were part of a world he wanted to leave behind. All were gone. Soon, those of more recent vintage, like Bob Tisch and Allie Sherman, would be gone as well.

Ross began to develop a fanlike fascination with the stars. They seemed to tap limitless stores in him; he could not do enough for them. The treatment they received, however, was not really different in kind, only in degree, from his romancing of the Rosenthal family nearly two decades earlier. Ross would now rationalize it as having business purpose, but the instinct—to court, engulf, and win—was unchanged.

In 1970, Warner Bros. president John Calley was dating Barbra Streisand. Calley and Ashley were well aware that Ross, though he was embarrassed to ask, would be thrilled to meet her. So on one of Ross's trips to Los Angeles, Ashley arranged a small dinner party, including Streisand, Calley, and Ross. That evening, as one participant would recall, Streisand began to complain at great length about having just bought a house in New York which to her horror she now discovered needed a new roof and a new heating system. She was desperate. She couldn't afford to keep it, doubted she could sell it; it was an insupportable burden; it was ruining her life.

"How much do you want for it?" Ross is said to have asked.

"Four hundred and fifty thousand," Streisand reportedly replied.

"I'll buy it," he's said to have rejoined.

He—or rather, the company—did so, and in a month or so managed to sell it at a small profit. Had it lost money, however, and had his board asked for an explanation, he would have justified it as the cultivation of talent. But that would have been so patently after-the-fact, when in truth it had been a spontaneous gesture, utterly characteristic—as telltale as a fingerprint. Years later, Streisand, looking back on what was by then a long friendship with Ross, reportedly remarked to a mutual friend that Ross's courtship, which had never ceased, had always had such an exaggerated quality. Every Christmas, year after year, she and her friend agreed, they had known that their most lavish present would come not from their lover but from Ross.

It was in late 1971, just as Ross was embarking in earnest on this great new venture, that he found his perfect companion and soulmate. Jay Emmett, the nephew of Jack Liebowitz, who had been the chairman of National Periodical Publications, was the president of a marketing business, Licensing Corporation of America (LCA). National Periodical had bought LCA just before being acquired by Kinney in 1967; so LCA, and Emmett, had been part of the acquisition. He and Ross had never exchanged much more than pleasantries, however, until one day in late 1971 when Emmett appeared before the company's budget committee.

These meetings were monthly events, which Ross loved. He knew every division in depth, and presented with a wall of numbers, he could isolate a figure that suggested some problem with a precision that dazzled most of his associates. Now, Emmett showed some figures for LCA, which purported to be projections for the coming year; he insisted, however, that they were more conjectural than not. How was he to know what licensing deals he would make?

Ross pointed out that it was hard to project in the movie business, too, but that the movie people did a pretty good job of it. Then Al Sarnoff, the company's sober, methodical treasurer, began to ask some rather piercing questions. Emmett postured, remarking with good humor that if he had known when he sold his company that he would have to answer questions like these, he'd never have done it. Ross started to laugh. Emmett continued his routine, managing to poke some fun at the assembled executives, interspersing a couple of jokes, giving an animated presentation about his business—without the numbers.

Ross seemed not to mind; he was having too good a time. Emmett was a live wire. He was very funny, stand-up comic material almost, with a humor more rapid-fire and incessant than Ross's. He would certainly liven things up in the executive offices. After the meeting, Ross pulled him aside and said, "We have to bring you upstairs, to corporate." Emmett was made a vice-president and given an office directly across from Ross's.

The two became inseparable—"welded at the hip," or "like Velcro," others in the company would say. Emmett was not gifted in the ways Ross was; but that said, they were in many ways remarkably similar. Both were preoccupied with a desire to have a great deal of money, far more than they already had. Both were taken with the stars; they rivalled each other in their infatuation with Sinatra. Both were immensely attractive to women. Neither one drew sustenance from an inner life; they were so fundamentally non-reflective and easily bored that they lived lives filled with motion and, in its inevitable pauses, games. Backgammon was their favorite: they played it in the office at lunchtime, on the company plane, in hotel rooms. Emmett, like Ross, loved football; Emmett now joined the weekly betting pool (placed with bookies) that had existed for years at Kinney.

Always needing a great deal of external stimuli (to fend off boredom, to feel alive), both were happiest in a group—how be the life of the party if there is no party? From the time he'd married, Ross had nearly always taken vacations with an entourage, and now he needed Emmett; if Emmett couldn't come along on a vacation, Ross was less inclined to go. While Ross knew how to cultivate people, he could, in certain situations (and certainly with the Hollywood stars), be a little shy; but Emmett drew him out, made him feel more himself. Emmett was *never* shy.

Their early histories were quite similar. Emmett had grown up in the Bronx; it was a household in which his father struggled to make a living and his mother—beautiful, intensely ambitious for her only son—dominated. His father had died when he was a teenager. His wife, Martha, who met him when she was twenty and he nineteen, recalled that he was already the handsome, funny, irrepressible extrovert. She fell in love with him, she would say, the moment that wave of warmth first hit her.

But the slightly overheated charm—Emmett was always in high gear —apparently covered a crippling insecurity, the only hint of which (to Martha's eye) was a severe facial tic, one that would diminish over the years but never disappear altogether. When she married him just a few months after having met him, she believed (because he had told her) that he was twenty-four (not nineteen); that he was Christian (not Jewish); that he was a college graduate (he was not); that he had grown up in a mansion in Great Neck, Long Island. He had even driven her past that estate so she could see it; he said they could not stop because he was not talking to his mother at the time (it was in fact the home of his uncle, Jack Liebowitz). All these discrepancies Martha Emmett discovered when she was seven months pregnant with their first child. She considered leaving him and going home to her parents, but her father, a Presbyterian minister, counselled forgiveness.

Ross had not gone to such lengths to alter his past. But he had for years had a tendency to embroider or even create out of whole cloth in order to make a story, or himself, more interesting. His references to having played for the Cleveland Browns seem to have started as a gag; that, at least, is how Stanley Feldman, who was friendly with Ross when they were in their twenties, would remember it. "It was a fantasy, something he'd kid about," said Feldman. And Louis Marx, who became Ross's friend in the seventies, said that whenever Ross started describing his supposed Cleveland Brown experiences, he too understood it was all in fun. By that time, however, Marx was an anomaly; most people who heard these stories from Ross—including his wife and dozens of colleagues at WCI—believed them.

Indeed, by the early seventies, this tale had become part of his résumé. A *New York Times* profile of him on August 13, 1972, described Ross as "a six-foot New Yorker who has a plate in his left arm to prove his honorable discharge from a short-lived career as an end for the Cleveland Browns. 'It was a lucky break,' he now says." Emmett would often refer to Ross's having played for the Browns—say, in conversation when they were in Hollywood with the movie studio crowd—and Ross would, with seeming modesty, assent.

In most of his fabrications, Ross started with at least a grain of truth. He *did* have a plate in his arm, the result of having broken it in a football game—but it was at Paul Smith, not with the Browns. In later years, when describing his early life for the press, he would embroider here and there; he would say that when he was growing up, they were sometimes so poor and yet his mother so elegant that she would set the table with fingerbowls even when there was only a roll for dinner (she did use fingerbowls, but only for company, and they sometimes had only cereal, but never just a roll). He would say, too, that he had had a "football scholarship" to Columbia Grammar (he had a scholarship—Columbia Grammar, a small private school, didn't give football scholarships).

And a story that was printed in that same *New York Times* profile, and that Ross retold numerous times over the years, concerned his having decided that they should ally their car rental operation with a parking company. As the story always went, he was driving down Third Avenue with Abe Silverstein to go to a small lot, when he realized, why not go to the biggest? So he stopped at a phone booth, looked in the Yellow Pages, counted to see which parking lot operator had the most locations—and called Kinney. "Well, I got one guy, and I started to make my pitch," Ross would say, "and then he passed me on to another, and then another, and finally I got to Caesar Kimmel. It was good, because now I'd practiced my pitch three times, so I really had it down. . . ."

Nothing particularly dramatic, just a way of building a narrative about something quite prosaic—but also, none of it true. Silverstein had thought of allying with a parking lot business as a way of expanding, and had called Kimmel. Silverstein made the appointment, Ross accompanied him, and Ross took over from there.

In these instances, Ross's fabrications were not a matter of taking credit for ideas that had been someone else's—Ross was a bona fide fount of ideas, and in most instances the credit rightly his. They seemed to spring, more, from a fear that he, as exemplified by his earlier life, was rather ordinary and monochromatic; he would add some color, here and there. And as he began to travel in more and more rarefied circles, his need to color seemed to increase.

As for Emmett, by the time he and Ross became close in the seventies, he was not given to the kind of all-encompassing deception that he had practiced on Martha at nineteen; but what he called "exaggeration" was his stock in trade. In this, he and Ross were in complete accord. Both would say (if honest) that telling a good story was more important than strict veracity, any day. Sometimes, if Martha brought up the subject of his early deception, Emmett would smile and say, " 'Oh, what a tangled web we weave, When first we practise to deceive!' " Both he and Ross liked to throw off such lines occasionally. Ross's standard (which he would offer whenever Emmett became angry about something, as a way of telling him to calm down) was, "He whom the gods would destroy, they first make mad."

This, then, was the matched pair who in the early seventies were setting out, arm in arm, for the time of their lives. Their shared experience would be social as well as business—more than that, it would be seamless.

In the office, Jay Emmett was Ross's consort, typically spending hours a day in Ross's office. The movie division reported to Emmett, but his involvement there was sporadic. What he did, more, was to function as an administrative extension of Ross: all the details, organization, and people that Ross didn't want to deal with, Jay Emmett did. He was widely viewed as an honest broker: employees who wanted to ask Ross for something often went to Emmett, who would advise them on the best way or would do it himself. Executives wanting to use one of the corporate planes would typically see Jay (one, asserting after a sharp question from Emmett that he really did need the plane for a business meeting, was told, "I'm sorry. This plane is *only* for pleasure"). He had his enemies, who derogated him as nothing but a jester; but there were more who liked and respected him, and perceived his role, with Ross, as indispensable.

"To say that Jay was a lightweight is to look only at the exterior of his performance," commented Jason Berman, who was in charge of governmental affairs at WCI in the seventies. "What Jay did was to administer this amorphous thing that was WCI—and to do it with an invisible hand. There were all these diverse parts, tugging at Steve, but somehow it all worked and everybody was happy. Jay was the glue that held everything together, under Steve.

"And," Berman added, "he gave new meaning to the word 'fun.' "

Outside the office, Emmett's role was much the same. At Ross's side, tending to details, handling what Ross didn't want to handle—and keeping Ross in stitches much of the time. While Ross was still married to Carol he met a woman in Los Angeles named Cathy Mitchell. They began an affair that lasted for more than a year. Ross, accompanied by Emmett, would meet her in Las Vegas, where Ross nearly always stayed at Caesar's Palace, in the Frank Sinatra Suite (complete with piano), his $200 tips making him popular with doormen and bellmen. Often, they went to Las Brisas together. It was quite a contingent: Jay with whatever woman he was seeing covertly at the moment; Steve; Cathy; and, on occasion, Cathy's mother. Ross, naturally, lavished gifts on Cathy. He also was said to have paid for plastic surgery for her (and her mother). On one Las Brisas outing, the plastic surgeon and his girlfriend came too.

Emmett and several other WCI executives who met Mitchell considered her a blatant golddigger, and by late 1974 they had succeeded in persuading Ross to end the affair. Carol had just left him for what would be the final time (while she would be the one asking for the divorce, he had made it virtually impossible for her not to do so). And he had recently met an attractive blonde named Courtney Sale—a Texan new to New York, working in an art gallery, and a habitué of a wealthy partygoers' circuit. He asked Emmett to invite Courtney to meet them in Las Vegas and to explain, somehow, that Steve's girlfriend was going to be there (Ross, of course, hadn't been able to tell her not to come), but that she was nevertheless history. Sale came. Since Cathy was staying in Steve's room, Courtney slept (in her robe) in Jay Emmett's room. And after that weekend, Ross gave Emmett $10,000 in cash to give to Cathy Mitchell, to end the affair.

Now that Ross was separated and his outings no longer had to be surreptitious, they took on a different character. Often, Emmett would bring his wife, Martha, and Ken Rosen would come with his wife, Lou. Rosen had had a couple of jobs with brokerage firms, and had allied himself with Arthur Carter, a sharp financial adventurer who had been one of the founders of a brokerage firm, Carter, Cogen, Berlind & Weill, and who had subsequently formed the Arthur Carter Group. Ross, through his connection with Rosen, had been able to buy a great deal of the company's stock at a low price, and Ross and Rosen had both gone on its board. Indeed, although Rosen was ostensibly working for Carter in these years, a person close to Ross would later say that Rosen was always taking direction from Ross. Now, Rosen was working as a deal-broker in a firm called Brisbane Partners, which he had started with Henry Silverman. They were on a $15,000 monthly retainer with WCI; any transaction fees were additional (for a deal in 1976, for example, they would receive $1 million).

Ample as his income was, Rosen was nonetheless living beyond his means, with a huge apartment on Park Avenue and a baronial estate in the country. ("It's important to live this way, we have to *look* like winners," he would say.) It was also important to try to imitate Steve Ross's style of living, to the extent he could. From the start—and it had only intensified over time—Rosen had been fixated on Ross: he wanted to be what Ross was, to have what he had. Rosen had even named his first child Ross.

The psychodynamics of these jaunts, with the three couples, were not simple. Ken Rosen, who was extremely protective of his relationship with Ross and seemed to view anyone (even, until they were separated, Carol) as an intruder, must not have been pleased with Jay Emmett's emergence on the scene. And Emmett seemed to feel, at times, a little slighted by the intensity of the bond between Ross and Rosen. None of this, however, was expressed overtly. It emerged in small ways. (Once, when Rosen visited Emmett's home, a rustic converted farmhouse in Westport, Connecticut, he asked, as he stood on the front porch, "Where is the main house?")

Their wives' presence probably tended to mitigate the tensions between the men. Martha Emmett had had a nervous breakdown in the sixties, and had subsequently been diagnosed as manic-depressive; her husband, who had been her mainstay, remaining devoted if not faithful through all her travails, characteristically made light of her state. "Martha," he loved to say, in and out of her hearing, "is two sandwiches short of a picnic." In fact, he was unmistakably proud of her, seeing her as better educated and more literate than he was; she had written a novel, more or less autobiographical, about her breakdown (published by Warner Books), and she had become a therapist.

Lou Rosen, while she looked the part of a storybook wife (she and Rosen had been featured as the latest golden couple in a recent issue of *Avenue* magazine, photographed in their sumptuously appointed apartment), was very fragile, given to debilitating mood swings. Rosen was extremely protective of her, treating her in many ways like a child. Rosen himself, for all his cockiness and swagger, was subject to a variety of maladies which some thought to be psychosomatic. Each tended to function as caretaker for the other, and sometimes Lou felt they were so symbiotic that they barely drew a separate breath.

In November 1975, William vanden Heuvel, the former U.S. Ambassador to Switzerland, who was on the board of a small company with Rosen, suggested that Ross ought to go out with a friend of his, Amanda Burden, the socialite daughter of Barbara ("Babe") Paley who had been divorced from Carter Burden. Rosen agreed that it was a fine idea, but said that Ross hated blind dates. So they agreed that they would all meet for dinner at "21," and vanden Heuvel would bring Burden.

For Ross, that first encounter with Burden—luminous, somewhat ethereal, a breed apart from any woman he had known—must have seemed like a romantic scene in one of the old movies he adored. The next week, the two went to spend Thanksgiving with Louis Marx and his family at their Saratoga, Florida, estate (Marx had known Amanda well because she'd been going out with another friend of his), and after that, Ross moved into her apartment with her at 10 Gracie Square. Burden had two small children, Flo-Belle and Carter ("C.B."), who was especially fragile in the aftermath of his parents' divorce. Ross—who was wonderful with children generally, though available in a somewhat limited way to his own—immediately embraced him. For Burden, who had been under some strain—caring for her children, finishing her undergraduate degree at Sarah Lawrence, struggling through generally tempestuous affairs—Ross, steady, intensely protective, and adoring, seemed a safe harbor.

Burden was apparently unaware that Ross had a girlfriend, Courtney Sale, who was fully ensconced in his life and even working at WCI. Ross had given her a job in marketing and promotions at Jungle Habitat, where Sale antagonized her fellow employees with her high-handedness, and when her ideas were rejected (as being too extravagant for the park's promotional budget, for example), would call on Ross to intercede.

Courtney Sale had been away on a trip when Ross met Amanda at "21";

by the time she returned, they were living together. This was apparently one occasion on which Ross had to deliver the bad news himself. He is said to have told Amanda one evening that he had something to take care of and he would explain it all to her when he returned. And that, reportedly, was when he broke the news to Courtney. Shortly thereafter, Steve and Amanda left for a long weekend at Las Brisas; Sale, enraged, is said to have flown to Acapulco and repeatedly phoned Ross at Villa Eden from her hotel. But Ross reportedly declined to come to the phone.

One person who shared Courtney Sale's rage, somewhat surprisingly, was Ross's son. Mark Ross, now thirteen, had spent time with Courtney and his father during the past year or so, and she had been very attentive to him. Suddenly, one day, Ross announced that instead of seeing Courtney that evening they were going to be meeting someone else. Ross brought his son to Burden's apartment, where he was living with her and her children. For Mark, it was insupportable: not only was Courtney being supplanted, but his father (whom he felt he never had enough time with) was now living with someone else's children. He hated C.B. and Flo-Belle on sight—a feeling that would not diminish much over the next few years, and something that Amanda would deeply resent. Now, picking up the chocolate pudding pie that Amanda had set on the table for their first family get-together, he pushed it into her face.

Much later, as Burden tried to analyze the source of her attraction to Ross, she would tell friends that she wondered whether she had seen Ross, in some ways at least, as analogous to her powerful stepfather William Paley; wondered whether she was trying to be more like her mother; whether she had imagined, in some way, that she and Ross would be a couple as legendary as "Babe" and Bill Paley. (Burden had always thought she was destined to occupy a special role in life; from the time she was a little girl, she confided to one person, she had dreamt of being First Lady.) Ultimately, though, she would discount the Paley-like hypothesis, deciding that the men were just too obviously different for her to have sought to replicate the one with the other.

While Burden, in retrospect, would be somewhat bemused by her infatuation with Ross, what Ross saw in Burden seems far less enigmatic. Ross had for years been awed by Paley; he was, as Bob Daly, who would leave CBS in 1980 to work for Ross, expressed it, "an icon for Steve." Paley had not only built a communications empire, but he was a Jew who had, eventually, become a denizen of a social and cultural world that Ross could only glimpse from afar—a world in which Burden moved quite effortlessly. Indeed, as the impeccably bred daughter of "Babe" Paley, her every gesture and inflection bespoke that world. There was, surely, more to it, as there always is, but this was probably sufficient to create the chemic action. If all Steve Ross's adult life had been a tireless ascent, Amanda Burden was—at least in the personal aspect of his life—the summit.

So intent was Ross on thriving in this new sphere that there were even moments when Jay Emmett, who had been until now his perfect sidekick, seemed wanting. One evening they were all at Paley's, surrounded by his dazzling collection of modern art, and Emmett, pausing before a seven-foot-high painting—Picasso's *Boy Leading a Horse*—remarked, "You know, Bill, I really admire you for this. I mean, most people would be embarrassed to hang a cheap copy of a famous painting in their living room, but not you. . . ." Ross pulled him aside at the first opportunity and hissed in his ear, "You have gone too far! This is *Bill Paley* . . ." Paley, for his part, made no secret of his displeasure at Burden's choice of Ross; he was "contemptous" of him, as Frank Stanton, Paley's long-time friend and colleague, later recalled, and felt that "he was not suitable for Amanda's hand."

However diminished Ross may have felt by Paley's reaction to him, his public persona betrayed no self-doubt. Indeed, with Burden at his side, he was entering new social and political worlds at a breathtaking clip, and with brio. Ross, working with Arthur Krim, the head of United Artists, who had been close to Presidents John Kennedy and Lyndon Johnson, had been a major fund-raising force for Hugh Carey in his campaign for the governorship of New York in 1974. In the process, Ross and Carey became good friends. Now, in 1976, when Jimmy Carter was running for President, Ross decided to assume a role in national politics; once again working in tandem with Krim, he organized a fund-raising event for the Democratic National Committee (DNC) at New York's Waldorf-Astoria Hotel, which raised $1 million. As one Warner colleague later said, "At that point, Steve saw himself assuming the kind of role that people like Arthur Krim and Lew Wasserman played—spokesmen for the industry, advisers to Presidents."

Shortly after the event at the Waldorf—the first ever million-dollar fund-raiser for the DNC—Ross and his associates were invited to the White House to meet President Carter. Warner executive Jay Berman, who had worked on the event, later recalled the moment of introduction as an example of what he perceived as Ross's instinctual generosity. "Steve was introduced to the President—and then he immediately turned to me and said to Carter, 'This is my colleague, Jay Berman.' " ("He didn't have to introduce me at all, or he could have said, 'This is the schlepper who carries my bags,' " Berman interpolated.) "But he said, 'Whatever success the event had is owed to him.' "

As exhilarating as these new venues were for Ross, none of them were as exciting to him as the Cosmos. Ross, of course, had fantasized since his youth about owning the Giants, and in 1970 had entered into discussions about buying the New York Jets. After those negotiations fell through, however, Ahmet Ertegun and his brother, Nesuhi—both rabid soccer fans since their days as children in Turkey—prevailed upon Ross, Emmett, and a handful of other executives at the company to buy the Cosmos soccer team. All chipping in, they paid $35,000 each for the team in 1971. Soccer, however, was a little-known sport in the United States, and the games they played at Downing Stadium on Randall's Island attracted only about 4,700 spectators, on average. As it became plain that the team was losing money (about $225,000 a year, at the start), Ross and the rest sold it to WCI for a dollar.

In June 1975, the Cosmos underwent an overnight metamorphosis. WCI signed a three-year, $4.5 million contract with Pele—the thirty-four-year-old Brazilian player idolized by soccer fans worldwide, who had retired the year before. The acquisition of Pele was followed by that of Giorgio Chinaglia, of Italy, and Franz Bekenbauer, of West Germany. By 1976, the Cosmos had moved from Randall's Island to Giants Stadium and they were playing to crowds of more than 60,000.

Ross assigned Rafael de la Sierra—the architect who had worked on the redesign of the new WCI building and also Villa Eden—the job of managing the Cosmos. At about the time those earlier projects were completed, Ross had asked the architect to join the company. De la Sierra was flattered but pointed out that he was an architect—what would he do? "You'll do whatever I do," Ross had told him, warmly.

But what did that mean? asked de la Sierra.

"We'll see. Take it a step at a time," Ross had responded.

De la Sierra had had no illusions that he would be Ross's understudy (as he would later say of their relationship, "Steve liked me, I was a nice guy, I didn't challenge him"), but he decided to join, anyway. In the homogeneous populace of WCI, where the executives were largely Jewish, from lower- or middle-class backgrounds, de la Sierra, a native Cuban of aristocratic lineage who spoke imperfect English, was an oddity. He had an easy, urbane charm, however, and Ross seemed to think he would add a trace of refinement and foreign flair to the corporate suite.

In hiring de la Sierra for he knew not what, Ross was engaging in what would become a signature practice over the years: drawing people whom he found attractive into the company and, in effect, warehousing them until it became plain (if ever it did) what job they could best perform. He would do this at relatively low levels (Armand Wittenberg, a handsome young man from Los Angeles, was brought in as an assistant to Ross in the early seventies, though it was unclear to others in the office what his duties were), and at high levels (Harvey Schein, for example, the former CEO of Sony, would join in 1977 with some vaguely defined, never fulfilled, notion of becoming Ross's number two).

Ross and de la Sierra had become fast friends. They vacationed together with their families when Ross was still married to Carol; then, when Ross began living with Amanda Burden, the tie grew even stronger, because Amanda and Alina de la Sierra, Rafael's wife, became very close. De la Sierra, who had emigrated alone to the United States when he was twenty, leaving his family behind in Cuba, began to think of Steve as an older brother. And Ross knew that his young friend was strongly devoted to him—which enhanced the value of de la Sierra's role with the Cosmos. For as the team became a phenomenon, it became the object of a frequent tug-of-war between Ross, on the one side, and Nesuhi and Ahmet Ertegun (its chairman and president, respectively), on the other. In the intrigue that ensued, Ross knew he could count on de la Sierra to be loyal to him.

Odd as it may seem, by 1976 Ross had become more fixated on the Cosmos than on any other part of the company. As Clive Toye, the Cosmos general manager who had courted Pelé for years before succeeding in signing him, recalled: "The Cosmos were easily the most visible part of the company, a much bigger name than Warner Bros. I remember Steve talking about a trip he'd made to talk to bankers in Europe. He said that he could talk about the Hollywood stars and it was okay; but talk about the Cosmos and every door opened!" Indeed, Ted Ashley, the head of Warner Bros., is said to have commented to a Warner colleague that he was relieved that Ross's attention had finally been diverted from the movie studio and its stars.

Toye found Ross's absorption in the Cosmos a distinctly mixed blessing. Ross was immensely supportive; he was in the Warner box for every home game, and he travelled in the company jet to most games that were played away. Once, the Cosmos were in Florida, preparing for a game and staying at a Marriott adjacent to an airport. When Ross overheard one of the players complaining that he had not been able to sleep because of the noise of the planes, Ross immediately ordered that the team be moved to the Americana Hotel in Bal Harbour, where a chef, too, was personally assigned to the players.

The price of such solicitude, however, was Ross's frequent interference. There were furious debates between Ross, the Erteguns, Emmett, and Toye about who should play key positions in each upcoming game. And following the games, Toye often had to contend with a very different Ross ("Jekyll and Hyde, I used to think") from the generous, thoughtful person who was so upset at a player's losing a night's sleep. "I'd get a call to come look at a tape of the game, where maybe we'd lost by a goal," Toye recalled. "The camera angle wouldn't be conclusive, so that, from the tape, it was impossible to tell. But Ross would go into a tirade, ranting, 'Protest the game! This is wrong!' But it was completely unreasonable— you *couldn't* protest the game."

Paul Gardner, a journalist who had covered soccer in England for many years and was reporting on the sport for ABC, recalled one episode where the press was told that the Cosmos, in the midst of a playoff, had been "screwed by the referee." "They herded us into the 'multimedia room' at Warner—and there, showing us all the bits and pieces of film in the previous game, to prove what went wrong, was Steve Ross! It was such a flimsy exercise. I remember thinking that even the mildest of questions will bring this all crashing down.

"If anyone was going to do that, it should have been the coach," Gardner continued. "Soccer is peculiar—it's not like football, where there is a thick book of rules. In soccer, the rule book is very thin, and there is tremendous latitude for the referee. You really have to have a detailed knowledge of the game. In that group, the only one you could have a real soccer conversation with was Nesuhi. Ahmet, to a lesser degree. Steve Ross, not at all."

Fluent or not, Ross was going to make himself heard. De la Sierra found Ross difficult in these situations, but he felt he understood the psychology of his friend: Ross was an incessant competitor in virtually every moment of life—and he *had* to win. It was to this end that Ross was constantly, instinctively, sizing up others' strengths and weaknesses; he always knew what vulnerability he could exploit, if the need arose. (With de la Sierra, for example, who had a single-minded devotion to his three children, Ross had said to him, "I know how I could always get to you— through your children.") It was so much a part of Ross that he did not seem to discriminate. He approached every business deal this way, of course; but there was no contest, however small, that he could accept losing.

Once, when Ross, de la Sierra, and their wives were playing canasta on the Warner jet, Ross and his partner lost just as they were preparing to land; he ordered the pilot to circle the airport while they played another game. If he lost a tennis match (as he often did, being a poor player), he always wanted to play again, and again; and if he were forced to end with a losing game, it took him hours to recover his equanimity. Now, with the Cosmos—*his* team, at long last—he would not brook a defeat.

"The Cosmos had nine coaches in five years," de la Sierra said. "We won four championships; we must not have lost more than six games—but the man would not lose! If the Cosmos would score a goal and the referee nullified it, we had to hold him back—he wanted to punch the commissioner and the referee. He had a saying, 'Show me a poor loser, and you'll show me a winner.' "

Ross was very superstitious, de la Sierra continued. As a joke, someone had a harness made, ostensibly to prevent his throwing himself out of his seat and over the railing in his excitement. Since the Cosmos won the game that day, the harness became a good-luck charm; it was kept for him at the stadium, and he picked it up at the start of each game. He thought of de la Sierra and his family as lucky, also, and he always liked them to be present at the games. Once, when the Cosmos were playing in Toronto, Ross sent the company helicopter for one of de la Sierra's daughters, who was at boarding school in Connecticut.

"He would always go the extra length," de la Sierra said. "Supposing we wanted a certain player, and I would tell Steve, we can't get him. We have a budget of $50,000. He would say, 'What does he want?' And it might have been $200,000. He would say, 'Do it!' We had the best players in the world. But every year, he wanted to get more players, make it more exciting. He always wanted to go the extra yard, and never stop."

Among the players, it was Giorgio Chinaglia who forged the closest tie with Ross. His reputation in Italy, before he signed with the Cosmos, had been poor; he was still popular with the fans of Lazio, a club for which he had played, but he was widely considered a player in decline and one who was rumored, moreover, to have ties to the Italian Mafia. ("His good friend had been shot to death just the week before I signed him," recalled de la Sierra.) According to one colleague, whenever he went out to dinner with Chinaglia, generally at some restaurant in the vicinity of Fort Lee, New Jersey, there would be "two or three guys with their guns bulging under their jackets, watching the door. I would say, 'C'mon, Giorgio, this is not Sicily!' "

Paul Gardner would later recall that in his first interview with Chinaglia, when he had just arrived, Chinaglia repeatedly stressed that Ross was a "very close friend," causing Gardner to speculate that they had a preexisting relationship. Certainly Chinaglia's words were quickly borne out. Warner executives later recalled that Ross seemed "infatuated" with Chinaglia, who would often meet with Ross in his office behind closed doors; and other players, marvelling at Chinaglia's influence, would often say, "What do you have on Ross, Giorgio?" After Chinaglia joined the Cosmos, his subsequent contracts were negotiated privately with Ross; while de la Sierra, who was the executive vice-president in charge of the

Cosmos, saw the other players' contracts, he never saw Chinaglia's. It was rumored that Ross had given the player a large amount of stock, in addition to his other compensation.

Chinaglia was apparently a person who saw ubiquitous opportunity in the Cosmos operation. De la Sierra recalled that on one occasion Chinaglia had said to him, impatiently, "You are very stupid. Why don't you take under-the-table money? You can do it when you sign players—when you make deals with advertisers. Tell Ellesse, yes, our players will wear your uniforms, but give me $100,000 in a Swiss bank."

By the early eighties, the Cosmos would be disbanded; Chinaglia would be generally viewed as having accelerated the team's demise (nonetheless he received a payout from WCI for years more); and he would flee the United States, supposedly after defrauding a group of Italian-Americans who invested in Lazio, an Italian soccer club. But for five heady years preceding this denouement, the Cosmos were Ross's obsession and Chinaglia his favorite. WCI was losing as much as $5 million a year on the team, but, as one executive said, it was never disclosed because Ross and his associates took the view that "anything under $10 million was 'not material.'" Once, when Ross at a shareholders' meeting was asked if it was true that the company was losing a lot of money on the Cosmos, he replied, casually, "Maybe two cents a share."

For Ross, it was a small price to pay (out of the corporate treasury, in any event) for the magic of these events. As he sat in his box at Giants Stadium with Amanda, who had become an ardent Cosmos fan, at his side, he may well have felt that he'd surpassed his and his friend Heckler's youthful dream. By 1977, the stadium was filled with 78,000 spectators—among them Henry Kissinger, Bjorn Borg, Mick Jagger—who would head for the locker room to mingle with the players after the game. As one participant recalled, "Chinaglia would be out on the field, scoring goals—and then he'd run to the halfway line and wave to Steve Ross. Homage being paid to Nero."

The rest of Ross's life with Burden was concomitantly regal, and tinged with fantasy. When the couple, accompanied by the Emmetts and the Rosens, went to Las Brisas for Christmas in 1976, the trip required two corporate planes: one for them and one for their gifts. On one of their trips to Los Angeles, Ross accompanied the three women to Giorgio's, the famed boutique on Rodeo Drive. After Ross had a word with the manager, the store was promptly closed to all other customers.

One of the women said she felt like she was enacting a childhood fantasy, set loose in a toy store and told that anything could be hers. As they tried on one outfit after another, it was Ross—with a sureness that bespoke his years in the garment trade—who decided which style was right, which color wrong. The bill, to be sent to him, was said to run to over $30,000.

Leaving Giorgio's—in two limousines, one stocked with their purchases—the couples drove to a lodge overlooking the Pacific where, that evening, the fantasy continued: Steve called for a fashion show, and the women happily complied, sweeping down a circular stairway to the men's applause. The star of the show, they all tacitly recognized, was Lou Rosen, exquisite in a floor-length, robin's-egg blue Halston that Ross had unerringly chosen. Amanda seemed uneasy; it appeared that she felt outshone by Lou Rosen—and impelled to keep a watchful eye on Steve.

Ross, meanwhile, orchestrating ever more grandiose scenes on the stage set of his life, still seemed dogged by the fear that—seen without these elaborate props—he was inadequate. He referred frequently to his experience with the Cleveland Browns, and soon the bedrooms of Burden's two children were filled with Cleveland Browns memorabilia. Though no one in this group—Burden, the Emmetts, the Rosens—questioned that he had played for the Browns, they did occasionally comment among themselves (though not in front of him) about his being an embellisher; sometimes Amanda and Martha Emmett would roll their eyes at one another when he said something that seemed particularly egregious. Once, they heard him recommending a certain book to someone as the best book he had ever read; after that, they would joke about that line among themselves, because they all knew he *never* read ("nothing but the Tax Code," as one long-time associate commented).

Powerful as he was, Ross apparently needed to become more so, in Burden's eyes. On one occasion, she returned home to their apartment at 10 Gracie Square and complained to Ross that a man had followed her along the city streets and now was loitering across the way. He immediately made a phone call and spoke in a terse, coded way, describing the man and the location. Then Ross, who was intensely protective, told her that she need never worry, that he would always be able to handle any situation, and alluded, mysteriously, to some high government connection. Describing this situation much later to a friend, Burden would say that at the time she had accepted it—though she would ultimately marvel at her own gullibility.

Perhaps the most extraordinary of Ross's declarations occurred once when he and Amanda reportedly were in his limousine, listening to a hit song on the radio. Suddenly, he turned to her and asked her if she liked it. She did, indeed. "I wrote it for you," he told her. Burden stared at him, astonished, as he explained that there were many creative things he did which, because of his position, had to be done in total secrecy.

## 1

Steve Ross, in 1964, a couple of years after he had engineered the merger of two rather byzantine corporations–the Kinney Parking and Riverside funeral businesses–which became, in turn, the foundation for his ceaseless acquisition spree, through the heady sixties.

Ross's close cohorts were Caesar Kimmel (center), whose father, Emanuel Kimmel–a major bookmaker, gambler, and associate of mobster Longie Zwillman–had started Kinney Parking, and (left) Jay Emmett (2). While Ross and Kimmel had been cronies since the merger of Kinney and Riverside, Ross did not meet Emmett until the early seventies. Almost instantly, they became friends.

Ross married Carol Rosenthal, the daughter of Eddie Rosenthal–head of his family-owned Riverside funeral business–in 1954, and they had two children, Toni and Mark (3). With the acquisition of Warner Bros. in 1969, Ross entered a new world. Studio denizens Frank Wells, Gerald Leider, Richard Shepherd, John Calley and Ted Ashley on the studio lot (4).

2

4

## 5

By the mid-seventies, the funeral business had been sold, parking spun off to a subsidiary—and Ross was chief executive of Warner Communications, with its main properties a movie studio, record companies, and cable. And once the Cosmos, a WCI-owned soccer team, signed Pelé, the world-famous Brazilian star, the Cosmos became Ross's obsession. Here, he and Emmett are pictured with Pelé and his wife (5), and Ross and Emmett (his constant consort) are seen at a Warner Bros. sales conference in Palm Springs (6).

The metaphor was the greatest show on earth, which captured the spirit of WCI in the mid-seventies, and Ross was indeed the undisputed ringmaster.

David H. Horowitz
Executive Vice President
Records, Music Publishing
Cable TV

Ed Silvers
President
Warner Bros. Music Publishing

Gustave M. Hauser
Chairman
Warner Cable Corp

W. Spencer Harrison
Exec. Vice President
Warner Cable Corp

Joel M. Friedman
President
WEA Corp

Charles A. Agemian
Chairman of the Board
Garden State National Bank

Mel Posner
President
Elektra/Asylum/Nonesuch Records

Gerald L. Greenberg
President
Atlantic Records

Nesuhi Ertegun
President
WEA International

Caesar P. Kimmel
Executive Vice President
Shareholder Relations

Joe Smith
Chairman
Elektra/Asylum/Nonesuch Records

Ahmet Ertegun
Chairman
Atlantic Records

Mo Ostin
Chairman and President
Warner Bros./Reprise Records

Steven J. Ross
Chairman of the Board

William Sarne
Chairman
Warner Publishing

In November 1975, Ross, who had separated from his wife, Carol, met Amanda Burden, the daughter of Babe Paley and stepdaughter of William Paley, and became instantly enraptured (8); in 1976 Burden and Ross attende a party with Bella Abzug (9). The two would live together for the next severa

years and marry in November 1979. This period happened, also, to be the golder age at WCI–the major businesses were so stron that Ross was free to experiment with smaller ventures that appealed to him–from a video-game business named Atari to a fragrance campany, started with Ralph Lauren. Here (10), Ross is pictured with Warner/Lauren executives George Friedman and Robert Ruttenberg, and Lauren.

There was a great deal to celebrate at Ross's fiftieth birthday party, in September 1977, a gala at the Waldorf Astoria. The theme of the evening was how far Ross and his merry Kinney/Warner band had come. Emmett (11) was one of the emcees. By the mid-seventies, Ross had entered the political world with brio; he was a major fund-raiser for Hugh Carey in his campaign for the governorship of New York in 1974, and in 1976 he organized a spectacularly successful fund-raiser for the Democratic National Committee. Here (12), he is pictured at a Washington, D.C., party with Senator Birch Bayh and Robert Redford, who had starred in the Warner Bros. movie *All the President's Men* and had an office in the WCI building.

The idyll of the mid-seventies drew to a close once the government's investigation of the mob-run Westchester Premier Theatre and, particularly, its ties to WCI began. In September 1976, Frank Sinatra, who had become a member of the Warner extended family in the course of Kinney's acquisition of Warner Bros., and who gave several performances at the theater, posed with Gregory de Palma, Thomas Marson, Carlo Gambino, Jimmy ("the Weasel") Fratianno, and, in front, Richard ("Nerves") Fusco (13).

Ultimately, the investigation resulted in the downfall of Emmett (center), who pled guilty and became a government witness against Solomon Weiss (left), a WCI assistant treasurer who had worked for Caesar Kimmel in the Kinney Parking days and had become, over the years, Ross's trusted aide. At the close of Weiss's trial, where the government lawyer was assistant U.S. attorney Nick Akerman, Weiss was convicted (14).

15

In the early eighties, Ross re-did his life. After
Burden left him, he immediately resumed a
relationship he had been having, before he met
Burden, with Courtney Sale; they married in
October 1982. And he began to create a new
social circle of Hollywood stars. Here, he is
pictured with singer Bette Midler (15); with
his wife, Courtney, director Steven Spielberg
(who would in some ways take Emmett's place
as his closest friend), and David Geffen, who
had joined the Warner family in 1972 when he
sold his company, Asylum Records, to WCI
(16); and with Spielberg and Courtney Ross (17).

## 19

In the galaxy of stars with which Ross surrounded himself, some were closer than others. While Ross gave Dustin Hoffman (18) the usual royal treatment, Hoffman and Ross never fully meshed. Clint Eastwood, pictured here with S.I. Newhouse, the chairman of Advance Publications (19), and Barbara Streisand (20) responded strongly to the Ross charm.

21

22

23

Beverly Sills (21) met Ross when she came to ask for money for the New York City Opera, and he asked her to join WCI's board. Here, they are pictured with Barbara Walters and her then husband Merv Adelson, who became a WCI director in 1988 following WCI's acquisition of Lorimar Telepictures Corporation.

Ross, with Courtney and James Robinson (22) of American Express, seemed friendly enough in public, but Robinson had been the loser and Ross the far-ahead winner at the end of their cable joint-venture, Warner-Amex—and Robinson was said by associates to have ultimately felt badly misled by Ross. Quincy Jones (23) was another in the coterie of stars who considered Ross a close and irreplaceable friend; in September 1993, nine months after Ross's death and at about the time of Ross's birthday, he left flowers on Ross's grave with a note that read, "How Do You Keep the Music Playing?"

The open and fierce acrimony in Ross's long-running war with Herbert Siegel, the chairman of Chris-Craft (25), was unique in Ross's career. Lawyer Arthur Liman (26), Ross's close friend and adviser, who had long been close to Siegel as well, brokered the "marriage" in which Chris-Craft became a major shareholder of WCI, thus thwarting the advances upon WCI of Rupert Murdoch's News Corp. Ross, however, found Siegel's threat to his hegemony intolerable. And, in the boardroom battles that ensued, Beverly Sills (24) was one of Ross's most impassioned loyalists.

With the Time-Warner merger, consummated in January 1990, Ross reached an elevation so high that even he, at the start of his extraordinary climb, might not have been able to envision it. Here (27), the ink on the deal not quite dry, he celebrates triumph with associates from WCI and Time Inc. (left to right: Dick Munro, Carmen Ferragano, Ross, Jerry Levin, Marty Payson, Ed Aboodi, Nick Nicholas, and Jodi Kass).

Levin (right) and Aboodi (left), whom some in the company called "Ross's Rasputin" (28), got to know each other as the deal's negotiators, and apparently saw the future in each other as well; over the course of the next year or so they would become, as an associate would later say, "like brothers."

28

Some of the WCI division heads, like Warner Bros.' Bob Daly (left) (29), pictured with Nick Nicholas (center) and Barry Meyer, had been opposed to the merger, fearful of any change in their autonomous way of life at WCI. But Ross had succeeded in persuading Daly and others that that would not change, and that the merger would provide the size required to compete in an ever more global world. Ross had long been thinking in such terms, and had been actively cultivating people like Jack Lang, France's minister of culture (31). Ross's most critical job of persuasion in the merger, of course, had lain with his counterpart, Time Inc.'s Nicholas (30)—whom Ross courted assiduously, promising Nicholas that he would become Ross's successor.

31

33

While Ross showered the stars in his circle with attention (both Spielberg and Streisand said they thought of him as a father), his own children Mark and Toni suffered from a lack of such attention; (left to right) Mark Ross, his wife, Sally, Ross, Toni Ross, and her husband, Jeff Salaway (32).

In his last couple of years, Ross tried to do better with them, and also with his and Courtney's daughter, Nicole (34). Here, Ross and Courtney are pictured with Elaine de Kooning (33).

37

CELEBRATION OF A LIFE
STEVEN J. ROSS
WARNER BROS. STUDIOS
MARCH 30, 1993

Ross's funeral was
held on December 23, 1992,
in East Hampton's Guild Hall; it was a
service, organized by Courtney Ross (35), in
which various stars spoke and performed. At the cemetery, mourners were
each given a flower to place on the casket; here (36), Quincy Jones and
Steven Spielberg go to bid farewell to Ross. The funeral was followed by a
memorial service at Carnegie Hall in January, which was, in turn, followed
by a third memorial in March, at the Warner Bros. studio Ross loved. On
the cover of the program (37) were a yellow pad and pencil—items that Ross
(who disdained calculators) was rarely without.

Surprisingly, it was the admiring Ken Rosen who was the first in this group to express a suspicion that Ross might be practicing deceptions that were more dramatic, even exotic—not just garden-variety misstatements. When the three couples went together to Las Vegas, they followed a routine. Ross would tell them, in the afternoon, that he was going to the blackjack table and had to go alone so as to concentrate on his card counting; he would return a few hours later with $10,000, $20,000, even $30,000 in chips pouring out of every pocket (he purposely wore three-piece suits so that, he said, he had places to put his chips, rather than letting the mounting piles attract the attention of those who watched from above the gaming tables). He then distributed the chips to the others to play with that night. On one of these trips, Rosen turned to Emmett and said, "What makes you think he doesn't *buy* those chips?"

That kind of skepticism, however, was rare. Skepticism requires detachment, and each of these people in his or her own way was enamored of Ross, eager for the heightening effect of his presence. Jay Emmett loved him and was happiest when they were together. Ken Rosen was obsessed with emulating him. Amanda Burden found him a different breed from the men she was used to (a diamond in the rough, she would sometimes say), and, perhaps, someone with whom she could abandon restraint; once, on the corporate jet, when he began showing the group rather extraordinary Polaroid photos of her with him, she just laughed, not seeming to disapprove. Martha Emmett was working on a second novel, in which she had a character, based on Ross, who emitted such sexual energy that she had him "moving like a panther." To Lou Rosen, Ross was like a drug; she felt that he drew people in with his enormous vitality and made them feel intoxicated with the possibilities of the moment, unbound; he was a catalytic agent.

Ever since Rosen had left his position as Ross's assistant at Kinney Service back in the mid-sixties, he and Ross had flirted with the idea of his return. As Ross would later tell me, Rosen had been intent on making far more money than Ross could pay him as a corporate executive. He *was* able to pay him extraordinary sums, however, in his role as outside consultant to the company—especially in transaction fees. This arrangement suited both of them. Rosen drew enormous income from his relationship with Ross and remained close to him; still, he could feel that he was not simply Ross's protégé but was making it on his own. And Ross had his favorite type of construct, one he would seek to recreate in years to come: a relationship with an ostensibly "outside" consultant, who was in fact wholly loyal to and controlled by him.

Ross never trusted those outside advisers who were truly independent; but he loved using someone who only seemed to be. That person, once removed, gave Ross the added edge, in negotiations, of deniability: the adviser functioned, in effect, as a decoy. It was a principle Ross had learned from Eddie Rosenthal. As Ross would later say, referring to his having been sent by Rosenthal to negotiate with Percy Uris, "It was Eddie who suggested that it would be better if I went alone, because I couldn't make a decision.

"That's always a good maneuver."

Now, by the summer of 1976, Ross and Rosen agreed that Rosen would join WCI. Reviving the idea he had presented to Alan Cohen several years earlier, when Cohen had been lobbying to be named president, Ross decided that he would create an "Office of the President," with not two but four members: Jay Emmett; Emanuel Gerard, the Wall Street analyst who had assisted in the acquisition of Warner-Seven Arts and then joined the company in 1974; David Horowitz, a lawyer who had been general counsel for Columbia Pictures, Inc., and had joined WCI in 1973; and Ken Rosen.

Ross would attempt to explain this decision in a deposition he gave some years later, in 1984, during litigation of a shareholders' suit: "It was developed instead of having one man as the President since the operating decisions were not made up by corporate but down at the divisional level, I thought it would be best if we had three, four individuals that were very capable and could relate to the divisional people, and would watch the divisional people. Since we were in entirely different businesses that would be a much better way to operate and that is the genesis of the Office of the President."

With this stroke, Ross, who had been chairman of the board, CEO, and president (a too-obvious hoarding of power) now made an apparent distribution of that power—while in fact doing no such thing. By naming four people to the Office of the President—but not one of them a true contender—he dismissed, for the foreseeable future, the notion of a successor, or even a second-in-command. In later years, Manny Gerard liked to recount how his fellow presidents had appeared in his doorway, soon after being apprised of the creation of this new structure, and said they were on their way to Ross's office, just down the hall, to ask whether Ross was going to be in the Office of the President, as well. "I laughed, and said, 'I'm saving my shoe-leather, guys. Don't you get it? Nothing's changed!' "

The only thing that did change, dramatically, was compensation—another advantage to Ross in forming this office. Ross had always been a lavish spender; even when married to Carol Rosenthal he had lived in such high style—particularly after the Warner-Seven Arts acquisition—

that his closest associates, aware of his moderate salary, used to speculate about his other sources of income. Moreover, Ross's use of cash (never credit cards) only fuelled such speculation. He typically carried a roll of hundred-dollar bills—perhaps fifteen or twenty.

In a deposition in 1981 (given during the litigation of shareholders' suits, which alleged that Ross was defrauding shareholders by causing WCI to pay his personal expenses), Ross would offer his often-repeated, albeit unwieldy, explanation of his reliance on cash. "I believe in paying cash for dinners when I go out. I don't want people thinking that it is business, even though it is business," Ross would testify.

"When you use credit cards, even if it is your own, they are always suspect [sic] that it is for business purposes for those things."

To one person close to him who questioned his practice, Ross offered another explanation. He claimed that his reason for dealing in large amounts of cash rather than using a credit card harkened back to the deprivation of his childhood—that he had vowed then that someday he would have so much money that he could pay, outright, for whatever he wanted; and that it gave him, now, a sense of long-awaited satisfaction to deal in cash.

After he had left Carol Rosenthal, moreover, his style had grown more grand; and now that he was courting Burden, it was positively imperial. Much of the luxury was provided by the company, of course: the private jets, Villa Eden, the trips to Europe, where he and his associates ate only at the finest restaurants and stayed only at the most luxurious hotels. But even the most severe abuse of corporate expense accounts would be hardpressed to cover the more than $30,000 reportedly spent at Giorgio's, or the $20,000 or so in cash that friends recalled his routinely bringing along to Las Vegas, or the $3,000 he would frequently spend on an evening at home, when he invited the Emmetts over for dinner, providing a six-piece band because they all loved to dance.

Furthermore, Ross, in sworn testimony, insisted that he had not gone into debt to support his spending habits. He testified that he had "never had a loan from the company," and had "never had any loans guaranteed by the company . . . as a matter of fact, I have no loans to [from] anyone, to the best of my knowledge. No loans to [from] banks." And his divorce settlement with Carol, in 1979, was $1 million—a sum the Rosenthals considered extremely generous given what they, and Carol's lawyer, understood his means to be.

How Ross had managed to support his fabulous lifestyle, then, remained something of an enigma; he was utterly close-mouthed about his personal finances even with those close to him. These matters were handled for Ross by Solomon Weiss, the former bookkeeper from Kinney; and it is possible that Carmen Ferragano, Ross's secretary, who had become his executive assistant, would have been privy to them as well, since she was well versed in all aspects of his life. However Ross had maintained himself in the past, in any event, he was now positioning himself to build a far more sizable net worth from WCI. And in this, Ken Rosen —as usual—was his decoy.

When the designated members of the new Office of the President met to discuss the arrangement, it was Rosen who put forth a proposition for their compensation—one that seemed so inflated that one of these executives would later recall he thought Rosen, characteristically, was overreaching, and he began to object that it was so rich they would never win board approval. However, Arthur Liman, the lawyer who by the mid-seventies had become Ross's ever present counsel and close friend, took this executive aside and told him to relax. "Then I realized, This is a set-up! Because if the OP's contract were '$x$,' Ross's would be '$x$' plus '$y$.' "

It was only a more specific application of the general principle at work when Ross had created a world of untrammeled luxury for his executives: in so doing, he had legitimized all that—and more—for himself. Cyril O'Neil, Jr., a lawyer representing Rosen, recalled that there was some discussion about whether these contracts for the four co-presidents should be submitted for shareholder approval. "Arthur [Liman] said, 'Absolutely not! You get it into the proxy material and people have an additional handle on you to claim that it is terrible for the company.' Then, later, Steve's contract did go to the shareholders for approval—but that one *had* to, because of the magnitude."

The members of the Office of the President received packages of salaries, bonuses, deferred compensation, options, and "incentive units" (keyed to the growth rate of the company). An unusual provision of these contracts—which was Ross's idea—was that these executives could choose to be released from their contracts if Ross were no longer to be the company's chairman and CEO. Ross, for his part, received a multiple of the co-presidents' package, and, in addition, a huge grant of "bonus units"—which, unlike the "incentive units" (which he also received), were not keyed to the growth rate. (By 1978, the benefits of his new employment agreement had begun to be manifest: his cash and cash equivalent remuneration would total $2,540,721.)

And, as Liman had indicated, everything passed muster with the sixteen-member board—eleven of whom were insiders, and virtually all of whom profited in some way from their association with WCI. It was the kind of board where even the outsiders were, in the truest sense, insiders.

Lawrence Buttenweiser, for example, was an "outside" director in the same sense that Rosen had been an "outside" adviser; one whose usefulness lay in his technical independence—and in fact was devoted, and unstintingly loyal, to Ross. The two men had met in their early twenties, when they were dating sisters; they had become good friends, and had remained close over the past two decades. When Kinney Service went public in 1962, Buttenweiser, by then a partner in the law firm Rosenman Colin Freund Lewis & Cohen, became a director; and, like most of the board members in this company that still seemed, in many ways, the family-owned company it had once been, Buttenweiser was family.

Now, commenting on the richness of these contracts, Buttenweiser reportedly said, "If we get sued, we'll just have to give back 'A,' or 'B,' or 'C.'" Indeed, the company and its directors were promptly sued in a shareholders' class action, but Warner would fight that suit, and subsequent related actions, for the next ten years.

Rosen's role in the formulation of the contracts for the co-presidents was easy for his colleagues to grasp; he had been carrying out Ross's agenda in a way that also benefited himself, as usual. What was surprising, to many people who knew him well, both within and outside the company, however, was that Rosen should be reentering WCI at such an exalted level. While each of his co-presidents would have designated areas reporting to them (Emmett, movies and publishing; Horowitz, records and cable; Gerard, an assortment of others, including a newly acquired electronic-games division, Atari), Rosen had no divisions reporting to him; he was to work on "deals." Insofar as dealmaking had been his vocation during the previous ten years or so, that might have been appropriate. But many who had been involved with him in the business world would later comment that Rosen had good presentation skills but little financial acumen (even Ross is said to have acknowledged that on numerous occasions); he was, essentially, a "finder." And he was so aggressive that many were wary of him.

A venture capitalist close to Ross, who also dealt with Rosen, described what he perceived as the difference between the two men: "Ken was someone always out for himself, you had to watch him around the edges. Steve was *never* that way. He always wanted to be fair." This person paused and then added, "I will admit that I never understood why Steve had some of these 'deal' people around him that he did—like Ken. I think Steve just didn't *get* it."

But surely that was the beauty of having Rosen as his covert agent—someone who would instinctively do those things that Ross wanted to but would not do himself, and who would always allow Ross deniability. Ross, in any event, was well aware of Rosen's way of operating. Shortly before Rosen was to join the Office of the President, Cy O'Neil recalled, Rosen had come to him and said, " 'Steve feels it would be helpful if I cleaned up my act.' We were to try to make sure before he joined the company that there was nothing outstanding that might hurt WCI."

Asked what Ross would have had in mind, O'Neil said, "There may have been transactions that cut corners. Ken moved quickly, without benefit of counsel."

To his critics, Ken Rosen seemed a thin caricature or, more, a knock-off of Steve Ross. Like him, Rosen was handsome, assiduously seductive, manipulative (with an instinctive preference for indirection), ambitious, money-hungry; but he lacked the grace and talent that, in Ross, tended to obscure, and counterbalance, these more negative traits. And his appointment to the Office of the President was attributed not to merit but, rather, to the strength of his personal relationship with Ross.

Just what had created that extraordinary bond was something that nearly everyone around Ross puzzled over. Some developed theories. Rosen was the younger brother Ross never had, or it was a father-son relationship (Ross had at this time a rather distant relationship with his own son, Mark). One close colleague of Rosen's believed that it was fuelled by a sexual adventurism, involving voyeurism and exhibitionism, in which, this person claimed, Rosen and Ross (without their wives) participated. A high-level executive at WCI believed that it was Rosen's malleability that Ross so valued: "If Steve said, 'Go jump off the Empire State Building,' Kenny would have jumped off. Steve liked that—somebody who would do *anything*."

Whatever the nature of their bond, it was hardly a reason for someone to be made co-president of a public company; but by this time at WCI, what Ross wanted, he received—a corporatized version of *droit du seigneur*. At the board meeting at which the directors were to vote on the appointments to the Office of the President, Eddie Rosenthal voiced strenuous objections to Rosen—but Ross had his way. Rosen, for his part, told at least one friend that this was to be only a brief interim arrangement; he claimed that he and Ross had agreed, privately, that he would shortly become sole president, under Ross.

Several months after he joined the company, on April 3, 1977, Rosen suffered a severe and somewhat bizarre injury. A couple who had been strolling in a relatively deserted area of Central Park would later say that they had seen a rider on horseback; had heard a couple of sounds, like gunshots, and had seen the horse bolt wildly; and, some minutes later, further on, had come upon the rider lying on the ground, bleeding heavily from the head. From the force of the blow it was ultimately concluded that Rosen had been thrown and, in the trajectory, struck his head against a tree.

When his wife, Lou, arrived at Lenox Hill Hospital, she was told that he had first been classified "D.O.A.," but he was now in surgery. Steve and Amanda and the Emmetts arrived, and, after many hours, they were told that Rosen would live. Martha Emmett asked, "But will we want him to?"

Ross kept a vigil at Ken Rosen's bedside for weeks. Rosen was in a coma during much of this time, and others would recall Ross shaking the bed in an attempt to wake him; it seemed to them that Ross was trying to bring Rosen back by the sheer force of his will, that it had become a personal test, a fight he *would not* lose. Doctors were flown in from other parts of the country, and around the world. Eventually, Rosen did come back, but only part-way; when he woke, he did not know his wife —all that had gone before was wiped out—and he entered a rehabilitation center where he began the arduous process of relearning enough to function, in a limited way, in daily life.

Ross became Lou Rosen's mainstay. For the summer, he rented a house for her in East Hampton, just down the street from where he and Amanda were living. Drawing on his years of experience with the bereaved as a funeral director, he talked to Lou Rosen about his having come to understand the importance of the ritual of burial for achieving closure; that was why, he said, it was so important in wartime that bodies of servicemen be brought home to their relatives. "But with Kenny," he added, "we will never have that." Meanwhile, Ross's solicitude for Lou Rosen was making Amanda Burden increasingly uncomfortable. According to friends, Burden had always been slightly wary of Rosen; now that Rosen was alone, and so dependent on Ross, Burden suspected a budding romance.

In September 1977, Steve, Amanda, and their entourage accompanied the Cosmos to China. En route, they stopped in Japan, where Steve—in a gesture that by this time seemed almost routine—bought pearl necklaces, reportedly valued at about $20,000 each, for Amanda, Martha Emmett, and Alina dé la Sierra. The Cosmos played local teams in Peking and Shanghai, in stadiums packed with about 80,000 spectators. Ross and his friends celebrated his fiftieth birthday, on September 19, in China. At the party, one of his friends—aware, as they all were, of his vanity (Ross typically started each day at WCI by having his hair blow-dried by the barber on the thirtieth floor)—pointed out teasingly that Ross's hair was now completely gray, almost white, while Emmett, just one year younger, had a full head of black hair. Ross, laughing, retorted, "That's because Jay doesn't have to live with Jay!" But the real celebration was held when they returned, in a huge gala at the Waldorf-Astoria.

The tragedy of Rosen aside, there was a great deal for Ross to celebrate that night. His company, whose contours he knew so intimately that it was like a physical extension of himself, had been growing and thriving ever since he had rid it of all it had been before his acquisition of Warner Bros. Those unfortunate businesses, grouped within National Kinney were dying; but Ross had announced in 1975 that Warner intended to dispose of its stake in National Kinney.

That disposal was facilitated when, in mid-1977, National Kinney finally succeeded in selling the Uris properties—prime New York office build-ings which National Kinney, at Ross's direction, had bought in 1973, just before the New York City real estate market collapsed. History would prove this sale of the Uris properties to have been a colossal financial mistake, inasmuch as the buyer, the Reichmanns' Olympia & York, paid about $334 million for eight buildings which, six or seven years later would be worth roughly $3 billion. It was, moreover, one of the few instances in Ross's dealmaking career where he did not take a back-end piece, thus preserving his upside potential in the future. Some close to Ross would later say that he would feel publicly humiliated as the value of the Uris properties skyrocketed, since it meant that this deal became emblazoned as the single megadeal where he had *not* won. At this point, however, the sale of those properties, after three years of exhaustive effort, lifted an enormous weight from Ross.

Thus unburdened, he could concentrate on his beloved WCI, which, under his increasingly sure hand, was besting its own record year after year. By the end of 1977, revenues would exceed the billion-dollar mark for the first time. Net income, $70.8 million, would have increased 16 percent from the prior year, while earnings per share would rise 33 percent (they had risen every year for the past five).

These results were attributable mainly to the strength of WCI's two largest operating groups, records and music publishing, and filmed enter-tainment. WCI's record division—which Ross had rightly recognized as the strongest part of Warner Bros. at the time of its acquisition in 1969—would have grown six-fold since then, its revenues, in 1977, $532 million, and its operating income $84 million. It was bolstered, both domestically and also worldwide, where sales had increased dramatically, by WEA, the Warner distribution arm formed in 1971, which was affirming Ross's conviction about the signal importance of distribution. And, by now, WCI's three record labels—seen as upstarts just five years earlier—had a combined artists' roster that was the strongest in the industry, and had overtaken the leader, CBS Records.

In support of his record business, Ross was being drawn, albeit unwill-ingly at first, into manufacturing. As a rule, he considered manufacturing businesses tedious, and dull; it had suited him that Warner's records were made in factories owned by CBS Records. But the oil crisis in late 1973 had resulted in a shortage of polyvinyl chloride (vinyl), and Ross and his record executives began to feel that they had created a situation where CBS, their most formidable competitor, was in control of their destiny. They entered, instead, into an agreement with Capitol Records, to manu-facture their discs and tapes. By 1978, however, WCI would announce its intention to enter into that business itself, and would acquire a record-pressing plant in Pennsylvania.

The movie industry, which had been almost dormant when Kinney had acquired Warner Bros. in 1969, had rebounded with vigor. U.S. box-office grosses had risen more than 70 percent since 1971, and Warner Bros.—Ross's favorite among all his businesses—had become a leading studio. Its revenues in 1977 were $353 million, and its operating income, $58 million, which eclipsed its previous record year, 1974, when *The Exorcist* had been released.

WCI's publishing operations, while a minor part of the company and the least interesting to Ross, would have an increase of 31 percent in operating income—$7.2 million. And the strength of the rest of the company would make it possible to absorb easily the decline in earnings at Warner Cable, which was about to launch QUBE—an enormously expensive but futuristic, "interactive" pay-TV service.

The strength of the company's core businesses was also enabling Ross to do what he loved best: take risks on new ventures, especially those that he thought had gold-mine potential. One that was showing early promise was the brand-new division called Atari, which made home electronic video games, and had been acquired in 1976. Atari was the first acquisi-tion WCI had made in four years; from 1973 to 1976, WCI had used a significant amount of its excess cash to buy in its common stock, which had been selling at very depressed prices. Now, however, it was em-barking on acquisitions once again. About a year after the Atari acquisi-tion, it acquired Knickerbocker Toy and also Malibu Grand Prix, a chain of mini-amusement centers with three-quarter-scale racing cars. Warner/Lauren, which had been started in 1976 with the designer Ralph Lauren, was introducing new fragrances. And the Cosmos in 1977—while they were, of course, losing an undisclosed $5–$8 million a year—were the North American Soccer League Champions, drawing 75,000 fans to their home games.

How far Ross and his Kinney/Warner band had come was the theme of this triumphal evening in September 1977. Appropriately enough, no excess was spared. The walls of the corridor leading to the Starlight Room in the Waldorf were lined with blown-up photographs of Ross's youth (Governor Hugh Carey, lending a hand to this event, had contacted the Cleveland Browns to obtain some film shots of Ross, one person said, but had been told that no one by that name had ever been with the team). There was a huge likeness of the marquee—featuring *Gunga Din*—from Ross's old neighborhood Loews (which some of Ross's fellow ex-Brooklynites in attendance that night pronounced "Lo-ees"). Guests (among them, Carey and Frank Sinatra) were being served caviar from pushcarts.

The emcee was Joe Smith, now chairman of Elektra/Asylum/Nonesuch, who in a company long on quick-witted and voluble people was probably the quickest-witted of them all. This night, even he seemed sensitive to the momentousness of the occasion, however, and his toasts were slightly more subdued than usual. He claimed that Ross—this tall, silver-haired, handsome character—was not Steve Ross at all but someone sent over from Central Casting to pose as a CEO. He also said that since Ross hadn't been to the Beverly Hills Hotel for some time, the room-service people had had to give up their trips to Hôtel du Cap and sell their Mercedes. (More typical of Smith's style was what he had said at a smaller, more intimate Warner gathering, when he was making his way around the room one by one and had come to Carmen Ferragano, Ross's right-hand assistant, whose devotion to Ross made her vocation seem more a calling than a job, and whom Ross appeared to trust more than anyone: "Carmen Ferragano—if she ever talked . . . " Smith skipped a few beats, for the idea to sink in, "the G3 would take off for Rio, with so many Warner executives hanging from the landing gear that it would look like the last plane out of Saigon!")

Norman Samnick, a lawyer at Warner who had worked on the whirl-wind negotiations to sign Pelé, which had taken him from Brazil to New York to Bermuda in a space of thirty-six hours, would later say, recalling the spirit of this night, "I grew up in Brooklyn, went to City College. Now, here I was, a senior executive at a major entertainment company, with all the attendant glitz, making a lot of money, working for a guy who was also from Brooklyn, who had the most amazing charisma—he gave that smile, put his hand on your shoulder, and you didn't care how tired you were, you'd get it done. And everything was doing great—movies, re-cords, the beginnings in cable and Atari. It was like living a fairy tale, as though we were Patton's army, going through Europe, taking on every-thing we could and turning it into gold!"

Amidst all the euphoria, Ross and Burden were caught up in a private conflict that night that would be reflected, later, in photographs of the event. Again and again, Ross would be pictured with both Amanda and Lou Rosen; he had escorted both women to the party. Burden, convinced that the guests, observing this threesome, would conclude that Ross and Rosen were having an affair, was openly upset; later, she told a friend she felt she had been publicly humiliated. Ross, who felt unjustly accused, was angry with her; but after that night, for the sake of peace with Burden, he stopped his visits to Rosen. Rosen, for her part, would blame herself for not having realized how Burden would react to her presence on Ross's arm that night. The wiser course, she thought in retrospect, would have been to stay home. But that summer she had felt almost as diminished as her husband, and she was desperate to reenter what had been their world.

After several months, Ken Rosen recovered sufficiently that, with a young man provided by the company as an escort, he could come to WCI each day, where he still had an office. (All his expenses were covered by WCI, according to the disability provisions in his contract, and further arrangements which Ross authored. "I remember someone saying that there might be some criticism about corporate resources being devoted to Ken," Cy O'Neil observed, "and Steve said, 'I'll take the heat on that one, any day.' ") Rosen's coming to work was a sad charade, however; eventually, Lou Rosen sent him to a home for the mentally disabled in Charleston, South Carolina; and some time later she remarried. She believed that Ross would have kept Rosen at WCI forever, but she thought it too cruel to the person he had been to have him paraded through the corridors—an object of pity, a testament to Ross's loyalty.

The loss of Rosen must have caused Ross to suffer. That said, however, Ross found a way to transmute the tragedy into something useful—as he did with virtually all the events and people in his life. In my first interview with Ross, back in 1989, he introduced the subject of Ken Rosen, and spoke at some length about having essentially moved his office into the hospital in order to remain at Rosen's side—an oddly public airing of something that was, presumably, a private ordeal, but that he seemed to be proffering as evidence of his being a good and giving person.

As the years went by and no potential successor appeared on the scene, Ross—in a slightly oblique way of explaining the absence of any successor—would frequently harken back to Rosen. He would remark, as he did when interviewed for an oral history of Eddie Rosenthal's life, "Ken Rosen was the young fellow I was grooming to be my successor someday."

4

$M$uch later, those who had been in the upper echelons of WCI in the seventies would recall that era, feelingly, as the best of times. Greater individual wealth, greater corporate growth, greater business triumphs would come later—but life at WCI would never be as sweet as it was then. And, even as Ross and his hundreds of guests were celebrating his fiftieth birthday, the events that would bring the idyll to its close had begun to unfold.

Earlier that month, an FBI agent had appeared at the door of Leonard Horwitz's home in Norwalk, Connecticut, and had told the startled, frightened Horwitz that he wanted to talk to him about the Westchester Premier Theatre. He had emphasized, however, that the government was not so much interested in Horwitz as in the information he could provide. Horwitz responded that he wanted first to talk to his lawyer.

Until that moment, Horwitz thought that the theater was a closed chapter in his life. He had been a stockbroker at a small New York firm, Ferkauf, Roggen, when, in early 1972, a fellow broker there, Eliot Weisman, had told him that he wanted to start a theater in Westchester that would book big-name recording artists—much like Long Island's Westbury Music Fair. Shortly thereafter, he had asked Horwitz to help him sell some "seed stock" in a private placement, to raise about $150,000 for an option on the land, near the Tappan Zee Bridge, and for start-up costs. Horwitz agreed, and chose to take an equity participation in the theater rather than a broker's commission.

One of the first people Horwitz approached was Jay Emmett, who agreed to buy $15,000 of stock ($1.50 a share). Emmett and Horwitz had been friends for about fifteen years, having first met back in the mid-fifties, commuting on the train from Connecticut to New York; it had become their habit on these train rides to play cards, usually gin rummy, for stakes that ranged from about $10 to $30. While he and Emmett did not generally see each other socially, they were good enough friends that Emmett frequently loaned him up to a couple thousand dollars to pay off gambling debts (they both bet on professional football).

Emmett was also one of a five-member stock investment group that Horwitz ran; they called themselves "The Flaky Five." A stress between Emmett and Horwitz had occurred after Horwitz, in 1971, had become enthusiastic about a cable company, TVC. He had bought TVC stock for "The Flaky Five," and he had also told Emmett that he thought it would be a good acquisition candidate for Kinney (about to be renamed WCI). When Kinney did in fact acquire TVC in late 1971, Horwitz argued that he deserved a finder's fee; but Emmett insisted that he had never conveyed Horwitz's idea to Ross, and that TVC had been brought to Ross's attention by Felix Rohatyn of Lazard Frères. Horwitz considered suing, but did not —and his friendship with Emmett continued.

By the late spring of 1973, a public stock offering of the Westchester Premier Theatre—at $7.50 a share—was faltering and seemed unlikely to reach the minimum required for the offering to proceed. Horwitz, who was once again selling the stock and, at Weisman's behest, offering inducements to various people (additional "seed" stock, for example, or, to an insurance broker, the opportunity to write Weisman's life insurance policy), decided to try Emmett again. Weisman had suggested that he propose to Emmett that Emmett borrow $50,000 in cash from the theater owners and add $25,000 of his own money in order to purchase 10,000 shares of stock.

Horwitz went to see Jay Emmett at his office at WCI, carrying (as he would later testify) $50,000 in cash in a brown paper bag. Emmett said he was not interested, but that he would check to see if there was anyone in the company who might help. As Emmett, too, would testify, he then went across the corridor to Ross's office (indeed, according to one person to whom Emmett recounted the story, he had taken the bag of $50,000 and thrown it, as a gag, on Ross's desk—something which it is difficult to imagine Emmett *not* doing) and described Horwitz's proposition. Ross, according to Emmett, said that Horwitz should see Solomon Weiss, the bookkeeper from Kinney Parking, who by 1973 was not only WCI's assistant treasurer but Ross's trusted designate, who handled Ross's personal finances.

Emmett returned shortly with Weiss, introduced him to Horwitz, and departed. Horwitz repeated the proposition, and, as he would later testify, Weiss "said he thought the company could help. The company always had a need for cash." Then, "Weiss sat down and started to count the money," after which he said he would return in a few minutes. "I made some mention about are you going to see Steve," Horwitz would say, referring to Ross, and Weiss said, " 'Don't use that name' or 'we don't use that name around here.' "

When Weiss returned a few minutes later, Horwitz would continue, Weiss said that the company would purchase not 10,000 but 20,000 shares, and that Horwitz would have to provide an additional $50,000 in cash, for a total of $100,000. And that, according to Horwitz, was the beginning of a series of illegal transactions that would continue over the next four years.

During that time, the theater would be eviscerated by the mob, and by 1977, it would be closed. Weisman had been an effective "front." He was a former accountant and stockbroker, with no criminal record; and he had apparently had some illusion that he could control the overall situation, while allowing his partners to run the parking lot and concessions. Those partners, from the very start, were organized crime soldiers Richard ("Nerves") Fusco, with the Colombo crime family, and Gregory De Palma, with the Gambino family (he would become a "made" member in 1976). Later, Salvatore Cannatella, who, the government would allege, was connected to the Genovese family, would put $1.4 million into the theater and assume a dominant role. The Westchester Premier Theatre was nothing if not eclectic.

What transpired there lent new credence to the old line about organized crime—in at least some of its operations—being anything but organized. From the start, there was illegal dumping on the site ("Every wiseguy in the world was dumping there," said one former partner in the theater). There were enormous cost overruns on the construction of the theater. Fusco and De Palma (who liked to refer to his handgun as "Pearlie") routinely delivered large amounts of cash to the theater. One former participant would later recall the two men arriving, one evening, with their shirts stuffed with cash, all fives, tens, and twenties—totalling about $35,000.

Despite the flow of cash from Carlo Gambino and others, by the time the theater opened its doors, after nearly two years of delays, it was $3.5 million in debt. Skimming was incessant, with cash looted from the box office to pay back some of the "shylock" money that had been used to start the theater, and to line the pockets of those at the theater. Another, more creative form of skimming was accomplished through the theater's sixty-one "phantom seats." After the auditors had come, one of the theater's hidden owners had added sixty-one chairs. As he would later explain, "the theater was practically empty during the week. But those sixty-one chairs were always the first ones sold—I promise you, there was never an empty chair in those seats. We used to make about $4,500 a week on those. We'd put it in a separate envelope, and split it four ways."

Even without the skimming, however, the theater would have been doomed. Its overhead was too high—it was closed for four months of the year, but still had to cover its expenses during those winter months. And entertainers were paid far too much for this 3,500-seat facility ever to be viable. Diana Ross, for example, received $225,000 for a week's performance. (Another performer was paid about $150,000, which she demanded in cash; when De Palma, Fusco, and a couple others went to deliver the money, they were held up for more by several of her associates. According to one witness, the exchange ended with De Palma and Fusco drawing their guns and disarming the others.)

In the fall of 1974, when the theater was deeply in debt and Weisman and his partners were struggling to meet construction costs, Ross, Emmett, Weiss, and Sylvester Gerard Benford, a WCI vice-president who concentrated on acquisitions, met to discuss the possibility of WCI's investing an additional $500,000—as a secured loan, which would carry equity kickers—in the Westchester theater. Milton (Mickey) Rudin, Sinatra's lawyer and manager, who was visiting WCI offices on other matters, also joined the discussion. Subsequently, as Benford researched the investment, he met at the theater with Weisman, Horwitz, and Weiss— Weiss, Benford would testify before the SEC, "was there because I believe he had contact with the theatre personnel prior to my getting involved in it. I believe he knew Mr. Horwitz and Mr. Weisman."

After several weeks, Benford recommended to Ross that WCI not proceed with the investment. During the same period of time, Eddie Rosenthal was asked by someone at WCI—he would later testify that he could not remember exactly who, though it was either someone in the executive group or Weiss—to look into the situation at the theater and see if he could help Weisman with some problems he was having with town officials in Greenburgh, regarding construction. Rosenthal lived in Greenburgh, and, since he had recently financed the construction of a day-care center there, he was well acquainted with the officials. He decided that what the officials were exacting from Weisman was appropriate, and also that WCI should not invest further in the theater. Indeed, he wrote a letter to Weiss in which he stated: "Don't put any more dough into the theater (if you can keep from doing so)."

Rosenthal, however, had taken a liking to Weisman, who had mentioned when they met that he was a two-handicapped golfer. Rosenthal loved golf. So he invited Weisman to play, and they did so several times. By the spring of 1975, Weisman was urging Rosenthal that WCI invest $1 million in the theater. Rosenthal brought in a retired accountant from Florida to go over the books; another meeting was held at WCI—and, once again, it was decided not to make the investment. But Rosenthal was inclined to lend Weisman $250,000 personally; he prepared to do so, then thought better of it and lent him only $35,000 (of which only $3,000 would ever be repaid). When he was later questioned repeatedly at the SEC about why he should have considered lending Weisman $250,000, in light of his conviction that the prospects of the theater were so bleak, Rosenthal would respond, "I felt sorry for him. I have loaned forty other people in the town of Greenburgh because I feel sorry for them and because I felt I could afford it and because I am lucky to have it."

While Weisman did not get the $1 million he wanted from WCI, his partner, De Palma, did succeed in raising $1.4 million from Thomas Marson, who had made a fortune in the plumbing business in New York and then moved to Rancho Mirage, near Palm Springs, California, where he had become friendly with Frank Sinatra. Among Marson's other friends were mobsters De Palma, Jimmy ("the Weasel") Fratianno, Mike Rizzitello, Dominic Brooklier, and Frank ("the Bomp") Bompensiero. By early 1977, FBI agents had become sufficiently interested in the activity at Marson's home in Rancho Mirage, which they viewed as a congregating place for members of the Los Angeles mob, that they sought authorization for a wiretap.

That authorization was based on information the FBI submitted about its investigation of the Alfa Chemical Company, which manufactured detergent and offered cleaning services, and was said to be owned by Marson, Fratianno, Teamsters head Jackie Presser, and Las Vegas mobster Tony Spilotro. Alfa closed down before conclusive evidence was accumulated. But the wiretap—its product known as the "Alfa tapes"—opened a window on a world peopled by mobsters from not only Los Angeles but Chicago, Cleveland, and New York, discussing extortion, loan sharking, land frauds, bribery, and bankruptcy frauds. Among these were conversations between Marson, De Palma, and Fratianno about Marson's investment in Westchester Premier Theatre.

Meanwhile, the FBI in New York had a convicted check-kiter, Charles Ross Carino, who, facing a new set of bad-check charges, was offering information about the theater which was run by his lifelong friend Eliot Weisman, and was controlled by the mob—and about bribes paid to officials of Warner Communications to induce them to buy theater stock. Carino told his story to assistant U.S. Attorney Nick Akerman. By May 1977, the FBI in New York (with the Alfa tapes as support) had gained authority to place a wiretap on the theater's offices and De Palma's home phone.

Leonard Horwitz's reaction to his visit from the FBI was immediate. He had no inclination to resist the government and seek solidarity with his erstwhile associates at the theater; he had worked there for about a year after the theater had opened, selling subscription seats, but he had always been an outsider, not one who benefited from any of the copious skimming. Indeed, one former theater partner recalled that he, Weisman, and their cohorts used to deride Horwitz as someone who barely understood what was going on. Horwitz had learned from the FBI agent, moreover, that a major focus of their probe was Warner Communications. He knew he could help them there. He would give up Solomon Weiss, to whom he felt no allegiance. Indeed, in the course of their many meetings over the previous four years he had developed a healthy dislike for Weiss who, he felt, had dealt with him in an insulting manner.

Horwitz called Jay Emmett, now in the Office of the President at WCI, and told him about the visit from the FBI, and his decision to cooperate and inform on Weiss. It was Emmett, of course, who had introduced Horwitz to Weiss, but Horwitz felt that he could protect Emmett, since, as he would later testify, all his transactions had been with Weiss. Emmett asked him not to talk to the FBI yet and said that he would get back to him shortly. Horwitz would later recall that a series of discussions followed, all ending inconclusively with Emmett's saying he would have to get back to him. Horwitz believed, in each instance, that Emmett was relaying their conversations to Ross. Finally, after about a month had gone by, they reached an accord: Horwitz would not cooperate with the FBI. And he would be given a job at WCI.

The way Horwitz looked at it, it was not a bribe; he had smarted for a long time at not having received what he believed was his deserved finder's fee in the TVC acquisition, and he liked to think of the job offer now as delayed payback. But he knew, at the same time, that WCI executives had dismissed his claim as invalid more than five years earlier and that, to them, the job was simply the price of his silence. He joined the company on January 1, 1978, as an executive with a salary and bonus that totalled $75,000 a year. His responsibilities were undefined. Initially, however, he was to work on Warner's investment in iai alai.

. . .

The jai alai venture had been brought to WCI by Caesar Kimmel, who, in 1978, was casting about for a new project. Kimmel had become a seeming anachronism in the upper corporate echelons of WCI; this was, after all, an entertainment company, and Kimmel had made his way in the parking business. After he had turned over the day-to-day running of Kinney Parking to Dan Katz, Kimmel had continued to monitor it for several years, and he had also been in charge of the administration of the new building. But by the mid-seventies there was relatively little for him to do at WCI. In collaboration with Saul Bass, who had designed the new WCI logo, Kimmel went to Los Angeles to make a short film about WCI for advertising and recruiting purposes; but Ross and others rejected it as inappropriate—there was a lot of slapstick humor, reminiscent of Kimmel's Al Kelly prank. Kimmel blamed Ross's reaction on Burden (who, he knew, had found the movie frivolous) and her highfalutin' ways.

However purposeless Kimmel felt, his power and position were secure. He owned as much of the company's stock as Ross; he was a director and an executive vice-president, receiving in 1978 a salary of $125,000 and an "incentive bonus" of $37,594 (less than the compensation of those in the Office of the President, but more than the company's general counsel). And, according to one corporate executive, Kimmel escaped any general oversight because he refused to report to anyone but Ross. Others knew better than to intrude. "We all knew we'd get a black mark from Steve if we annoyed Caesar," this executive said.

Now, Kimmel had become keen on the business of jai alai. He seemed drawn to the same areas of life that so lured his father, Manny, though always from a somewhat different angle: while his father was a bookie at the racetrack and "straightened out" the jockeys, according to his old friend Hand, Kimmel owned racehorses; and now, whereas his father had been and would remain an inveterate, obsessive gambler to the day he died, Kimmel wanted to own the gambling enterprise. Whatever the psychological affinity may have been, the economics of jai alai alone were probably sufficient to whet his appetite. The typical fronton in the seventies was estimated to bring in about $200,000 in bets a day, which (operating about 150 days a year) would mean roughly $30 million a year in revenues; about 12 percent of that ($3.6 million) would go to the fronton owners.

Kimmel's close friend and partner in various business ventures, Leonard Meyers—who had for years been involved in his family's company, Meyers Parking—in 1976 became the owner of record of 5 percent of the shares in a jai alai fronton opened in Bridgeport, Connecticut. That fronton had a history of corruption from its inception so intense (its chief promoter was indicted for perjury and embezzlement) that state licenses were withdrawn and its opening delayed for more than a year, while other prospective owners tried to gain approval of the Connecticut gaming regulators. The fronton had been built with a loan of $11 million from the Teamsters Pension Fund. According to *The Teamsters,* by Steven Brill, Anthony ("Tony Pro") Provenzano, the notoriously violent captain in the New Jersey–New York Genovese family, who would ultimately be convicted of having murdered a rival New Jersey Teamsters official, and who ran that racket-rich union, had received a $100,000 finder's fee for arranging the loan to the Bridgeport fronton.

One state investigator maintained that Provenzano was increasingly upset about the fronton's sitting empty and revenueless; Meyers then came in and bought 5 percent of the fronton. The owner of record of the remaining 95 percent of the fronton's shares was A. Robert Zeff, a lawyer from Detroit, Michigan. "We were very unhappy about Meyers," this investigator continued. He added that Meyers was pressured to withdraw— he relinquished his holdings in the Bridgeport fronton in November 1977 —with the understanding that he could reenter the Connecticut jai alai scene at some later date (he would do so, in 1983). Also, according to several people, Kimmel had indicated to them during this period that not only Meyers but he, too, had a stake (hidden, if true) in the Bridgeport fronton.

Now, Kimmel and Meyers wanted to develop jai alai in New Jersey, with the backing of WCI. Ross at least initially seemed enthusiastic about the idea, but other executives were appalled; with the company being investigated in connection with the Westchester Premier Theatre, it seemed foolhardy and almost brazen to become involved in jai alai, which was widely understood to be linked to organized crime. (Indeed, to one investigator experienced in this area, the shooting murder in 1980 of Roger Wheeler, chairman of the Telex Corporation—a company that *did* invest in jai alai—was proof of the proposition that one could not survive in jai alai unless one had some relationship with organized crime.)

While senior corporate executives believed that the company was not going forward with Kimmel's jai alai proposition, Kimmel and Meyers continued to pursue the venture in New Jersey. In league with David Friedland, a New Jersey state senator who would later be convicted of stealing from the Teamsters Pension Fund, they organized a campaign to legalize jai alai in the state. Friedland would later recall that Kimmel had told him that WCI was committed to the project (indeed, promotional materials were generated there, and numerous state officials attended meetings with Kimmel at WCI, where some were quite struck at being served by a white-gloved butler), but that the company could not assume that stance publicly. He would recall, too, that Kimmel had repeatedly assured him of his power to deliver, saying, "I can get anything I want from Steve Ross."

In fact, when Friedland told Kimmel and Meyers that it would take $500,000-$750,000 to gain public officials' support to place the measure on the ballot, and then to win at election, Kimmel (according to Friedland) had said that that was no problem, and he promptly made the funds available. Paul Byrne, a veteran of Jersey City politics who was working with Friedland on this measure, recalled that Kimmel's only caution on their spending was to paraphrase the words of Joseph Kennedy, joshing, "I don't mind buying an election, but I don't want to pay for a landslide." He, too, recalled Kimmel's having stated that WCI was behind it but would need to stay in the background.

Friedland would later assert that the political effort he spearheaded was utterly corrupt—involving payoffs to himself, as well as to local officials, state legislators, lawyers, and wardworkers. About $80,000 was handed out in "street money" in one ward alone, to bring out the vote. With it all, however, the proposition lost, in November 1978.

After WCI had, at least officially, ceased pursuing an investment in jai alai, Leonard Horwitz worked for a time with Warner Cosmetics, and then with Atari. But it seems plain that he drifted from one area to the next because there had been no real job for him at WCI; his job, in effect, was to stonewall the government in its probe of WCI and Westchester Premier Theatre, and, as it developed, to aid his former theater associates in their efforts to do so too.

A record of exchanges involving Horwitz and his erstwhile compatriots was provided to the government by one of them, a former partner in the theater, who became an informant and taped conversations for about five months. In the initial exchanges with Horwitz, in December 1977, the informant was pressing Horwitz to help fabricate an explanation for a $30,000 WCI check, made out to Dennis Konner, a lawyer, and the informant's former partner; he was insisting that he needed a file from WCI that would support the notion of work performed, as well as two names of WCI employees with whom Konner could claim he had dealt. Konner —who was never charged with any wrongdoing—was soon to go before the grand jury, and if he were not provided a plausible story, then, his former partner threatened Horwitz, Konner would tell what little of the truth he knew: that no services had been performed, and that the check had simply been a means of generating cash that was returned to WCI.

At first, in a conversation recorded on December 14, 1977, Horwitz appeared intensely nervous, and stridently noncommittal; he was, in all likelihood, frightened of saying anything that might jeopardize his new-found position at WCI. "I know nothing and nobody knows nothing," Horwitz insisted. "All they know is that somebody did some services for them." Four days later, however, his former cohort was increasing the pressure. "Hey, Lenny, let me tell you what's going to happen here. He's [Konner] going to go down there and say we didn't do the legal work. I'm going to go down there and then, I'm going to go right behind him and tell the truth. You know. That you gave me the fucking check for a phoney bill. I'm not going to get stuck for this. I'm willing to work it out. But I ain't getting fucking stuck for it all by myself. . . ."

By mid-January 1978, Horwitz, now formally ensconced at WCI, was making a gesture of conciliation. He said he "had an attorney spend three days going through different trade journals, different magazines" in order to compile something that might pass for a file. He had not yet been able to produce the requested names, however. Describing the position being taken at WCI, and, specifically, their response to an IRS investigator who had come to the company, Horwitz said: "When the guy came and asked about bills, it took them weeks to even get an answer to him. . . . We don't have this fucking file, ba ba ba, we do a billion a year."

Eventually, Horwitz continued, WCI had taken the position that "all we can find is this bill. That five years ago or whatever, there was some work done for us by Konner. Cablevision, somehow we don't have any papers, we don't know nothing. We know nothing. . . ."

Asked whom the investigator had come to see, Horwitz replied, "The treasurer. They came to see the guy who, who knows really," he said, apparently referring to Weiss, who was the assistant treasurer.

A short time later, describing his conversation with Horwitz to Weis-man, the informant said, ". . . I gotta tell you something, if I was in War-ner's position, I gotta tell you the honest truth, I wouldn't say a word, either. They got Lenny scared shit. They give em money from time to time. He said it before. This is not the first time about the 75 [his salary plus bonus]. He's, he's, he's got other money from them too from time to time. So they're saying to em we'll, we'll, ya, Lenny says he just paid his lawyer an awful lot of money. Where's he got a lot of money. I'm sure that he went to Jay for the money or somebody for the money. He's, they're gonna feed him money. They got no position. They, I'll tell ya, they're taking the right attitude. If Lenny's gonna stand up for them why should they ah come up with a name. Why should they get involved in some sort of conspiracy if Lenny gonna stand up for them."

Some time later, however, Horwitz approached these two again and, in a three-way conversation, did volunteer the name of Peter Goldmark, the former head of CBS Laboratories who had joined the company in 1971, and who had recently been killed in an auto accident. And, about a month later, in another taped conversation, Eliot Weisman, who had been trying to wrest further cooperation out of Horwitz, mentioned "one guy in a coma," who was, as it developed, Ken Rosen.

The use of both names was reportedly authorized by Ross—despite objections raised to him that using the names of one person who was brain-damaged and another who was dead might seem, at best, suspicious. On the other hand, no one at WCI was taking that position for the record; it was merely being fed to others, by Horwitz.

Judging from these taped conversations, Weisman began to take an increasingly active role not only in soliciting Horwitz's cooperation but in doing whatever else he could to further the obstruction of the government's case. Initially, he had given some thought to cooperating, and at one point, in September 1977, when he was arrested for making a false statement on a mortgage application, he had started to give Nick Akerman some information about skimming at the theater; but once Akerman asked him to wear a body recorder, he had stopped talking.

Weisman, more than his other Jewish associates, had always been afraid of his mob partners. One former associate recalled that when he had urged that the theater go into Chapter 11, Weisman had at first resisted, repeatedly declaring that if they tried that, they would only end up going into "Chapter cement." In the course of these conversations, too, Weisman remarked that "'fuckin' Richie [Fusco] don't scare me ... but the other guy [De Palma] scares the living piss out of me."

Referring to De Palma's occasional remarks about the possibility of someone's going before the grand jury and "doing a job" on him, Weisman added, "You know, he's not sure of me 'cause I'm not, I'm not, I'm not Italian. You know what I mean?"

Weisman and his partners at the theater had been surprised, at first, that a major corporation like WCI would be willing to risk dealing with people like them, in illegal transactions, for relatively paltry sums of cash —in the end totalling $170,000. What they had soon concluded, as one former partner later explained, was that the accumulation of cash through such transactions must have been a way of life at WCI, and their contribution, therefore, part of a much larger picture. Now, Weisman remarked to his former partner that he had said to Horwitz, "I want to tell you something, I said, you know, the shit's going to hit the fan, over Warner, and I say, you know, the Westchester Premier Theatre is only one small part of it, O.K., and I says, your fucking friends are going to be blown out of that fucking building."

". . . Yeah, they were fucking around with everybody else," Weisman's former partner agreed.

To which Weisman replied, ". . . There got to be nine million of them, right."

Weisman stated repeatedly in these taped conversations that he was talking to Eddie Rosenthal and keeping him fully apprised of everything. Indeed, according to Weisman's former partner, when Weisman went to Rosenthal back in the spring of 1975 to ask him to persuade WCI to invest $1 million in the theater, he also informed Rosenthal about the illegal transactions that had been taking place between the theater and WCI.

By early April 1978 (when these taped conversations would end), Weisman was solidifying his bond with Mickey Rudin. Sinatra had been recruited to appear at the theater by Louis ("Louie Dones") Pacella, who worked for Frank ("Funzi") Tieri, head of the Genovese family; and, beginning in April 1976, he had given several performances there. Sinatra's September 1976 performance was memorialized by his posing for a photograph, in his dressing room, with a rather striking group: Carlo Gambino, Joseph Gambino, Paul Castellano (who would later become head of the Gambino family), Tom Marson, Salvatore Spatola, Weisman's theater partners Fusco and De Palma, and Jimmy Fratianno.

In late 1977, Fratianno—with a mob contract out on his life, and close to indictment on a murder charge—turned to the government for protection. He would be described by law enforcement officials at the time as the most important organized crime figure ever to cooperate with the government. One of those whom Fratianno would implicate in the skimming at the Westchester Premier Theatre was Sinatra. Fratianno told prosecutors that De Palma had paid Sinatra $50,000 or $60,000 in cash, in Las Vegas, to persuade him to play the theater in 1977.

Also, in one of the conversations the FBI recorded from De Palma's phone, De Palma told Cannatella that he had given Rudin a cut from the money that had been skimmed from sales of Sinatra concert paraphernalia.

Now, in the conversation on April 5, 1978, recorded between Weisman and this former partner, Weisman reported that he had spent three hours on the prior Sunday with Rudin, discussing the theater investigation. "Sinatra and Warner are very close," Weisman remarked, mentioning the benefit for Governor Carey, Ross's friend, at which Sinatra had just performed.

"Anyway, ah, Warner's lawyers called, ah, Mickey to ask him his opinion," Weisman continued. Rudin, Weisman later stated, had become "one of my attorneys." To which his former partner, who had also been a lawyer, responded, "Mickey, he's got privileged information." (It is not clear from this exchange, what this former partner was suggesting with respect to Weisman's statement about Rudin. It is also not clear that Rudin was ever retained by Weisman.)

At one point, striking an optimistic note, Weisman said, "Mickey, ah, said that however we arrived at what we did here is ingenious. What can they prove?" Still, a few minutes later, when Weisman was asked whether Rudin felt he had a legal problem, Weisman responded, "Mickey is, ah, very nervous about the whole thing."

In early April 1978, both Emmett and Weiss were subpoenaed to appear before the grand jury that was investigating WCI and the Westchester Premier Theatre. Horwitz had already appeared in March and asserted his rights under the Fifth Amendment—as he had planned to do ever since he had agreed not to tell the FBI about his transactions with Weiss but, rather, to remain silent and take a job at WCI. It was what his lawyer, Jonathan Lubell, whom he had known for a number of years, had advised him to do.

Now, before Emmett and Weiss's scheduled appearances, Mickey Rudin—who had been on retainer as a consultant to the company since it had acquired Warner Bros. in 1969, and who was close to several of WCI's top executives, including Ross and the company's general counsel, Martin Payson—is said to have flown in from Los Angeles for the specific purpose of conferring with the company's other lawyers (as Weisman, too, mentioned on the tape). Rudin is also said to have strongly advised Jay Emmett, with whom he was especially friendly, that he should invoke the Fifth.

Arthur Liman, of the Paul, Weiss firm, was directing WCI's legal strategy. Paul, Weiss, of course, had been the company's outside counsel from the time it had gone public in 1962, and Judge Simon Rifkind, one of the firm's founders, had had a relationship with Eddie Rosenthal that went back even further. Allan Ecker had been the Paul, Weiss lawyer closest to Ross in the sixties; but by the early seventies, Liman had replaced Ecker at Ross's side.

As WCI had grown dramatically in the seventies, its account had become one of the most important corporate accounts at Paul, Weiss; this, in turn, helped to augment and solidify Liman's power at the firm. While Liman, who was Rifkind's protégé, was widely regarded as a highly intelligent, skilled attorney, and much in demand, still Steve Ross was the single client most critical to his success. Liman brought to this relationship, moreover, a devotion that suggests that the bond was intensely personal, as well.

Emmett, who was inclined to follow Rudin's advice, was reportedly urged by Liman not, as co-president of the company, to invoke the Fifth. Also, Solomon Weiss was reportedly advised by Liman that Paul, Weiss would only represent him if he were prepared to cooperate with the investigation. (Liman denies talking with Rudin at all, claims that he advised Emmett only that Paul, Weiss would not represent him if he took the Fifth, and that one of his partners, not he personally, gave similar advice to Weiss.) In their appearances before the grand jury, both Emmett and Weiss were represented by Max Gitter from Paul, Weiss; they had no independent counsel. Prior to their appearances, Gitter had phoned Nick Akerman to inquire whether either client was a target of the grand jury's investigation. Akerman replied that neither was a target within the meaning of the Department of Justice guidelines (which defined a target as "a person as to whom the prosecutor of the Grand Jury has substantial evidence linking him to the commission of a crime and who, in the judgment of the prosecutor, is a putative defendant").

Two months later, Leonard Horwitz, Eliot Weisman, and eight other defendants were charged in twenty-four counts with violations of federal law that ran the gamut of the theater's short-lived existence, from defrauding investors who bought securities at its inception to looting the theater while it was in bankruptcy. Horwitz and Weisman were also charged with having attempted to obstruct the grand jury's investigation by counselling others to give false testimony. Horwitz took a paid leave of absence from WCI to prepare for the upcoming trial.

The two "unnamed executives" referred to in the indictment were Emmett and Weiss, as Liman learned from Akerman. At that point, Liman told them that Paul, Weiss lawyers could no longer represent them, and Liman directed Emmett to Robert Morvillo and Weiss to Robert Kasanof. (Solomon Weiss was at home recuperating at this time. Several weeks after his grand jury appearance, he had suffered severe angina and had undergone a triple-bypass heart operation.)

In September 1978, Emmett and Weiss were named publicly in connection with this case for the first time, in pre-trial documents filed with the court; there, Akerman alleged that they had taken a $50,000 bribe for influencing WCI to buy 40,000 shares, or 4 percent, of the theater's stock, for $250,000. Although mentioned in pre-trial documents, neither Emmett nor Weiss was indicted for any wrongdoing, and both denied that they had taken bribes.

In its quarterly report filed with the SEC in early November, WCI stated that these matters—involving Emmett, Weiss, and Horwitz—had been referred to the company's audit committee. The audit committee consisted of three outside directors: Bess Myerson, the consumer columnist, who had just joined the board; Eugene Black, the elderly, long-retired chairman of the World Bank; and Lawrence Buttenweiser, Ross's devoted friend of roughly thirty years, who had joined the board when Kinney Service first went public, and was a partner in the Rosenman Colin law firm. The committee, in turn, had retained Michael Armstrong as its counsel in this matter. Armstrong was to do his own investigation, but he announced that he would not begin until the Westchester trial ended, and until the U.S. Attorney's Office had completed its inquiry of WCI.

These moves—orchestrated by Arthur Liman—achieved a duality of purpose; they conveyed a sense of corporate responsibility at work, while also serving as a shield for Ross. Like the rest of Ross's board, the audit committee was a dependable adjunct. Its chairman (and lone decision maker) was Buttenweiser, who, as a lawyer, and one from a prominent New York family at that, lent it legitimacy. Buttenweiser, however, was "family," his loyalty to Ross beyond question. Armstrong, moreover, was an ideal choice inasmuch as he had a fiery reputation for ferreting out police corruption from his days as chief investigator on the Knapp Commission. But he was also one of a fraternity of prominent New York lawyers, including Liman, who, in a generally benign symbiosis, referred cases to each other, acted as co-counsel in multi-defendant cases, and tried never to cross one another.

The strategic benefit of the audit committee referral would be highlighted in an SEC deposition by Ross taken on September 25, 1979. By this time, the theater phase of the government's criminal investigation was essentially finished. The trial of Horwitz and his co-defendants had ended in a mistrial; on the eve of the second trial, in March 1979, several of the defendants had pled guilty, leaving Horwitz, Weisman, and a couple others to be retried; and in May, Horwitz, Weisman, and Cannatella had all been found guilty. Horwitz had appealed that verdict and, in August, had been granted the right to a new trial. Odds and ends of the theater phase, therefore, remained to be resolved. But the second phase—WCI—had now begun in earnest, in investigations by both the U.S. Attorney's Office and the SEC (which had opened its investigation in April 1979).

At Ross's deposition, where he was represented by four attorneys, including Liman, he began by giving direct responses to a few of the usual résumé questions but then, seizing the opportunity ("Well, I think the best way to tell it, if I may tell it from this point"), launched into a full-scale autobiographical recitation. It was one (punctuated with the same throwaway lines) into which, over the years, he would always throw himself, unbidden, in any deposition where the questioner allowed it, and in interviews, too—a way, it would seem, of subtly wresting control of the situation from his interlocutor, using up time that might be spent on other sorts of questions, presenting himself as an open and forthcoming person, and, of course, succeeding in putting on the record, one more time, the story of which he was so proud. When, seventeen transcript pages later, Ross had made his way only to 1969, Michael Nelson, the SEC enforcement division lawyer, interrupted him, saying that he would "like to expedite it a bit."

Even in his expedited version, Ross managed to articulate a theme that he and his lawyers would repeat, mantralike, in the course of this investigation, one that would attempt to explain how whatever had happened could only have been unknown to him. "We are somewhat of an unstructured—we could be considered one of the most unstructured companies and that is how you have to survive in the entertainment business. What you have to do is give everyone autonomy. We are dealing with a lot of creative people. We have a very enviable record. To my knowledge we have never lost a key executive to a competitor since we have been in business. And the way you do that is by giving total authority.

"Our concept as has always been stated we would want the mailroom boy to order pencils, if we want to get a decision on the single lowest possible level, we would keep pushing."

It was, of course, true that this had been one of Ross's early, golden precepts—he did indeed give his division heads extraordinary autonomy. But Ross ruled at corporate, and he had, moreover, never been a detached CEO. As Allan Ecker had said of him, "Steve was into the nuts and bolts of everything."

Asked whether the retention of an outside lawyer at the division level would have to be approved by the general counsel's office—a question that was clearly heading in the direction of the fee paid to the lawyer, Dennis Konner—Ross answered, "I wouldn't know that."

"Mr. Ross doesn't get involved in that," interjected Martin Payson, WCI's general counsel.

". . . Let me put the question," Liman said. "Mr. Ross, this is a highly decentralized company, is it not, Warner?"

"Yes." Ross replied.

"With a very small executive staff?" Liman continued.

"Too small," responded Ross.

At times, the deposition seemed less a deposition than a well-rehearsed, skillfully-executed *pas de deux* between Liman and his client. The only moments when their synchronicity was imperfect occurred when Ross slightly overplayed his part in a way that clearly strained credulity—and then Liman was always there to rescue him. Asked when he had become aware that there was a grand jury investigation under way that involved Horwitz (who had, of course, been engaged in constant conversations with Emmett about these developments, beginning in the fall of 1977), Ross testified, "Whenever my counsel informed me."

Queried whether that had been before or after Horwitz was indicted, in June 1978, Ross replied, "I wouldn't know whether it was just before, after—"

"Before," Liman interjected.

"Before," said Ross.

"You learned this from whom?" Nelson asked, again.

"From counsel," Ross replied.

"I will help you with the time frame," Liman again interjected. "It was after Mr. Horwitz was employed, correct?"

"Yes," said Ross.

It further emerged, from Ross's testimony, that once he had learned "from counsel" the substance of the charges against Horwitz—including the allegation that Horwitz had passed the $50,000 to Emmett and Weiss —counsel had instructed him not to talk to Emmett (his best friend, and constant cohort) or Weiss about the matter. And Ross testified—repeatedly—he had not done so. Instead, the matter had been turned over to the audit committee ("... as a matter of fact I think you turned it over to the audit committee," Ross said to Liman in their ongoing exchange), and there it remained.

As the deposition evolved, it became clear that Steve Ross's defense was two-pronged. On virtually all questions relating to the substance of the investigation, Ross either testified that he had no knowledge of these matters, and he had never inquired because counsel had instructed him that that was the province of the audit committee, or, that while he had no knowledge of these matters, Jay Emmett would.

Only on one issue—the decision to purchase the Westchester Premier stock—did Ross describe a shared responsibility. He said that the "ultimate responsibility" at the company for the purchase of securities was his, and while there was an executive group that generally discussed such purchases, in the instance of the Westchester Premier Theatre stock, "To the best of my recollection it was Jay Emmett and I," Ross testified. As to whose idea it was, "I believe, once again to the best of my recollection, it was Jay Emmett."

When Nelson asked what information he had on this investment, Ross replied that other than perhaps from a prospectus or having seen the theater site, which was near his country house, "Only probably what was told me by Jay."

Asked if he knew who had hired Horwitz, Ross testified, "Mr. Emmett."

Nelson also asked if Ross knew who had retained Horwitz as a consultant—since by now the government was investigating checks written to Leonard Horwitz, as a consultant, during the 1974–76 period. Ross testified that he had only learned that Horwitz had been a consultant from counsel, and that he understood from counsel "that Mr. Emmett retained Mr. Horwitz as a consultant."

"You are the chief executive officer of Warner," Nelson persisted. "Who would know what Mr. Horwitz did as a consultant to Warner?"

"I assume Mr. Emmett would have knowledge of that," Ross responded.

Queried again, he replied, "In light of everything I have been reading and everything told me by counsel, I would ask Mr. Emmett."

Asked to whom Horwitz reported, Ross said it was Emmett. He didn't know if anyone worked for Horwitz, or reported to him. Asked what Horwitz was hired to do, Ross testified, "Mr. Horwitz was just hired to work for Warner Communications, I don't know anything else but that . . . Jay Emmett just told me that he was hired because he thought he would do a good job for Warner Communications."

Ross also mentioned, now, that Emmett "also told me we owed him because he brought to the attention of Jay Emmett a company called TVC in the past."

The issue of Horwitz's continued employment at WCI was a delicate one. He had after all been hired just five months before his indictment, and had remained at the company even after his second trial had resulted in a guilty verdict. Horwitz was appealing that verdict, and Ross testified that he, with counsel, had decided to await the outcome. Asked whether any decision had been reached as to whether Horwitz would be discharged if the verdict were upheld, Ross said simply, "No."

Liman, however, did his best to leaven Ross's stark and surprising response. "Mr. Nelson, let me say on the record, the problem you are presenting is not one that is an easy one for counsel, because we are all brought up in a tradition of due process and not passing judgment on someone or engaging in an act which would be taken as the equivalent of concluding that an appear [sic] either had merit or didn't have it. So in advising Mr. Ross on this, it has not been an easy job for counsel, nor has it been an easy responsibility for Mr. Ross." In a less high-toned moment, a little later, Liman did his best to convey his disdain for Horwitz. Ross was being asked (as he was many times) what Horwitz did at WCI, and Liman broke in, saying, "The record ought to reflect the fact that one thing he has done is he has learned something about the rules for criminal procedure... he is now a resident expert."

After a break in this lengthy deposition, Stanley Sporkin, then the messianic director of the SEC's enforcement division, resumed the questioning of Ross. Sporkin was his aggressive self, demanding to know how it was possible that Ross could have not spoken to his number-two executive and friend about these matters, how it was possible that in over a year he had made not a single inquiry. (It emerged that the audit committee had also done nothing, so as not to interfere with the criminal investigation.)

Responding to Sporkin's question about how he could have never raised these issues with the people involved, Ross said, "The person [Emmett] came in a rage and said it's all untrue. Number two, Mr. Sporkin, who in the world that knows my association with these people, and they have been long-term associates, and I want you to know and on the record I believe them innocent of the charges, because I can't believe they would do anything wrong. They are diligent, they are hard-working, they are honest individuals. They have devoted their life to this company, 24 hours a day, 7 days a week. I would be the worst one to sit and judge and who is going to believe me if I come up with all the evidence in the world?"

"Mr. Sporkin, can I ask him one question?" inquired a suddenly diffident Liman, who for hours had been interrupting the examination to ask questions of Ross.

"Sure," said Sporkin.

"Why didn't you ask Mr. Weiss his response to these charges?"

"Because he quit," Ross replied. "He walked out. He had been so insulted that I even had one little suspect that he would do anything like that."

Liman—who in all likelihood could not have anticipated that Ross would so reach for the dramatic—tried again. "Tell Mr. Sporkin about Mr. Weiss."

"Mr. Weiss is a fellow who when he does anything, anywhere, anyplace and you attempt to give him the smallest gift, it could be a candy bar, it's thrown back in your face with tremendous insult in any way, shape, or form. He is one of the finest people I have ever met in my entire life, and to suggest anything to Sol Weiss would just be wrong by me. I couldn't get myself ever to do it in a million years."

Sporkin responded by asking if it were not true that Emmett and Weiss, when called as witnesses in the second Westchester Premier Theatre trial, had asserted their rights under the Fifth Amendment. Ross said he had been told that that was so. Then Sporkin (who would continue to belabor this point in what Liman would counter was "the greatest assault on the Fifth Amendment since 1954") declared, "And here is a person named Weiss who you say would not take a candy bar and yet when called in a trial on a case, in a public trial, asserted his rights under the Fifth Amendment to the Constitution, is that correct?"

Despite all the sturm and drang, Sporkin did not succeed in eliciting much more information from Ross than the staff lawyers had. As he had done earlier, Ross repeatedly pointed to Emmett, in response to Sporkin's questions about the decision to employ Horwitz and about his function at the company. He also pled, once again, an ignorance engendered by high position ("Mr. Sporkin, as the chief executive officer of maybe not the largest company in this world but a pretty substantial company, I don't know those facts").

But the major difference in the effect of Sporkin's examination of Ross, as contrasted with the low-key earlier one by Nelson, was that the hotter Sporkin became, the more intent Ross seemed to become on winning him. At one point, when Sporkin had been excoriating him at length for having made no inquiry, Ross interrupted Liman and said, "Can I ask Mr. Sporkin a question? How would you recommend a situation like this is handled, Mr. Sporkin? I would really like to know. I mean, this is thank God the first time I am through something like this and I hope the hell it's the last, but I would really like to know the recommendation from you, Mr. Sporkin, and how to handle this."

Sporkin, however, was not so easily disarmed. "Mr. Ross, I certainly am prepared to respond at the appropriate time and place. This is not, as far as I can see, this is not a very difficult question that other executive officers haven't met over the years. What I am trying to find out is how you reacted to this."

From Ross's deposition, the shape of his strategy in this investigation began to emerge. He would protect himself, at all cost, and he would use Jay Emmett as a buffer. In one sense, it was really not so different from the way their relationship had always been. Emmett had generally handled for him those things he did not want to do himself; what he presumably did not want to do himself, in this instance, was to go to jail. It was, of course, extraordinarily cold-blooded, in that Emmett was his best friend. That said, the pure logic of sacrificing Emmett, if need be—by utterly isolating him with Horwitz, in that (according to Ross) Emmett alone had retained Horwitz as a consultant, alone knew why, alone had hired him, alone knew for what reason, alone knew what he was doing at the company—was unassailable.

Horwitz, after all, was Emmett's friend. Emmett had brought in the idea of investing in the theater (when Horwitz came with his proposition). He had signed some of the vouchers for checks made out to Horwitz as a "consultant." And he had hired Horwitz (reportedly, at Ross's direction). There was, therefore, a conceptual neatness to a scenario that coupled Emmett and Horwitz; it was persuasively self-contained, with no intrinsic need to reach beyond the two men.

It is interesting to note that Ross did not attempt to use Solomon Weiss similarly. He never volunteered Weiss's name. When asked direct questions about him, his answers were sparse, sounding as though he barely knew what Weiss did (he said Weiss was "in the accounting department," but he didn't know to whom Weiss reported, and when asked if he knew Weiss's areas of responsibility, Ross answered, "I am familiar with one . . . where he helps the individual executives on their personal tax planning").

Weiss, of course, had gone to the theater for meetings with Weisman, Horwitz, Benford, and others, when WCI was considering making a further investment in the theater (Weiss was there, according to Benford, because he was, essentially, the contact person for the company's dealings at the theater). But at Ross's deposition, when he was asked whether Weiss had "any responsibilities as far as overseeing, or in any other way maintaining contact with the operation of the Westchester Theater on behalf of Warner," Ross said, "I wouldn't know." While Ross professed to know little about Weiss's functioning in the company, on a more personal level he had (at Liman's prompting) offered that impassioned testimonial to Weiss's integrity. He made no comparable declaration for Emmett.

From a strategic standpoint, Ross would have had good reason to be much more protective of Weiss than of Emmett; for while Emmett could be used effectively as a shield by Ross, Weiss offered no such benefit. Indeed, there was an inverse relationship: the more implicated Weiss became, the weaker the shield of Emmett would be. Weiss and Emmett were polar opposites—a devoutly Orthodox Jew and a Don Juan—who had little liking for, and only minimal dealings with, each other. For these two, alone, to have combined in some scheme defies credulity; they would have required a third party as a catalytic agent. And given the nature of the role that Weiss played *vis-à-vis* Ross, Ross would be the most likely person.

From the beginning, when Weiss had come to the company from Kinney Parking in Newark, where he had been the accountant—and through the sixties when payoffs in the parking business, especially, were endemic—Weiss was the accountant who could be trusted with everything. By the early seventies, Weiss had become Ross's personal book-keeper and check-writer, as well as his most trusted assignee for specific financial tasks within the company. There were certainly people in the company for whom Weiss had greater affection than he did for Ross—he is said to have loved Eddie Rosenthal, for example, and Rosenthal made him co-executor of his estate, as well as naming him in his will. But Weiss would unfailingly do Ross's bidding.

In September 1980, a year after Ross's SEC deposition, Emmett was indicted. He was charged with having accepted bribes from Horwitz to induce WCI to buy Westchester Premier Theatre stock, misappropriated funds from the company, and created fraudulent documentation in an attempt to hide the theft. Now that Emmett had been indicted, Liman suggested that he—with an eye to going to trial—switch counsel, from Robert Morvillo to Edward Bennett Williams.

Horwitz, who earlier had been tried on the charges of having partici-pated in a scheme to defraud investors and skim funds from the theater, as well as obstruction of justice, but had not been charged with bribing anyone at WCI, now was indicted on the bribery charge. Remarkably enough, even when in December 1980 Horwitz's guilty verdict from his second trial would finally be reinstated following a lengthy appeals process, he would continue to be employed by WCI—something that was, indeed, presaged in Ross's careful refusal to commit himself on that issue, before the SEC. Now, Horwitz commenced yet another leave of absence (his third) in order to prepare for his defense in this trial, with Emmett.

Although both Emmett and Weiss had been named in the pre-trial documents Akerman filed with the court in September 1978, he did not have enough evidence at this point to seek an indictment of Weiss. Ini-tially, two informants from the theater had told Akerman that they had learned in conversations with Eliot Weisman and Leonard Horwitz that Emmett and Weiss had been bribed, and that a series of phony bills and checks had been generated. And when Akerman subpoenaed Warner records, he had found Solomon Weiss's name, either as a signer or a co-signer, on most of those that were suspect. There were also repeated references to Weiss in the Weisman tapes. But apparently the only person who had had first-hand dealings with Weiss in these transactions was Horwitz; and Horwitz, of course, was not cooperating.

Weisman, however, was. Shortly after his conviction in the second Westchester Premier Theatre trial had been upheld on appeal, in April 1980, he had begun to cooperate in hopes of reducing his six-and-a-half-year prison sentence. He didn't have to testify against his mob associates, the people he most feared; they were already convicted. But Weisman did testify before the grand jury to conversations that he said he had had with Emmett (on occasions when Emmett visited the theater for performances), which included references to the illegal transactions. At Emmett's trial, Weisman would be the key witness.

Akerman considered Weisman's cooperation partial, but he was grateful, nonetheless, and told the court so; Weisman's prison term was cut to eighteen months. Given Weisman's apparent selectivity, it is interesting to note those about whom he did not testify. Weisman did not testify about Sinatra and Rudin and stated to Akerman that he knew of no wrong-doing on their parts. He had begun booking acts for Rudin clients even while he was on trial, and after his prison term he continued to do so for clients including Liza Minnelli. If it were true that Weisman had told Eddie Rosenthal about the stock-for-cash transactions back in 1975, and also that he kept him fully informed of the cover-up attempts, as he repeatedly said he was doing on the tapes in early 1978, then he also protected Rosenthal.

And one may wonder why Weisman chose Emmett—and not Weiss. It was Weiss, after all, who was the theater's contact at WCI, and it was Weiss who had attended the meetings with Weisman at the theater about Warner's increasing its investment. But Weisman claimed that he and Weiss had never discussed the cash transactions. And what he knew about Weiss's role from Horwitz was only hearsay. Whatever the reason, Weisman ultimately only helped in the case against Emmett.

On February 9, 1981—the day that Emmett and Horwitz's trial was to begin—the two men pled guilty and agreed to cooperate with the government. Had Emmett, facing a racketeering charge, gone to trial, he would have risked not only a stiff prison term but the forfeiture of about $7 million of WCI stock, the bulk of his net worth. Moreover, his grand jury testimony had committed him to a strongly implausible course; Williams would later say that he had counted sixty-seven lies in the transcript. Emmett pled guilty to two felony counts, and Horwitz pled guilty to two charges of tax evasion and filing a false tax return. Horwitz had been sentenced to three years in prison on his earlier conviction at the West-chester Premier Theatre trial; now, that sentence was reduced to nine months (of which he would actually serve four).

Late on the morning of February 9, while Williams was negotiating various points of Emmett's plea bargain with Nick Akerman, Emmett (who had been told that as part of his cooperation he would have to tape-record a conversation with Ross and attempt to elicit incriminating state-ments from him) called Ross from a pay phone in the courthouse. He warned Ross that he would be calling again, later, and that in response to his questions Ross should say that his attorney had told him not to discuss the case. Emmett did call back that afternoon, and Ross did, indeed, repeat that Arthur Liman had told him "a million times" that he could not discuss it.

Shortly thereafter, Liman informed the U.S. Attorney's Office that Em-mett had warned Ross. Liman argued that that action was proof of Em-mett's unreliability as a witness; and, furthermore, that he should be indicted for obstruction of justice. Ed Williams is said to have called Liman and said that Emmett had "walked through minefields" for Ross, and that this was a sorry way to repay him. Ross made Williams apoplectic. Wil-liams had become very fond of Emmett and thought that what Ross had done—using his best friend to shield himself—was unconscionable; it enraged him far more than the violent crimes that some of his other clients had committed. As a confidant of Williams's would recall, "Ed hated the injustice to Emmett. He just thought it was *wrong*. He used to call me every day, saying, 'That goddam Ross . . .' "

While Jay Emmett would not attempt to entrap Ross, he did, in the days following, record a conversation with Weiss. Weiss was guarded; when Emmett said something about his (Emmett's) having supposedly received all the money, there was what Akerman would later argue was "deafening silence" from Weiss. Weiss had now become the government's immediate target. Horwitz had described all his dealings with Weiss—as had been his first inclination, when the FBI agent had appeared at his door in September 1977—and Emmett had corroborated those in which he had been involved. Soon they would testify before a grand jury; and, in Sep-tember 1981, Weiss would be indicted.

Within a day or so of his plea bargain, Emmett again called Ross, from home. According to another person, this conversation, in which they briefly discussed Emmett's resignation, ended with both men crying, in such great, gasping sobs that they could not speak. It was the last conver-sation the two would ever have.

For Jay Emmett, the rupture was profound. The loss of Ross, for him, was incalculable. He was, furthermore, being extirpated from his professional life, which, Emmett being Emmett, mainly involved people. The last decade at WCI had been the best time of his life; and, as he would later say to friends, he had loved every single day of it. *Loved* going to work every single day. He had his enemies, but countless people at WCI —and not just the high-level executives—considered him their friend. He had a quip for nearly everyone he encountered (you could track Emmett's passage through the corridors by following the laughter), and the atmosphere was brighter for his being there. "When Jay left," commented Norman Samnick, the WCI lawyer, "the glue was gone. The place was never the same."

For Ross, it was altogether different, inasmuch as he was losing his closest friend, but not the professional world that comprised his life. Still, it must have been wrenching. Steve Ross's world would expand mightily in the coming years, and his friendships, mainly with the famous, would increase in number, too; he would have advisers, such as Liman, who would be business intimates; but he would never again have a friend as close as Emmett.

In the world that Ross and Emmett had so enjoyed together, there were many people who had been fond of the two men and who continued to be. It was a difficult and painful matter; if one believed that Ross had sacrificed Emmett, it hardly spoke well of Ross. And if one further believed that Emmett had, within the context of striking a deal, done his utmost to protect Ross—and yet was now totally cut off by him—it was even worse. Indeed, it gave the lie to Ross's much-vaunted reputation for loyalty.

There were few who would raise the matter with Ross. One who did was Cy O'Neil, who had been Ken Rosen's lawyer, and who had become a very good friend of both Ross and Emmett. As to the justification for Ross's having severed all ties with Emmett, O'Neil said, "I understood from Steve that Jay had tried to set him up, after he copped a plea. Steve never wanted to talk about it—we probably didn't exchange more than ten sentences about it—but he did tell me that."

Informed that something quite opposite was true—that in fact Emmett had warned Ross, and that Liman had gone to the U.S. Attorney's Office with that information, arguing that Emmett should be indicted for obstruction of justice—O'Neil said that he had not known that. He had accepted Ross's explanation, and he had hoped that maybe, unbeknownst to the world, Ross and Emmett did continue to have some relationship. That would make it less terrible for Emmett, and it would also mean that

Ross, though he had sacrificed his best friend to save himself, was unwilling to take the final step and close him off forever. But it was not so. And, as O'Neil said, "I have *nothing* to base it on—I guess it was just wishful thinking."


In his opening statement at the trial of Solomon Weiss in November 1982, Nick Akerman said that he would be presenting an essentially two-part case: first, focusing on Weiss's participation in a fraudulent scheme to create a "cash fund" at WCI; and second, Weiss's attempts to obstruct the grand jury that was investigating that scheme. Akerman also told the jurors —in words that would become headlines in the next day's newspapers— that "in the course of this trial, you will learn how the chairman of the board of Warner designated the defendant, Weiss, as banker or overseer of a secret cash fund at Warner."

Several more times during the trial, Akerman would similarly invoke Steve Ross's name; Ross became the conspicuously missing defendant, his absence so palpable that Akerman might as well have placed an empty chair at the defense table. On one occasion, U.S. District Court Judge Mary Johnson Lowe would rebuke Akerman in a sidebar conference, saying that "Mr. Ross is not on trial. You have painted that picture. Let's move on to something else, okay?"

That Ross was not on trial was not due to any lack of effort or conviction on Akerman's part. The U.S. Attorney for the Southern District, John Martin, had recused himself from all decision making in this investigation, because, years earlier, he had represented a defendant in the first phase of the Westchester Premier Theatre case. It was Acting U.S. Attorney William Tendy, therefore—a conservative, career prosecutor in that office— who was Akerman's superior. And Tendy had not granted Akerman the permission he sought to seek an indictment of Ross from the grand jury. Tendy favored a more cautious and traditional prosecutorial approach: first, convict Weiss; then, with Weiss's presumed cooperation (as he would be facing a substantial prison sentence), indict Ross.

Now, Akerman sketched the government's case. The proof would show, he said, that in May 1973 Leonard Horwitz, representing Westchester Premier Theatre, had come to see Jay Emmett at WCI, offering him a $50,000 cash loan—which he had with him, in a brown paper bag—to use toward the purchase of theater stock. Emmett refused the proposition, but went to see Steve Ross, who directed him to bring Horwitz together with Solomon Weiss. Emmett did so. Horwitz and Weiss then negotiated a deal whereby WCI would purchase 20,000 shares of theater stock, in return for which Horwitz would give Weiss $100,000—$50,000 of which (in the paper bag) he gave him in that meeting.

  Shortly thereafter, Akerman continued, Weiss asked Horwitz for the remaining $50,000; but the theater, at that time, did not have it. So Weiss agreed, instead, to accept only $20,000 in cash; and, in order to make this possible, WCI would issue two corporate checks to theater representatives—$20,000 to Horwitz and $30,000 to Dennis Konner, the lawyer—for services never performed, and the company would receive cash back.

About a month later, in early July 1973, Weiss and Horwitz struck another deal. This time, WCI would again purchase 20,000 shares of theater stock, in return for which Horwitz promised that when the theater opened—then set for early 1974—he would deliver $100,000 in cash. By late 1973, it was apparent the theater would not be opening as scheduled, and thus would not have ready cash; so Weiss arranged, instead, for the same modus operandi (WCI checks out, cash back) that they had employed before. In return for these checks—made out to Horwitz and a purported consultant, for a total of about $150,000, issued in 1974, 1975, 1976, and 1977—Horwitz would deliver a total of $100,000 in cash. And, Akerman continued, Weiss created phoney internal documentation at WCI—both in the earlier check to Konner and in these later checks—to justify the payments.

The second part of the government's case was more succinctly stated. Akerman said that Weiss had lied before the grand jury when he had been called to testify in April 1978, and also that he had concealed documents subpoenaed by that grand jury.

The series of transactions outlined by Akerman was then testified to by the government's key witnesses, Horwitz and Emmett. Their recollections of shared events did not gibe perfectly. Horwitz testified that when he brought the bag of cash to Emmett's office, Emmett "made some gag about the bag of money, picked it up in his hand, dropped it like a hot potato and made some funny remark, I don't recall anymore." Emmett, on the other hand, did not recall that Horwitz had the bag of cash with him.

The only substantive references to Steve Ross in their testimony occurred when Horwitz said that after Weiss had counted the money and said he would return shortly, Horwitz had "made some mention about are you going to see Steve," and Weiss had replied, "Don't use that name or we don't use that name around here." And Emmett, for his part, testified that when he had described Horwitz's proposition to Ross, Ross had told him that "the company couldn't take a loan to buy a publicly traded issue," but "perhaps Len ought to meet with Sol Weiss and maybe he could be helpful in the Warner cash fund."

About other conversations that would seem to have naturally followed, between these two best friends, as events unfolded—regarding Horwitz's wanting to cooperate with the FBI, and his intending to tell them about Weiss; Horwitz's being hired instead; the creation of alibis, with the names of Goldmark and Rosen; decisions about how much to tell Liman of what had actually occurred—Emmett volunteered nothing. More, when he was asked directly, by Akerman, whether the hiring of Horwitz had "anything to do with the grand jury," Emmett replied, "No, sir."

When it did not require his implicating Ross directly, however, Emmett did testify about moves that were made at the company to support Horwitz surreptitiously. Both Emmett and Weiss had arrangements with WCI whereby the company would pay their legal fees unless they pled guilty or were proven guilty. In March 1979, Horwitz's lawyer, Jonathan Lubell, had gone to see Arthur Liman to ask that Horwitz be given the same arrangement (Horwitz was about to stand trial for the second time, and was unable to pay his legal bills; there was still an unpaid balance of $45,000 from the first trial). Liman had consulted Lawrence Buttenweiser, chairman of the audit committee, who in turn had met with Lubell, along with Michael Armstrong, the committee's counsel in this affair. Ultimately, it was concluded that it would be inappropriate for WCI to pay Horwitz's legal bills; he was, after all, alleged by the government to have bribed Emmett and Weiss.

Emmett had loaned Horwitz money in the past (including a recent $165,000 loan as a mortgage on his house), but in this instance he felt it would look terrible, as though he, the putative bribee, were paying Horwitz to remain silent. Emmett now testified that Liman had come into his office and asked him—after it had been decided that WCI could not do it—to lend Horwitz $100,000 for his legal bills. Emmett testified that he did so only on Liman's request. His lawyer at the time, Robert Morvillo, is said to have exhorted him not to do it, but Emmett, who barely knew Morvillo, was not about to refuse to do what he said Liman, in confidence, had urged him to do.

Later in the trial, Liman took the stand and emphatically denied Emmett's testimony. Liman testified that he had not been at Warner's offices at all during the month Emmett claimed he had met there with Liman. Recalling a phone conversation he said he had had with Emmett, he testified: "I said that his lawyer, Robert Morvillo, had telephoned me, and that Bob Morvillo had said to me that Jay was considering making a personal loan to Leonard Horwitz for Horwitz's legal fees, that he was considering that because I, on behalf of the corporation, had refused to have the corporation advance legal fees toward Horwitz. And Morvillo said that he was very much opposed to Jay making this loan, that Jay was not about to follow his advice on this, and he asked me, because I knew Jay longer, if I would call Jay and urge Jay to listen to him, Morvillo.

"So I picked up the phone and I called Jay and I told Jay of the conversation that I had just had with Robert Morvillo. And I urged Jay to listen to his attorney. And I said to Jay, 'Jay, it will just look wretched if you make a loan to Leonard Horwitz.' "

Their testimony was, of course, conflicting. (Morvillo would later claim attorney-client privilege when I asked him about this situation.) While Emmett was awaiting sentence on his guilty plea and thus had some motivation to fabricate, one might question why he would choose to fabricate on *this* matter, so tangential to the government's case, when there seemed to be far richer areas concerning Ross about which Emmett could have testified and pleased the government so much more. On the other hand, if Liman had made such a request of Emmett, its logic would have been plain. He would have asked Emmett himself, rather than allowing Ross to do it, so as to insulate Ross. And he would have asked this of Emmett because, as Lubell had been told, the company could not; because Liman may have been concerned about whether Horwitz, without the money, would cut a deal with the government; and because it was such an easy alternative—Emmett was Horwitz's friend, and would surely have done it voluntarily under any other circumstances.

In any event, Liman's version of the circumstances under which Emmett loaned Horwitz the money was consistent with the strategy that Ross would employ six months afterwards, in the SEC deposition where he used Emmett to shield himself and stressed the notion that *only* Emmett had made decisions about Horwitz. If the entire scheme had been carried out by Emmett and Horwitz alone, what better supporting evidence than that it was Emmett who not only gave Horwitz a job but also—without prompting from anyone—lent him $100,000 for his legal fees?

Not long after Liman delivered his rebuttal, the subject of Horwitz's legal fees—and, more, their surrounding discussions—was raised again, in a rather extraordinary way. More than halfway through the trial, as the government's case was drawing to a close, Michael Armstrong, the audit committee's outside counsel, was called to the stand as a witness for the defense, and a memo, dated March 5, 1979, which he testified he had then written, was introduced into evidence.

In the memo, Armstrong recounted his recollections of the meeting held with Buttenweiser and Lubell, in which Lubell was urging that WCI lend Horwitz the money to pay Lubell's bills. In its most pertinent part,

Armstrong had written: "Lubell indicated that if Horwitz could not come up with the money to pay for his defense, he would 'make the best deal he could.' The Government has been pressuring defendants to cooperate, relying upon the financial hardship caused by the mistrial and the need for a second trial. He said that the Government had offered to accept a plea from Horwitz to two felony counts in return for Horwitz's telling the Government everything he knew; but Lubell said that, in fact, Horwitz had nothing to tell. Lubell said that Horwitz was in no frame of mind to plead even to a 'traffic ticket' on the facts of this case."

"It was pointed out to Lubell that the Audit Committee was interested in finding out what happened and might, indeed, have an interest in seeing pressure brought to bear upon Horwitz. Lubell then emphasized that Horwitz had nothing incriminating to say but that he might be forced into saying something that was not true under the financial pressure that was being brought to bear by the prosecutor."

As Armstrong had stated in a closed session in chambers the day before, he had placed this memo in his files, back in March 1979, and had not thought of it again. His own investigation had been sporadic; he had been asked to defer to this or that government investigation at various times, and his investigation now had been in abeyance since sometime in 1980. He did, however, have an associate, David Frankel, monitoring the trial, and just the day before, Armstrong said, the trial proceedings had stirred Frankel's recollection of that memo, and they had dug it out of the files.

Since he had resisted a government subpoena for his investigative files, arguing that they were covered by attorney-client privilege, Armstrong now had to explain his appearance with this document. The distinction, he argued, was that this document was not part of his investigation; rather, it had been generated in the performance of "kind of a side service." In addition, Armstrong noted that Lubell knew that the conversation, unlike the Audit Committee's other conversations, would not be confidential. Armstrong seemed intent on drawing this distinction not only so as to explain his present action, but, also, to ensure that that action would not be construed as a waiver of the attorney-client privilege, lest his files be subpoenaed anew.

Reactions on the defense and prosecutorial sides were predictably polar. Kasanof could barely contain his glee. "I think that the government now has a significant report that one of its key witnesses has threatened to fabricate in exchange for money, and I think that the government ought to reflect on that . . . I am shocked, I am appalled . . . and I think it is ominous for the integrity of the government's case."

Akerman, for his part, grew heated. "... I'm somewhat disturbed that this came up at this point in the trial.... It's been known for well over a year that Mr. Horwitz was going to testify. The Audit Committee, in effect, is an arm of Warner Communications. One of the prime focuses of this investigation, as is clear from the trial, is on the chairman of the board of that company, who is in charge, presumably, of this Audit Committee. Here we are, about to finish off this trial. This memo has been sitting in these files all these months...."

Akerman's fusillade, of course, triggered a protest from Armstrong ("Mr. Ross is not the head of this Audit Committee. Mr. Ross is the chairman of the company that we are charged with investigating"), as well as a rejoinder from Kasanof ("I don't understand Mr. Akerman's remarks, except as they seem to divert from the issue here. If Mr. Akerman wanted to try Mr. Ross, then he should have indicted him").

None of these fireworks took place before the jurors, of course. Armstrong's appearance on the stand was free of drama, and the memo was presented to the jurors. In the end, however, the memo would appear to have had little discernible impact on Horwitz's credibility, although its sudden appearance causes other speculation.

Armstrong did not say that he or Buttenweiser actually believed that Lubell's client would lie if WCI did not pay his legal fees; rather, he described the memo as an attempt to "get this meeting memorialized." Had Armstrong and Buttenweiser believed at the time Lubell's alleged remark that Horwitz might lie, they might have decided or perhaps even have been obligated to take some further action—perhaps to notify the court or to refer the matter to a lawyer disciplinary committee.

More likely, they probably understood that Lubell—a scholarly, well-regarded attorney whose specialty was more First Amendment than criminal law—was simply remarking, in passing, about Horwitz's desperate state. Nonetheless, when Armstrong's memo of the meeting was produced during trial, it was a gift to the defense—one that inflicted considerable damage, of course, on Lubell, for it raised grave questions about Lubell's conduct in a public forum where their truth or falsity would never be ascertained, or even closely examined; they would just be aired, and allowed to linger.

In Solomon Weiss's first few minutes on the stand, Kasanof led him to the heart of his defense: Emmett and Horwitz were lying, because they'd been caught in their crooked scheme. Weiss, a slight, gray-haired man, wearing a yarmulke as always, opened on a note of piety: he explained that he was affirming, rather than swearing, "for religious purposes." Almost from the start of his testimony, however, there was a persistent incongruence, for he was presenting himself as a wholly innocent bystander, victimized by his one-time colleagues who had turned out to be criminals—but the affect was missing. The only expressions of outrage emanated from Bob Kasanof, while Weiss remained stiff, pallid, recessive, barely less guarded in his direct testimony than he would be on cross-examination.

"When witness Horwitz says that about May 29, 1973, he met with you at the offices of Warner Communications and paid you a $50,000 cash bribe, is that true?" demanded Kasanof.

"No, it's not," said Weiss.

"And that's not a question of mistake or anything else. You're saying it didn't happen?"

"I'm saying it didn't happen."

"And he said it did happen. You heard him say that he did it, Mr. Horwitz."

"Yes, I did."

"And either you're lying or he's lying?"

"That's correct."

After a similar recitation of Emmett's allegation, Kasanof continued his litany. "Either Mr. Emmett is a liar when he testified in this courtroom or you're a liar."

"That is correct."

"And are you saying that when Mr. Emmett says that, he is a flat-out, bald-faced liar?"

"Yes."

Weiss grew no more forthcoming as his testimony continued. Questioned by his own attorney about whether he had destroyed documents as the government was alleging (in a question simply intended to place his denial on the record), Weiss so lowered his voice as to make his response inaudible—and then, in a second try, he responded, still muffled, "No, didn't." Only the third time did he speak clearly. At one point, after Judge Lowe had repeatedly cautioned Kasanof about leading his witness, Kasanof defended himself, protesting, "I have to lead a little in order to elicit."

As though to compensate for his client's emotional flatness, Kasanof grew more and more volatile—at one point, in his excitement, referring to the theater as the "Westchester Criminal Theatre." Near the end of Weiss's direct, as Kasanof was attempting to bootstrap Weiss to a stirring finish, he demanded: "And when they . . . were crooks, did you help them, did you try and be a crook with them, did you take their money? Were you a participant in their crookedness?"

"I did nothing illegal," Weiss responded.

Weiss was almost certainly hurt by his demeanor. (One of his own lawyers acknowledged later that Weiss was "terrible" on the stand. "But no amount of preparation could have changed that," this person added. "Sol was who he is.") Probably his greatest handicap, however, was his own prior testimony before the grand jury in April 1978—so vastly at odds with the testimony he was delivering here.

The posture that Weiss had struck before the grand jury in 1978 was precisely what had been described, repeatedly, on the tape recordings of Weisman and Horwitz. Each had reported (based on their conversations with those at WCI) that when called before the grand jury, WCI executives would testify that they no longer recalled what services Konner had performed, five years earlier; all they could point to was what had been written on the check request.

When Weiss had been asked to tell the grand jury what the Konner transaction "was all about," he had testified: "The only thing I can tell you is that this—I had a request for a check. It said consultation services in connection with the cable acquisition and other matters."

"Who was it that requested that you make that check request?"

"All I had was a request signed by Jay Emmett."

"Did Mr. Emmett request you to make this check out?"

"It only had—I don't recall who would have asked me to make the direct check request but I had the voucher so that I would have prepared it from the statement. I would have prepared a request for check."

"You prepared the request for a check, is that right?"

"Yes."

"You would have prepared it based on the letter that was signed by Mr. Emmett?"

"Yes."

"Dated July 11, 1973?"

"That's correct."

"So is it true that Mr. Emmett asked you to prepare this particular check for $30,000 to Dennis Konner?"

"I can't answer that."

"Why not?"

"Because it could have come in any number of ways."

"What would be the other ways it could have come?"

"It could have been sent in through the inter-office mail. It could have gone from one secretary to my secretary."

"But it certainly would have come from Mr. Emmett at any rate, isn't that right?"

"I would believe so."

What the government did not have at the time of Weiss's grand jury appearance in 1978 was a letter Weiss had written to Horwitz (a carbon was never produced by Weiss, but once Horwitz had cooperated, he provided it to the government), reminding him that he was awaiting "the bill for legal services that you indicated you would get for me." However, the letter had been written roughly two months after Weiss had drawn the check request. Now, at trial, he explained this odd sequence by saying that "I was instructed . . . by Mr. Emmett to draw the check for $30,000 and await for a supporting document."

This was, of course, something Weiss had said he could not recall at the grand jury. Addressing this discrepancy, Weiss said that "at the time, I really didn't focus in or concentrate on the grand jury appearance. . . . However, obviously, as a result of all this trial going on, it has become a very significant part of my life, and I certainly have had much more time to reflect upon it and to hear testimony about it, and certainly to discuss it with my counsel, and I could say, without reservations, that I did get instructions from Mr. Emmett to prepare that request for check."

In the grand jury, Weiss had been interrogated as to what services Dennis Konner had provided. Repeatedly, he referred to the words written on the voucher, about "cable acquisition"—but insisted he knew no more. He repeated that he had asked Jay Emmett, who also could not recall. Asked whether there was any connection between Horwitz and the Konner bill (as would subsequently be manifested by Weiss's letter to Horwitz, asking for a bill from Konner), he had testified that there was not. Now, however, Weiss remembered. Referring to the $30,000 fee to Konner, Weiss testified: ". . . Mr. Emmett told me that he owed a fee for having TVC being purchased by Warner Communications, Inc."

"That he owed a fee to whom?" asked Kasanof.

"He indicated he owed a fee to Mr. Konner and Mr. Leonard Horwitz."

In his grand jury appearance, Weiss had been questioned repeatedly about WCI's two purchases of Westchester Premier Theatre stock, on which he had filled out the check requests. Asked what his role had been, Weiss had testified, "Just fill out the request for check."

"Who was it that asked you to fill out the request for check?"

"I do not know, sir."

"Was it Mr. Emmett?"

"Possibly."

"Have you ever discussed this with Mr. Emmett to try and refresh your recollection?"

"Yes, I have."

"Did that help refresh your recollection?"

"No, it didn't."

". . . Do you know who it was that approached Warner Communications to ask them to buy this stock?"

"I do not."

"Do you know who it was in the company that approved the purchase of the Westchester Premier Theatre stock?"

"Said 'Okay for Jay Emmett,' I assume that must be the individual."

"Did you discuss this with Mr. Emmett to try and refresh your recollection?"

"Yes."

"What was your conclusion after discussing it with Mr. Emmett?"

"Had no conclusion."

Now, Kasanof asked Weiss, "As far as you know, whose deal was the purchase of Westchester Premier Theatre stock?"

"Mr. Emmett's."

"And did you—was there a reason why you prepared [the check request]?"

"Yes."

"What was the reason?"

"He instructed me to."

As for all the checks Weiss had written to Leonard Horwitz and Bruce Kosman, he testified that he had believed they were performing legitimate services for Jungle Habitat, WCI's animal park in Milford, New Jersey —something for which Emmett had responsibility; and, asked by Kasanof why he had gone to Jungle Habitat on one occasion, with Horwitz, Kosman, and others, Weiss testified: "I was instructed by Mr. Emmett to go out to Jungle Habitat."

At another point, Kasanof, referring to a number of checks that Weiss had prepared for which there was no approver, asked: "Does that mean there was no approver?"

"No, it does not."

"Or were there approvers?"

"Yes."

"And who were those approvers, if you recall?"

"I remember some of them would be Mr. Jay Emmett."

"And as to the other approvers in 1973, do you recall?"

"No, I do not."

Near the end of his testimony on direct examination, Weiss delivered his own terse summation of his defense: "My only role in the entire thing was to prepare a request for checks."

"And basically at whose direction, if anyone's, were you acting?" Kasa-nof prompted.

"At Mr. Jay Emmett's direction."

Had Weiss taken this tack when he had first testified before the grand jury (or had he invoked the Fifth, and so not committed himself), his current story, with its positive identification of Emmett as the culprit at every possible juncture, would have seemed more plausible. As it was, however, his current testimony and his grand jury testimony—much of which Akerman read into the record at trial—formed a devastating coun-terpoint, each contrasting with and resonating in the other: the current testimony making the earlier testimony sound evasive and deceptive, and the earlier testimony making the current testimony sound blatantly revisionist.

This was the greatest source of dissonance in the defense that Sol Weiss and his lawyers had constructed—and its effect was only heightened by the introduction of a "memory expert," who attempted to explain Weiss's prior forgetfulness by theorizing about "a basic forgetting curve." But, in addition to the grave problems Weiss had created for himself by his own earlier testimony, he also had to contend, now, with the testimony of others. As for Emmett and Horwitz—both of whom had withstood cross-examination very well—he simply said they were liars. There were other witnesses in the government's case, however, witnesses from WCI, unwill-ing witnesses against Weiss, who nonetheless gave testimony that called his story into question.

James Henry, a manager of corporate accounting at WCI, testified that out of the hundreds of millions of dollars of stock in the WCI portfolio, the only stock confirmations that were signed by Weiss were for these two purchases of Westchester Premier Theatre stock.

Albert Sarnoff—the WCI treasurer whom Eddie Rosenthal had once described to me as "*too* honest, if there is such a thing"—in random inspections had questioned three of these checks that Weiss had written, and then, after receiving some explanation from Weiss (which Sarnoff said he could not recall), had okayed them. Two of the check requests—one to Horwitz and one to Kosman—had said, "real estate consulting fee," which struck Sarnoff, since he was in charge of real estate at WCI. In fact, when Sarnoff had been asked at the SEC whether anyone else at the company had the authority to hire a real estate consultant, he had testi-fied, "Not that I'm aware of." After Sarnoff questioned these check re-quests, Weiss wrote many more checks to Horwitz and Kosman, but he never again wrote on the requests "real estate consulting fee."

Weiss's version of events was also contradicted by the testimony of his secretary, Linda Horns, who seemed at trial to be doing her level best not to hurt him but was herself constrained by her prior testimony. On the subject of Leonard Horwitz, for example, Weiss in the grand jury had acknowledged knowing him but, it would have seemed from his testimony, only as the most passing acquaintance. When he had been asked if Horwitz had done any work for WCI prior to being employed there in 1978, Weiss had replied, "I believe so. I don't know."

"Did he or didn't he do any work for them?"

"I don't know."

"When did Mr. Horwitz do work on the Jungle Habitat, do you know?"

"I believe in '77."

"Now, did Mr. Horwitz do any work for Warner Communications prior to 1977?"

"I think, yes."

"And what was that work?"

"Some consulting work that he was doing for them."

"For whom?"

"I don't remember."

"Do you know who it was for?"

"I'm not sure."

"Do you have any guess as to who it was for?"

"I believe in the cable industry."

"In the cable industry?"

"I believe."

"Do you have any idea who it was that he was doing it for in the cable industry?"

"No, I wouldn't."

"Was it Mr. Stern?"

"I don't know."

"Do you remember what year it was that he did that?"

"No, I would have to check."

"Was it 1972?"

"I don't know."

"Was it 1971?"

"I don't know."

"Was it 1973?"

"Could be."

"Was it 1974?"

"Could be."

At trial, however, it emerged from Horns's testimony that during a period in 1973, Horwitz was a visitor to Weiss's office as often as twice a week, and he called him four or five times a week. When Kasanof asked Weiss about this in his direct examination, Weiss testified that Horwitz used to drop by to attempt to interest him or other executives in real estate investments, and also because Horwitz's daughter and Weiss's nephew both suffered from Hodgkin's disease, and Horwitz wanted to share notes on treatment.

Horns, however, had testified that the subject matter of their exchanges was "to deal with the Westchester Premier Theatre," and, also, "concerning an investment in the Westchester Premier Theatre." (In later years, she testified, they were involved together with Jungle Habitat.)

Confronted with Horns's testimony, Weiss said, "I don't know if that's correct," and suggested that she was telling the truth "to the best of her ability."

Other parts of Horns's testimony, while not directly contradicting Weiss's version, were potentially damning. There were two letters that Weiss had sent to Horwitz, requesting Konner's bill; he had, of course, testified to the grand jury that he knew of no link between the Konner bill and Horwitz. At that time, Horwitz was employed by WCI, and Weiss would have felt assured that Horwitz would not be turning over these letters to the government; Weiss had produced no copies of them in response to his subpoena. But when Horwitz cooperated, Horwitz turned over the originals. Now, Horns testified that she had typed both letters, and that her practice would have dictated that she placed the carbons in a file marked "Leonard Horwitz." Asked by Akerman where the carbons were, Weiss testified that he did not know.

Even the small, everyday details that the government had elicited from Horns, in her SEC deposition back in 1979, proved to be troublesome. She had testified that while Weiss kept both a pocket diary and a desk diary, it was the pocket diary—"the small appointment book that he carries with him at all times"—that was the far more reliable of the two, in which he entered everything, and that he had been keeping these diaries since 1973.

The government had subpoenaed Weiss's diaries, and his lawyers had waged a fierce battle to keep them from being produced. Indeed, on May 6, 1981, Weiss had been held in contempt of court for not having produced them; the penalty of imprisonment was stayed pending a ruling from the Court of Appeals. Later that night, a fire broke out in the basement of the brownstone which housed Kasanof's office (the diaries were kept in a safe in the basement), and the building was destroyed. The diaries, however, were retrieved from the safe.

At a court hearing on the morning of May 7, Lawrence Iason, an attorney who was working on the case with Kasanof, told the judge that "the origin of the fire is unknown and we have been told that it may be suspicious." It was never proven that the blaze was arson. But at least one lawyer in this case—who knew that Caesar Kimmel's brother, Charles, was known as Charlie ("the Torch") Kimmel because he had had restaurants in New Jersey that burned down—always remained convinced that it was.

When Weiss had finally been compelled to produce the diaries, however, the all-important pocket diaries for the more important years— 1973, 1974, 1975—were missing. (As for those diaries that were produced, they offered information helpful to both sides—for example, Weiss was in California on one of the days when Horwitz recalled he'd brought him cash; and, on the other hand, a meeting with "L. Horwitz" was noted on a day when Horwitz said they were negotiating the Westchester Premier Theatre stock purchases. So their effect was essentially neutralized.)

And it was Horns, finally, who testified that Weiss's boss was Steve Ross. In the course of this investigation, every effort had been made by WCI lawyers and executives—Ross foremost among them—to insulate Ross from Weiss. Weiss himself had meticulously adhered to the "we do not use that name around here" principle. In his grand jury appearance, when asked to whom he reported, the transcript of his response reads: "Blank."

"If you had a boss who would you say your boss was?" Akerman had continued.

"I would say my boss is Jay Emmett." This was sensible enough in light of all the check vouchers that Emmett had signed, but it was not so. While Weiss's role was formally ill-defined enough that some employees might not have been sure who his "boss" was—and might have postulated Ross, or, conceivably, Sarnoff, or Bert Wasserman as the chief financial officer —Emmett would not even have appeared on the list.

When questioned further by Akerman, in the grand jury, about who his "immediate superior" had been in 1973, Weiss said it had been Albert Sarnoff.

Again, reasonable enough, inasmuch as Sarnoff was the treasurer of the company and Weiss assistant treasurer; but, again, not so. When Sarnoff, in his SEC deposition, had been asked if Weiss reported to him, he had replied, "Not on a line function." Asked to whom Weiss did report, Sarnoff had answered that he didn't know. Sarnoff had described his functions as treasurer—responsibility for banking relationships, real estate activities, cost control. But he added that he dealt with Weiss on none of them.

Moreover, when Eddie Rosenthal was asked at his SEC deposition in 1979 whether Sol Weiss was within Jay Emmett's chain of command, he answered that he was not. And he was uncertain, furthermore, to whom Weiss did report. He said that Weiss did "personal bookkeeping" for him, and he believed also for Ross, Sarnoff, and some other executives. And he gave the best thumbnail description of Weiss's duties: when he had first met Weiss, Rosenthal testified, he "was the bookkeeper for Kinney Parking . . . [and] he is still the bookkeeper."

Weiss's origins at Kinney Parking and his closeness to Caesar Kimmel were subjects that he studiously avoided and even, to a degree, denied at trial. He testified that he had worked for a small accounting firm, Wortzel, which had the Kinney Parking account; when that account was purchased by another accounting firm, Bronson, Tuber & Bloom, he said, he had gone along with it; and then he had joined Kinney Service in December 1962, about nine months after it had gone public. When Akerman began to question this, Kasanof interrupted, saying, "I object to further inquiry about 1961 and 1962 events, your Honor." Akerman pressed, with a single question—asking whether Weiss had ever worked for Kimmel. Weiss testified, "No."

While it was true that Weiss had moved, with the Kinney account, from Wortzel to Bronson, Tuber & Bloom, as one person at Kinney Parking recalled, Weiss had been only nominally an outside accountant. "He was working within our organization, doing accounting for us—he was there most of the time. We were probably his only account."

Just as every attempt had been made to distance Steve Ross from Weiss, so now similarly strenuous efforts were being made to distance Sol Weiss from Kimmel. Understandably—for it was a nexus that, fully understood and explored, could only be damaging to Weiss's defense. As Judd Richheimer, Ross's college roommate and close friend who had worked at the company until 1972, had told me, cash payoffs to Teamsters, city inspectors, and others were routine at Kinney Parking in the sixties, in a total amount of as much as $1 million a year. Akerman had been alerted to the possibility of labor payments by Rosenthal, who had a habit of saying the most remarkably direct things, and who must have been the bane of the WCI lawyers. Akerman stated, in a sealed sidebar conference with Judge Lowe, that Rosenthal had testified in the grand jury that "he had heard that there was at one time money paid to labor people in Kinney," in a time period that extended from the mid-sixties through the early seventies. Akerman was seeking the judge's permission to cross-examine Weiss on this subject, but she refused.

Apart from the perils of exploring the parking business and labor payoffs, there was a further reason to attempt to minimize Weiss's relationship with Kimmel. After Sarnoff had questioned Weiss's check requests, Weiss obtained Kimmel's signature, as approver, for the next check in the fraudulent series of checks he was requesting. To forestall any further questioning from the diligent Sarnoff, Kimmel was an obvious choice for Weiss to make; he was high in the corporate hierarchy, as an executive vice-president—and he was also the person that WCI executives knew better than to tangle with, lest they incur Ross's displeasure.

Now, however, that well-reasoned selection of Caesar Kimmel as approver was another threat to the integrity of Weiss's story. For, as Akerman would demand in his summation, if this were a scheme conducted by Emmett and Horwitz—and Weiss, unknowing, was Emmett's pawn—why would Weiss have taken the initiative (after Sarnoff's questioning) to obtain the approval of Kimmel, with whom he had had a close business relationship for more than twenty years (and who, moreover, would have understood the company's need for cash as well as anyone)?

There were more fundamental questions about Weiss's story, and Akerman posed them repeatedly in his summation, not only addressing them to the jurors but challenging Kasanof to answer them. It had been established through documentary evidence that in five instances, Horwitz had delivered the cash first, and then received the checks. (Indeed, Horwitz had resented this, because it imposed a considerable burden on him and, more important, because it showed, so inescapably, that Weiss did not trust him.) Now, Akerman asked, if these transactions were taking place between Emmett and Horwitz, why would Emmett have demanded of his long-time friend, Leonard Horwitz—to whom he lent large sums—that he bring the cash first?

Moreover, if this were merely a scheme between Emmett and Horwitz designed to get money for Emmett, why would Emmett have involved Weiss at all? He did not need Weiss. Emmett had greater check-writing authority, and, given the far wider scope of his responsibilities, more plausible pretexts for hiring consultants or lawyers. Why would he have involved Weiss in the purchases of Westchester Premier Theatre stock? Why—if Weiss's only role was to sign the stock confirmations at Emmett's direction—was Horwitz, during that period, visiting Weiss twice a week, and calling him almost daily?

These discrepancies were striking enough, based on the trial record. But the more one knew about the characters and the cultural context, the more hopelessly contrived Sol Weiss's story became. Weiss did Ross's bidding; he moved in and out of Ross's office almost as unobtrusively as did Carmen Ferragano, Ross's omnipresent assistant. But he had little to do with Jay Emmett (he did not even do Emmett's personal banking, as he did for Ross and some other executives); there was no affinity between the two. Indeed, Weiss was one of the last people that Emmett would ever have included, even as an unknowing participant, in an illicit scheme that he was trying to hide.

An equally far-fetched scenario, too, would be evoked by Bob Kasanof, in his summation, when at one point he demanded, rhetorically, why—if indeed there were a cash fund that Weiss was managing for the company —would Sarnoff, the treasurer, who had questioned those checks, not have been in on it? (For Rosenthal and others from WCI in the courtroom audience at that moment, it must have been all they could do to suppress their mirth.)

Kasanof's summation—like his cross-examinations of Emmett and Horwitz—was long on vitriol but short on substance. He denigrated them, calling them "crooks" and "liars" again and again, while, by contrast, speaking reverentially of Arthur Liman and Michael Armstrong. He used the Armstrong memo as a centerpiece, moreover, referring to Lubell's alleged action as "the one-hundred-thousand-dollar perjury shakedown." Beyond these *ad hominem* attacks, however, there was nowhere to go. In Kasanof's sole attempt to deal with Akerman's questions, Kasanof declared: "When Mr. Akerman says, how come this, and how come that? We do not know. Why cash? Why this, why that? We don't know. We were not part of that crookedness but it may well be that these crooks or some other crooks that were in it didn't trust each other. I don't know."

When Akerman rose for his rebuttal summation, he asked the same, unanswered questions again.

After four days' deliberation, on November 27, 1982, the jury found Solomon Weiss guilty on seven of the thirteen counts charged. He was convicted of conducting the affairs of an enterprise through a pattern of racketeering activity (under RICO), mail fraud, and perjury. Upon hearing the verdict, Weiss turned ashen, and Judge Lowe, urging him to be seated, summoned paramedics. His lawyers, too, felt stricken; as two of them would later tell me, they had expected Weiss to be acquitted.

Despite the formidable heft of the government's evidence, there was in the defense camp an abiding hope that the issue of character—Weiss's (buttressed by Liman's and Armstrong's), in contrast to Emmett's and Horwitz's—would tilt the scales. Although in other, less intensely secular and materialistic settings, Weiss might not have seemed so unusual, at WCI he was regarded as something of an anomaly. And once he became a target of this investigation, his defenders tended to focus on his religious piety, as though that might be, in itself, exoneration. In a story that would become legend, they recounted, again and again, how Weiss had been driving home to New Jersey with other WCI employees on a snowy Friday late afternoon, amidst very slow-moving traffic; so slow, in fact, that they were still driving when dusk fell and the Jewish sabbath (on which driving is prohibited) began. Weiss, miles from home, got out of the car and walked the rest of the way in the snow.

Weiss was most anomalous, of course—in this company where Ross's largesse was infectious and gift giving a fact of life—for his refusal to accept a gift. This despite the fact that he often went out of his way for others, rendering personal services—such as preparing the tax filings for widows of WCI executives—for which he received no compensation. Ross, Weiss, and the lawyers apparently hoped that this behavior would be interpreted as a sign of Weiss's incorruptibility, for it was a note struck repeatedly in testimony. Ross (prompted by Liman) had done so in his SEC deposition, and at trial, John Calley, the head of Warner Brothers, had followed suit.

Calley testified that "one particularly grueling year which we had a lot of complicated tax stuff to do, he [Weiss] worked through the Christmas holidays and as a consequence of it, I wanted to send him something as a demonstration of my gratitude, so I sent him, I think, a case of wine. And he returned it to me with a note saying that he thought it would be inappropriate for him to accept any gift from me, and if I wanted to make a donation to his temple, I was welcome to do that, but he couldn't accept anything from me, and I thought that was bizarrely honorable. I thought it was extreme."

Indeed, it seems that Weiss so rigidly adhered to this self-imposed ban that anyone's attempt to transgress it provoked him. At the SEC, Weiss's secretary, Linda Horns, had testified (under questioning by Liman) that business associates would "call me and ask what they could possibly send Mr. Weiss for a gift and I tell them that they absolutely cannot send him a gift because it will just, it will anger him and he'll send it back."

Paradoxically, the greater the public perception of Weiss's rectitude, the more perfect an agent he was for these cash transactions. And with all the trumpeting in court of Weiss's refusal to accept gifts, exactly why he considered it so improper was never clarified; did he fear that it might be seen as having compromised his objectivity as a preparer of individuals' tax returns? Or was it a discipline he imposed on himself for other, private, perhaps religious reasons?

Whatever the nature of Sol Weiss's personal code, it had not prevented him from functioning as a bookkeeper for Kinney Parking, when, as one former partner told me, it was being used to launder cash for Manny Kimmel, who was a hidden owner (perhaps along with Longie Zwillman, as was rumored for many years). It had not prevented him from being the financial person at the company closest to the parking division through the sixties and the early seventies, when cash was skimmed and payoffs to Teamsters and others routinely made. And, as these jurors had decided, it had not prevented him from engaging in these various transactions with Leonard Horwitz and the Westchester Premier Theatre, to amass cash for the company. As Horwitz had testified, when he appeared with his proposition and his $50,000 in cash, Weiss had set about methodically counting it, saying that "he thought the company could help. The company always had need for cash."

Upon reflection, there was not even an apparent inconsistency here. It was indeed inconceivable that Weiss would have taken the money for himself; but the government, although it had begun this investigation with a theory of bribery, had amended it to the "cash fund" theory, and so informed Weiss and his lawyers, long before trial. He was convicted of having operated a secret cash fund, with all the creation of fraudulent documentation that that required: a subversion of the bookkeeping function. And as to that, one might argue it was what he had been schooled in, from his early days as an accountant; keeping the books for a company steeped in secrecy, with hidden ownership connected to organized crime, money laundered, cash skimmed, payoffs made, all as a way of life. Indeed, Weiss—far from being incongruous—was the person in the company most ideally suited for the task.

Years after Weiss's trial, when I interviewed Eddie Rosenthal in 1990, he spoke warmly of Weiss, whom he had made a beneficiary and a co-executor of his will. "Weiss came from Kinney," Rosenthal said. "Dearest friend of mine, dearest friend of Caesar Kimmel. Loveliest guy you would ever want to meet."

As for the substance of the case against Weiss, Rosenthal said, "I believe there *was* a cash fund—to pay union leaders when you need their help, when they do some special favor. In the garage and cleaning businesses, you need it. And Sol Weiss would have been in charge of it."

At trial, Akerman had never articulated a theory of what the $170,000 in cash was used for; the closest he had come to that was when, based on Rosenthal's statement to the grand jury, he had sought Judge Lowe's permission to question Weiss about "labor payoffs." Among executives at WCI, this was merely one of many theories, and in fact it had less currency than others (by 1973, the garage and cleaning businesses were part of

National Kinney, so once removed—and the parking lots had always been able to generate plenty of cash themselves).

Many believed that the cash was used by Ross—who dealt only in cash —to finance his munificent lifestyle. Some, that the cash was needed for payola in WCI's record business. Or, also, for entertaining WCI's performers, which would include providing them with their drugs of choice. At the SEC, there was a theory that cash was used to pay Cosmos players over and above the amounts stated on their contracts, and that deposits were made to their foreign bank accounts. (Weiss was also in charge of bookkeeping for the Cosmos.)

That money was needed for campaign contributions was another popular theory. One lawyer for a WCI executive subpoenaed in the investigation reportedly asserted that some of the cash from Horwitz did go to Nixon. Interestingly, Tony Provenzano (an associate of Caesar Kimmel) in early 1973 collected about $500,000 in cash for Nixon and arranged to have it delivered to Charles Colson, according to *The Teamsters,* by Steven Brill. And Colson, during this period of time, was a highly paid consultant to WCI (though it was so private a relationship that even Colson's partner then, David Shapiro, would later say he had not known it existed). The purpose of the cash fund was never established; whether any of the activities it might have been used for actually occurred is beyond the scope of this book.

There was, in any event, no dearth of likely uses for cash, beyond the labor payoffs that had been a company custom. Nor was the existence of a cash or "slush" fund an aberration in corporate America in the seventies —a point that Weiss's lawyers would emphasize in their post-trial motions, referring to an article in a journal, *Business Crime,* which stated that "some 500 corporations reported to the Securities and Exchange Commission that they had cash funds during the period in question here." It was because of the prevalence of this practice that the Foreign Corrupt Practices Act was passed in 1977 (a law which Sporkin would so zealously enforce).

The cash fund became a keystone of Weiss's appeal. Some in his defense camp would later say that they had always believed there had been a cash fund, operated by Weiss at Ross's direction—although Weiss reportedly had never acknowledged even to his counsel that this was the case. It was only on the appeal, after all else had failed, and when the notion of a cash fund could be couched in theoretical language, that it was tendered. With WCI still paying Weiss's legal fees, he was represented not by Kasanof but by Leon Silverman (Alan Dershowitz was also asked to read the brief, for which he was paid $10,000). And one of the issues

Silverman presented was "whether the undisclosed creation of a corporate cash fund . . . constitutes a breach of fiduciary duty—and thus a mail fraud and RICO violation—by a participating corporate subordinate who has no disclosure duty and who acts on the orders of the corporation's chief executive officers."

In January 1985, the U.S. Court of Appeals for the Second Circuit would affirm Weiss's conviction on all counts. At one point in his opinion, Senior District Judge Robert Kelleher, summarizing Weiss's newly struck posture, wrote: "On appeal, Weiss contends that he established the cash fund pursuant to orders from his superiors, and that he never personally retained any of the cash. Yet Weiss never presented such claims at trial."

Nor did he ever offer to strike a deal with the government and so testify, despite the fact that he was facing the possibility of a substantial prison term. However, at his sentencing, on March 13, 1984, Judge Lowe declined to send Sol Weiss to prison; she fined him a total of $58,000 and placed him on probation for five years, during which time he was to perform community service, full time, for the Essex County Division of Youth Services. He was also ordered to forfeit WCI stock worth approximately $411,939 at that time.

For Nick Akerman, it was an abortive end to the investigation he had begun seven years earlier. While he had not focused on Steve Ross at its inception, he had been fixed on him at least from the time Jay Emmett had plea-bargained. It was subsequent to Emmett's cooperation that Ross, subpoenaed to appear before the grand jury—and, in all likelihood, informed that he was a target—had invoked the Fifth (by this time, Liman had brought in Peter Fleming, a well-known criminal lawyer who was part of his circle, to represent Ross). And there had been several points during Akerman's investigation when he must have felt he was coming tantalizingly close to Ross.

Sometime between Emmett's plea and the start of Weiss's trial, a WCI corporate vice-president in charge of public relations, James Abernathy, was alleged to have told someone that upon entering Ross's office one day, he had overheard a conversation between Ross and Weiss, concerning a cash kickback from the United Jewish Appeal. When Abernathy was questioned about this alleged conversation before the grand jury, however, he denied any knowledge of it. Also, there were WCI contributions to Weiss's synagogue so conspicuously large that they caught the attention of Akerman and his investigators. While they reportedly found no documentary evidence of what had been done with the money, Weiss's rabbi is said to have claimed that it had been used to smuggle Jews out of Russia.

One lead that did not eventuate in a dead end for Akerman, however, was a "credit card" for Ross at Caesar's Palace in Las Vegas. It indicated that Ross had lost $40,000 in cash playing blackjack during the weekend of June 1–3, 1973—immediately after Horwitz, as he testified, had delivered the $50,000 in cash to Weiss. However, since Acting U.S. Attorney Tendy had forestalled Akerman from seeking an indictment of Ross, and since Ross did not take the stand at Weiss's trial, Akerman was never able to use this piece of information.

Akerman's frustration at Ross's elusiveness was all too evident. Not only had he evinced it in his remarks about Ross at trial, but he repeated it at Emmett's sentencing, in December 1983, declaring that, "In our view, the real culprit has not yet been brought to justice." And he then added, "The real culprit was the chairman of the board of Warner Communications, Inc., and the investigation of him continues."

Akerman would subsequently assert that he had made these remarks in order to inform Emmett's sentencing judge that, despite the fact that Emmett's indictment portrayed him as the kingpin in this corporate fraud, the government no longer viewed him that way. Nonetheless, Akerman's remarks seemed inappropriate, inasmuch as he was speaking with the authority of the government but had won no indictment of Ross. And his intemperance lent some credence to the criticism of him that Liman, Armstrong, and others had been levelling since the start of this investigation.

That Liman would have waged what was essentially a public relations battle against Akerman, on behalf of his client, Ross, was not surprising. Altogether remarkable, however, was the fact that, in the aftermath of the Weiss conviction, Liman, in seeking a public relations advantage for Ross, went so far as to sacrifice one of his own defense teammates, Bob Kasanof.

In the June 1983 issue of *The American Lawyer,* Steven Brill wrote a piece entitled "Trading Up—How to Hang a Tycoon," which—in a ringing denunciation of the evidence, the government's witnesses, the defense lawyer, the prosecutor, and the jurors—found for Weiss and exonerated Ross. Liman was an important source for the piece.

Brill argued that Weiss had been convicted because Kasanof had failed to bring out two points. First, that Emmett's net worth was allegedly less in 1973 than had been stated at trial, thereby increasing the likelihood of his having wanted the $50,000 in cash. And, second, that while it had been brought out by Akerman that Weiss was named in Ross's will, Kasanof had failed to elicit from Weiss the information that (according to Brill's sources) about twenty WCI employees were named. (The theory being that Ross's beneficence *vis-à-vis* Weiss was not unique and, realizing that, the jurors might have been less inclined to conclude—as they had—that Weiss was protecting Ross.)

Also, Liman was quoted attacking Kasanof for having agreed, in a robing-room conference, not to cross-examine Emmett on his extramarital affairs. " 'Bob is kind of an old-world gentleman,' says Liman. 'He left out that line of questioning when few of us would have.' " In fact, when Kasanof raised his desire to address this subject, Judge Lowe had ruled that it had nothing to do with the merits of the case. Kasanof did win Judge Lowe's permission to broach it in a single question, about Emmett's having paid for plane tickets and hotel bills for women.

While Kasanof declined to comment, Liman was voluble. "Liman says, 'Bob decided to try what you could call a lean case, something that all good trial lawyers do when they think things are going their way. Bob thought he had it won. I guess you could say he was wrong.' " Adding his own stamp to Liman's knifework, Brill wrote, "Kasanof's laissez-faire optimism seems absurd."

It is, however, highly unlikely that presenting the above points would have made a difference in the jurors' decision; even seen in their best light, they do not perceptibly shift the weight of the government's evidence. Moreover, while it is certainly possible that Kasanof left out a question or two that Liman, in his place, would have asked, the fact remains that this was a *joint* defense, in which Liman was an intensely active partner. As several of the lawyers who worked with Kasanof have told me, Liman received daily copies of the trial transcript. Someone from Paul, Weiss was always observing in the courtroom. Kasanof consulted with Liman constantly. And no major strategic decision was made without Liman. Liman denies that his statements to Brill were intended to disparage Kasanof's handling of the case and asserts that he and Kasanof remained friends. However, according to Kasanof's colleagues, Kasanof was so pained by what he viewed as treachery by Liman that the rupture between the two had not healed by the time of Kasanof's death, in 1992.

It is ironic that while Liman was the only defense lawyer involved in this case to publicize his criticism, the consensus among most of Weiss's lawyers was that the greatest disservice done Sol Weiss, the one which created the handicap that was ultimately impossible to overcome, was Liman and his firm's—in allowing Weiss (along with Emmett) to testify before the grand jury, and in allowing him to do so in a way that seemed, on its face, so patently unbelievable.

In court motions, Weiss's attorneys would argue repeatedly (but unsuccessfully) that Akerman had misled Max Gitter about whether or not Emmett and Weiss were targets. Akerman's ambiguous statements aside, it is plain that Liman and his firm gave advice here that some lawyers (Rudin, for one) would not have. And while Liman may or may not have been able to foresee its long-term consequences, in the end Weiss's self-immolation had served Ross: his body stood between Ross and the government.

Having dispatched Kasanof, Liman also helped Brill dispense with a troublesome source, Eddie Rosenthal. Brill had obtained copies of two letters, ruled inadmissible at trial, that Rosenthal had written to Emmett after he had been indicted but before he pled guilty. Brill quoted portions of the letters. The first began:

Jay, with a deep feeling of guilt in my heart that you must suffer because of what you did for me and my company and all of us at WCI, including my family, I write to beg your forgiveness for what we have put you through. . . . We just pray that the knowledge of your innocence, that what you did, you did for us . . . not for yourself, will help you continue the great courage you have shown. . . .

And the second began: "Since you took the rap for all the WCI [sic], I can't get the thought of you out of my mind. . . ."

When Brill asked Rosenthal about the letters, Rosenthal had said, "Jay took nothing for himself. He did it to set up a cash fund. . . . Every major company has a cash fund. . . . We needed cash for record deals, for unions at the parking lots. . . . It's standard. And now they're trying to cover it up. Steve is. And the lawyers are, too. The letters I wrote are beautiful letters."

Toward the end of the piece, Brill said that when he returned to Rosenthal to ask him if he had proof of a cash fund, or proof that Emmett hadn't stolen, Rosenthal did not. "I then found out that Rosenthal, 80, is articulate but widely believed to be capable of the kind of erratic behavior and judgments that might be called senility," Brill explained. "For example, he recently wrote to Ross advising him to name his son the next chairman of Warner and to designate his grandson [Ross's son] as the next chief executive. Mark Ross, 20, is a freshman at Tufts University."

Liman was a likely source for what Brill asserted was Rosenthal's "senility"—both because Liman was an eager supplier of so much else in the piece that served his ends, and also because it is difficult to imagine who, other than Liman, would have had reason to say it. It was not true. Of the dozens of people I have interviewed who knew Eddie Rosenthal, not one believed—or had ever heard anyone say—that he was senile. When I interviewed Rosenthal seven years after Brill had (and when he made a similar statement to me about the cash fund), Rosenthal recounted the history of the company, with recollections dating back to the 1950s and spanning the succeeding thirty years, accurately. He was cogent, lucid, and—the trait that had always marked him—outspoken in a way that was, at moments, startling.

As for the letter to Ross that Brill offered as evidence of Rosenthal's senility, that letter was consistent with (and considerably less outlandish than) the one Rosenthal had fired off back in the early sixties to Frank Stanton, CBS's then-president, suggesting that his son-in-law, Steve Ross (whose major work experience at that time was as a funeral director), should become president of CBS. (Liman denies that he told Brill that Rosenthal was senile.)

Liman made Ross available to Brill, who asked the question Ross wanted to answer: How could Emmett have done all this stealing without Ross's knowledge?

Ross explains: "I do not get involved in the operating divisions. My job is to dream for tomorrow. To come up with an idea to take Atari out of the arcades and put it into homes. We let our operating division heads and our creative people make the day-to-day decisions. It's a system that's under attack here. [Warner has been beset by bad publicity not only because of the Weiss/Emmett cases but because of sharp declines in Atari's earnings.] But it works. And I continue to believe it's a system for fostering entrepreneurship that the country needs."

Brill did not press beyond this oratorical response, nor point out that the criminal acts at issue here did not occur in "the operating divisions" but within corporate, Ross's sovereign domain. But for the spirit of cooperation that suffused the article, it might have seemed strange that Ross, who had invoked the Fifth before the grand jury (this was not publicly known at the time), who had not testified at Weiss's trial, and who was still under investigation, would discuss the case with a reporter. Regarding Ross's not having testified at Weiss's trial, Brill wrote: "Ross says he was available and willing to testify to rebut Emmett but he was not called, a decision that Liman ruefully attributes, again, to Kasanof's 'lean' case method."

According to several lawyers familiar with the case, the idea of Ross's testifying was much discussed among Kasanof, Liman, Fleming and, on occasion, Ross; and all ultimately agreed that he should not testify. Kasanof, moreover, is said to have concurred in this decision that Ross not be called not only to accommodate Liman but also, more legitimately, because Kasanof (aware that once Ross took the stand, the government would be able to introduce the Caesar's Palace "credit card") believed it would badly damage Weiss. That "credit card" would serve as a vital piece to the puzzle, evidence—indeed, the government's only evidence—of where Horwitz's initial delivery of cash might well have gone.

For Steve Ross, the *American Lawyer* article became a kind of public certification of his innocence, countering what was at least implied by the Weiss conviction. And it would for many years be viewed in some circles as the most definitive word on the subject, since the other document which purported to be definitive—the "Armstrong Report," a 663-page treatise, accompanied by 88 exhibits and nearly 8,000 pages of testimony, which was submitted to the WCI audit committee in 1986, capping an eight-year-long investigation—was never made public.

According to the rules created by Ross and his board, only the two directors then comprising the WCI audit committee, Raymond Troubh (an investment banker who had known Ross since 1966 and was a close personal friend of Liman's; Liman had asked him to join the WCI board in 1979, expressing the view, according to Troubh, that in light of the company's troubles it needed more "outside" directors) and Lawrence Buttenweiser, were to read the report and then summarize their conclusions to the rest of the board. Having done so, they decided that it was in the best interests of the company and its stockholders that no one else— not even their fellow directors—read it.

One could see why, in an excerpt of the report that later became public. (It was included in a confidential letter to the court, written in 1987, by a lawyer on behalf of a WCI director seeking expanded access to the report; the letter was sealed but, later, disseminated through a court clerk's error.) The excerpt included reference to the Caesar's Palace "credit card," which had not previously been made public (as well as Ross's denials of the card's accuracy). And it confirmed that it had been Kasanof's fear of the damage the government could inflict with that evidence that had led him not to want to call Ross as a witness at the Weiss trial.

It also contained a rather startling statement, made by Ross to Armstrong, that the government in its investigation had never heard. After over the course of three interviews having denied that he maintained any "cash reservoir," Ross in the fourth interview, in January 1985, "when pressed on this point . . . asserted for the first time, that he had kept excess gambling winnings in a briefcase in his office." Ross, moreover, stated that he had done so between 1973 and 1975—contemporaneous with Horwitz's largest deliveries of cash. He claimed that he used the cash for "various purposes," including "cash and gifts" to a woman with whom he had a "relationship." (This was Cathy Mitchell, for whom Ross supposedly paid for plastic surgery, and to whom Emmett had given $10,000 in cash on behalf of Ross when Ross ended the relationship.)

Ross further claimed that the source of the cash was gambling, and that he "regularly won $60,000 to $90,000 each time he engaged in card counting." Armstrong and his investigators were skeptical of this, writing that "the weight of the credible evidence indicates that Ross probably won between $10,000 and $40,000 on a consistent basis."

Armstrong suggested that Ross might have exaggerated the amount of his winnings in order to explain how he funded the woman's expenses. Armstrong asked Liman to explain why Ross had not mentioned this briefcase full of cash in three earlier interviews, and Liman seemed to try to call into question Ross's statement, saying that "he was under considerable strain from other events and was also taking heavy amounts of medication for health reasons. . . . They argued . . . that his demeanor, as well as the surprising content of his answers, were largely attributable to the side effects of medication."

After further discussions, including Liman, Ross, and Ross's other lawyers, the briefcase story was modified, not disowning the practice but asserting that Ross had been mistaken about the dates: the lawyers said, "he had not initiated that practice until 1976 or 1977. We [Armstrong and his associates] were told that Ross associated his first such use of the briefcase with a gambling trip he had taken with [Ken] Rosen." (It is curious that Rosen should have emerged—again!—as a useful reference in a tight spot.)

What Armstrong's investigators did note was that these dates—"1976 or 1977"—no longer jibed with Ross's explanation of his use of the cash. His relationship with Cathy Mitchell had indeed spanned the 1973–75 period that Ross had first indicated. But Mitchell was long gone by 1976, having been replaced in the beginning of 1975 by Courtney Sale, who was in turn replaced by Amanda Burden in November 1975. "Ross's 'revision' as to the timing of his use of the briefcase had the effect of placing its use as a cash repository beyond the Mitchell period and during a time when Ross would not have had as strong a motive to accept cash. At that later time, he was separated from his first wife and was in a considerably stronger personal financial condition."

Liman had been trying for some time to wrest from the U.S. Attorney a public statement that the investigation of Ross was closed (a practice rarely followed). Finally, according to one attorney, Liman had agreed with U.S. Attorney Rudolph Giuliani that Ross would give a private, sealed interview to the prosecutors—and, if it proved satisfactory, Giuliani would make such an announcement. Ross had given the interview. And, in February 1985, Giuliani had announced that the office had "insufficient evidence" to file charges.

Now, Armstrong and his associates, who had access to the transcript of Ross's interview, stated:

> We are also troubled by the fact that Ross's explanations are inconsistent with his statements to the U.S. Attorney. When he was questioned by the prosecutors about his gambling successes, Ross said that he had not reported any gambling winnings on his income tax returns because: "I felt at the end of the year that I netted out. I was neither a winner or a loser with all my gambling." Ross's statement that he "netted out" could not have been true if a substantial portion of his winnings were used to pay for Mitchell's expenses or to buy her gifts.

Furthermore, it was only after Armstrong and his associates had located Mitchell, and she had told them about Ross's giving her substantial amounts of cash, that Ross acknowledged that he had done so. He claimed to Armstrong that he had not recalled it before. It also seems plain from this excerpt that Armstrong surprised Ross in that January 1985 interview, either with Mitchell's statements or something else about Ross's use of a large amount of cash—which triggered, from Ross, his story about a briefcase in his closet stuffed with cash from gambling, something which, he also said, no one else knew about. (Indeed, some who moved freely in and out of his office in those years were never aware of it.)

It was only Ross, then, who divulged to Armstrong the existence of the briefcase; this was confirmed, too, by someone familiar with the investigation. Which suggests—knowing Ross—that there was no briefcase. For he would only have proffered such a provocative piece of information in a sudden, spontaneous effort to divert an investigator from something which, if discovered, would be far more damaging. Indeed, if the company were operating a cash fund (one that served Ross's personal needs as well), which by the mid-seventies might well have been as large as several million dollars a year, it is highly unlikely that it would have been run out of a briefcase in Ross's closet. Given Ross's consummate cultivation of deniability, elevating it almost to an art form—in negotiations, as well as in the company's history of cash funds and payoffs—his closet is the last place that such cash would be kept.

Armstrong's investigators harbored similar doubts about the briefcase story. In conclusion, they wrote:

> We are not convinced that Ross maintained a briefcase in his office throughout the Mitchell period into which he deposited cash from gam-

bling winnings. We believe that Ross might have exaggerated his use of a briefcase to store cash in order to explain where he must have kept the surplus from his claimed winnings of $60,000 to $90,000 per each gambling trip. We simply do not believe that Ross regularly won that much money playing blackjack, and suspect that he made such estimates in an effort to explain how he funded the Mitchell expenses.

On the other hand, they continued, " . . . if Ross maintained a receptacle for cash (as it seems that he must have done if his gambling winnings had been his source of cash), he could have also kept a portion of the kickbacks in the same place."

Tangled in a web of what they took to be Steve Ross's half-truths or outright lies, Armstrong and his investigators laid them all out—and then, essentially, threw up their hands. Their mandate had been to explore, and that they had done. They had found a CEO who, when questioned on these core issues, was, in their view, deliberately misleading them. But had they unearthed the smoking gun that irrefutably tied the Westchester kickbacks to Ross? No. They could, therefore—after an eight-year-long investigation—deliver the predictable conclusion.

Armstrong's report found Ross's "inconsistent statements regarding his own gambling and uses of cash . . . troublesome. There were instances in which Ross was not

completely candid. Despite our reservations about Ross's credibility, however, we have been unable to establish that any of the alleged kickbacks made by Horwitz were intended for the private benefit of Ross or for an entertainment slush fund.

In summary, we continue to believe that the weight of all the available evidence does not support the charge that Ross received or knew of the [Westchester Theatre] cash kickbacks.

The "Armstrong Report" could not have been unwelcome to Ross, even though it raised some question about his conduct. Its length alone suggested diligence, and Armstrong's past as an aggressive prosecutor, as well as the provocative nature of some of its contents, lent it an aura of credibility—but since its contents were never to be disclosed there would be no real damage. And the ultimate conclusion was exactly what was needed. Based on that conclusion, Troubh and Buttenweiser were able to assert in a brief public statement that "there was insufficient evidence of illegal conduct."

They further stated—and this, quite amazingly—that there was "insufficient evidence. credible to the committee. to conclude Solomon M.

Weiss engaged in illegal conduct in connection with kickbacks." Of this conclusion, which contradicted not only Weiss's conviction but also its affirmance on appeal, Troubh would say years later, "Yes, it *was* extraordinary. I guess we were, in effect, one of two juries." Thus, with the corporate slate effectively wiped clean of Sol Weiss's criminality, WCI was able not to seek reimbursement from Weiss of the $2 million the company had spent for his legal bills and expenses. (Weiss had remained on the WCI payroll while on a leave of absence throughout the period of his trial and subsequent appeal; in fact, he had received a salary increase while he was on leave.)

In years to come, Ross would continue to take care of Weiss. Weiss's successor, handling Ross's personal financial matters—as well as assisting Ross on the company's financial transactions—would be Oded Aboodi, the canny tax specialist who for years had worked on first the Kinney and then the WCI account at Arthur Young, and who had also put together tax-shelter deals for Ross and other WCI executives. In 1980, Aboodi had left that firm to establish his own small company (by that time, Weiss's usefulness to Ross was at an end). As Ralph Peterson, the treasurer of Warner Brothers and a good friend of Aboodi's, would say, "Ed went out on his own because Steve wanted Ed to work for him." Peterson also added, regarding Aboodi's departure from Arthur Young, "Public accounting is not a place for creative minds—and Ed can get pretty wild."

Aboodi would operate in that position most favored by Ross: a completely loyal and dependent person, in the guise of an outside adviser. Since Aboodi's firm, in the WCI headquarters, was nominally independent, it was there that Weiss would work—thus, he never had to really leave the company. According to several people close to him, he would be paid a couple of million dollars out of large fees that Aboodi would garner over the years. He would remain a beneficiary of Ross's will. And he would be accorded not just wealth but tribute: at the end of his five-year probation period in 1989, WCI would celebrate the event with an evening in his honor at the Jewish Museum.

Still, Sol Weiss grew increasingly withdrawn and bitter, several of his friends maintained. His relationship with Ross, which had been intimate only in a sense of shared business dealings, dwindled to nothing. According to one person, Ross (never able to confront someone whom he was disappointing, or hurting) could not tolerate being in a room alone with Weiss. And Weiss, who had so kept his silence when it counted, even became slightly truculent. Once, when Ross was late to a funeral of a WCI colleague, Weiss is said to have muttered, "Steve Ross can't do *anything* right."

Much as Ross tried to compensate him, the toll on Weiss's personal life apparently proved insusceptible to subsidy. After his conviction, his wife —who is said to have experienced it as an insurmountable public disgrace—suffered a bout of hysterical blindness. Weiss's son, an engineer, is said by friends to have responded to the ordeal with some resilience. But Weiss's daughter dropped out of Yale Medical School after the trial, and never resumed her medical training.

Years after the trial, Jay Emmett reportedly was walking up Sixth Avenue toward his apartment on Central Park South when he became aware of a woman shouting over the din of the traffic. For a time, he paid no attention. But as the noise grew louder, he reportedly turned and saw that it was Weiss's daughter, and he realized that she was shouting at him. He quickened his pace slightly as she continued in pursuit, screaming: "You! It was you! You! You ruined my father's life!"

On a midsummer day in 1980, Jay Emmett, Manny Gerard, and David Horowitz (the three co-habitants of the Office of the President at that time) took a company helicopter to East Hampton to visit Steve Ross. In a period of enforced lassitude, recuperating from a heart attack he had suffered in June, Ross was under considerable strain. The West-chester investigation was closing in ever more tightly—indeed, by September 1980 Emmett would be indicted, and several months later, on the eve of his trial, he would plead guilty and begin cooperating with the government. Ross, however, kept his anxiety largely to himself; though he was at home for a prolonged period of time, together with Amanda Burden, she is said to have had no idea of the gravity of the Westchester investigation, nor of its import to their close friend Jay Emmett, or to Ross himself. When he mentioned it at all, it was only as a casual aside about an overambitious prosecutor who wanted to make a name for himself, and had therefore targeted Frank Sinatra.

One leavening influence in this trying time was a development at WCI so large and exciting that it was beginning to engender a kind of corpo-rate euphoria. The company's video-game division, Atari, had lost money for several years. But in 1979 Atari had licensed "Space Invaders," a program for coin-operated machines, and produced it for its VCS (Video

Computer System) 2600, the game machine which operates by being plugged into a television set. Until this time, Atari's marketing strategy had been that of a hardware business; now, with the "Space Invaders" hit, it became clear that it was the software that would drive its sales, and that advertising should focus not on the player but the games. In 1979, Atari made a profit of $6 million; for 1980, it would escalate ten-fold, to nearly $70 million. And the people running Atari were convinced that there was no plateau in sight.

Ross, who had been only mildly interested in the Atari division (though he loved the games, and had at home several favorites, which he sometimes played far into the night), now became an enthusiastic booster. Not only were the profits mounting at breathtaking velocity, but Atari had such wide appeal that it had entered the popular lexicon; a *Time* magazine writer dubbed the period "The Age of Atari," and Thomas ("Tip") O'Neill, Speaker of the House of Representatives, referred to new young congressmen as "Atari Democrats." This delighted Ross. For he loved best those WCI products that, in addition to making money, achieved a cultural visibility; they allowed him to think of his own role in a more romantic way, to imagine himself more as a patron and protector of creative spirits than simply the CEO of a workaday corporation.

Notwithstanding the excitement of Atari's success, Ross now wondered aloud whether they ought not to find a partner for Atari—IBM, say, which could provide technological expertise (vital to Atari's fledgling home computer operation) and, given Atari's prospects, perhaps $100 million in capital.

"But Atari is a gold mine!" Emmett protested. "Why should we share it?"

Ross shook his head and responded, in effect, that nothing is a gold mine forever.

According to several close to Steve Ross, he would continue to nurse a strong ambivalence about Atari over the next couple of years, believing that it was simply too good to be true. Indeed, witnessing the growth of Atari from 1980 through the beginning of 1982 was like watching a pyrotechnics display; there had probably not been another company, in the history of American business, that grew as large, as fast, as Atari.

In 1972, Nolan Bushnell had started a small company, Syzygy (which then became Atari), to design computer games for arcades; "Pong" was his first big hit, followed by "Tank" and others. By 1976, Atari—based in Sunnyvale, California, and run by Bushnell and his associates, a free-wheeling, entrepreneurial group of computer engineers—was thriving, with sales of $39 million. The company had created the VCS, and the cartridge games to be played on it. But there was insufficient capital to fund its growth.

An analyst named Gordon Crawford had joined California's Capital Group investment funds in 1971, and had begun to follow the entertainment industry—an area so depressed at the time that it was largely neglected by other analysts. In 1972, Crawford bought 10 percent of WCI's stock for Capital, making it the company's largest institutional shareholder, and thus inaugurated what would be a long-term, mutually cultivated relationship with Ross and other WCI executives. An arm of the Capital Group, moreover, had financed Bushnell in his start-up of Atari; and, in 1976, Bushnell told Crawford that he was intent on gaining capital for expansion and thus wanted either to bring Atari public or to sell it (and continue to run it). Crawford contacted Emanuel Gerard, who, after looking into it, urged the deal on Ross.

In later years, after Atari had become the stuff of business legend, Ross would often recount how it had all come to be: he was visiting Disneyland with Amanda, her children, and his son Mark, and, struck by how mesmerized the children were by the video games, he had written down the name of the manufacturer—Atari—and instructed his executives to find out about it. While it is true that the children were avid for an Atari game at Disneyland, Gerard's discussions with Bushnell were under way by that time. Gerard would later recall that he was startled when, reading one of Ross's depositions, he saw that Ross had given, under oath, this revisionist account. He said he commented on it to WCI's general counsel, Martin Payson, who responded, "I know that it didn't happen the way Steve says, Manny. But Steve *believes* it did."

Gordon Crawford became a confirmed Ross admirer, if not an acolyte, while witnessing the Atari deal. What struck him was that Ross, as a dealmaker, not only had extraordinary conceptual talents but, "more than most, he understands what drives the egos of the people on the other side of the table."

In this instance, Crawford continued, Bushnell—at the same time that he was having discussions with WCI—was considering selling Atari to a semiconductor company instead. "Nolan [Bushnell] and Don Valentine [a partner] were going to fly to New York to see Steve. They were met at the San Jose airport by the Warner jet, and were told there would be an intermediate stop; Clint Eastwood and Sondra Locke were on board, and they had to be dropped off at location, where they were making a movie. Clint talked to them, made them sandwiches. Then, in New York, Nolan and Don went to check into the Waldorf-Astoria, where they thought they were staying; but they found, instead, that they were in the Waldorf

Towers, in a palatial suite. From there they went to Steve's apartment, where they had a great dinner, and watched an unreleased Clint movie. Then they negotiated all night—and WCI bought it on terms Nolan never would have sold it on before that trip."

Gerard was the person in the Office of the President to whom Atari reported. And from the outset, he was more heavily involved in Atari than his corporate counterparts were in their divisions—Horowitz, say, in records, or Emmett in the studio. Atari was a relatively small bet for WCI to have made, and in the beginning Ross paid little attention to it; but Manny Gerard was a believer from the start. It lost money for the first couple of years. In 1978, Gerard fired Bushnell—whom he considered a poor administrator in the best of times, and now fatally distracted by the riches he'd gained from the sale of Atari—and hired Raymond Kassar, who happened to have been a Harvard Business School classmate of William Sarnoff, head of WCI's publishing division, and who had been a high-ranking executive at Burlington Industries for many years.

Kassar imposed a certain degree of structure on what had been the free-form environment of Atari. ("When I arrived, there was no infrastructure, no financial reporting, nothing," he would later claim.) He reorganized Atari into two parts: coin-operated games, and consumer electronics (which included home computers). He increased Atari's advertising budget. He also hired and fired people with great rapidity, and encouraged, with his shows of favoritism, a workplace rife with corporate politics. He never cultivated the company's "talent"; there was a steady exodus of some of Atari's most creative computer engineers. Still, within about a year of his assuming control, the business began to surge. After achieving a ten-fold leap to what seemed like stratospheric profits of $70 million in 1980, Atari's revenues more than doubled in 1981, and its profits were nearly $300 million.

By 1981, it was Atari that was driving the price of WCI stock, and to unprecedented heights. In December of that year the stock traded at $61 a share, roughly twice its level a year earlier. While both the movie and record divisions were flagging in 1981–82, Atari's plenitude appeared almost infinite. By 1982, it would be producing more than half of WCI's $4 billion in revenues and over 65 percent of its profits. Indeed, one former Atari executive would later claim that the disproportion between Atari and other WCI divisions was even greater than disclosed. He insisted that in the company's published breakdowns in 1981 and 1982, at least $100 million of Atari's earnings were distributed to other WCI divisions, so that outsiders would not know how palsied they were.

Toward the close of 1981, Ray Kassar came to New York for a WCI budget meeting, at which he delivered his five-year projections for Atari. By 1986, he predicted, Atari, fully ensconced in a worldwide market, would be generating $6 billion in revenues and $2 billion in earnings.

If Kassar's projections were Panglossian, they may be best understood in the light of what Atari had come to mean to him. Ross, for whom lavish, performance-based bonuses were his stock in trade, was not stinting with Kassar. According to several former Warner executives, Kassar received a bonus of $4 million in 1980 and $6 million in 1981. The company bought him a grand apartment in Trump Tower, with panoramic views. He—and his favored executives at Atari—emulated the Warner style, travelling by limousine and Warner jet, staying in the most elegant hotels. As one former executive would later emphasize, it was not so much a matter of extravagant perks as, rather, a storybook lifestyle that was almost wholly subsidized.

To celebrate Atari's having broken the $1 billion mark in sales for 1981, Kassar elected to hold Atari's annual sales meeting, in the spring of 1982, not at a California resort as in prior years but in Monte Carlo, where they stayed at the fabled Hôtel de Paris. At Atari headquarters, Kassar installed a dining room, attended by waiters in formal attire, that was the culinary rival of the most exclusive restaurants in Silicon Valley. Atari's buildings were scattered over many different locations; so, in late 1981, Kassar and Gerard came up with a plan to build a fifty-acre "Atari campus" at a projected cost of about $300 million.

For Gerard, too, Atari was the mother lode. Other Warner executives would later recall that, in 1981, Manny Gerard was fond of remarking, "Atari is bigger than WCI." Some would argue to Gerard that the profit margins at Atari were excessive (cartridges cost $4 to $5 to produce, and sold wholesale for $20 to $23), and that they should be reduced, to forestall price competition. But Gerard would dismiss such suggestions, pointing out that Atari had 80 percent of the market. Brash and cocksure, Gerard had all the answers. And to the extent that Atari was to continue its nearly vertical trajectory, Gerard's star would rise concomitantly. Some in the company believed that by early 1982—based primarily on Atari— Gerard was the single executive in the company who might be positioned to succeed Steve Ross, someday.

Many in the company whose personal fortunes were not so bound up with Atari's, however, observed it with increasing skepticism. Roger Smith, who by 1981 was a vice-president for corporate affairs, wrote a memo in November 1981 urging that the company make a major acquisition for stock (then at an all-time high), because of the "inherent volatility" of Atari's earnings.

Smith would later recall that Ross agreed with this assessment. For as Atari, quarter by quarter, had risen to dizzying new heights, Ross continued to feel that it was apt to be a fad which one day would (perhaps suddenly) subside, and so, even in its most halcyon times, he had contemplated ways of hedging WCI's bet. During 1981, he had considered taking Atari public (a variation on his earlier notion of forming a partnership with another company, such as IBM); by early 1982, in fact, Salomon Brothers prepared a preliminary prospectus, in which 20 percent of Atari would be sold to the public for roughly $600 million—and the plan was, eventually, to sell up to 50 percent. But none of these hedging maneuvers to protect the company was ever carried out—and Atari, meanwhile, continued to grow to the sky.

By the end of 1981, however, Ross began taking steps that (though they may have been influenced by other factors as well) would result in protecting himself, financially, if Atari were to suffer a reversal. He moved WCI shares he owned into a family partnership, in preparation for their sale in a way that would benefit the company from a tax standpoint, and also would provide an advantage to him. This would be the first time since Kinney Service had gone public in 1962 that Ross would sell his stock. His intention was disclosed publicly on April 30, 1982, when the WCI proxy stated that "in December 1981 the Company was advised by Steven J. Ross of his intent to sell approximately 360,000 shares of Common Stock of the Company for personal financial and tax planning reasons." As one long-time WCI executive commented of Ross generally, "I have watched Steve play blackjack—and it always impressed me that he knew when to leave the game."

By the time Ross disclosed his intention to sell, there was a growing conviction on Wall Street that Atari's star was falling; in May 1982, the *Wall Street Journal*'s "Heard on the Street" column echoed a wide refrain, asking: "Is the home video game market close to saturation?" Many traders, convinced that Atari would not be able to sustain its growth, were aggressively shorting WCI stock. And Capital's Gordon Crawford—who had brokered the sale of Atari to WCI, and had been so close to WCI management for the past decade that he was treated almost as part of the family—was foremost among the pessimists.

He would later say to me that he had started selling Capital's WCI stock in January 1982, and by August he had unloaded the entire position. Crawford claimed he was reacting primarily to what he had seen at the Consumer Electronics Show (CES) that February (although he began selling the month before). "There were three or four new video hardware systems, and about fifty new software systems—all the warning lights went on for me. Then, at the June CES show, it was worse! There were about two hundred software systems. This was a business where the year before it had been essentially a monopoly, and now there were literally hundreds of new entrants." By this time, WCI stock "was almost a game stock," Crawford added. "When you went to a meeting, no one talked about the movies the studio was making; they talked only about Atari." Crawford said he was able to sell WCI stock at prices ranging from about $60 to $45 a share.

Atari's boosters, attempting to counter the ever more prevalent dooms-day view, pointed to the record earnings of Atari's first quarter, produced in large part by the overwhelming hit of "Pac-Man"—12 million car-tridges were shipped, with sales of over $200 million. Later, Gerard would say that the "Pac-Man" experience "lulled us into a false sense of security." But that singular bonanza was no convincing rebuttal to the arguments of Wall Street; nor did it mitigate the growing concern of many executives within WCI.

As Atari had grown mammoth, its system of distribution had become a bone of contention at WCI. Atari's products were being distributed through a network of independent representatives—in flat contravention of what had become, over the years, one of Ross's bedrock precepts: that WCI should control its products from inception through distribution. Not only would owning the means of distribution maximize control over the products' destiny, but it would enhance the company's power in a variety of ways; for example, a distributor can become so important to a retail outlet that it will accept the company's weaker products as well. Shortly after WCI had acquired Atari, the idea of its products being handled by the record companies' distribution arm, WEA (Warner Elektra Asylum) had been discussed with Nesuhi Ertegun, the president of WEA Interna-tional, and Henry Droz, the president of WEA's domestic unit. At that time, however, there was no hint of what Atari would become, and the WEA executives had been unreceptive. After Atari achieved its metamor-phosis, Droz and others urged that WEA handle it, but by then Atari had developed its system of independent representatives, and Gerard and Kassar both vigorously opposed the idea.

Atari's was a system that appeared, superficially, to be working well enough in good times—millions of cartridges were being sold, after all —but was susceptible to many different varieties of exploitation. Ac-cording to Michael Moone, president of Atari's consumer electronics divi-sion, Atari customers were stealing truckloads from other customers. A company which was entitled to a half-truckload of product would instruct its employees to pull up to an Atari warehouse and say they had authorization to pick up a full truckload—and it would be done. Moone said such practices were occurring in March and April 1982.

Moone told me that he believed at the time that it would be better if WEA were to take over Atari's distribution, but that Ray Kassar had disagreed—a decision that Moone attributed to Kassar's exceeding protectiveness of his domain. As it was, the ills in Atari's distribution only spawned greater ills. Demand was enormous; but, in part because of the system's poor controls, distributors were not assured of receiving as much as they wanted. Therefore, Moone continued, "distributors would say to themselves, 'I think I can sell 100 dozen. If I order 100 dozen, I'll only get 50 dozen. So I'll order 200 dozen.'" Since they were all independent agents, their attitude, he added, was "Live for today, the hell with tomorrow."

As long as demand was outstripping supply, the damage done by such over-ordering was not so conspicuous. But to sharp eyes, there were signs of a build-up of excess inventory, certainly by the beginning of 1982. It was then that WEA had started distributing for Atari on a limited basis, only to music outlets. Even from this partial vantage point, however, Droz said he could see that "there *was* a glut in the marketplace. Throughout the entire year of 1982, there were signs that there was overselling. If you looked at the inventory, relative to the turns of that inventory, you could see it." In the spring, Droz outlined his concerns to Ross, and to Gerard. "We did have some discussions about it, but Atari insisted on calling its own shots. They were reluctant to accept outside comments," Droz added.

Given Atari's inadequate controls and torrential revenues, it is perhaps not surprising that the company was rife with stories of corruption. Distributors, operating in their own peculiar demimonde, were amassing great sums of money; one New York representative drove around the area in a black Mercedes limousine with the license plate "ATARI," another in a mauve-colored stretch limousine. An Atari executive based in the Orient was said to be making millions in secret arrangements for himself, so much that he could never be prevailed upon to return to a position at Atari headquarters, even at a much higher salary ("He couldn't take the paycut," his colleagues would deadpan). At one point, WCI's general counsel, Martin Payson, travelled to Taiwan to investigate reports he had received of Mafia intervention in Atari there.

According to several former executives of both WCI and Atari, Atari's head of marketing left for a time, and then returned as head of sales and distribution and turned his position to particular advantage. A former Atari executive told me that he discovered at one point that this person had sold an amount of inventory to his own marketing company at a very good price, and then to Macy's for twice that amount. "Atari had shipped it from its own warehouse straight to Macy's, so [the marketing] company never even took possession of it. When I questioned it, though, I was told, 'Well, that is a special arrangement that [he] had with Mr. Kassar.'"

Jac Holzman, who had sold his company, Elektra Records, to WCI, had become a director of Atari when WCI acquired it ("We used to hold our board meetings in Nolan's hot tub," Holzman recalled) and was a consultant to the division in 1981–82. In June 1982, Holzman says he wrote a letter to Ross in which he declared, among other things, that he was troubled about Atari—there was too much inventory mounting, as anyone in the record business could easily see, and he thought they should consider selling Atari. "I thought the game business was going to fall apart," Holzman said. "Anything that spikes like that is going to come down again. They had these clearly bloated inventories. They believed that cartridges would have a long shelf-life, but I was in the record business, and I knew better."

Holzman added that Bert Wasserman, WCI's long-time chief financial officer who had joined the Office of the President after Emmett's departure but would never truly relinquish his job as CFO, shared his pessimism. Another WCI executive also said that Wasserman had begun questioning the inventory excess by February. "Bert had experience with the record business," Holzman continued. "Games, unlike the record business, was a no-returns business—up until this point, Atari had not taken returns. But Bert knew it would have to. That should have been built into the structure, as it was in records—we *dealt* with returns."

The alarums that were reaching Steve Ross from within the company, then, were louder and even more compelling than those that were being sounded on Wall Street. Several executives close to him at the time recall, however, that he often seemed distracted, and was not nearly as focused on the business as he had been in earlier years. They attributed this, at least in part, to the ever-intensifying pressure of the Westchester Premier Theatre investigation: by 1982, Emmett had pled guilty, Solomon Weiss was facing trial, and Ross—who had only narrowly escaped being indicted along with Weiss—was still facing the very real threat of indictment. (Indeed, that threat may have been another factor in his determination to cash out a major proportion of his stock; a conviction could have compelled him to forfeit his WCI stock holdings.) And as the stock continued its downward slide in the late spring of 1982, moving into the 40s price range by June, Ross—who had recently announced his intention to sell but had not yet begun to do it—seemed to his lieutenants increasingly nervous about the stock price and generally disinclined to hear any bad news that might further affect it.

WCI's stock price was inextricably linked to Atari's profits. The two had risen in tandem, in an extraordinary levitation: the stock had shot up over 3,000 percent in just over six years. When WCI's earnings for the second quarter of 1982 were announced in late July, they had declined slightly from the spectacular first quarter (fuelled by "Pac-Man"), and, more importantly as far as securities analysts were concerned, they fell slightly short of the company's informal projections. As a former WCI executive explained, "What we did with the analysts was, we led them to predict earnings of, say, 27 cents when the earnings were going to be 29 cents. The idea was not to come in *under*, certainly, but also not to come in too much over, so as to make them look stupid. So we led them up to the edge.

"It was a very carefully managed system," he continued. "Typically in the fourth quarter, we would take writeoffs for films, predicting that they would be bombs, and then we would have extra earnings on hand when we needed them. I remember Steve once telling Fred Tepperman [who had been one of the company's auditors at Arthur Young prior to becoming its chief financial officer for a short time], 'Look, no one ever went to jail for understating earnings.' "

It was Bert Wasserman, he went on, who over the years had "masterminded" this process, holding back earnings in such a way as to "produce the even, stair-step progress that Wall Street loves—and that entertainment companies, by the nature of their businesses, just don't have." By 1982, Wasserman must have refined this to an art, for WCI had had an unbroken streak of seven years of quarters which beat the record of the same quarter in the prior year.

While the second quarter of 1982 comfortably cleared the hurdle set in 1981, it fell slightly short of the informal projections the company's representatives had made earlier to the analysts. This former WCI executive explained that they were fearful that the level of profits they'd been achieving was fast becoming unsustainable, and they were trying to draw back slightly. But there was to be no painless withdrawal. The Street reacted negatively, and the stock declined further, into the 30s.

One major securities analyst who—as a broker for large institutional holders—controlled a very significant amount of WCI stock, had been recommending it for years, and had a strong relationship with Ross, decided that he had to take WCI off his "recommended" list. "My guidepost was this: if after a long run a company's projected earnings were off even slightly for one quarter—no matter how management might explain it—I had to take them off the list. I called Roger Smith and I said, 'I'm taking you off.' He said, 'No! You can't! Steve will be so upset! You and Steve are so close—you can't do this to him!' "

While Smith invoked Ross, Ross himself did not call—something which impressed this analyst greatly, and made Smith's case all the more persuasive. "Steve in all the years *never* called to complain, or to suggest that I was wrong, that I should do something about the company. A lot of managers would complain to the Street, saying that the stock is priced too low, or whatever. But Steve never did. He was a very classy guy."

Against his better judgment—and without sharing his thoughts with any of his partners—the analyst broke his self-imposed rule and left WCI on his "recommended" list. Later, he would fault himself for having grown so close to the company, and especially to Ross, that he had allowed that emotional connection to cause him to deviate from what he was convinced, professionally, was the right thing to do.

At the end of July—with Ross still not having started to sell—WCI announced that it had been authorized by its board to buy in as much as 6 million shares of its outstanding stock. Such a decision reflects a bullish outlook on the part of a company's management, and will generally drive up the price of its stock, or at the very least keep it from falling further. As it turned out, the company purchased little of its stock; but in terms of bolstering a stock price, the announcement is generally the catalyst.

By August, the signs of trouble at Atari were increasingly plain to executives in corporate headquarters back in New York. The inventory problems that Droz and Holzman had reported months before now began to be reflected in financial documents. One budget projection prepared at WCI in July reflected an adjustment of $65 million for excess inventory at Atari. An inventory report, dated August 11 (and circulated to Manny Gerard, among others) stated that Atari held substantial excess inventories of virtually all of its cartridges. It was at about this time, too, that a WCI executive learned that, in an Atari warehouse in Milwaukee, there were "hundreds of thousands of these games, just sitting there." He told Gerard about it; Gerard first insisted it was not true, and then, after a conversation with Kassar, admitted that it was.

In mid-August, Bert Wasserman and Fred Tepperman, who had recently joined WCI as its chief financial officer, went to Sunnyvale. "They went out there," one of their colleagues said, "because they weren't getting the numbers." Kassar would later testify in an SEC deposition that "Mr. Tepperman and Mr. Wasserman came to Sunnyvale, to kind of get a financial update, and I think that the August revision developed from those meetings." The revision, dated August 24, cut Atari's projected earnings for 1982 by 23 percent from the level Atari had projected the previous May.

Kassar attributed this reduction to the presence of competition—something which had, of course, been plainly visible six months earlier. "Suddenly, Coleco was out with a new game which they announced in February," Kassar testified. "The Donkey Kong was beginning to get shipped. It was doing extremely well. Parker Brothers had introduced Frogger, a very big cart. Mattel was very active with rebates. Suddenly, you know—we had a pretty dominant market position and suddenly everybody was coming after us. It was generally known, back in the summer."

Two days after the August 24 revision—and weeks after the company's announced intention to buy in its stock—Ross began to unload his shares, and he continued to do so through early November. Another major seller in the upper corporate ranks of WCI during this period (according to documents in subsequent shareholders' suits) was Wasserman, who had also sold 8,000 shares the previous March but who, in June, above all July, and the beginning of August sold over 40,000 shares, for gross proceeds of over $2.2 million. Gerard was the other biggest seller in this period: from March through June, he had sold 21,000 shares; then, in July, he sold 50,000—roughly $3.5 million worth of stock. Additionally, six other high-ranking corporate officers (at least several of whom, like Ross, Wasserman, and Gerard, were cognizant of the trouble at Atari) sold in the July–October time frame, though in far less significant amounts. (One who may not have heard the emanations of concern was Caesar Kimmel, who in May, August, and September sold a total of 18,000 shares—a fraction of his large holdings—for gross proceeds of nearly $900,000. Kimmel was said to have been angry, later, that he had not been alerted to what Ross and others apparently knew.)

Meanwhile, steps were being taken, at WCI corporate headquarters, and also out in Sunnyvale, to ensure that the third quarter would be a recordbreaker. "After we saw how badly the Street reacted to our drawing back in the second quarter, we pumped it out for the third quarter," a former WCI executive said. It would subsequently emerge, in shareholders' litigation, that Atari had asked one of its major retailers, K mart, to accept shipments earlier than had been scheduled by receiving its full order on October 1. It was also decided at WCI, sometime in September —very late in the third quarter—to add a week to that quarter: 1982 was a 53-week year; one quarter, therefore, would necessarily have 14 weeks.

Typically, however, the extra week would be put into the fourth quarter. What was particularly resonant here was not only the fact that it was put into the third quarter instead, but that the decision to do so was made in the last weeks of that quarter.

Gerard would subsequently testify in a deposition in shareholders' litigation that Wasserman and Tepperman had discussed this decision with him in September; he said he did not know if Ross had had input into it. But, as one former Warner executive said, "That year, the message from Steve was, 'Guys, make sure the stock stays up, I've got to get my house in order.' Steve may not have *had* to tell Bert to put that extra week into the third quarter. Bert and Fred may well have just been responding to the psychological climate. Believe me, nobody wanted to walk into Steve's office with the news that the third quarter wasn't going to be what they'd said."

When the third-quarter results came in, they were record-breaking— as a WCI press release on October 18 trumpeted, "the best quarterly earnings in WCI history." The release quoted Ross saying, "Atari's continuing rapid growth resulted in another outstanding performance for the Consumer Electronics division . . . [it] continued to experience dramatic growth, as retail demand for its Video Computer System programmable game and related cartridges increased substantially in both domestic and foreign markets."

With these results, the stock price was finally boosted into the high 40s and, within a week or so, the low to mid-50s. Ross, who had begun unloading in late August in the $39–$40 price range, had continued to sell through September and early October, mainly in the $40–$41 range. A week before the announcement of the third-quarter earnings, the stock price had finally jumped into the mid-40s (in well-cultivated anticipation of what was forthcoming), and Ross continued to sell. In the peak price period, from October 19—the day after the announced earnings— through November 2, Ross sold more than 193,000 shares. In all, he sold roughly 479,000 shares, for total proceeds of more than $21 million. Furthermore, he sold about 120,000 more shares than the proxy had stated was his intention.

As Atari moved into the fourth quarter (historically its strongest, because of Christmas), its biggest new product, being introduced through an enormous, costly marketing campaign, was a game cartridge, "E.T."— a take-off on the movie, which had opened in the summer of 1982 and was the largest-grossing motion picture ever made. Its director and co-producer was Steven Spielberg. By mid-1982, Spielberg and Ross had become good friends; and, according to several people involved with

Atari at the time, it was Ross and Spielberg who made Atari's deal for "E.T."

The two men had met in 1981. By that time, Spielberg was an established wunderkind, who had directed *Jaws*, written and directed *Close Encounters of the Third Kind*, and directed *Raiders of the Lost Ark*, among others. Spielberg had started out at the age of twenty with an exclusive term contract at Universal, and over the years he developed an almost filial relationship with Sidney Sheinberg, the CEO of MCA (Universal's parent company). Virtually all his movies (with the notable exception of *Close Encounters*) had been made there.

According to several people close to Ross, he was determined to find a means to loosen the Universal-Spielberg bond and bring Spielberg to Warner Brothers. Spielberg would have been an alluring asset for the Warner studio at any time, but the early eighties were especially fallow. Ashley, Calley, and Wells, the triumvirate who had led the studio to banner years in the seventies, had departed. In the late seventies, WCI had formed joint ventures with Orion (created by five former executives of United Artists Corporation) and Ladd (created by three former executives of Twentieth Century-Fox Film Corporation) to produce feature films to be released by Warner Brothers. Robert Daly, whom Ross brought in from CBS to run the studio in the latter part of 1980, soon concluded that the arrangements with Ladd and Orion had only led to warring factions in what had become a tripartite studio, and movies that were unimpressive; the Orion and Ladd deals were eventually terminated. In any event, it was not until 1983 that Warner Brothers began to regain its luster, after several very lean years.

In the WCI family, the studio was the favorite child. Employees in other divisions would often resent this favoritism; even at Atari, the company's star performer, Steve Ross was a legendary but rarely glimpsed personage. But the studio was his home away from home; he loved everything about it—its romance, its product, its stars. By now, Ross had become more of a movie maven than ever. In his leisure time, he never read—but he always watched movies; from the early seventies on, his homes featured elaborate screening rooms, where he watched movies on 16-millimeter film, never videotape. And when the studio was faltering, in the early eighties, he assumed (far more than during the Ashley regime) the role of an anxious parent.

Indeed, in a deposition taken from Ross several years later, he would testify that during 1982 he spent more of his time on Warner Brothers than any other division. Jay Emmett, who had left WCI when he pled guilty in February 1981, had, of course, been the person in the Office of the President who had overseen the studio. By way of explaining his own preoccupation with Warner Brothers during this period of time, Ross testified that "a prior fellow who Warner Brothers reported to was no longer with us so there was a dramatic shake-up so that I followed Warner Brothers very closely."

The idea of wresting Spielberg away from his home base at MCA would have had an added charge for Ross, moreover, because MCA—presided over for decades by Lew Wasserman, the unrivalled patriarch of the entertainment industry—had long been the paragon, the one against which other entertainment companies measured themselves. Wasserman, too, had always viewed Ross rather coldly, with a hint of disdain—and more than just the natural wariness of a competitor. So, while it would be sweet indeed to win Spielberg for Warner Brothers, it would be ineffably sweet, in so doing, to uproot him from MCA. One former Atari executive recalled being in Steve Ross's office in New York when Ross learned that Universal had just hired Kathleen Kerry, Spielberg's then-girlfriend, who had previously been in music publishing at Warner Brothers, to work at its Backstreet label. "Steve slammed the phone down in a rage, and he said, 'They've hired Kathleen Kerry! I can't believe it! Now, what can we do?' "

Spielberg and Ross met at a four-day weekend at Villa Eden in Acapulco in early 1982. It had been arranged by Terry Semel, who had been a good friend of Spielberg's since the mid-seventies (someone Spielberg describes as "kind of an older brother"), and who, after running Warner Brothers' distribution for years, was made president of the studio in 1981.

"Terry said, you should meet Steve Ross," began Spielberg, recalling that first encounter. "I had typecast what a CEO was—I'd never met one before, and I wasn't far off, because I've met them since—and in my mind, they looked like J. C. Penney. And suddenly here was this older movie star. We quickly found out what we had in common: my favorite movies were made between 1932 and 1952 and those were his favorites, too. Steve to me was a blast from the past. He had silver-screen charisma, much like an older Cary Grant, or a Walter Pidgeon. He had style in a tradition that seems to have bred itself out of society. He had flash. He was a magnetic host—eventually, that became his calling card. And at Acapulco, he *was* the weekend.

"I asked him, how did you get started—and he sort of smiled, and said, 'Well, it's a long story'—and then he told the story from the funeral homes on. It went through lunch, cocktails, dinner—that was my primer in Steve Ross. I thought it was a movie! Rags to riches—or, riches to rags to riches—because Steve had such natural style, to start with."

The friendship evolved from there. And while Spielberg would indeed come to do movies at Warner Brothers, he would adamantly insist, years later, that it was a "friendship without agenda," that Ross had not set out to romance him with a business purpose. "I had been told, 'Watch out for Steve Ross, he is only being your friend so you'll make movies for Warner Brothers.' And I was cautious for the first year. But he never did ask me. Over the years, I had Bob [Daly] and Terry [Semel] coming, saying, 'When are you going to do your next picture?' Steve never did."

In the summer of 1982, when the issue arose at MCA of licensing *E.T.* to a video-game manufacturer, Sidney Sheinberg would later recall, "Steven [Spielberg] had promised Steve Ross that he would have the first opportunity to acquire it. Steven wanted Atari to have it." Sheinberg said that he had had discussions with Coleco Industries, as well as another manufacturer, and he believed that he might be able to make a deal in the range of $15–$20 million. That, in any event, is what he told Charles (Skip) Paul, the president of Atari's coin-operated games division, when Paul came to see him.

"I offered MCA $1 million and 7 percent of royalties, which was far more than Atari had ever paid before for a license," Paul said. "And I was thrown out of Sid's office.

"Then I was told that the deal had been done over a weekend, at East Hampton, between Steve and Steven—and that it was for $23 million," Paul continued. "I thought, 'Yes, I understand the $1 million. But what is the other $22 million for? It must be for some other reason.' "

Kassar, who had very little contact with Ross, learned about the "E.T." deal when Ross called him. "He said, 'I've made a deal with Spielberg to make a game out of *E.T.*—what do you think?'

"I said, 'Okay. We've never made a game out of a movie before. But, okay.'

"Then he said, 'Part of the deal is, Spielberg says it has to be out for Christmas.'

"I said, 'It *can't* be.' This was July. With the lead time of delivery, it meant doing the game in four or five weeks, instead of our usual six months.

"He said, 'Also, I've guaranteed a $23 million royalty.'

"I said, 'We've never guaranteed a royalty! This is terrible!'

"And he said, 'Well, it's done.' I think he was annoyed at me for not saying how wonderful it was," Kassar concluded.

What Atari had bought was the right to use the title, "E.T.," and also its image; engineers at Atari, with Spielberg's input, were now to design a game. The project, however, was blighted from inception. Its engineers told Kassar the movie wasn't suited to become a video game ("They said that it was a lovely, sweet movie, and kids like to *kill* things," Kassar recalled). Once the game was done, it was established in focus groups that, in all likelihood, the company would be able to sell only one third of the 4 million that were slated for production (a quantity that Atari needed to sell in order to make a profit, considering the costs of the guaranteed royalty, production, and advertising).

"E.T." exceeded the most dire predictions. According to Kassar, of the 4 million they shipped, about 3.5 million were returned. "It wasn't a game," Paul recalled ruefully, "it was a thing waddling around on a screen." It was shipped in time to be on stores' shelves for Thanksgiving weekend—typically a significant retail weekend, the start of the Christmas season. But the news on "E.T."; on another new cartridge, "Raiders of the Lost Ark"; and on the rest of Atari's games, as well as its new, much-delayed home computer, known as the "5200," all became increasingly stark by the beginning of December. .

On November 17, Atari revised its projections downward for the fourth quarter by $81 million; this reduced Atari's predicted fourth-quarter net income by more than 50 percent from the August forecast. Now, Gerard asked for another fourth-quarter forecast, and on the evening of December 7 he was given it. There was a further revision downward of $53 million.

While the November reduction was considerably larger—and while that forecast had predicted that Atari's fourth quarter would be its worst quarter since early 1981—WCI had issued no press release, as Gerard would later testify, because even after the November revision, "the corporation's earnings per share were in the range of the Street's estimates. You were not wildly out of range." But after the December revision, Gerard continued, "we clearly were in another ballgame."

As late as December 7, WCI executives—despite the November 17 revision at Atari—were still assuring analysts of a strong fourth quarter and a 50 percent earnings rise for 1982. On December 8, however, the whole overreaching, ill-supported construct gave way.

WCI issued a press release, stating that its earnings for 1982 would be well below previous expectations, and that a major factor was lower earnings in its consumer electronics division; instead of profits increasing by 50 percent, they would increase by only 10–15 percent. It was estimated that WCI's earnings for the fourth quarter would be roughly half the level of fourth-quarter earnings in 1981—thus ending a dramatic, unbroken string of thirty quarters, each of which had beaten the record of its analogue the previous year. Overnight, WCI's stock—which topped the most active list on the New York Stock Exchange, even though it opened late for trading—fell a dizzying 17 points.

Since the summer of 1982, Ross had been involved in an attempt to acquire the Madison Fund, Inc., a closed-end investment company. The deal, in which Madison shareholders would exchange their stock for WCI securities, and WCI would then sell off Madison's portfolio of stock, had been conceived as a way for WCI to gain access to about $500 million in cash—something that Ross had been prescient enough to target as a priority back in July. The transaction had been announced on October 7, and a definitive acquisition agreement—based on the market value of WCI stock, then trading at about $55 a share—reached on November 12. In the aftermath of the Atari crash in mid-December, however, with WCI stock trading at about $35 a share, the deal—and the $500 million in cash —were hanging in the balance.

It was George Gould, CEO of the Madison Fund and former chairman of the Wall Street firm of Donaldson, Lufkin & Jenrette, who had approached Ross with this proposal. "I asked my investment bankers to find a company which had had up-earnings for five years and a double AA-rated balance sheet, and they came up with Warner Communications," Gould recalled. "It just happened that Warner's had had *seven* years up."

Gould, who would later become Under Secretary of the U.S. Treasury in the Reagan administration, spent a fair amount of time with Ross. They socialized a little; Gould and his wife were Steve's guests at a gala dinner, held in September 1982, where Ross was honored by *Ad Age* as "Adman of the Year." But Gould, easygoing and genteel, found Ross consistently opaque. "He was somewhere different than where I've ever lived. I had great trouble understanding him—his standards, the way he looked at life, what was important to him. He's *different.* Even when you make a lot of effort to get at Steve Ross, and talk to him about his children, or his marriages, or public policy issues, he seemed not terribly interested in any of this. He was clearly talented and bright, but he lived in a narrow world—entertainment. He was Hollywood, flamboyant—there's something about having those jets and helicopters, walking around with this big bodyguard, like a character in a movie...."

Gould's sense of Ross as essentially alien and impenetrable only served to exacerbate his uneasiness about the Westchester Premier Theatre investigation. Solomon Weiss's trial—and Nick Akerman's charges in his opening statement about Ross, which made headlines—occurred while the Madison Fund negotiations were taking place. "My directors were very concerned," Gould said. "But Liman, who had been my lawyer in the past, reassured me that Steve Ross was not involved. Arthur said he'd dealt with Ross for a long time and never had seen a lack of integrity. And Arthur had warned me off of deals or people before, so I trusted him."

Although Gould and his advisers had been conducting their due diligence investigation of WCI, they had seen nothing that hinted of trouble at Atari. (After the announcement on December 8, Gould recalled, "My own directors said Ross must have been lying to me.") When the price of WCI shares plummeted, it decimated the value of the warrant in the securities package that the Madison shareholders were to receive. "We couldn't agree on a revised set of terms because we couldn't quantify the problem," Gould continued. "Ross was dead wrong. It was clear to me that the first stumble was not going to be the last, but I couldn't get him to see his numbers were wrong.

"It was so hard to get him to focus on what Atari was going to mean, analytically. He just didn't see the dynamics of the deterioration of the business. They hadn't *sold* those video cassettes, they had shipped the dealers potfuls of them on what I would call consignment—because what the dealer didn't sell he had a right to return. It was plain they were going to get potfuls of returns—and they had not calculated for that.

"But Ross thought it was a blip. He couldn't see that it wasn't a blip—it was a sea-change."

Finally, feeling compelled to abort the transaction, Gould had a long lunch with Liman on the day before Christmas. "Arthur pleaded with me not to cancel the deal. He said, 'George, you and I are old friends—let me talk to you here. . . . I am telling you that Steve will turn it around.'"

Despite Liman's exhortation, Gould refused. By mid-1983, the sea-change that Ross had professed not to see was engulfing WCI, and Gould felt that he and his shareholders had only narrowly escaped disaster.

For Ross, there was an unhappy convergence between the news from Atari—deniable no longer—and the latest outcome of the Westchester Premier Theatre investigation. Solomon Weiss had just been convicted, and on December 13, 1982, five days after the Atari announcement, Akerman declared at Emmett's sentencing that the "real culprit" was Ross, and that the investigation of him was continuing. It was a delicate moment. Only a month before the Atari news broke, Ross had finished selling his WCI stock for roughly $21 million—something he had done while he and his executives had been zealously touting the stock to securities analysts. Had the SEC commenced an investigation of Ross for stock manipulation and insider trading at the same time that he was under threat of indictment in the Westchester scandal, the odds of his prevailing on all fronts—against the U.S. Attorney's Office, the SEC, and the most cataclysmic crisis of his business career—would have been significantly diminished.

As it happened, however, there was a far more clear-cut (albeit comparatively insignificant) case of abuse for the SEC to focus upon. Raymond Kassar had sold 5,000 WCI shares on December 8, before the public announcement was made, and Dennis Groth, Atari's chief financial officer, had sold some 6,000 shares on December 1. There had also been selling by four other high-ranking Atari executives in the several weeks before December 8.

That WCI would report these trades to the SEC, given the surrounding circumstances, was appropriate. Ross, in a display of concerned corporate citizenship, took the matter a step further. On December 24, he announced that Kassar, Groth, and some other Atari executives had sold; and he said, further, that at his instructions, representatives of WCI and Atari had met with members of the SEC to disclose the trades. For its part, the Commission then released a statement saying that its policy was not to comment on what might or might not be the subject of an investigation.

The SEC commenced a thoroughgoing investigation of the Atari employees' trading. One former executive would later recall that in 1983, this investigation occupied about two thirds of his and other executives' time. "It was a very gut-wrenching time for the business, the worst possible time for something like that to be happening. People were there going through our files. Arthur Liman seemed to be always there—he spent a lot of time preparing us." This person added that 1982 bonuses were withheld from the Atari employees until after they testified at the SEC.

The investigation culminated with consent decrees entered into by Kassar and Groth, who were also compelled to disgorge the profits from their illegal trades. That the SEC focused only on trading that had occurred from mid-November on—ignoring what was done slightly earlier by so many high-ranking WCI executives, Ross foremost among them (and never even taking Ross's deposition in the course of their investigation)—was attributed, by several close to the investigation, to the deftness of Liman, who is said to have so successfully steered the SEC's inquiry that it amounted to an almost collaborative effort.

It was therefore left only to the plaintiffs' lawyers in the shareholders' litigation to explore what motivated Ross and some of his colleagues to sell their stock in 1982, and whether they were deliberately misleading shareholders while they sold. These suits never came to trial, however; by September 1984, the parties had reached an agreement in principle to settle. And while Ross's deposition *was* taken here, he was made available only after the settlement accord was essentially in place, roughly two weeks before both sides appeared in court to present it. As one of the plaintiffs' lawyers, Melvyn Weiss, explained to me, it was a "confirmatory" deposition—where it was understood by all sides that they were adversarial no longer.

What transpired, therefore, was more shadowboxing than a real match. At times, Weiss, who conducted most of Ross's examination, seemed to be prompting him quite as helpfully as Liman was. Questioning Ross about the meeting with Gerard on December 8 when Gerard told him of the latest numbers from Atari, Weiss asked, "Do you recall your emotional reaction to what he told you?"

"Shock," Ross replied.

"Shock?"

"Yes."

"How about anger?"

"Anger, shock, upset."

"But definitely anger?"

"Yes."

"What were you angry about?"

"That this could happen."

"Were you angry at not being made aware earlier of things that were happening?"

"I was angry that something like this could happen. How could it happen? I think the most shocking thing, and it was much more shock than anger, and perplexing thing was that I had remembered vividly being told that everything is great, we just shipped 98 and a half million dollars in a one-week period.

"It was an unbelievable shipment. I don't know of many companies that could make that shipment in the world, that amount of goods, and for Atari it was a great shipment.

"It happened several weeks before that, so I was shocked."

Even in this friendly match, however, Ross's sworn statements about his lack of knowledge or, at least, recollection, were striking. He claimed not to have been aware that an extra week had been put into the third quarter of 1982 until the day before his deposition, when he was shown a document illustrating that. Asked if he knew who had made the decision to include the extra week, Ross replied, "I assume the accountant."

He testified that he had no recollection of anyone's telling him that the income results for WCI for the summer of 1982 (July 1–August 31) were low. The earnings for the second quarter (with only one month remaining) were only 9 cents by August 31, and it was a quarter for which earnings were projected to be in the $1.09 range—but he had no recollection of that. Nor did he recall a $65 million writedown of Atari inventory in July 1982, or an internal audit report, written in early November, that discussed that writedown. He also had no recollection of having discussed with anyone what the third-quarter results might be; or the decision that was made then to reverse certain writeoffs, totalling roughly $6 million; or the impact of adding the extra week (which, once again, he testified he had never known about).

In response to questions regarding documents which showed that inventory and receivables' levels were remaining high at Atari in mid-1982, Ross repeatedly attributed these high levels to Atari's expanding business.

Weiss, in a sudden, reflexive surge of combativeness, asked: "Did anybody ever suggest to you that inventory levels can remain high because of a slowing down in business?"

"No," Ross testified.

"Because you can't push the inventory out the door and because customers aren't paying their receivables in as timely a fashion as they previously had. Nobody ever discussed that with you?"

"No," Ross repeated.

Ross clung tenaciously to his sworn conviction that Atari's increase in inventory denoted only expansion. Weiss then showed Ross documents indicating that sales forecasts were going down as inventory was increasing, and read aloud a note on one document: " 'Atari's inventories were up due primarily to the purchase of raw materials under purchase commitments which could not be cancelled and inventory imbalances.'

"Why," Weiss continued, "would one want to cancel purchase commitments in a booming enterprise?"

"I haven't the slightest idea," Ross replied. And though this document had been sent to him, Gerard, Wasserman, and Tepperman, he testified that "I have no recollection whatsoever of anyone discussing it with me."

The issue of Ross's sale of WCI stock was taken up only at the very end of the deposition, by Weiss's colleague, Ralph Ellis. Ross testified that in 1981 he had determined to sell roughly 350,000–370,000 shares of WCI stock because "I owed a considerable amount of money and will on taxes due to the exercise of tax [sic] options. A considerable amount. The options I had to exercise." He added that he had to exercise them because they were expiring, either in December 1981 or January 1982.

Ross further stated that he wanted to garner $18 million—"to reduce my liabilities of which a large part were tax liabilities." And he said that ultimately he had sold about 100,000 more shares than he had first planned, because the price of WCI stock had fallen—so he had to sell more to achieve his requirement of $18 million.

Ross also took this occasion to register a protest about the change in the tax laws which, he declared, defeated the purpose of stock option plans—to enable employees to own equity in the company over a long period of time. Since the tax liability now ensues when the options are exercised, he continued, one is forced to sell in order to pay taxes on the exercised options—as he, in this case, had had to do.

All reasonable enough. Except that it was not true. Ross had had no options left to exercise by December 1981; he had exercised his last batch about a year before. These options, moreover, had been a type that did *not* incur any tax liability upon the date of exercise—only upon their sale. He had transferred them into a family partnership, Tomaro, in December 1981, which did result in his incurring a tax liability at that time (the transfer triggering the liability as a sale would have), but that transfer had been a purely volitional act.

Volitional and, of course, advantageous. Once he had decided that he wanted to sell a major portion of his stock, Ross had had a choice. He could have sold very low-basis stock he had held for a long time, on which he would have had to pay capital-gains taxes (roughly 30 percent on the gain, which would have been large because of the low basis). Or he could have sold his option shares, which—since he would not be waiting the requisite three-year period from their date of exercise— would be taxed not at capital-gains but at ordinary-income rate (roughly 50 percent). By his selling these option shares at this time, however, the company would be enabled to take a $12 million tax deduction.

Ross sold the option shares. The company—in appreciation of his affording it the tax deduction—agreed to pay him $1.8 million (the difference between the capital-gains rate at which he would have been taxed had he sold his low-basis stock and the ordinary-income rate at which he now was taxed). Thus, Ross was able to hold on to his low-basis stock, which in the event someday, say, of a tax-free merger, could be exchanged for full value (and the tax avoided). He was able to pay no more tax than he would have paid if he had held the option shares for three years; and, this way, he was able to cut his downside risk in WCI stock and diversify his holdings, three years earlier. A cursory reading of the disclosure of this transaction in the WCI 1981 proxy statement would suggest that the company gained and Ross was made even, but that was not quite the case; it was, rather, that the company gained and Ross came out ahead.

When an objector to the settlement of the shareholders' litigation, Professor Elliott Weiss of Cardozo Law School in New York, pointed out that Ross's testimony about the need for about $18 million to exercise his options and meet his tax liability was inaccurate, Liman—after first declaring that Weiss was "mak[ing] up facts"—subsequently acknowledged that Ross's sworn statements about *why* he needed the $18 million were wrong. But Liman stuck to the notion that Ross had required the $18 million. He said that the tax liability Ross had incurred upon transferring the shares to Tomaro, combined with "Mr. Ross's other obligations, amounted to approximately $18 million, and to meet this indebtedness, plus the interest that accrued and was continuing to accrue, he needed over $20 million."

What was most bemusing here was that Ross and Liman, who had so many perfectly orchestrated performances to their shared credit, did not get their stories straight. Perhaps they had barely rehearsed, since they knew the case was to be settled. And while their versions were different, the theme was the same: both conjured up an image of Ross as someone whose actions—selling stock for a gross of $21 million just before the collapse—were dictated by circumstances beyond his control.

It is possible, however unlikely, that Ross, despite having received cash compensation in 1981 of over $10 million (more than $3.2 million in salary and bonuses, and about $7.4 million from his exercise of bonus units), found himself in a financial squeeze in 1981–82; and therefore possible, however unlikely, that his initial decision to sell a major portion of his stock was not primarily influenced by his doubts about Atari.

Even if that were true, however, it would not cure the problems inherent in his actions following that decision, which, taken together, are so suggestive of self-serving manipulation: ignoring his executives' warnings about trouble at Atari; bringing about the announcement that the company was authorized to buy in its shares; starting to sell after that announcement, and just two days after the August revision; letting it be known that everything should be done (as, indeed, it was) to make the third quarter a recordbreaker; continuing to drive the stock with raves on Atari while the evidence of the slowdown, at least, was mounting; and selling, selling, as the stock was driven ever higher. Which is, perhaps, why WCI paid about $17.5 million not to have to take this case to trial.

Melvyn Weiss, who has taken the depositions of hundreds of CEOs in his practice, would later say that Ross stood out from that crowd. "He didn't let his ego get in the way of his intelligence," Weiss said. "It is very hard for men in that position to continually say, 'I don't know,' or, 'I don't recall.' But he certainly did. Also, in a conversation that we had at the break, we touched upon his ability to predict the future, and immediately, instead of trying to portray himself as knowledgeable about public taste, he portrayed himself as a dummy. He said, 'I'm the worst at it! For example, the movie that I thought would do the best did the worst.' "

"I said, 'Really? Which one?' "

" '*Frisco Kid,*' he said."

"I said, 'Are you kidding? That's my favorite movie!' "

The next day, a videotape of the movie was delivered to Weiss's office.

O ver the years, Ross's family and friends would often remark on how extraordinarily lucky a person he was. They were not referring, as a more objective outsider might have, to his good fortune in not being indicted in the Westchester Premier Theatre investigation, or in not having been charged by the SEC in the Atari episode. They meant, rather, that in those situations altogether outside of his control, where there was no influence to exert, no plethora of levers to work—a sunny day for a planned picnic, say, or the right choice in roulette—Ross nearly always came out a winner. "Steve must have had a hot line to God," Spielberg said.

It was, moreover, an image of himself—that of the ultimate winner, really—that he cultivated. But even those who suspected an element of contrivance at times—his daughter Toni would note that she sometimes thought the reason he won so many raffles was that he purchased hundreds of tickets—ascribed to the notion that Ross's luck verged on the uncanny. It seemed, almost, as though he had charmed fate itself.

By the time of the Atari debacle, however, Ross's preternatural luck seemed to have deserted him. For the collapse of Atari came hard on the heels of successive traumas in his personal life. In early 1980, his son Mark, who had earlier been expelled from boarding school, continued to behave rebelliously at nineteen in ways that distressed Ross. While Ross's divorce and subsequent marriage to Burden were extremely difficult for both his children, Mark's reactions, as Toni would later express it, were "louder" than hers.

Then, in June of 1980, Ross had his heart attack. (He ordered that it be kept a secret, saying it would be "bad for the company," if it became public. Burden reportedly was instructed to tell people who called that he had a "bad back." The fact that he had had a heart attack at all was only acknowledged three weeks later, after he had been released from the hospital.) Until Ross suffered that attack, at fifty-two, he had lived as though he were exempt from basic physiological principles: he smoked several packs of Parliaments a day, exercised only sporadically, gorged on steak and eggs for breakfast. Now, however, he seemed to have recognized his mortality, if only in a glancing way; and, to the surprise of some family members, when Ross's doctors told him that he had a choice—he could go on smoking, or he could live—he believed them. From this time forward, Mickey Rudin's gold Dunhill lighter, which Ross still kept on him, was only for lighting others' cigarettes . . . and for luck.

Roughly six months after his heart attack, Amanda Burden left him. She would later tell friends that even during the excitement of their long courtship she had had misgivings; she would recall, for example, that on the long plane trip to China, when they travelled with the Cosmos, Ross and Emmett had played backgammon for endless hours and she had thought, then, that she would find it trying to be married to someone whose diversions were so limited. Another friend claimed that during this period Burden would sometimes disparage Ross for not having the cultural tastes that she did.

Burden had married Ross in a private ceremony in November 1979, after they had lived together for four years. About a year later, as part of Ross's recuperation, they went on a cruise aboard the QE2—an event that Burden would later tell friends was one factor in the break-up of their marriage: everything that he loved about it, she hated—and he didn't even realize it! Upon their return, they planned to move into a palatial apartment at 740 Park Avenue, which Ross had bought from Edgar Bronfman, Sr. Just as Ross, ten years earlier, had added a third floor to his Fifth Avenue apartment, building a terrace and screening room, so here, too, he added a third level—but since his apartment already occupied the top of the building, he had had to construct an additional level, making the building one floor higher.

Ross, as usual, was extending his reach toward something more unique, more outsized. But Burden reportedly began to see the apartment differently. Living there would mean she would have to maintain a large staff, much as her mother had done; she considered her mother's life extremely unhappy, and she is said to have worried, now, about recreating a similar lifestyle for herself. In the past year, she had begun working for the first time, in urban planning, and the experience had provided her a new sense of her own competence and potential. The apartment, on the other hand—and, increasingly, Ross himself—symbolized everything she didn't want. As she would tell a friend later, she felt that Ross and she had never really meshed as a couple. She remarked that she wished he could have been her uncle—he was so protective!—rather than her husband.

Ross is said to have believed that Burden was having an affair with her boss—something that he found even more maddening since he had helped her get her job. In any event, about a week after they moved into 740 Park, Burden moved out. Ross, who was unable ever to be alone, asked Guy Salvadore, whom he had known from the car-rental days, and who was now in charge of the company's fleet of limousines, helicopters, and planes, to move in with him. Some long-time friends were so protective of Ross, and so angry at Burden for what she'd done, that they stopped speaking to her. (Louis Marx, for one, who had been friendly with Burden before he met Ross, and who had entertained them at his Sarasota estate, never spoke to her again.) When it came to a divorce settlement, Ross abandoned his characteristic generous posture. Burden reportedly would later say that her settlement had been in the negative range, inasmuch as she had not even been able to retrieve her furniture from the apartment.

It was only about three weeks after Burden had moved out, moreover, that Jay Emmett pled guilty. Many of Ross's friends would say, years later, that these losses—of his most rapturous romance and of his best friend—were irreplaceable, and that Ross never regained the measure of happiness he had had when these two people were part of his life.

Ross moved instinctively to fill in the blank. Having been badly bruised—indeed, having *lost*, with Burden—he made what was widely interpreted as a safe move, one that would not entail emotional risk. Within less than two weeks of Amanda's exit, he asked Lou Rosen, who had remained friendly with Courtney Sale, to call her for him; he was abashed, having dropped her so precipitously. (Sale, for her part, had never lost touch completely with Ross; she had continued to see Mark, taking him out for lunch often in the intervening years.) Once the way had been paved by Rosen, Ross called Courtney himself, reaching her at a birthday party for her friend, Anne Ford. It was late in the evening, but Ross told her he was leaving shortly for Villa Eden, near Las Brisas; would she come? Sale is said to have hesitated, as a matter of pride, and consulted Anne and Charlotte Ford, who said, "Go!" And she did.

With Courtney Sale ensconced at his side, Ross embarked upon a new chapter. Carol Rosenthal and Amanda Burden had been dramatically different in many ways, but they had shared a marked imperviousness to the trappings of wealth. Both had been raised in families where there was an abundance of money (albeit in varying degree), and they had neither any hunger for it nor illusions about what it could provide. Indeed, each probably exerted a somewhat restraining influence on Ross. His daughter Toni, who took after her mother in this regard, was so embarrassed by his display that she used to beg him not to pick her up at school when she was attending New Lincoln (then on 110th Street) in his limousine. Later, when Ross was coming to speak to her film class at Wesleyan, she asked him not to land his helicopter on the campus; he obliged.

Sale, however, had a background that was in some ways much more similar to Ross's. Both came from families dominated by their mothers, where those strong, willful women, disappointed in their respective husbands' failures to provide the material comforts they coveted, fixed high expectations on the child that was the acknowledged family star—Steve, in the Ross family, and Courtney, or "Cody," as she was called, in the Sale family.

Courtney grew up in the small town of Bryan, Texas. Her mother, Gloria, had married E. B. ("Chick") Sale very young, and by the time Gloria was in her late twenties they had three small daughters. According to Vera Wyatt, who grew up with Courtney, Gloria's father bought a Coca-Cola bottling company; when he died, Gloria took over the business. "Gloria handed her children to the maid and took over the bottling company. She managed men and trucks all day, relegating E.B. to being a truck driver and Mr. Mom," Wyatt said.

"Gloria was this dynamo, with enormous physical charm. Bryan, you must understand, was a poor town, and most of the women dressed in clothes from Sears. But Gloria would come to work in alligator spike heels, a black Pauline Trigère suit, wearing gloves in the heat of a Texas summer.... Gloria had a collection of knock-out eighteenth-century silver. They lived in this modest ranch house—but they were the first ones in town to have dressing rooms.

"Gloria was one of the original strivers in the universe," Wyatt continued. "She was the first woman I ever saw to say, basically, I want control —this man [her husband] does not have the drive I do. Courtney ... was always her mother's favorite, and I think in a way Gloria was the harshest on Courtney, in terms of her expectations of who she would marry. I think she put on Courtney all her own disappointment that she hadn't married someone rich."

Sale, who had graduated from Skidmore in 1969 and pursued an interest in art, working in galleries, organizing exhibits, had dated many wealthy men over the years but had never married. Now, with Ross, for the first time she was able to begin to fund her proclivities. She was producing a documentary about the artist Willem de Kooning. Elaine de Kooning, who had been separated from Willem for many years, had recently returned to live with him and manage his affairs (about which de Kooning, in his late seventies, was increasingly vague). Soon, Courtney and Steve were courting Elaine de Kooning, inviting her to dinner in East Hampton and to accompany them on trips to Europe on the WCI jet; and soon, too, they were buying, mainly for WCI, a large number of extremely well priced de Kooning paintings. When Ross was with Amanda, he had bought a couple of paintings for the company, but art had never been his interest; now, under Courtney's tutelage, he began to build a collection with WCI funds, and within a couple of years, the company would have spent at least $8 million.

Courtney began to redo every available surface in Ross's life. He bought the house in East Hampton where he had lived with Amanda, and Courtney decorated it. She deplored the triplex that he had bought to live in with Burden as too ornate (it had been decorated in a traditional style, with French antiques). Instead, Ross bought a duplex in the same building and he and Courtney set out on European forays, mainly in Paris and Vienna, buying Art Deco pieces for the new apartment—as well as for his office at WCI. (According to one person, there were storerooms of additional pieces of Art Deco furniture that Ross had WCI buy at this time.) She also redecorated Villa Eden.

With Sale, then, Ross for the first time had a partner who ratified and even amplified his instincts for style and display. Hers was an informed sensibility, and his was not, but they shared a dedication to the acquisition of material objects, and to living on a grand scale, commensurate with the surroundings they created—in a way that neither of his former wives had.

Moreover, while neither Carol nor Amanda had sought the company of the Hollywood stars, those were the people with whom Courtney most wanted to socialize. Some who had befriended her when she had been supporting herself modestly, in the seventies, she is said now to have dropped. Instead, soon after she had rejoined Steve, Terry Semel, the president of Warner Brothers, was arranging weekends at Villa Eden with Steven Spielberg, Quincy Jones, and Barbra Streisand (the group made a movie of these outings). While Ross had always been infatuated with the stars, and had courted them lavishly when the occasion arose, he had not so assiduously cultivated them as friends before. Now he did so, and they became his circle.

There was a nice confluence, moreover, of Ross and Sale's art collecting, and their burgeoning relationships with the Hollywood set. Semel, describing the attraction that, in his view, Ross held for Spielberg at that time, began speaking of the allure that Ross had held for him, as well. "Steven [Spielberg] was a young man, in his early thirties, with no business sophistication," Semel began. "He found Steve, who was much older, so fascinating. Steve Ross was into things we knew only a little about— art, planes, homes.

"Courtney and he took some time off for a month and travelled through Europe and bought a lot of art—paintings, French Deco. She was an expert in collectibles. Steve and Courtney knew how to locate every painting—going with them to an auction was a great education. I remember in the early eighties Steve and I had to go to Paris, and my wife and I wanted to buy French Deco furniture. He knew everyplace to go. He knew every art dealer. Everyone knew him. He was totally wired. I would go to their apartment, and Courtney would say to me, 'Look at this artist. Go to this gallery.'

"Steve taught me how to buy art," Semel declared. "He always said, 'Buy the best—in furniture, in art, in real estate, in people. It will appreciate. A Picasso will appreciate. Why shouldn't you buy the best, when that's what you want?' "

If Spielberg was enthralled by Ross's talent for life, he was, of course, meant to be—Ross was courting him intensely, and the $23 million Atari deal for "E.T." was only one of many gestures. Spielberg would later declare that Ross was "the single most generous person I've ever met in my life. There are two kinds of generosity, the kind which involves putting names on buildings, and another kind, which is selfless and done in complete anonymity."

Describing the period in the early eighties when he and Ross were just getting to know each other (and when Ross, of course, had been frustrated to learn that Kathleen Kerry had been hired away from Warner Bros. by MCA), Spielberg continued: "My girlfriend, Kathleen Kerry, had become a 'special friend' to a very difficult nine-year-old boy, whom she would take out of the Holly Grove orphanage from time to time. She had been telling Steve and Courtney about him. Well, one day she got a call from the orphanage: why have seven color TVs, seven VCRs, and eight hundred pounds of Christmas presents arrived here with your name on it? She had no idea. She asked me if I'd done it. We wanted to make sure it wasn't a clerical error. And then I thought—could it be Santa Steve?

"I called him, he said, 'No. no.' Then there was this deep chuckle, and he said, 'Look, don't look a gift horse in the mouth.'

"He was like a Frank Capra movie."

And when Ross decided that he wanted Spielberg as a neighbor out in East Hampton, it was all arranged with one almost magical gesture. "Steve said, 'I want you to live here, to be my neighbor,'" Spielberg recalled.

"I said, 'But people live in these houses.'

"So we walked two doors down, rang the bell, and a woman in her eighties came to the door. Steve said, 'Hi, how are you? This is my friend, Steven Spielberg. I wanted you to know that I have a buyer—him—if ever you want to sell your house.' He had heard rumors that she might want to. Well, a week later, Steve's phone rang, and it was the broker for this woman. He said, 'I don't know what you did but she wants to sell to Spielberg.' Steve closed the deal that afternoon." Indeed, Ross did not wait for Spielberg to make up his mind definitively; according to one former WCI executive, the company bought the house immediately (much as, at Ross's direction, it had purchased Streisand's apartment from her several years earlier) and later sold it to Spielberg.

Spielberg did not move in for three or four years, however. Ross introduced him to the architect Charles Gwathmey, who designed a new structure on the property. During the construction, Spielberg said, "Steve would walk over and check on it once or twice a week. He would call me and say, 'Listen, I don't want anybody knowing that this came from me, but I think the windows are too small . . .'" And its interior was decorated by Courtney Sale, to Spielberg's great satisfaction. He declares her "the best decorator I've ever known."

Sale's attention to detail—and, always, to the very best, in true Ross tradition—was in full evidence at their wedding in New York, in October 1982, roughly twenty months after he had summoned her back into his life. Many claim that Courtney, at thirty-five, had grown nervous about losing Steve for a second time. Organized in just a few weeks, the wedding was a formal affair with over three hundred guests, among them the mainly familiar roster of celebrities, including Spielberg, Sinatra, Quincy Jones, Barbara Walters, and Cary Grant, as well as a sampling of New York's powerbrokers—Governor Hugh Carey, American Express chairman James Robinson, *New York Times* vice-chairman Sidney Gruson, Manhattan District Attorney Robert Morgenthau. Ross had wanted Arthur Liman, who was his best man, to perform the ceremony as well. Liman would recall later that Ross had been insistent, despite Liman's telling him that this was one rule they could not find their way around. When Nicole was born the following June, Liman would be her godfather.

The Grand Ballroom of the Plaza Hotel was transformed into an almost bucolic setting, decked with flowers, plants, and small trees. The music—ranging from a classical string quartet to an all-women's band playing forties pop—had been arranged by Quincy Jones. The dinner had been planned by the chef at La Côte Basque, and it was served not on the hotel china but on place settings purchased specially; the table linens, also, were Courtney Sale Ross's own, bought for the event.

One old friend of Courtney Ross, who later saw a wedding photograph of Gloria Sale dancing with Ross, commented on what a dynamic pair those two made—and how deeply gratified Gloria must have been by her daughter's match.

With his personal life thus reconstituted, Ross returned from a three-week honeymoon in Italy in early November 1982. One month later, the Atari announcement—and the avalanche of selling of WCI stock that it triggered—marked the opening of a period of deep, tectonic struggle, the most taxing by far of his career.

In January 1983, Ross was pictured on the cover of *New York* magazine, under the heading: "Steve Ross on the Spot—Can the Wizard of Warner Rebound?" Ross, who had always been leery of the press, cooperated with the writer, Tony Schwartz. (A former Warner executive told me that he had told Ross that he thought Schwartz was "susceptible to glitz" and that Ross should give him the royal treatment; Ross did so.) The piece was immensely favorable (Ross even managed to omit the fact that he had been a funeral director). It also gave considerable play to Ross's relationship with Spielberg—an early display of what would be the continued usefulness of that relationship to Ross. The article said that Spielberg "has several movies under way for Warner Bros., and . . . is inclined to do more." At one point, Spielberg, emphasizing what he said he saw as Ross's "child-like quality," declared, "I think of him as a six-foot-three E.T."

Schwartz afforded Ross every opportunity to present himself in the best possible light. With Atari, he had undeniably stumbled; but Schwartz included excerpts of statements Ross had made during the summer of 1982, which described his general philosophy and were his best defense (and it was far more advantageous for Ross to be quoted as having made these comments when the company was riding high than now when he would sound defensive).

I keep looking at businesses with a potential for a high return. I want room for error, and there's no room when you have a 1 percent margin. With a 15 or a 20 percent margin, you can overcome mistakes. If you look at the chief executives of most companies, you'll see that they're all managers, not people who built their own companies. A manager who hasn't built anything is more concerned with conserving his market share than he is with growing. He just wants to make sure his business doesn't get hurt. Well, that's the surest way of getting killed. It's like a car going up a hill. The first time you go into neutral, you're going backward.

If people complain that we're on a fast track, then we plead guilty to that. That goes with our management style. This is an autonomously run company. We do make mistakes, but that's because we believe in taking risks. The funny thing about the staid companies, the Rock of Gibraltar companies, is that a lot of them are having financial troubles today. Look at Chrysler and G.M. and International Harvester. Our balance sheet is as strong as it's ever been, and our growth record is hardly equalled.

(Interestingly, the posture of the outsider—and, especially, the derogatory references to "the Rock of Gibraltar companies" of the corporate establishment—echoed the kinds of statements that were already scriptural for Michael Milken, the Drexel Burnham Lambert financier who would soon be challenging that establishment. According to a former Warner executive, it was Liman who introduced Ross to Milken in mid-1982, and the two men quickly developed an enormous mutual admiration.)

Ross also took the opportunity, in the *New York* magazine article, to express his continued optimism about Atari. He was portrayed rallying the Atari team, like a good coach, at the January 1983 Consumer Electronics Show (CES) in Las Vegas. He emphasized, not surprisingly, that the trouble at Atari had come without warning. (" 'The week before Thanksgiving was the biggest in Atari's history,' he says. 'There was no hint that things would turn around so fast.' ") Mainly, though, he dismissed the dramatic shortfall as primarily a problem of perception rather than a harbinger of worse to come. " 'We made a fundamental error,' says Ross. 'If I'd said at the beginning of last year that we'd be up 10, 15, even 20 percent, our stock would be 45 or 50 today, instead of 30.' "

Several weeks after Ross's performance at the CES, which Schwartz witnessed and featured as the piece's lead, Ross flew out to Sunnyvale. It was one of the few occasions he visited there. WCI had held its annual meeting there in 1982, and Atari employees recalled that Ross had stopped a couple of times on his way to or from vacations in Hawaii, but there had been a general feeling that their glamorous chairman paid them little mind—despite the fact that they were the people who were pumping out nearly 75 percent of WCI's revenues by 1982.

Now, he excoriated the troops—and Manny Gerard and Ray Kassar, personally—and then departed. Several hours later, though, he was back. He said he'd told his pilot to turn around, because he was afraid he had demoralized everyone. One Atari employee recalled: "He came back and tried to give a Knute Rockne speech. But we just thought the whole thing was bizarre."

Kassar continued to give Ross rosy projections, and Ross continued to use them—even though Michael Moone, the president of Atari, would later say that he had told Ross he did not believe them. The first quarter saw a loss of more than $45 million at Atari. Roger Smith, who had been assigned to write Ross's opening remarks for the annual meeting in May 1983, recalled that Ross made it clear he intended to promise shareholders that Atari would return to profitability and that WCI's earnings for the second half of 1983 would exceed those of the second half of 1982. Before the annual meeting, in a meeting attended by company executives and outside lawyers, Smith continued, he had challenged Ross, saying that there was no basis on which to make such a promise.

"Steve said, 'But I have the projections.'

"I said, 'From the same people who gave us last year's projections. So far our ability as managers is questioned but not our credibility. We have to say we don't know.'"

Smith, of course, did not prevail. Ross made his promises—and was shortly proven wrong to a shocking degree. In the second quarter, Atari lost a staggering $310.5 million. For the year, the company lost roughly $500 million.

By mid-1983, it was plain that not just Atari but the whole video-game industry had crashed: Mattel had suffered enormous losses; Imagic was laying off a fourth of its work force; and many others who had entered the field the previous year had gone bankrupt. Ross, who had revived his old idea and started looking for a partner for Atari in early 1983, had been unable to find one. So, in the summer, efforts were made to take remedial steps at Atari. Kassar was fired, and James Morgan, a former executive vice-president of marketing at Phillip Morris U.S.A., took his place. Thousands of employees were laid off. And, too late, in what proved to be only a costly move, many of Atari's independent distributors were let go in favor of a better-controlled distribution network.

With Atari in this morbid state, there was a lingering bitterness among many of its employees about "E.T." and Ross's having forced it upon them. Years later, Charles Paul, who had become general counsel at MCA, would recall that "when I was at Atari, I believed 'E.T.' had been a terrible mistake. I knew it hadn't caused the downfall of Atari but it did throw gasoline on the fire. You *had* to build huge volumes, you *had* to get it out fast—all your chips were out, because of this incredible guarantee. And then, when the game was such a flop, there was this loss of faith with consumers. Now, they wanted to know if a game was going to be fun before they bought it; before, they just *wanted* it."

"But, today, I think it was a brilliant move by Steve Ross. He succeeded in breaking MCA's hold on Spielberg," Paul continued, pointing out that in the past decade, Spielberg's two major relationships had been with MCA and Warner Bros. "Steve's viewpoint was, so what if I overpay by $22 million? How can you compare that to the value of a relationship with Spielberg? And I think he was dead right."

Paul had fond memories of his own brief glimpse of what it was like to be courted by Steve Ross. It occurred at the gala Atari conference that was held in Monte Carlo in the spring of 1982. "I was a twenty-nine-year-old kid, and Steve invited me to come out for the day on this *big* boat. It was just Steve, Mickey Rudin, Manny [Gerard], and me. We sat around talking all day—Steve, Mickey, and Manny telling stories about the old days. Then we went back to the hotel and Manny called me and said, 'Put on a jacket and meet us downstairs in fifteen minutes.' I did—and Steve was there, and he took us with him to the Palace, to meet Princess Grace, Prince Rainier, and the children. And I just thought, 'Wow! What an incredible day!'

"I was completely seduced," Paul concluded. "He had me. That was Steve, thinking, 'Okay, I will have *this* heart, over here.'"

As 1983 wore on and Atari's losses mounted, however, Ross's expansive, romantic persona seemed to recede. Withdrawing behind a battery of secretaries, he became difficult for even senior-level executives to reach. Joe Smith, who had left Elektra Records and moved to New York to work on developing sports programming for cable: recalled, "Steve was spending a lot of time in the bunker in the spring of 1983. Bert [Wasserman] couldn't get to him, Marty [Payson] couldn't. But, on maybe four, five, six occasions, we'd walk uptown together, at the end of the day. And he was never despondent, always up. He'd be saying, 'Let's buy the Chicago Sports Channel!' And I'd be thinking, 'That will cost $30 million, how can we possibly do that?' "

In a sense, though, he should not have been so taken aback, Smith continued, inasmuch as he had always known that Ross felt compelled to keep up the morale of his troops. "The stock was always on a roller coaster—and I remember when it went way down in the early seventies, Steve said, 'This is great! The stock is down, now the company can buy it in!' And I said, 'Great, Steve. Should we root for it to go to fifty cents?'

"He was a charmer," Smith concluded, "but a little of the snake-oil salesman."

As much as Ross was trying to boost morale, of course, he was also putting on a brave front. Even those who knew him well for many years felt discomfited, at times, at not being permitted beyond the impregnable facade. But not showing vulnerability was Ross's self-imposed dictum, and WCI, his rationale—as it so often was—for his own idiosyncratic needs and desires. As one person who had a close personal relationship with him said, "Steve felt that he always had to be strong, that he could never show any crack. He would often tell me, 'If I show any vulnerability, the company will suffer.' "

Even in the good times, there had been unpleasant situations that Ross had not wanted to face. While the more senior-level employees who were not doing well at their jobs were rarely fired, but rather, shifted within the company, there was occasionally someone for whom there was no place. Harvey Schein, for example, had entered the company with the notion, encouraged by Ross, that he would join the Office of the President. After two years it was clear that Schein never would, and there was nothing for him to do; he tried to see Ross, to discuss his situation, but for about a year he could not get an appointment. Finally, he left the company.

In the past, too, Jay Emmett had always been there as Ross's buffer, and as the person who could ease a difficult situation. Now, that role was needed more than ever, but no one else had been able to assume it. As Terry Semel said, "Jay was the fun in Steve's life—and he also could tell Steve the truth. He could take the most horrendous situation and in ten minutes have everyone smiling. He could deliver the bad news to Steve —no one else could—and he didn't have to be politic, because he was secure in his relationship. They were like brothers. We all missed him."

With Atari losing more than $1 million a day, it was clear that the ranks at corporate headquarters, which had become bloated in the last several years, would have to be cut. But not, of course, by Ross (a person who so shrank from bringing bad news that he had not even been able to ask someone who had inadvertently taken his seat at a Cosmos game to move, but would ask Emmett or de la Sierra to do it, instead). Following his frequent practice of warehousing people, Ross in 1982 had hired Robert Morgado, formerly Governor Carey's chief of staff—although he had no clear idea of what Morgado would do. Now, it became clear: Morgado would be the company's hatchet man.

Ross, for his part, distanced himself from those who were marked for elimination. And, because of the intensely personal rapport that he tended to strike with so many of the people who worked for him, his withdrawal from them tended to be both unnerving and, ultimately, quite painful. After Emmett's departure, Ross had tried moving Roger Smith into that empty niche. Smith would start most days by spending a half-hour or so in Ross's office, and they took a few vacations together. Smith introduced Steve and Courtney to the glorious Hotel San Pietro, set in a cliff in Positano, Italy ("I knew Steve liked it when I came downstairs the morning after we'd arrived and found him negotiating to try to buy the hotel," Smith commented). For Smith's thirty-ninth birthday, in 1982, Ross gave him a watercolor of the hotel, painted by Elaine de Kooning. And at Steve and Courtney's wedding, Smith had been seated at their table.

By mid-1983, however, things had changed. Smith no longer started his day with Ross; in fact, he saw him very little. His office, which had been located nearby, was moved to a different floor. Carmen Ferragano, increasingly the medium through which Ross spoke, had told Smith, "Steve says, 'Tell Roger not to have a personality collapse; it's just office logistics.' But I knew better." He knew that his star had fallen; indeed, he was soon working out with Morgado his arrangements to leave the company. But what he did not know was why. He told himself, at the time, that it was because he had challenged Ross in front of others on the promises Ross was about to make regarding Atari at the annual meeting; but much later Smith would decide it had been nothing so specific. He and Ross would never discuss it.

Rafael de la Sierra, too, fell out of favor. After Chinaglia had taken over the Cosmos, de la Sierra had created a new position for himself: vice-president, international coordination. The various WCI divisions were run so autonomously that there was a great deal of duplication, and de la Sierra saw an opportunity for cost savings if the international branches were to share certain functions. Ross had had only a lukewarm response to his proposal, but when de la Sierra approached the executives in the various divisions, they supported the idea, so he was put in charge of its coordination. "Steve did not like it, though," de la Sierra recalled. "Let's face it, if people talk to each other, they know what is going on. He felt, unity creates strength—if you disperse them, they are weak. He *wanted* it completely decentralized. As it was, the left hand didn't know what the right hand was doing—only Steve knew."

For de la Sierra, a warm, emotional person, Ross was family. They had socialized a lot when Ross had been married to Carol, and they had done so even more when he was with Amanda because she and Alina de la Sierra grew so fond of one another. Now, however—with the Cosmos about to be folded, Amanda gone, and Ross socializing with his Holly-wood set—de la Sierra "had outlived his usefulness," as one of his peers expressed it. It may be, too, that Courtney Ross, now increasingly royal in demeanor, found him an unpleasant reminder of her plebeian past when she had worked under him in marketing at Jungle Habitat.

De la Sierra, in any event, was history. As was the case with Smith, however, his termination began with indirection. After he had been asked whether he wished to be included in the tax shelters fashioned by Ed Aboodi and offered to Ross's privileged circle of executives, and replied that he did, he was subsequently informed by an enigmatic Aboodi that he was "not on the list." He knew then that something was wrong, but when he tried to see Ross (in the old days he would just walk into Ross's office, unannounced), he was stopped by secretaries. He called Ross; Ross never returned his calls. He would pass him sometimes in the corridor, and Ross would say, heartily, "Raf! How are you?" and move on.

Eventually, Morgado told him the news: they were disbanding the international coordination post, and he could stay, but in a dramatically diminished position. He chose to go. But years later he would insist that it was the emotional rupture—and Steve Ross's strange evanescence—that was hardest of all.

"I loved the man," de la Sierra said. "My father was not available to me—my parents had divorced when I was eleven, and then I was in this country from the time I was twenty years old. Steve had given me opportunity, he had been kind to me. Then, suddenly, he withdrew. Why? I wanted to know. For years, I wanted to know."

Another person, describing Ross's pattern of pursuit and abandonment, commented: "He treated you like you were a mixture of son and trusted confidant and girlfriend—and then he dropped you! It was like he had cast out his net, and he'd caught you, and he'd gotten everything from you that he could until you were no longer of interest to him—and then he moved on."

In August of 1983, Rupert Murdoch, the Australian publishing magnate, asked Stanley Shuman of Allen & Co., who had advised him in several of his U.S. acquisitions, to arrange a meeting with Ross. "Steve wouldn't come in from East Hampton to see him. He said, 'Come out here'—and he sent the helicopter," said Joe Smith "Someone close to Murdoch told me, after their meeting, Murdoch was horrified. He said, 'This guy is living like Midas out on the Island, while his company is falling apart.' " In the course of their conversation, Murdoch said he would like to buy some WCI stock and Ross said, "Be my guest."

Several months later—when Murdoch's News Corporation had acquired 6.7 percent of WCI, in apparent preparation for a hostile raid—Ross would say that his gracious words that August day may have led Murdoch to "mistake kindness for weakness." Over the years, Ross had cultivated an extreme politesse, a kind of courtliness, that overlay the vestigial edges of the hustler; and that was indeed the manner in which he had responded to Murdoch's declaration of interest. Except, Ross surely had done so not primarily out of innate courtesy, as he was suggesting, but rather his instinctive calculation that to ask Murdoch *not* to buy the stock would have been an admission of vulnerability.

In December, Herbert Siegel, the chairman of Chris-Craft Industries, Inc., proposed to Ross a transaction in which Chris-Craft would become Ross's "white knight." Siegel, who in the sixties had owned and run a Hollywood talent agency, General Artists Corporation (which would later become ICM), had a proven instinct for entertainment and broadcast properties; he had acquired a major stake in Paramount Pictures in 1965 and had gone on the board; after being bought out, he had acquired Chris-Craft, the boat manufacturer which also owned television stations. Siegel and Ross had been neighbors in the Imperial House apartment building during those years and had known each other casually, but their real connection had come through Arthur Liman.

Liman had been Siegel's lawyer and friend for many years, and Siegel regarded him as a brother. Shortly after acquiring Chris-Craft, Siegel had made a tender offer for Piper Aircraft, which had turned to Bangor Punta as its white knight. Siegel had sued, charging securities law violations. "Herb had made a hostile bid for Piper, it was hard-fought, and he was perceived to be the loser," recalled Liman, who represented Siegel in that suit. "I desperately needed a businessman to testify about how someone in a 38 percent position could never win control—but you couldn't get many to testify for Herb. I brought Herb up to talk to Steve, and Steve testified. He was brilliant. Herb was very grateful, and very respectful of Steve's abilities." Even with Ross's assistance, Liman lost that case at trial; then he won on appeal, but ultimately lost in the U.S. Supreme Court.

Now, with Liman as the broker, Siegel and Ross agreed on a complicated transaction in which WCI would give Chris-Craft's TV subsidiary, BHC, 19 percent of its voting shares in exchange for a 42.5 percent interest in BHC. Chris-Craft's stake in WCI would make a takeover by Murdoch much more difficult; and, furthermore, WCI's entry into broadcast TV would in all likelihood pose a regulatory impediment to Murdoch, since U.S. regulations prohibit foreigners from owning TV stations. While other lawyers, including Joseph Flom of Skadden, Arps, Slate, Meagher & Flom, were involved in crafting this transaction, the primary representation—for both WCI and Chris-Craft—was by Paul, Weiss. It was an unusual approach, in which a law firm attempted to divide itself in order to assume, and then deal with, a position of conflict of interest—signalling the degree to which both sides trusted Arthur Liman, and recognized him as the author of the deal.

Murdoch responded angrily, declaring that Ross had entered a "marriage of convenience" in order to save himself and the company from a takeover. He sued, asking the Delaware federal court to order the WCI–Chris-Craft transaction reversed. News Corp. also sued WCI under racketeering and fraud statutes, citing the Westchester convictions, the insider trading at Atari—as well as Ross's own selling—and the salaries and compensation given WCI executives.

Murdoch, who owned the *New York Post,* assigned a couple of investigative reporters to examine the Westchester Premier Theatre situation as well as other details of Ross's background; these reporters then briefed the lawyer who was preparing to take Ross's deposition. And Murdoch carried on his campaign in the pages of the *Post,* too, where Eddie Rosenthal's letter to Emmett, expressing his sorrow for what Emmett had "done for all of us at WCI," was reprinted.

Ross mounted his own publicity campaign. Barbra Streisand, David Geffen, and others were called upon to avow their loyalty, stating that if Murdoch were to take over they would sever their connection to WCI (Geffen by this time had started a film and music company 50 percent owned by WCI, and Streisand had starred in several Warner movies). According to one friend of Streisand, with her the quid pro quo was clear. "At Barbra's, paintings, statues—costing maybe $50,000, $100,000—were always arriving. Then the call would come—Steve would say, talk to this reporter. With Murdoch, though, she got nervous, because he owned all those newspapers. But I know that at least two or three different times, Steve asked her to, and she did." Asked whether the process—a gift, followed by a request—did not offend Streisand, this person replied, "So what if it was obvious? She didn't care—she's a taker. She loved it."

In Ross's deposition, he had testified about his relationships with the artists, and the likelihood of their leaving the company or making their movies elsewhere if Murdoch were to take over the company. Murdoch, at his deposition, testified that Ross had first raised this issue with him at a meeting they had had in early December 1983, when Ross "claimed that there was concern from some of their artists about any possibility of changing control of the company." In connection with that, "Mr. Ross did talk about the—about the possibility of him having a long-term contract . . . I think he said the company wanted him to—it would be reassuring to the artists."

Murdoch also testified that the lawyer Joe Flom "said that if I got the company there would be no company there, no one would work for me, Barbra Streisand writing a letter to all the shareholders." However, he added, he had had one of his executives check with Streisand's manager. When asked whether Flom's statement about Streisand were true, Murdoch continued: "Mr. Lefrank [Streisand's manager] said he would inquire; called back and said there was absolutely no truth to it . . . that she was neither going to make any statement or write any letter against me, and that my presence wouldn't change her attitude or her relationship with the studio." Streisand denies that either Rupert Murdoch or any of his intermediaries ever checked with her or her representatives or that she responded in such fashion.

Ross was unnerved by Murdoch's onslaught. It may have been the specter of Westchester; it was, after all, barely more than a year since Sol Weiss had been convicted and Nick Akerman had made his statements about "the real culprit," and the government's investigation, while apparently inactive in the face of Weiss's continued silence, had not been closed. Despite the fact that Murdoch had made no headway with his court challenges, and that there was no aperture remaining through which he could reasonably gain control of the company, Ross rejected the advice of his fellow executives, his biggest shareholder at the time, Siegel, and a large assemblage of lawyers, and insisted that WCI buy out Murdoch's block of stock.

It was an act so clearly born of Ross's psychological need, rather than any legitimate corporate purpose, that even his loyal directors bestirred themselves. "I disagreed with the buyback of the Murdoch stock—I did view it as greenmail," said Ray Troubh, who argued against it but, in the end, voted in favor of the move. In March 1984, WCI announced that it was buying back Murdoch's block at $31 a share (for a stock valued at that time at about $22), giving Murdoch a profit of roughly $40 million. Even in the heat of the fray, Murdoch had always allowed that he might sell his stake. When asked about that possibility by a *Los Angeles Times* reporter in January 1984, Murdoch had been quoted as saying, "Oh, we've got to keep our head. If someone else is prepared to pay a stupid price, we're not going to kill ourselves for it."

Meanwhile, Chris-Craft, in its support of the Murdoch buyback, had increased its stake in WCI to roughly 30 percent. And it was agreed that, at the annual meeting, WCI would nominate three Chris-Craft directors, including Herbert Siegel, for election to the WCI board. Back in January, when he had still been in the throes of the Murdoch fight, Ross had responded to speculation about his losing control of the company to Siegel by telling *Los Angeles Times* reporter Kathryn Harris, "Herb is a passive investor. His philosophy is the same as ours. He wants to do his thing with the broadcast side, and he understands we want to do our thing."

The notion that someone owning such a major stake in a company—one that had lost a half-billion dollars the previous year, and was continuing to lose at a comparable rate currently—would be a "passive investor" was clearly specious. While it was almost certainly true, as Siegel always contended, that he had no designs on Ross's job, what he surely wanted was to be treated as a partner, and to have some say in how the company was run.

That, however, was impossible. Ross had never truly shared authority since Kinney Service had gone public, and he had given up even the appearance of doing so more than a decade earlier, when William Frankel had died. Someone who could not countenance the existence of a president as his designated second-in-command could hardly tolerate a partnership with another strong-minded businessman—who, furthermore, owned about 30 percent of the company's stock, while Ross himself owned less than 1 percent.

Later, when the battles between these two men became the talk of the business world, there was much comment on their evident incompatibility. Ross was seen to be a builder, always focused on the "big picture," Siegel, a canny investor; Ross, a mercurial free-spender, charismatic suitor of Hollywood talent, Siegel, a hardheaded businessman with a sharp pencil at the ready; Ross, someone who demanded the most luxurious perks the corporate till could provide, Siegel, inhabitant of a spartan corporate suite, fastidious in his cost accounting for shareholders' money. While there was a great deal of truth in this counterpoint, and while it did determine some of the grounds on which the two men would square off, it was not dispositive.

One might even argue that if Siegel had shared more of Ross's traits, Ross would have found him more threatening. But, in any event, no composite would have been acceptable, because Ross could not share authority with anyone. (Indeed, at one point some months after the deal had been made, Herb Siegel, realizing they were at an impasse, reportedly offered Ross a list of names of other investors who could be substituted for Siegel, if Ross wanted. Ross declined them all. Siegel even suggested to Ross that he bring in Liman as his president, to carry out the needed restructuring of the company—Liman, whom Ross presumably trusted as much, if not more than, anyone. Ross instantly refused.)

Knowing Ross as well as he did, Liman should have foreseen how untenable the situation would be, for both men. Ross, however, was in extremis—and Siegel was at hand. Ultimately, as events played out, and as Liman was seen to have been not an impartial arbiter but rather Ross's ally in this transaction, the price for Arthur Liman would be his long-time friendship with Siegel. That, no doubt, Liman would regret. But the falling-out between Liman and Siegel—while very public and painful—was not unique. Over the years, Jay Emmett, Robert Kasanof, George Gould and others would feel a similar bitterness toward Liman, all over Liman's representation of Steve Ross and Warner.

Some who knew the two men believed that Liman was so protective of Ross that, in matters involving him, Liman lost his sense of proportion. Some commented, too, on Liman's seeming infatuation with Ross; on the way this highly sophisticated, middle-aged lawyer seemed more a starry-eyed adolescent when he talked about his friend. As Liman once re-marked to me, "Steve is a dreamer. Part of the magic of our relationship is dreams. I've always encouraged him to dream, because some of those dreams come true."

Of his role in bringing Siegel to Ross's aid, Liman said that he had been careful to apprise Siegel of the kinds of problems he would face. "Before the deal was finalized, I took Herb and Larry Barnett [a Chris-Craft direc-tor] to David Horowitz's office at Warner [Horowitz was then in the Office of the President]. He had just created a high-tech office for himself—*very* expensive. I said, 'This is David Horowitz's office. He is in charge of the record business, he's not the CEO. If it is going to bother you, then you cannot do this deal.'

"Larry said, 'It's going to bother me.' But Herb silenced him. He said, 'It won't bother me. I'm betting on Steve, and if he feels this is the kind of office David Horowitz should have, fine. I'm betting on Steve.'

"I felt I'd given him a Miranda warning," Liman concluded.

Siegel was almost certainly not prepared for what he found, however. At just about the time he joined the WCI board, in May 1984, he is said to have received a call from a *Wall Street Journal* reporter, inquiring about a WCI restaurant division called Warner Leisure. It had lost about $70 million, Siegel was told, and was run by someone named Robert Petrallia who had a criminal record. Siegel is said to have immediately gone to see Ross, to ask if this were true and to warn him of the press interest. It turned out that it was true. A short piece ran later in *Forbes,* and WCI, for the record, denied the investment of $70 million.

Warner Leisure was Caesar Kimmel's project. Ever since Kimmel had yielded the parking business to Dan Katz in the early seventies, he had been at loose ends; he continued to hold the title of executive vice-president and to collect a salary and bonus of hundreds of thousands of dollars each year, but he had no real role. The jai alai project, which would have been his to control, had fallen through. Now, in Warner Leisure, he finally had a division to run. Kimmel told me that someone named Robert Petrallia had brought him the proposal: to start a chain of family-oriented restaurants, called "Gadgets," which would feature video games (an Atari tie-in) and robotic figures, many of them characters from Warner Bros.' "Looney Tunes" cartoons.

Petrallia, a New Jersey lawyer, had been involved with a company called Investors Economic Systems, Inc. (IES), based in Irvington, New Jersey, which syndicated real estate limited-partnership tax shelters. In many cases, however, the real estate for which millions of dollars had been raised through the sale of securities to the public was never purchased; in 1977, IES filed for bankruptcy, leaving thousands of investors with claims of more than $38 million against the company.

While there was much that was strange about Warner Leisure, its timing was strangest of all. In July 1981, Petrallia, who had earlier filed a consent decree with the SEC, was charged with conspiracy and sixteen counts of mail fraud for drafting fraudulent promotional material for IES. And in June—one month before his indictment, which was expected—WCI bought 80 percent of his company, Leisure Development Corp. of America (LDCA), for $250,000 and a commitment to invest $2.75 million. LDCA, which Petrallia and three other principals had formed in 1980, was a shell—no restaurants yet existed. Neither Petrallia nor his colleagues, who all now signed employment contracts with WCI (replete with "signing bonuses," according to one former WCI executive), had had any experience in the restaurant business. Several months after the almost concurrent events of Petrallia's deal with WCI and his indictment, he pled guilty to a misdemeanor tax charge; he was placed on two years' probation, fined $1,000, and directed to perform 200 hours of community service.

During this period, the government's Westchester Premier Theatre investigation was at its height; Emmett had pled guilty in February 1981, and Weiss would be indicted the following September. Also at this time, according to one present and one former FBI agent, the FBI was investigating the possibility of a criminal association between Kimmel and Matthew ("the Horse") Ianello, who was subsequently indicted; the inquiry, however, led nowhere with regard to Kimmel. In any event, as several former high-level WCI executives agreed, it was "crazy" to allow a person with a record such as Petrallia's to assume a substantial position within the company—all the more so at this moment, when the company was under the government's microscope. It was, simply, a deal for which there was no colorable explanation.

Company lawyers, at least one of whom was convinced that Petrallia was lying in response to specific questions in his discussions with the company, fought against the deal's going forward. But Kimmel was intent on it, and Ross—for reasons unfathomable to his associates—overruled them and ordered it be done. Describing Petrallia's qualifications for this enterprise, Kimmel told me that Petrallia was "a good dreamer." "Dreamer" was a word much used by Ross (beginning with the anecdote about his father, and continuing from there), which had become a staple of the WCI lexicon. Ross could perhaps be forgiven its fatuousness because of what some of his "dreams" produced; but the situation became more problematic when others in his organization, seeking to emulate him, began to think of themselves as dreamers too.

Petrallia got right into the swing of things. His Warner Leisure brochure featured a rainbow, and its text began:

The commitment of Warner Leisure from its inception has been to see all the colors in the rainbow and to share the beauty with others—to imagine —to create. This philosophy is at the very heart of why we are different. It is why the inevitability of tomorrow beckons with such promise and excitement.... The magic begins with a unique philosophy that ... says, bring together an unusually wide range of people with specialized talents and give them total creative and working freedom. Original thinkers, designers, artisans, computer engineers, practical dreamers ... all working together, blending high technology with the kind of artistic talent and vision needed to produce works of great originality and purpose.

The first restaurant, at the Seaview Mall in Asbury Park, New Jersey, opened in the spring of 1982, and within the next two years ten more would be built, with an investment of at least $70 million. Although Al Sarnoff handled virtually all WCI's real estate transactions, these were the exception; Petrallia and one of his associates, Edward D'Angelo, made these deals, under Kimmel's supervision. Petrallia, his associates, and a few secretaries opened corporate offices in Rutherford, New Jersey, in early 1982; some say that over the next two years the staff grew to roughly 250 people.

"These guys had no experience in building or running restaurants, they chose locations on the second floor of malls—those were death," said Anthony Guissari, Warner Leisure's controller, who was sent to Rutherford after having worked at WCI. "They negotiated long-term leases, with Warner as the guarantor, and with huge minimum rents—the real estate deals were outrageous. There were overruns in construction costs. After buying an animation plant in Connecticut, they decided to drop the animated figures. They set up a design company in California. The staff multiplied. We were losing so much money. Even the secretaries used to say, 'Doesn't anybody realize what's going on out here?' "

Guissari insisted that he kept Wasserman and others at WCI fully apprised. "They were getting numbers every week from us. They saw the development of the corporate staff, and the businesses we were getting in. Bert Wasserman and Caesar had many, many conversations. But Bert could not butt heads with Caesar."

According to another person who worked at Warner Leisure, however, systems of controls were lax, and the records did not show where much of the money went. "The gross investment was much more than $70 million. Follow the money. I live in a two-bedroom condo and have no other houses; it didn't go into my pocket. But it went somewhere."

As a former WCI executive commented, referring specifically to Kimmel and "Gadgets," among other things, "There was so much dirt at the company. You didn't *know* it—if somebody's moving money, he's not going to come and tell you about it. But you would hear things—so much static."

In WCI's annual reports and 10Ks, there had been no mention of the restaurant division until its 1983 10K (issued in the late spring of 1984, after the *Wall Street Journal* reporter and then Herb Siegel had begun to ask about it). The outside directors had apparently been barely, if at all, aware of its existence. Later, director Ray Troubh would say, "Yes, we should have paid closer attention to Warner Leisure—but we were following a leadership that did things this way. And Ross was someone who could see around corners. The history was, there were successes more often than not." Efforts were made to sell the Gadgets restaurants, but they failed; by 1985, the division was shut down. Kimmel was forced out of the company, with a lavish retirement package, in the fall of 1984. Liman told people within the company that it was Herb Siegel who had insisted that Kimmel be ousted; but according to those close to Siegel, he had only insisted that Warner Leisure be sold, if possible, or shut down.

For Siegel, upon his election to the board, to have uncovered Warner Leisure and, inevitably, made it an issue, was not an auspicious beginning. It embarrassed Ross, focusing attention on something he clearly would have preferred remain hidden. Most important, he was being called to account for something, at *his* company, and being taken to task for it. No one but the U.S. government had ever tried to do this to him before; and the government had failed. Siegel would, too. Ross, being Ross, must have vowed that Siegel would lose, he would win.

Meanwhile, Siegel, focused on the task before him, seeing a company which was in greater disarray than he had suspected and was continuing to suffer punishing losses—and on which he had gambled roughly 42 percent of his assets—pushed on. Given what was at stake for him, he could hardly afford to be passive; and he took seriously, moreover, not only his responsibilities as a director of WCI but his obligations to his own shareholders. When Ross and Siegel had made their deal, they had agreed to what later was announced as the "asset redeployment program": personnel would be reduced, expenses cut, non-core divisions sold. Indeed, that general plan had already been in place before Siegel had appeared; Morgado had been firing people by the fall of 1983.

But by the summer of 1984 Siegel felt that what he often referred to as the "clean-up" of the company was moving much too slowly. He told friends that after Murdoch had been bought out, they had run into each other at "21," and Murdoch had said to him, "Want to save $100 million? Just turn the lock on Warner's corporate headquarters in New York—and throw away the key!"

That, of course, was Steve Ross's private preserve, a world unto itself that might well cause any outsider, having stumbled in, to wonder if he had not stepped through the looking glass. Ross had made good on his declarations about these headquarters being "home" for the "Warner family." Even with the recent spate of dismissals (which were without precedent in the company's history), there was still plenty to testify to the notion that this *was* home, and a home one never had to leave. The Cosmos' glory days were long over, but Pelé was still drawing a large salary and maintaining an office and secretaries here, as well as an apartment (as he would for the next eight years); Chinaglia, too (he had not yet fled to Italy). Allie Sherman, the former coach of the Giants who had been one of Ross's best friends in the sixties, and had joined the company then, was still here; he had done some work with the Cosmos in the mid-seventies.

The company had recently spent millions to buy an entire floor of sumptuous apartments in Trump Tower. The refurbishing of David Horowitz's office (which Liman had shown Siegel) had cost $750,000. Ross, aided by Courtney, within the past couple of years had not only purchased at least $8 million worth of paintings for the company but had also spent millions more on Art Deco furniture.

There were five or six people employed to administer the company's charitable contributions; from corporate headquarters (excluding the divisions), these totalled about $10 million a year. In 1983, even as the company was losing over a half-billion dollars, $1 million had been donated to the Dallas Museum—because of Courtney's ties there, according to one former WCI executive. In the fall of that year, Richard Kasholek, head of the Los Angeles Museum of Contemporary Art, had gone to see Ross at the Beverly Hills Hotel to ask for a donation. As Kasholek recalled, Ross had unhesitatingly whipped out a company check and written it out for $250,000. Siegel declared that he wanted Ross to cut WCI's four hundred-person corporate staff by half within thirty days. He wanted all but one plane and one helicopter to be sold; all the executives to give up their cars and chauffeurs and share one between them—Ross alone should keep his. (He pointed out that when Manny Gerard and his family had used the company plane to return from Hawaii in the midst of the Murdoch assault, it had cost the company $80–$90,000.) Siegel wanted the board to review and control the payment of salaries and bonuses to all employees making over $100,000 a year. And Siegel wanted Villa Eden to charge, at what would be rates for a comparable rental. He also wanted better expense accounting; in 1983, for example, records at Villa Eden indicated that $25,999 had been spent on tennis balls and sneakers. He is said, also, to have wanted Ross to forgo one of his trademark gestures: sending many hundreds, perhaps thousands, of gargantuan turkeys at Thanksgiving. (As Ross would explain to an executive years later, he *loved* sending the turkeys. A gift at Christmas, he explained, gets lost in the crowd. But at Thanksgiving, it's unique! And while turkeys are relatively inexpensive, they are appreciated, and used, by nearly everyone.)

In all this, Siegel was not so intent on tampering with the way the divisions, such as the studio and the record companies, were run. He appeared, rather, to be trying to follow Murdoch's advice regarding corporate headquarters—with the caveat that he was prepared to leave Ross's perks intact. He had almost certainly assured Liman of that when they first agreed that he would do the deal, although he probably could not have guessed, at that time, the extent of Ross's self-endowment.

As one former executive explained, Ross liked having lawyers at WCI, such as Martin Payson and those who worked under him, who were very straight; they had circumscribed tasks and they did not try to investigate any more than they had to to deal with specific assignments, but by being as conservative as they were, they "lent a patina of legitimacy. [They] were the blessers. Could the company pay for security systems for Steve's house in East Hampton, for his bodyguard, chauffeur, domestic help—for Carmen [Ferragano], from the moment she got up in the morning to the moment she went to bed at night? There was always an argument to be made, and Steve made it. He was his best lawyer."

Even if Siegel were willing not to infringe on Ross's sovereign perquisites, however, Ross had made the company—and its treasury—so much an extension of himself that it was hard to say where one ended and the other began. Was not the demand to sell the paintings, for example, so many of which hung in his office, his conference room, and, reportedly, his home, an infringement on that which he considered his own?

Far more important was the fact that any attempt to isolate what Ross bestowed on himself from what he bestowed on others threatened to subvert one of his bedrock principles in shaping this company—what one of his executives had termed the "$x$ plus $y$" principle. For if they received a munificent "$x$," then Ross—camouflaged, to a degree, by the lush surroundings—could receive that and more. But if this camouflage were torn away, and he, alone, left exposed—acquisitive, indulgent, pampered, grandiose—where would be his charm and where the loyalty which he valued above all else in his cohorts? The whole construct only *worked* if the largesse were shared—something Ross had known instinctively years ago.

Moreover, by carrying the distribution of largesse to extremes, he had succeeded not only in engendering loyalty but in building himself up to mythic proportions. He had increasingly become defined by the extravagance of his generous gestures—as Spielberg put it, Ross's being such a "magnetic host" became "his calling card"—and those gestures seemed, in a way, to affirm his own sense of his power. Who but a contemporary potentate, after all, could so afford to indulge every whim—sending the company plane across the country to bring Spielberg's dogs to East Hampton, for example, or back to New York from the Caribbean, where Ross was vacationing with Quincy Jones, to get Nathan's hot dogs?

In such instances, of course, the rationale, however attenuated, always was that he was courting the stars for the good of the company. But there were other situations in which there was no rationale—as in the case of the businessman who had known Ross for years but never had a single transaction with the company, who told me that Ross, in the early eighties, learned that this man's wife had had a back operation. Sympathetic, talking about how he'd been plagued by back problems himself, Ross had insisted that they go to Villa Eden for her to recuperate. "And he wouldn't hear of our flying commercially. He said we had to take the company plane. 'She *must* lie flat on the plane ride,' he kept saying. I—and my wife—will never forget it."

This self-image—warm, supportive, caring—that Ross was ceaselessly projecting to the world at large had also become woven into the fabric of the company. Robert Daly, the chairman of Warner Brothers, recalled one of his first visits to WCI corporate headquarters. "I attended a budget meeting there in December, and when it was over I heard Steve and Jay [Emmett] and Bert [Wasserman] arguing about a pension for someone at Warner Brothers, who was very sick. Now, at CBS, it would have been an argument about how little they could give. But these three—the CEO, the co-president, and the chief financial officer—were arguing about how much more over the normal pension they could give. Each one was topping the other! They were saying, what else can we do for him?"

Siegel's demands were reasonable, under the circumstances. Indeed, given the condition of the company, and the size of his investment, most were hornbook. But Siegel was challenging both Ross, with his idiosyncratic ways, and a surrounding environment so keyed to Ross that it was almost immunogenic; it repelled Siegel. With barely a signal from Ross, his directors and division heads, most of whom Ross knew like the back of his hand, would move into formation behind him. As one of them commented, "I never had a reaction that Steve Ross did not anticipate."

By early 1985, just a year after having finalized his deal with Siegel, Ross began maneuvering to try to extricate himself from it. The company had just survived two terrible years; it had lost more than $1 billion, wiping out nearly all its earnings since 1975. It had breached the covenants on its bank loans, and only the bankers' forbearance had kept it from being forced into bankruptcy. But several events had occurred that suggested that the worst was past.

While issuing consistently optimistic statements about progress at Atari through 1983 and early 1984, Ross had been looking desperately for a buyer since the spring of 1983. Years later, Nintendo—having learned from the errors of Atari—would prove that the video-game business was a real, enduring, and lucrative one. But Atari had grown so recklessly that it was unable to survive the 1983 downturn and await the next cycle. Finally, in July 1984, in a stroke of luck—just as WCI's bankers were reaching the end of their patience and considering pulling the cord on the company rather than see it through another Christmas season with Atari—a buyer for the division materialized. Alberto Cribiore, who had joined WCI in the summer of 1982, negotiated the sale to Jack Tramiel. Working with Cribiore during this period was Siegel's son, Bill, who had come to the company at the time of the Chris-Craft deal. "Tramiel had just left Commodore Computer, and he had gotten $100 million," Cribiore recalled. "He said, 'With $100 million, I'm a very rich man. With $50 million, I'm still a very rich man. With $50 million and Atari, I'm a happy man.' So, it was a risk he could afford to take. A very unique situation." Tramiel bought Atari's home computer unit at a fire-sale price; though that would later have to be renegotiated lower still, and payments made to Tramiel, WCI was able finally to stanch Atari's crippling losses. Meanwhile, the record companies and the movie studio, which had suffered a couple of very weak years, had rebounded. Warner Bros., especially, had had its best year yet, with revenues over the $1 billion mark for the first time. Ross had stuck to his credo, supporting these divisions in the bad times as well as the good, and it had paid off. "During Atari, he *never* would call and say, 'Watch the budget, we've got to cut back,' " said Bob Daly. "It was the opposite: 'Don't let this problem affect you. You keep doing what you're supposed to do, and that's how you'll help.' "

Also, by early 1985, other divisions in addition to Atari had been sold: Warner Cosmetics; Franklin Mint, a direct-response marketing company; Panavision, a producer of professional motion picture cameras and other photographic equipment; Malibu Grand Prix, the chain of mini-amusement centers with go-cart tracks; Knickerbocker Toy, in an exchange of its assets for securities of Hasbro Industries. Gadgets was, essentially, shut down, as were the Cosmos. WCI's 48 percent interest in the Pittsburgh Pirates was for sale. In transactions where it seemed there would be future value, Ross followed his favored practice of taking an equity stake in the newly constituted venture. "We sold about ten companies from 1983 to 1985," said Cribiore. "We cleaned up the whole house. Many of the acquisitions done from 1976 to 1982, we divested from 1982 to 1985."

Ross seemed to move in roughly ten-year cycles of accumulation followed by divestiture. It was not simply a repeated disgorgement, however, but a progressive process of growth. In 1972, he had divested himself of much that he had amassed since 1962, when he took Kinney Service public; now, he was staying with his core businesses, the entertainment and communications companies, but divesting himself of everything else. All else (and it was quite a potpourri) had been, in the end, nothing but a costly distraction—Atari, foremost.

With a far leaner company under his command, Ross began having discussions with Michael Milken about taking it private in a leveraged buyout which Milken, through Drexel Burnham, would finance with junk bonds. The deal held considerable allure for both men. At roughly $3 billion, it would be the largest LBO that Milken had yet financed; it was the dawning of Milken's era; and Milken liked and believed in Ross. According to one friend of Milken's, as Milken's relationship with Ross grew stronger over the years, he would often remark that he felt that Ross and he were very much alike.

For Ross, the deal promised emancipation. It would free him of Siegel. It would free him, too, from the disclosure requirements of a public company, which he was finding increasingly onerous (more so, no doubt, since he had Siegel as monitor). As Spielberg would later recall, Ross often said to him during this period, "Stay a dreamer and never go public." Ross's plan was to include his Hollywood friends in the deal along with key WCI executives: Spielberg, Streisand, and Eastwood would each own a piece of the newly private company. And, finally, while WCI had started on the road to recovery, it was still early enough that the public shareholders might be bought out in the kind of deal Ross always strove for: seemingly fair but, in fact, sublimely opportunistic.

A number of Milken's associates, including Leon Black, spent many hours working on the transaction with Cribiore and Oded Aboodi—who, by this time, was not only handling tax-related investments for Ross and other executives but was Ross's close adviser on deals. Finally, Milken came to New York for a meeting (unusual, inasmuch as virtually everyone, in that era, came to him). A large group, including Milken, Black, Ross, Siegel, his son Bill Siegel, Cribiore, and others met in a conference room at the law firm of Cravath, Swaine & Moore. (By mid-1984, Herb Siegel had realized that Liman and his firm had been on too many sides of this transaction and that he needed his own independent counsel. He had retained Samuel Butler of Cravath.)

"At one point, Steve and Mike got into an argument," Butler recalled. "Mike said he'd have to give 40 percent of the equity to the debt holders —of course, as we now know, that was actually going into his pockets. He said, 'That leaves 25 percent for you guys, 35 percent for Drexel.' Steve said, 'What are you talking about? All you're doing is financing this deal, and you get 35 percent?' They went back and forth that way for about ten minutes, about who was going to cheat the public more."

The price at which they were proposing to buy out the public shareholders (including Siegel) was about $30 a share (about $24 in cash, the rest in paper). From Ross's standpoint, it would have been sweet indeed. Years later, Terry Semel of Warner Bros. recalled this deal. "It would have been wildly profitable, if we had taken it private"—better, he added, than the deal that ultimately transpired about four years later. (Indeed. Ross and his cohorts were attempting to buy stock for the equivalent of $15 a share that, after a stock split, would later sell for $70 a share.) In those days, he continued, "Steve was constantly scribbling something on those yellow pads of his, drawing boxes and charts—he was figuring out the future of the company. But he always had to think of Herb [Siegel], and whether he would block it."

Siegel vetoed their suggested price (the stock price had been rising and was just a few dollars under $30 at the time). And from this time on, Siegel and Ross occupied plainly drawn enemy camps. Bill Siegel left WCI and rejoined his father at Chris-Craft, where, as a lawyer and his father's closest adviser, he drove their strategy *vis-à-vis* Ross.

Herb Siegel believed that Ross was intent on trying to steal the company—as was almost certainly the case. Siegel kept pushing for a stock repurchase program (something that Ross had done aggressively in the past), but now—because, Siegel is said to have believed, it would make the company more expensive to take private—Ross repeatedly refused. Siegel considered mounting a proxy fight to unseat Ross. While he would continue to contemplate the option over the course of the next couple of years, this was the time to do it, according to several of his advisers; later, the company strengthened and his chances of success became much less good. "In 1985, Herb could have won hands down—Steve's reputation had been so tarnished. There was Atari, and Westchester was still quite recent," one adviser said. "But the truth was that Herb didn't want to run the company, and he didn't want to have to put somebody else in there. He just wanted Steve to listen to him and to run it better. All Steve had to do, from the start, was to listen to him, cut back, sell some of the planes —and it would have been okay. But Steve was king."

During this period of time, many people—Wall Street analysts, journalists, members of the business community—vastly underestimated Steve Ross's resilience. After the Atari collapse and during the travails of the following couple of years, his imminent departure from WCI was predicted regularly in the press. But those who knew him well never counted him out, for they understood that he was a competitor above all: he would *best* adversity. Some suggested, moreover, that good times tended to accentuate his weaknesses (he became too laissez-faire), and bad times his strengths. "Steve Ross was the Pied Piper of that organization—he took off down the road with these big ideas and everyone scrambled behind him," commented one executive at another company who observed Ross at close range. "But the fascinating thing about him was that while he looked like the Pied Piper and acted like the Pied Piper, when he got into his periodic troubles, the other Steve Ross emerged—the deal guy who saved himself with some very tough negotiations."

Ross's supreme deal during these years of trial occurred in the summer of 1985, with the buyout by WCI of the American Express half of Warner-Amex, the cable joint venture which had been formed back in 1979. At that time, as an early and stalwart true believer in cable, Ross had been expanding steadily and wanted to do much more. He had even pursued his early enthusiasm for the concept of the "frame-grabber"—the device which, essentially, would enable a consumer to order everything from the TV screen, via cable—which his embarrassed colleagues had thought was sheer hucksterism. In this enthusiasm, Ross had found a kindred spirit in Gustave Hauser, whom he had brought in to run Warner Cable in the early seventies (after first having tried to recruit John Malone, who would later head the country's biggest cable company, Tele-Communications Inc.). In 1977, Warner Cable had gone on the air with a multi-channel interactive cable service to 100,000 subscribers in Columbus, Ohio, called QUBE. As WCI's 1976 annual report stated: "Subscribers will be able to communicate not only their program selections, but their opinions and choices in surveys. In addition they will be able to play interactive television games. . . ." Concerts and sports on pay-per-view; a subscriber movie channel, called the Star Channel; children's programming, called Nickelodeon; video clips of musicians, which would subsequently become MTV; home shopping; a vote by the subscribers in Columbus, after President Jimmy Carter's famous energy speech—all this was the fare in Columbus. Subscribers paid $11.95 a month to be hooked up to the system; those with personal computers could pay an additional $5 per hour to play computer games or receive information on stocks and bonds. Many years later, Hauser would say proudly that "what we did with those thirty channels is what cable is today. QUBE was really the mother."

It was clearly ahead of its time, however—the cost too great, the technology too imperfect, and the consumer too unready—to develop on a larger scale. Still, QUBE would prove to be a valuable asset in the contests for the big urban cable franchises beginning to be offered in the late seventies. Ross was intent on winning as many of the franchises as possible; these were one-time opportunities. But building cable systems required an enormous front-loaded investment. He wanted to obtain a partner and form a joint venture, thus moving the necessary debt off WCI's balance sheet to that of a separate entity.

Ross enlisted Felix Rohatyn, of Lazard Frères, to help find a partner. James Robinson of American Express seemed ideal. Ross believed that the respectability of American Express would lend image enhancement to WCI—something that would be particularly helpful in the franchise contests, where competitors were bound to make an issue of the intensifying Westchester investigation. Robinson was likely to be susceptible, moreover, inasmuch as he was smarting from a humiliating failed attempt to acquire McGraw-Hill, and would be eager to consummate a major deal. According to several former WCI executives, Rohatyn carried out his assignment so well that it was Robinson—believing it was *his* idea—who made the overture. Ross was an incessant suitor, but when it came to a deal, he always liked to affect the posture of the one being wooed (he had been doing this ever since the time he had maneuvered Eddie Rosenthal into asking him to join the funeral business, and probably before). Now, he responded warmly to Robinson, talking about the potential of interactivity, and about selling financial products through cable television. His excitement was infectious, and, as an article in *Institutional Investor* later said: "Robinson chattered away excitedly about the cable company being the foundation for a business selling products through television and computer terminals, using—what else?—the green card."

Even if this had been possible, the investment would probably not have been an optimal one for American Express. As many of Robinson's top executives later argued to him, their shareholders would always view them as a financial-services, not communications company (and, therefore, they would never receive a growth-company multiple). One of these executives said, "If you were going to sell financial products over cable, why did you have to own the cable? Steve Ross sold Jim a bill of goods. Jim bought a cow to get a quart of milk."

For the deal's celebratory signing, Ross insisted on travelling by the company helicopter downtown to the American Express Building. American Express invested $175 million for 50 percent of Warner-Amex Cable Communications; thus, WCI was able to recoup its entire investment in cable, and it still owned half of it. The new venture obtained a loan of $800 million—considered huge in the cable industry at that time—and embarked upon a new phase of franchise winning and construction. The franchise battles were hard-fought, and Warner-Amex won more than any other cable company. (Indeed, Time Inc. filed suit against WCI and the city of Pittsburgh, alleging improper bidding procedures there; and some Time executives were convinced at the time that Warner-Amex won Queens because of Ross's coziness with former borough president Donald Manes.)

For Ross, the Warner-Amex deal provided everything he had wanted. In fact, his conservatism, in wanting the debt moved off the WCI balance sheet (to that of a subsidiary where it was not guaranteed by either parent), would be proven wise; had the debt not been moved, WCI could almost certainly not have survived the aftermath of Atari. But for James Robinson, the experience was different. According to colleagues, he had been much taken with Ross, and envisioned the two of them, side by side, collaborating in this new enterprise. Ross's attention, however, had wandered, as it generally did once the deal was done; indeed, Robinson was said to have been quite offended when Ross did not even attend a small dinner Robinson threw at the Rainbow Room on the anniversary of their deal.

It soon became apparent, moreover, that although American Express had put in half the money, they had little control; the venture was steered by WCI. And while Hauser, in the franchise fights, was no doubt carrying out Ross's mandate to win, he made promises to cities that were excessive —promising up to 108 channels for subscribers, in addition to extensive community programming, for example. He also seems to have acted with the near autonomy that was a WCI tradition for division heads. "Promises were made in the franchise proposals that weren't reflected in the economic presentations to the board [of Warner-Amex]," declared a former American Express executive. "The mayors of the cities would see these guys coming and they'd say, 'Build us a studio, interactive between city hall and the fire department.'

Gus Hauser's attitude was, 'Let's wire up the nation and put this interactive cable into everyone's homes'—and based on his projections, Warner-Amex made commitments to invest over a billion dollars," this executive continued. "The costs kept going up and up, and the American Express side said, 'We don't think we've got a guy here who can manage costs. He's betting on a technology. But we can't build it at the cost he's telling us, and it doesn't look like the consumer is going to want to pay for the original cost, let alone the inflated one.' "

By 1983, Warner-Amex was experiencing losses that would total $150 million by the end of the year. At Robinson's insistence, Hauser was fired (he would start his own cable company and, ten years later, sell it for more than $600 million). Robinson recruited Drew Lewis, the former U.S. Secretary of Transportation, to run Warner-Amex. WCI, of course, was reeling from its losses at Atari, and Robinson was afraid that his partner would go bankrupt and American Express would be left morally—though not legally—obligated for the debt of Warner-Amex. In an effort to cut losses, Lewis began asking cities for dramatic changes in what Warner-Amex had promised. In Milwaukee, he succeeded in renegotiating the contract. In Pittsburgh and Dallas, Warner-Amex sold the systems it had fought so hard to win, and had partially built.

"Warner had done a great job of getting the franchises, but they had overpromised, and they were installing things that were beyond state-of-the-art. It was incredibly 'Buck Rogers' and unproven," said one competitor. Referring to the Pittsburgh system, where Warner-Amex had invested about $100 million and then sold it to Tele-Communications Inc. (TCI), he continued, "TCI tore out all the bells and whistles, made it into a plain vanilla system—and did very well."

Cable, more than any other part of WCI, reflected the overheatedness of Ross's enthusiasm—not surprisingly, since he had been that way about it from the start. And it provided a graphic illustration of what he would always tell his employees, when he was urging them not to be afraid: that it was sins of omission, not commission, that kill you in business. The force of Ross's conviction in cable led him to error, but even his errors provided fertile ground for future successes. QUBE, too futuristic, was a money loser—but then it enabled Warner-Amex to win more franchises. They had won more than they could handle, and so had to undo some of what they'd done; but what they kept was enormously valuable, and, in the future, would vault WCI to its highest leap yet.

If Steve Ross was viscerally connected to cable, however, Jim Robinson was not. And, despite Lewis's restructuring efforts, by 1985 Robinson only wanted to exit. "It was very emotional and bitter—American Express felt totally misled," said one of its advisers. "No set of numbers Warner had given them turned out to be even vaguely true. . . . [T]hey'd finally figured out they were the pigeon. Now, it was like a bad marriage where they just had to get out—they felt they couldn't trust the Warner people."

In the spring of 1985, reports appeared in the press that American Express was interested in selling its interest in the Warner-Amex cable operations—something Ross learned when he read it in the newspaper. By late May, American Express had worked out a deal with Time Inc. and Tele-Communications Inc.—two of the largest cable owners—whereby they were proposing to buy Warner-Amex for $750 million in cash and the assumption of $550 million in debt.

The original Warner-Amex agreement contained a "buy-sell" provision that worked like Russian roulette: to trigger it, either partner could offer to buy out the other at a given price—a price at which the second partner, however, declining to sell, could then buy out the first. Robinson and his executives, aware that Ross might well want to buy rather than sell, were banking on their assumption that Siegel would prevent that. When WCI had still made no response several weeks after the proposed deal was announced, a sweetened deal, now for $850 million plus the assumption of debt, was entered into by American Express, for its 50 percent of Warner-Amex. Part of this agreement was that if WCI continued to ignore the bid, American Express would trigger the buy-sell provision, by offering to buy out the Warner part of Warner-Amex—and it would then sell the whole to Time and TCI. So confident of the outcome was American Express that it promised to pay Time and TCI $10 million if the deal did not go through.

Siegel *was* opposed to WCI's assuming any more debt, in order to buy out American Express; but he was not opposed to the transaction if it were financed by finding a partner, or by selling assets to raise cash. Warner-Amex's debt had been reduced, its huge losses eliminated (for 1985 it forecast a profit of $17 million). And, with recent legislation, the outlook for cable's profitability was bright; the Cable Act of 1984 effectively deregulated the industry, allowing cable operators to raise their rates without local approval.

There were many permutations; but, in the end, WCI bought American Express's share of Warner-Amex for about $400 million and, almost immediately, sold two Warner-Amex ventures—a two-thirds interest in MTV Networks and 19 percent of Showtime/The Movie Channel (a pay-TV company that competed directly with Time Inc.'s HBO)—to Viacom, for about $510 million (plus warrants, so as to share in the upside). For Ross, as one American Express adviser later said, the history of Warner-Amex could be fairly encapsulated as "a great sell, followed by a brilliant buy." Siegel offered congratulations; Ross's juggling had been masterful. Just how masterful was not fully evident at the time—seven or eight years later, the cable venture then valued at $800 million would be worth about $4 billion. (To Ross's chagrin, on the other hand, MTV and Showtime/The Movie Channel would be valued at about $2.5 billion.) Ross, in any event, was mightily pleased with himself. About a year after the deal, he would refer to his having purchased that 50 percent of Warner-Amex as "the coup of all coups."


With Ross's prodigious deal skills and the company's intrinsic strengths (movies and records continued to perform outstandingly in 1985), WCI was beginning to flourish again. But for Siegel's intervention—and his ceaseless prodding to cut costs and sell assets—Ross might not have survived to enjoy this renascence. But, as far as Ross was concerned, Siegel was no more than a nagging vestige of that dark period, and as long as he was present, Ross could not enjoy what he thought of as his company; Siegel never allowed him that illusion. Ross was desperate to be rid of him. Spielberg recalled that in the latter part of 1985 they were shooting *The Color Purple* in North Carolina, and Ross visited them. "I had ten gospel singers come to the window of the cottage where we were, and they sang, 'Drive Herb Siegel away! Drive Herb Siegel away!' *That* brought a smile to Steve's face," Spielberg said. In early 1986, with the threat of a proxy fight looming, Siegel and Ross reached a compromise agreement, whereby certain provisions in their contractual agreement were revised and Siegel was allowed to add three more directors to the board—he would have six, including himself, out of sixteen. While this should have been a significant ratio, on this board Ross's directors (four of whom were part of management) voted as a bloc, so the addition of the Siegel directors (who did not always vote together, although they usually did) meant nothing.

Siegel continued to make his requests, and objections. He wanted to see monthly balance sheets. These, he was told, would be too costly to produce. He wanted more regular audits of the divisions; this, too, was not practicable. (Perhaps for good reason. According to one former WCI executive, much of the supposed cost cutting at corporate headquarters had simply consisted of moving costs to the various divisions. Also, another person said that the expenses of Ross's lavish gifts to the stars—like the works of art for Streisand—were buried in the studio's overhead.)

As one Siegel partisan who attended the WCI board meetings during this period recalled, "We were amazed at how little operating information from the divisions was given to the board. Steve's attitude was, 'I'm the boss, you have to trust me.' And every time Herb asked for something, Steve took it personally—how dare you question me? He took such umbrage. It was a *betrayal,* it meant this guy didn't trust him. Even in those days, most CEOs, at board meetings, were respectful, listened, gave responses to questions. It was bizarre."

Arthur Liman confirmed that Ross felt personally diminished by Siegel's actions. He said, "Steve felt, as he expressed it to me, that he was killing himself to make the company successful, to make money for everyone—and Herb was humiliating him."

Another person added that Ross, although he sometimes would give vent to his indignation, often chose to remain above the fray, while his directors—Martin Payson, William vanden Heuvel, Ray Troubh, Lawrence Buttenweiser, and Beverly Sills, most conspicuously—would wage the battle. Sills and vanden Heuvel vied for "most emotional." This may well have been due to their respective personalities; but it was also true that while Ross had made sure that all his directors were beholden to him in one way or another, these two, Sills and vanden Heuvel, were arguably the most beholden.

Sills (whom Ross always called by her nickname, "Bubbles") had, of course, first met Ross when she had come to ask him for a donation to the New York City Opera and he countered by promising that WCI would contribute if she would become a director (WCI had pledged $500,000). Vanden Heuvel, who had conspired with Ken Rosen to introduce Ross to Amanda Burden, had sided with Ross after their break-up and joined the board. For his role as a finder in selling Warner Cosmetics to L'Oréal in 1984, he received $950,000. So baldly stated, however, these examples risk assuming a disproportionate importance. Each of Ross's directors received some individualized bounty. But to say, as Siegel partisans did, that the directors were all "bought" by Ross, is to underestimate the power of Ross's hold over them. With Ross, "buying" became an art; the ordinary was transfigured. Instead of a crass transaction where both sides tacitly acknowledge what has taken place and feel demeaned by its occurrence, here it became, rather, an outpouring of goodwill and affection, by someone so likable and so clearly revelling in the giving that the recipients of Ross's largesse responded in emotional kind; and soon— where there might have been detected the sordidness of a quid pro quo —there was only warm effusion.

Siegel, however, could not be "bought": he stood, blunt, obdurate, and wooden, while all this eddied about him. But neither did he stand a chance against the romance of Ross. Ross's directors would never deviate from him when he was under attack; until Herb Siegel had appeared, their board had been one harmonious family, and Ross the benevolent patriarch. Moreover, in questioning Ross's judgment, Siegel was often questioning theirs as well, so there was an added incentive for solidarity. The stronger the company grew, the weaker Siegel's chances at a proxy fight. By mid-1986, those chances were no longer very good. But Ross— who had, after all, insisted upon buying out Rupert Murdoch when there had been no rationale for doing so—was not inclined to take any chances now, with Siegel.

In the summer of 1986, WCI announced it was going to effect a split in its common stock, and also issue a convertible preferred stock, to raise $500 million. The result of these two moves, in combination, was to reduce Siegel's voting position from 29 percent to 19 percent. While Siegel's lawyers at Cravath understood that the preferred offering would dilute Siegel's position, they found it strange that he should be diluted by the stock split; surely, they thought, anti-dilution provisions for his voting, as well as his economic rights, would have been part of the deal agreement. That was the agreement that had been prepared, in the main, by the Paul, Weiss firm representing both sides. Upon inspection, the "certificate of designation" did not, in fact, offer such anti-dilution protection; but the "term sheet," a kind of rough draft which had preceded the final version, did. Retracing steps, the Cravath attorneys, having interviewed Liman and others, pieced together a rough sequence of events as remembered. As part of the deal, Chris-Craft had received a special voting anti-dilution provision, but it was subject to approval by the New York Stock Exchange. Shortly before the agreement was to be finalized, Liman and others—without anyone representing Siegel specifically—had gone to the Exchange for this special approval. They had been told it couldn't be done, and no one had requested a standard voting anti-dilution provision (which would likely have been granted). Siegel was informed; and —with Murdoch looming and the need for dispatch great—the anti-dilution provision had been removed, and the "Certificate of Designation" signed. (Liman disclaims any responsibility for the drafting of anti-dilution clauses.)

"This story about the need to go to the Stock Exchange, and the Exchange's refusal, made no sense to us," one of Siegel's attorneys said. But the decision was made not to pursue it; it would have been difficult if not impossible to win a remedy in court, insofar as Siegel had been aware that the change was being made, and, although Paul, Weiss was primarily involved, Siegel did have another law firm which had reviewed the papers. "Liman was much too involved on all sides," this attorney said. "Both clients accepted it because they both trusted Arthur. But Herb was not as well protected as Steve Ross was in this agreement. Herb used to say to me, he couldn't believe that Arthur had done this to him."

There was a theory, too, this attorney continued, that Ross had achieved an additional safeguard, by issuing the convertible preferred. Siegel had argued, unsuccessfully, that it made no sense for WCI to issue this preferred stock, for which the interest payments would not be deductible, when it could issue debt, where the payments would be. Ross, however, had been adamant, and his directors had backed him. The offer was underwritten by Drexel and Lazard. And it seems altogether plausible, given Milken's practices, that he placed these securities in pockets that he controlled. Had Siegel mounted a proxy fight or made a hostile bid, the theory went, these securities could have been voted and thus marshalled by Milken to Ross's aid. Or, in the event that Ross was to undertake another buyout attempt, it would be helpful to have these committed. (Indeed, Ross and Milken had begun to organize another buyout attempt when Ivan Boesky pled guilty and the financial universe that Milken had created changed overnight.)

Ross's plans for a buyout were foiled, but still, once these maneuvers were accomplished, Ross was more secure than he had been in years. And it was only weeks before he was asserting himself, in a move that must have sprung, at least in part, from that childish, bullying urge to inflame an adversary when he is hamstrung and unable to retaliate. Ross announced that, of the $500 million raised in the preferred offering, about $50 million was going to be spent, promptly, to buy the company a new, expanded fleet of planes.

Several months later, in early 1987, Ross indulged in a more serious exercise of his newly entrenched power. His last contract had expired in December 1983; since the company then was approaching the brink of bankruptcy, it had not been an opportune time for him to renew. By mid-1986, however, the company had been doing so well that Ross had, finally, proffered what he had been preparing for some time. As Liman once said of his friend, speaking of his general approach to crafting a deal, "Steve is a customizer. He's always using the tax laws and accounting rules in some way where you take a deal where the numbers are one plus one and you get more than two. He would never be content to do something, even if it were good, if it were ordinary. 'Anyone can do that,' he'd say. 'I want something unique.' "

Ross's contract *was* unique: a ten-year employment agreement that would likely make him the highest-paid CEO in the country. Even its duration was unusual—and all the more significant since Ross had undergone surgery and radiation for prostate cancer in 1985. It was estimated, at the time, that if the price of WCI stock and the company's net income should rise 10 percent a year, compounded annually, Ross would make an average of $14 million a year in salary and bonuses—and an estimated $143 million over the next ten years.

If, on the other hand, WCI stock price and earnings were to remain flat, he would make an estimated $5.8 million annually. There was also a golden parachute provision: if the company were to be taken over at, say, $50 a share (a reasonable premium over the stock price in early 1987), Ross would get about $90 million; this would hold true even if it were a leveraged buyout that Ross initiated himself. Then there was, according to lawyer Cy O'Neil, who helped draft this contract, a "look-back" provision, truly unique—O'Neil said that in his practice of thirty years he had never before seen anything like it. Assume that Ross had options at $20 a share, and the stock price went to $40, and then fell back to $30; within a certain time frame, Ross could "look back" and exercise his options *as if* the stock price were still at $40.

There was much, much more. O'Neil, who worked on drafting it with Ross and Aboodi, recalled: "I looked at that contract and said, 'My God, this is a very lucrative contract!' But by my lights, the more money he made, the more value for shareholders. I always felt that Steve Ross to Warner was priceless. If Steve had decided to go do something else, the amount of money you could have raised around him was huge."

The contract was the product of the fecund financial imaginations of Ross and Aboodi. "Steve and Ed communicated in an almost unconscious language," O'Neil continued. "Some of the provisions in the contract relative to investment of retirement funds were unbelievably complex. No analysts ever focused on them very much. You put aside amounts for retirement, and how you treated the income from those funds—the gains and losses, taxwise and otherwise—could only be characterized as abstruse. Those provisions had evolved—and unless you had been present at creation and through evolution, you'd be a long time trying to understand them."

First confronted with this contract in June 1986, Herb Siegel had asked certain questions of WCI's compensation committee about how much Ross's lifestyle was costing the company. Ross—enraged, terming the questions "insulting" and "degrading"—had withdrawn his contract from consideration. He may have speculated that if Siegel were going to make an issue of his contract, it could precipitate a proxy fight—and Siegel at that time had not yet been diluted down to 19 percent. Now, in February 1987, Ross was again proffering the contract; the full board was given only a week to study it before voting.

Siegel and his directors objected that it was being railroaded through, and argued that the fifty-five-page agreement was so complicated that they could not possibly decipher it in a week. They argued, too, that it should be put to a shareholder vote (as Liman had originally promised it would be), and also that the four management directors had a conflict of interest and should be precluded from voting. They did not prevail on any of these points.

Vanden Heuvel, as chairman of the compensation committee, led the well-scripted charge for Ross on this contract. Much of his argument, interestingly enough, centered on Ross's relationships with the stars. Indeed, in the package that he sent with the draft of the contract to all directors, he included a recent *Wall Street Journal* article about Steven Spielberg which mentioned Spielberg's relationship with Ross. (It featured Spielberg, signing off from a phone call with Ross, saying, "Bye, I love you." It also mentioned that when Spielberg's mother—who ran a kosher restaurant in Los Angeles called the Milky Way—first travelled on the Warner jet, Ross had the cabin ceiling covered with Milky Way candy wrappers.)

However much affection Ross no doubt came to feel for Spielberg over the years, the pure utility of that relationship to Ross, in his business life, is unmistakable. One person who knew Ross well said that since the time of Murdoch's attack, Ross always felt that his relationships with the stars were his "armor" against any would-be acquiror. Now, in defending his contract, Ross was extracting value from these relationships within the company as well. So, while Spielberg and other stars tended to be overwhelmed by Ross's generosity—and to feel, quite naturally, that it was Ross who was the giver and they mere takers—the long-term benefit Ross received far outweighed what he gave (which derived, in any event, from the corporate treasury). As his erstwhile partner Caesar Kimmel once put it, "Steve gives peas for watermelons."

Vanden Huevel invoked the usual galaxy—Spielberg, Streisand, Jones, Eastwood—but he added a new name, too, that of Dustin Hoffman. Ross had recently returned from a Christmas trip to Paris, where he and Courtney had hosted Dustin Hoffman and his wife, Lisa, and Spielberg and his wife, Amy Irving, at the Ritz. Anouk Aimée, a friend of Hoffman's, had also joined them—and immediately hit it off with Ross. ("We *recognized* each other," she said repeatedly. "He is so sensitive, like a complete artist—he knows everything, he sees everything. It is so unusual, for a man of that dimension to be so sensitive. I wish he had been my brother. He would have protected me.")

Hoffman, who had been friendly with Courtney in the seventies and whom Ross was just beginning to pursue, still seemed somewhat dazzled, years later, when he recalled this vacation. "He was generous to an extent where you'd never come across it before in your life," Hoffman said. "We had two floors at the Ritz, there were Israeli secret servicemen—I think they were Mossad—walking up and down the corridors. We went to the Musée d'Orsay before it was opened to the public. My kid, drawing on the floor in the Musée d'Orsay, with nobody else around, is an image I'll never forget."

Spielberg, for his part, later recalled that he and his wife were amazed to find each of their names printed on stationery in their rooms and embroidered on their bathrobes. The sine qua non for Ross was that everything appear to be freely given. As Terry Semel said, "Steve *never* talked Warner Brothers business with the stars. He would never mix it. I used to say, 'You have the best job in the world—you talk drivel to these people, and I'm the cheap sonuvabitch who's taking all their money!'" Bob Daly confirmed that Ross believed in "relationships, and the natural flow that would come out of relationships—he *never* would say to Clint or Barbra, 'C'mon.'" Indeed, Daly added, it was Ross who had taught Streisand how to negotiate—something which had not redounded to the studio's benefit. As Ralph Peterson, Warner Bros. treasurer, explained, "Barbra is very difficult. We'd make a deal with her lawyer, and then she'd call and say, 'I've fired him, there's no deal.'

"I'd say, 'But we made a deal.'

"She'd say, 'He agreed, I didn't. I'm sending a new lawyer.'

"And I'd say, 'Will he be speaking for you?'

"She'd say, 'Maybe yes, maybe no.'"

While Ross would never exert pressure on the stars *vis-à-vis* the studio, he did ask them to do small favors—like meeting with business people who were going to make a deal with the company and were smitten with them; or making an appearance for a particular charity, or talking to the press. Streisand, now, made up for having allegedly backed down when contacted by Murdoch's agent; Siegel did not intimidate her. She was quoted in a *Wall Street Journal* article in 1987, saying that she would, indeed, leave the studio if Ross departed, and she added, "Who is this guy Herb Siegel? Doesn't he run a boat company?"

This was the first time that Ross—through vanden Heuvel—had so deliberately linked these relationships to his own compensation. It was, however, the kind of argument that could only be counted a winning one with a board such as this, with a majority so mesmerized by Ross, because the benefit to the company of these relationships was not easy to quantify. Streisand's recording contracts were extremely profitable, but those were with CBS; her movies, mainly with Warner Bros., were mixed. Spielberg made nearly all his movies at MCA and at Warner Bros.; it so happened that, with the exception of *The Color Purple,* his biggest-grossing movies were for MCA. Quincy Jones had not been a steady moneymaker. Clint Eastwood, on the other hand, generally had been.

But if the value that accrued to the company from Ross's sworn devotees was questionable, that which accrued to Ross was not. At the decisive board meeting, vanden Heuvel (who is said to have referred to Ross, at one point, as "godlike") delivered his paean to Ross, emphasizing not only Ross's Hollywood relationships but also the successful deals that Ross had orchestrated in the last couple of years. Ray Troubh seconded him—and he, too, went on to underscore the importance of Ross's rapport with the Hollywood set. He reported to his colleagues that he had spoken at length about this subject to Semel, who had said that if Ross were to leave the company, there would likely be a major defection from the studio.

It was not a bad gambit. Improbable as a walkout of talent from Warner Bros. was, it was a dramatic threat, with potentially disastrous consequences—something that could ease the consciences of any WCI directors who might be troubled (even if unwilling to say so) by the conspicuous venality of Ross's contract. In any event, the vote was 9 to 6: all of Ross's directors (including the management, without whom he would have lost) against Siegel and all of his.


Finally, it was in June 1987, at a WCI shareholders' meeting—Ross's perennial showcase, those events for which he prepared so assiduously that he would find himself at a loss on a shareholder's question only once in thirty years—that Ross formalized what was, to him, his unmitigated triumph over Siegel. There had been skirmishing between the two in the preceding months. A year earlier, in the spring of 1986, the board had ratified the authority of the "special audit committee," which consisted of Troubh and Buttenweiser—and had thus ensured that they alone, among the directors, would read the Armstrong Report. Now—perhaps beause of his outrage at the contract Ross had won, and because of his further outrage at the finding of the WCI audit committee that there was in the Armstrong Report "insufficient evidence to find Weiss guilty" (despite the findings of the jury and the Court of Appeals)—Siegel had argued that he needed to read the report in order to determine whether or not he should be voting for Ross and also Buttenweiser, who both were nominated for reelection at the coming annual meeting.

In response, Ross had initiated discussions to buy Siegel out. But Siegel —in a habit that exasperated some of his own advisers—had refused what Ross's negotiators were offering (about $40 a share), and also refused to counter with a price. This had been his approach to Ross's contract, too; he objected to it, but when Ross's representatives attempted to elicit specific objections from him (they might have given up one or two of the more outrageous provisions if they could have won his complicity), Siegel had refused. "Herb felt that whatever he said would become the ceiling. Ross would negotiate down from there, so that later he could talk about how he'd gotten the best of Herb Siegel," said one Siegel adviser. "But the result—since Herb wouldn't name anything—was that we couldn't negotiate. You could almost have been sympathetic to Ross at this point. He had this bee, buzzing around his head, and there wasn't any way to deal with him."

By this time, Siegel and some of his own advisers were clearly at odds. Frustrated as he was by his incessant battling with Ross on Ross's home court, where the fix was always in, Herb Siegel remained convinced that his greatest strength was that, inasmuch as he had incurred no debt in his transaction with WCI, he was his own master and could afford to bide his time. While some of his advisers, more attuned to the eighties mentality, were always trying to effectuate an exit strategy and get a deal done, Siegel believed this was a situation where patience would win out.

With the buyout discussions terminated, Siegel had sued for the Armstrong Report in Delaware Chancery Court, but then agreed to a compromise settlement: only he and certain of his lawyers could read the report, and they were bound to divulge its contents to no one. Having read it, Siegel had returned to court, asking that a wider circle, including a criminal lawyer, be allowed access to it, as well as to its thousands of pages of exhibits (it was his lawyer's letter to the court, using excerpts of the report, that years later became public, through the court's error); but his request had been denied.

At the annual June meeting, Ross led from his strength, which no one could refute: under his aegis, the company had recovered. Earnings in 1986 had been up 48 percent over 1985, with movies, recorded music, and cable enjoying the best year in their histories. "WCI's 1986 results attest, once again, to the fact that WCI, now twenty-five years old, is one of the strongest entertainment and communications companies in the entire world," Ross declared, with his characteristic emphasis on the word "entire"—that salesman's penchant for overemphasis and exaggeration which he never outgrew. Ross ticked off his achievements. The market value of Kinney Service, when it went public twenty-five years earlier, had been $12.5 million; now it was well in excess of $5 billion. Total compounded average annual return to shareholders between 1976 and 1986 was 22 percent per year. Warner Bros. had been "the most successful motion picture company in the world for the last seventeen years"— number one in 1984 and 1985 in box-office results; and the record company, the most profitable in the industry (including foreign competitors), in seven out of the past ten years.

Referring to all the businesses that WCI had sold, Ross said, "We adhered to a key WCI principle: Find the right buyer at the right time and retain an interest in that company's future. As a result, our residual holdings in the businesses we sold are worth approximately $700 million at today's market, yet are carried on our books for less than $75 million." He brought up, too, the Warner-Amex acquisition of which he was so proud, stating that the value of Warner Cable had risen by over $1.3 billion since they had acquired American Express's interest. Stepping back to survey the whole, Ross asserted that the company's comeback after Atari showed that the great years that had preceded that disaster had been "no fluke."

Finally, he keyed on his strong suit, the fact that "in an industry where long-term is usually defined as anywhere from three minutes in music to two hours in film . . . our people stay with us"—and what he apparently thought of as his trump (somewhat illusory though it was): "It is no coincidence that great artists like Steven Spielberg, Clint Eastwood, Barbra Streisand, and Paul Simon have chosen to work with WCI and to commit themselves to us."

If Ross had bought time through his control of his board and executives, using them as a shield against Siegel when the company and he were weak, it was his success, now, that made him invulnerable. And with his stated exposition of that success as a predicate, Ross moved on to the business at hand. He announced that since Siegel and Chris-Craft had not reaffirmed their commitment to support the slate (including Buttenweiser and himself) for reelection, WCI was withdrawing its commitment to fill the vacancy created by the resignation of a Chris-Craft director, Senator Abraham Ribicoff, and was withdrawing its renomination of another Chris-Craft director, Howard Arvey. Thus, the size of the board would be reduced from sixteen to fourteen directors (and the Ross/Siegel ratio, now 10:4).

Arvey made an impassioned objection, asking that shareholders cast a direct ballot for him, and concluded by saying, "Stepping on me is just Steve Ross's way of showing Chris-Craft that Steve can step on any shareholder or director. That, if you think about it, includes you." Siegel came to a lectern in front of the auditorium, also, to take exception to much of what was being said, and what had been said in WCI's proxy statement; during Siegel's brief remarks, Ross—standing at another lectern across the stage—turned his back to him.

As usual in this forum, Ross had all the answers—or, at least, answers that passed muster in this kind of setting. As for wider access to the Armstrong Report, he said: "Just recently, Mr. Siegel requested the documents for Westchester Premier. We were concerned about the confidentiality of the auditor's report, because it was handled by Michael Armstrong, an ex-U.S. Attorney, and on the audit committee were Larry Buttenweiser and Ray Troubh, two very highly regarded individuals in the country, if not the world.

"We were anxious to protect the confidentiality of it, because many people who gave testimony to the audit committee gave it of their—all gave it of their own volition, since the audit committee had no subpoena power, and they gave it freely and spoke very freely, so we were very anxious to protect that."

Ross delivered these remarks with a straight face.

On the defense of his contract, he essentially argued, briefly, that he would indeed do amazingly well if the company did. But he also said, with the seigneurial air that was increasingly becoming his, "I find this very distasteful, defending myself," and he passed the duty along to vanden Heuvel. (A shareholder questioned whether William vanden Heuvel could truly be "arm's-length," given the fact that the law firm with which he was associated did legal work for WCI. This shareholder was obviously unaware of the nearly $1 million that vanden Heuvel had personally received from the company, just three years earlier, for his role in the sale of the Ralph Lauren cosmetics company.)

Mac Schwebel, the long-time associate of Canadian stock swindler Lou Chesler and owner of Warner-Seven Arts stock whom Ross had successfully courted back in 1969, rose to offer an unctuous homily to Ross, as he had done at every annual meeting since Kinney's acquisition of Warner-Seven Arts. (Ross had shown his gratitude in the usual way: in 1982 the company had donated $500,000 in honor of Schwebel to the Solomon Schecter School in Westchester, New York, of which Schwebel was a trustee.)

But the high point of the show was the appearance of Steven Spielberg, who had even donned a white suit, for the occasion. "Oh, a familiar face. Please state your name," Ross deadpanned.

Referring to WCI's "storybook success," Spielberg told the crowd, "I am too secure in my line of work and too fat as a result of it, to be seduced by deals and perks and promises. I have settled down to live and work in only two houses. . . . MCA and WCI." His reason for doing so, he continued, was his "respect and admiration for people, for two people in particular, Sidney J. Sheinberg and Steven J. Ross. . . . Steve is as obsessed with the creative development of this company as I am in the making of my movies," Spielberg continued, "and I just wanted to come here and say, as long as Mr. Ross remains the skipper of this battle wagon, I will never leave my station and [will] continue to make pictures here that hopefully will please you and your families." After reading a letter of like affirmation from Clint Eastwood, Spielberg concluded: "There are hundreds of creative people in my hometown who second everything that Clint and I have just said. We really do love Steve Ross. We think Steve Ross *is* WCI."

That had always been the cardinal conceit—propagated subtly by Ross, and gradually adopted by most others at the company. Paradoxically, it had been the source of much of the company's strength; also, its weaknesses, and certainly its abuse. And it was the notion that had been challenged almost reflexively by Siegel—whose actions flowed, not unreasonably, from the premise that WCI was a public company. (In December 1987, when Ross would ask the board to grant 100,000 options, each, to Streisand and Eastwood, and 200,000 options to Spielberg, Siegel would charge that these grants were a "payoff"—essentially, a personal gift from Ross for their support of him against Siegel, funded by the corporate treasury.)

The saga would continue. Siegel would not be bought out for a couple years more, and he would continue to wrangle with Ross, and would, in fact, take him to court on one issue successfully; his investment would prosper, his initial stake of roughly $400 million amounting ultimately to $2.4 billion—hardly enabling Ross to cast Siegel as a loser. Indeed, as far as Siegel was concerned, he had by dint of patience and perseverance achieved most of his objectives: he had prodded Ross to do what was required to restore the company; he had prevented Ross from taking the company private and, essentially, stealing it from its shareholders; and he and his shareholders had reaped a fortune. But—on the issue that Ross cared most about—he would never again pose any threat to Ross's power.

The enmity between the two men never lapsed. It was a singular situation in Ross's life, inasmuch as he was the master of bonhomie, even with people he strongly disliked—"the king of making people think they had a good relationship with him," as one person said. He prided himself on keeping his cool, never losing control; he loved to describe negotiations with David Geffen, for example, where Geffen would be shouting at him, chain-smoking, and he would just keep extending Mickey Rudin's gold Dunhill to light Geffen's cigarettes.

Siegel, however, had done what no one else had: in contrast to Murdoch, who had attacked but then disappeared, Siegel had attempted, over a period of years, to call Ross to account, and he had interfered with Ross's dominion. For that, Ross paid him back. He put on "his fight face," as Arthur Liman once said. Or, he "cut Herb Siegel off at the knees," as Caesar Kimmel liked to express it. Years later, associates of Ross would remark on their surprise at the meanness Ross had exhibited. "Steve could have treated Herb with more dignity and respect," commented Ray Troubh. "If he had, I think there would have been less carping at the board meetings. It was so unlike Steve—you would go to a movie premiere, you would think Herb might have been given a better table, or not seated in the back of the room.

"I always had a soft spot for Herb," Troubh continued. "He did his homework, and he asked a lot of questions other people were afraid to. He was a nitpicker of sorts—but those were perilous days, and I don't think it was wrong to ask the kinds of questions he did."

At the time, however, Troubh did not break ranks; he voted with the Ross bloc. Abe Ribicoff, who had resigned after Ross's contract was voted through, later testified in a deposition about his reasons for resigning, which he had discussed at the time with Siegel but not divulged publicly. "I said, look, Herb, I have been [a director for] three years and . . . this is the worst association I have had in my lifetime . . . and I don't intend to spend any part of my life as an exercise in futility and that is what the Warner board is, it is an outrage, and I think that Steve Ross's contract is one of the most outrageous things that could happen. Nobody is worth that money.

"What you have," Ribicoff had continued, "you have a person who has exceeded his power with the greatest of arrogance and you have a bunch of myrmidons on that board completely manipulated by Steve Ross. . . ."

Ribicoff was a sophisticated veteran of American business and political life, but this experience, he emphasized, stood alone. "I have never in all my life been with a board so subservient to the chairman or the chief executive officer of any company. . . ."

# 7

Once all the diversionary ventures of WCI had been sold off or shut down, Ross was left with the core businesses that he had acquired in the late sixties and early seventies—movies, records, cable, and, to a lesser degree, publishing. He was ready to begin building again. As Spielberg later remarked, many businessmen "consolidate and play it safe, but that would have bored Steve. So he just kept doing Lego sets. He had to have the best Lego set on the block." Rather than adding on myriad odd parts, however, as he had done in the sixties and again in the seventies, this time he would build from the company's strength and concentrate on the core.

Since Ross had achieved his "coup of all coups" in the buyback of Warner-Amex, his attention had been increasingly riveted on cable. It provided the balance that he always strove for, inasmuch as it was the most stable of all WCI's businesses, not subject to the fluctuations of the movie and record businesses. It fit what had become his orthodoxy—that WCI must control its distribution. Cable was a valuable business in itself, but it was, further, an outlet for the company's product. And, with deregulation going into effect in 1987, it was primed for growth.

WCI's survival struggle of the last several years had cost it dearly in the cable competition, however; while other cable owners were acquiring systems, WCI had cut back, and sold off some of what it had fought so hard to obtain. "It was killing me," Ross said. "I knew, during the Atari period, that I had lost ground." Another of Ross's precepts—which, like the control of distribution, sprang from what he often described as the need to "control our destiny"—was that WCI should always be one of the biggest, in its key businesses; that way, its voice would be assured of being heard among its competitors, and also in Washington.

However, WCI was only middling in size in cable: it was about the sixth largest in the country, whereas in its other key businesses it was generally the first or second. And to be middling in anything—but especially something he cared about—was anathema to Ross. As he frequently remarked to his associates during this period of time, lamenting the fact that cable was a major part of their company but they were only a minor player in the industry, "We are too large to be small, and too small to be large."

Through much of 1986 and the early months of 1987, Ross explored various possibilities. He entered into negotiations to acquire Storer Communications, but could not come to terms; and he discussed entering into a joint venture with a number of companies. Time Inc.—its cable holdings making it the third largest in the country at the time—was an interesting candidate. At Ross's instigation, one of his executives, Edward Bleier, mentioned to Michael Fuchs, head of Time's HBO, that talks between their respective companies might prove fruitful. Fuchs told Nicholas Nicholas, then the newly designated president of Time Inc., that he ought to call Ross. And, one day in February 1987, Nicholas, just released from jury duty, called Ross from the courthouse and told him he would like to come see him. Ross—having arranged things as usual so that he was the one receiving the call—graciously agreed.

Their discussions proceeded, and by August 1987 the outlines of a transaction began to take shape for Nicholas. Flying back from a safari in Kenya, Nicholas stopped overnight in Zurich and stayed up most of the night, excitedly writing notes on a small hotel pad. When he returned to New York, he handed these notes to Gerald Levin (whom he had bypassed in the contest for president, and whose title was "chief strategist") and asked him to put them into the form of a memo.

The memo, which Levin addressed to J. Richard Munro, Time's chairman and CEO, declared that their "primary long-term objective" should be to bring about the consolidation of Time Inc., Warner Communications, and the Turner Broadcasting System (in which Time then owned a stake), so that "the new Time Inc." would be "an entertainment-oriented communications company."

That idea was a radical one for the journalistic Time Inc., and both Nicholas and Levin realized that a great deal of acculturation would have to take place before the company's senior management and its board would approve such a fundamental reshaping of the company. Moreover, as the memo also acknowledged, they would have to satisfy themselves and their directors that—contrary to persistent rumor over the years—there were no skeletons in Ross's closets. As the memo said: "Any inquiry of Steve's past must include an examination of the Westchester Premier Theatre scandal, although presumably that is behind him."

Unbeknownst to the Time executives, there was at that very moment a different investigation in the U.S. Attorney's Office for the Southern District that had been brewing quietly for months, and—depending on whether its target decided to cooperate and incriminate others, or, alternatively, was indicted—might shortly become public. It did not involve Ross directly. But it did focus on his company's past, giving substance to what had been rumored for so long. It also gave added resonance to the government's argument at Solomon Weiss's trial in the Westchester Premier case, concerning his maintenance of a cash fund. And, since it involved the company's early, well-entrenched relationship with organized crime—whose tentacles are, of course, both varied and tenacious —it was uncertain where, ultimately, it might lead.

The target of the government's investigation was Daniel Katz, the chairman of Kinney System, Inc. Katz had inherited Katz Parking when his father had died in the sixties, and in 1970 had sold the company to Kinney; he worked directly under Caesar Kimmel for a couple of years. Then, when National Kinney was spun off from WCI at the close of 1971 —with WCI still owning a majority of its voting shares—Katz had become chairman of the parking company (although, according to Morton Sweig, the vice-chairman of National Kinney, Kimmel had continued to oversee it until the late seventies). Martin Fischer, a lawyer who had joined the company in 1967 when he was hired by Kimmel and Richard Seley, had gone to National Kinney with Katz to become president of Kinney Parking. For more than a dozen years, Katz and Fischer worked closely together.

It was not until the end of 1978 that Ross was finally free of Kinney, when he sold WCI's majority ownership. The earlier spin-off had proved a blessing, since Kinney had been beset with problems of fraud and corruption; but Ross—despite his control of Kinney—had not suffered from his connection either in prosecutions or the press. In the price-fixing case that the government brought in 1976 against National Cleaning and ten other companies, National Cleaning's chairman, Morton Sweig, and its president, Morris Weintraub, were also charged; both these individuals and the company pled *nolo contendere* to a criminal information, stating that the defendants had engaged in a conspiracy since "at least as early as 1970" to 1974, to restrain trade by allocating customers among themselves, submitting non-competitive bids to customers, and compensating one another for customers lost to each other. This conspiracy did, of course, begin at a time when National Cleaning was a wholly owned subsidiary of Kinney Services, Inc., WCI's predecessor company, of which Ross was co-CEO and president. As Sweig insisted, "Steve had to approve *everything*. He didn't show his face but he knew everything that went on here."

National Kinney also had an electrical contracting subsidiary, National States Electric Corp. It was disclosed in National Kinney's 1980 annual report—when National States showed an operating loss of $11 million, and wrote off an additional $7.6 million—that National States' earnings had been overstated from 1972 to 1980, through falsification of its records. Consequently, National Kinney's consolidated financial statements for all those years "should not be relied upon." Arthur Young & Company, the historical auditors of both WCI and National Kinney, withdrew their opinions for those years, as well.

By the early eighties, National Kinney was being liquidated, its few viable parts broken off. Katz and Fischer decided to take the parking business public as an independent entity, Kinney System, Inc. Then, in the fall of 1986, it was sold in a leveraged buyout to a group of investors. Katz was to remain to run it, and Fischer became a consultant. (One of the investors, new to the parking business, commented to me that if anyone had wanted to exploit Kinney over the years—skimming it not only for labor and political payoffs but in order to put cash in one's pocket—it would have been easy. "When we bought Kinney in 1986, it had 160 locations and was making a gross of $65 million a year. To have one or two million a year stick to you would have been nothing.")

Within six months of the buyout, Katz became a target in the government's investigation—one that had grown out of the FBI's electronic surveillance of the Palma Boy Social Club, and the Social Club in East Harlem, from December 1983 to February 1985. Those whose conversations were recorded included Anthony ("Fat Tony") Salerno, previously the boss of the Genovese crime family; his brother Cirino, or Charles ("Speed") Salerno, a long-time official of the International Brotherhood of Teamsters' Local 272, which has jurisdiction over the parking and garage employees in New York City; and various other members of organized crime, including Vincent ("Fish") Cafaro, Louis Gatto, Giuseppe Sabato, and Sammy Santora—who are all members of the Genovese family.

The tapes proved a treasure trove for the FBI. Fat Tony Salerno—who was rated, in a 1986 *Fortune* magazine article, the most powerful and wealthiest gangster in America—was convicted in 1986 of racketeering charges in a case popularly known as "the Commission case" (the Commission was the ruling council of the five principal crime families in La Cosa Nostra). He was sentenced to one hundred years in prison. In 1988, Salerno would also be convicted of having allocated contracts and obtained payoffs for the construction of the concrete superstructure of sixteen buildings in Manhattan, including Trump Plaza and the Jacob J. Javits Convention Center (this conviction was reversed on appeal). Salerno would die in prison in 1992.

In mining the thousands of hours of tape-recorded conversations, FBI agents came upon nuggets, tangential to their major investigation, that led, eventually, to others. According to two investigators, Fat Tony Salerno was heard on the tapes saying words to the effect of "We *own* Kinney"— and bragging about how much money they (the Genovese family) made from the company.

That, of course, had been the long-held belief not only of various FBI agents but of some people within the company. While the origins of the Genovese connection were not crystal-clear, many speculated that Longie Zwillman had had an interest initially (as his widow, too, is said to have asserted), and that that had passed to Gerry Catena (to whom Manny Kimmel was close), who was for many years the head of the Genovese family operations in New Jersey. Whatever the origins of possible Genovese ownership in the company, the ongoing connections between the company and the family were plain: government investigators had long been convinced that Local 272, the parking and garage employees' union with which Kinney dealt, was controlled by the Genovese family.

Vincent Cafaro, one of the people recorded, began cooperating with the government after he was indicted in the Commission case, and he submitted numerous signed statements to the FBI. In one of his early statements, in October 1986, Cafaro—who claimed he had known Fat Tony Salerno for over thirty years—said, "In our brugad [the Genovese family], most of the members of La Cosa Nostra make their living from illegal gambling businesses, loansharking and labor racketeering. Control of the labor unions is what gives our brugad its power. However, there are instances when individuals are murdered based on the 'okay' of the hierarchy of our brugad."

Cafaro confirmed the common wisdom about Local 272. In a statement made in January 1987, he said, "I have known Charlie Salerno for many years. I have also known Salerno by the names 'Charlie' and 'Speed.' . . . Unlike his brother [Fat Tony], Speed is not a made member in our brugad.

Speed is a union official in the garage and parking lot Teamsters Union which is located in Manhattan.... This union represents garage employees and parking lot attendants ... the union is ours; it belongs to our brugad.

"Speed Salerno has the New York City garage and parking lot industry locked up through sweetheart contracts with the owners of these businesses.... Speed collects money from garage and parking lot owners and delivers this money to East Harlem. Speed used to deliver this money to his brother Fat Tony or to me in East Harlem. The cash ranged from two thousand dollars to five thousand dollars per score [garage].... Speed has never had problems negotiating or collecting payoffs from the owners of garages and parking lots in New York City. This used to be because Fat Tony was the 'power' behind Speed and 'our union' [Local 272]." Cafaro added that since Fat Tony had gone to prison, Speed delivered the money to Sammy Santora.

Cafaro was describing what Ross's one-time close friend, Judd Richheimer, had told me about: payments that were made routinely, as a way of life. Later, after reading Cafaro's statements, I asked Richheimer about Charlie Salerno, and Richheimer stressed that while Salerno collected the money, he was only a conduit.

"Charlie Salerno is a lovely gentleman. He's my neighbor down here," said Richheimer, who lost his job at Riverside after Kinney sold the funeral business, and is now living in Boca Raton, Florida, where he is a funeral director (when he gets very busy, he is apt to declare that "the angel of death has swooped low"). "But he was a front," Richheimer continued. "He wasn't 'made'—he didn't have the power. The guy who owned the union was known as 'Stretch'—Joe Stracci." One investigator confirmed that in the sixties, when Richheimer was with Kinney Parking, Stracci—an old-time mobster who was part of a group that included Thomas Lucchese, Frank Costello, and Vincent John Rao—"owned the rights" to the parking lot payoffs.

When Katz learned that he was under investigation in the late spring of 1987, he went to see former Federal Judge Harold Tyler and asked him to represent him. There was a great deal at stake for the forty-eight-year-old Katz. He had become enormously successful; he was said to be worth tens of millions. He had parlayed his expertise in the parking business into lucrative real estate investments; with his frequent partners, lawyer Leonard Boxer and developer Norman Segal, he had built the Montana, a luxury building on Broadway, for example.

He had also achieved standing in his community: he was chairman of the National Parking Association, a Washington-based trade group, as well as board chairman of the Metropolitan Garage Owners Association (in that position, he was the link between the industry and the union). And, according to one person who knew him well, it was extremely important to Katz that he held those positions, and that he was regarded as someone whom others relied on as a problemsolver. He was treasurer of his synagogue, Temple Israel, in Great Neck, where he and his family lived.

From conversations with a prosecutor at the U.S. Attorney's Office, Judge Tyler believed that the government had tape recordings of conversations between Charlie Salerno and Katz; and that the government's case would allege a "sweetheart contract" struck between Katz, for Kinney, and Local 272. ("Sweetheart contracts" in such situations take various forms, but among the more common is one where the company is allowed to hire non-union workers—paying them substandard wages and providing little or no benefit coverage—in return for which the company pays the union official a bribe.)

After his second meeting with Katz, Judge Tyler made his recommendation, and Katz said he wanted some time to think about it. He understood that if he did not cooperate with the government and implicate others, he would be indicted. Tyler said, later, that he had had the feeling that Katz was not telling him everything, and that there might be more than the payoff situation they had discussed.

It would appear, from Vincent Cafaro's signed statements, that there was indeed more to cause Katz concern. In one of Cafaro's early statements, in November 1986, he said: "Approximately a year and a half ago, I obtained a construction contract for Leon Morono of Marson Construction, Bronx, N.Y. The contract was on a project located at 86th St. and 3rd Ave., N.Y., N.Y. I call the location 'The Old Woolworth Building.' It is across the street from Papaya King on the northeast side of 86th St. and 3rd Ave. I obtained the contract for Morono through Speed Salerno and Steve Crea [a member of the Lucchese family]. Morono had already submitted a bid for the 86th Street project. I had Speed talk to a First Name Unknown Katz, a garage guy, with Speed and Fat Tony. Speed had previously introduced Morono to Katz. Katz told Speed that Morono had bid too high and that if he lowered the bid by about $1,000,000 that Morono would obtain the contract. I told Morono to lower the bid, which he did, and he was awarded the contract. I asked Morono what the contract was worth to him or what was a fair finder's fee for my help. Morono told me $100,000, which we agreed upon."

An investigator told me that he believed that the "Katz" referred to in the above statement was Dan Katz; and that it is not unusual for Cosa Nostra informants to know only partial, or rough approximations of, names. And in the following statement of Cafaro's, made a couple of months later, this investigator said that although "Katz" is now referred to as "Louis Katz"—thus filling in the "First Name Unknown" blank—he believed it was an error, and that Cafaro was talking about Dan Katz.

"Although Speed has the garages in New York City locked up, he [Speed] would get involved in construction. However, Speed only got involved in construction jobs which involved Louis Katz. Katz is one of the owners of Kinney and Meyers Parking Garage Company. I do not know if Kinney and Meyers is one or two companies. Katz knows Speed for over 30 years and is also very friendly with Fat Tony Salerno. Whatever Speed and Fat Tony wanted, Katz would do relative to awarding a bid to get a contractor who was building a parking garage for Katz so long as it was a 'competitive bid.' One of Katz's partners is an individual whose last name is Spiegel. However, the real 'scores' were made when dealing with sub-contractors who would have to kick back 30, 40, or 50 thousand dollars to get a job. Fat Tony and Speed did not discuss this area with me in any greater detail.

"Fat Tony was also very friendly with Manny Kimball, the former owner of Kinney Parking Company. Kimball was a short Jewish man who was in his mid to late 80's when he died."

Cafaro's confusion as to whether Kinney and Meyers were one or two companies is interesting. Caesar Kimmel and Leonard Meyers were close friends and business partners for many years, and some used to speculate that they may have collaborated, in competitive bidding situations, rather than competed. "Spiegel" may well be Norman Segal, who was Katz's partner in real estate deals. And "Manny Kimball" is clearly Manny Kimmel, Caesar's father, who died in Florida in 1982, at the age of eighty-six —leaving as his widow a Swedish woman, Ivi, who, friends said, Kimmel had married several years earlier, when she was in her twenties.

Cafaro's statements present a rough and imprecise sketch. If what they assert about Katz is true, however, then he was enmeshed in a web, spun over decades, of contacts and transactions—one that would appear to have been extensive, involving not only parking lot union payoffs but construction deals as well, and one that would have been difficult for him to extricate himself from.

On the morning of August 12, 1987, Dan Katz was found in the front seat of his Cadillac, parked a few blocks from his home in Great Neck, a shotgun propped between his legs. He had been shot in the chest, and he died at the hospital about an hour later. The gun, it emerged, had been given to Katz by his grandfather and had been in the basement of his house for years. He left no note. It was, however, almost immediately termed a suicide. The following day, local detectives told the press that Katz was "upset about a couple of bad business deals." Martin Fischer, who answered the phone at the Katz home, told a *New York Post* reporter, "I'm shocked and grieved. He was my friend for 15 years. He was a dynamic person, an active citizen and a leader. We're sad."

Because Katz had been a target of an investigation involving organized crime, the FBI also investigated his death, and they too concluded that it had been a suicide. Later, Katz's lawyer, Judge Tyler, who had last seen Katz about a month before his death, told me that the whole episode left him puzzled. "Dan Katz's wife had told the cops that she thought it was a suicide—that was her first thought. But then, about a month later, she came to see me. She was groping to understand. She really didn't think he had been *that* despondent and neither did I. He wasn't happy, of course. But, from the case the prosecutor had described, even if Katz had gone to trial and been convicted, he might have gotten a sentence of a couple years—not really reason to kill himself."

Where Fischer may have fit in the government's investigation is not clear. One investigator, when I asked whether Fischer had been involved, said that "that is too close to what we were doing, and I won't comment." Despite the fact that Fischer had had no tie to WCI since the end of 1978 when WCI had sold its majority interest in National Kinney, he continued to be treated as one of the Warner family. The year after Katz's death, when Oded Aboodi began to plan the opening of a small bank with which he, Ross, and other members of the Warner family would be involved, Martin Fischer was made one of its directors.

Katz's death short-circuited the government's investigation. It languished for several years. The assistant U.S. Attorney in charge was assigned another case and, subsequently, left the office; it was reassigned. In 1991, Charles Salerno was forced from the presidency of Local 272 by the court-appointed administrator of the Teamster International Union, Charles Carberry. And, in July 1992, in the Southern District of New York, what had been the Katz case finally culminated in the indictments of Charles Salerno, Victor Alfieri, and Eugene Bennett, all sometime officials of Local 272. They were charged with turning Local 272 into a racketeering enterprise and using it to enrich themselves with bribes from garage owners.

They were alleged to have extracted illegal payments from garage owners at Christmas and before their summer vacations; to have accepted bribes from employers who were seeking to fire union employees without interference from Local 272; and to have accepted bribes from garage owners in exchange for permitting those owners to hire non-union workers in union garages. The government charged that the conspiracy had taken place "from in or about 1973" up to the filing of the indictment. Presumably, the government chose to frame the conspiracy as beginning in the early seventies, rather than even earlier, because it was then that Salerno became an officer of Local 272.

In November 1992, Salerno, Alfieri, and Bennett pled guilty. Salerno, seventy-eight, was subsequently sentenced to three months in prison, followed by twenty-one months of home confinement; Alfieri, to twenty-four months in prison, and three years of supervised release. Bennett has not yet been sentenced.

The Salerno indictment did not disclose the identity of the garage owners who gave the payoffs. And there was no public report of the investigation of Katz and Kinney. Asked whether the government's investigation was continuing, Assistant U.S. Attorney Daniel Nardillo said, "I can't confirm or deny that."

Had Dan Katz lived, it seems plain that he would have either cooperated or been indicted. Had he been indicted, the role he and Kinney apparently played, *vis-à-vis* Speed and Fat Tony Salerno, would of course have become public immediately. Had he cooperated, it would have taken longer, but that role—and, perhaps, more—might eventually have become known. These revelations might have damaged Ross's courtship of Time, which would not be consummated until two years after Katz's death—for at a minimum they would have established, for the first time, what had long been whispered about Kinney's historic ties to organized crime (the story that *Forbes* had printed, and then retracted, with an apology, back in 1970).

In terms of a connection to the mob, this situation was far more weighty than that of the Westchester Premier Theatre—where one might argue that while the theater payoffs were clearly corrupt, the fact that they were made to a Mafia-run organization was in a sense incidental, inasmuch as the proposition had come in over the transom with the hapless Leonard Horwitz. Here, on the other hand, there was a long-established relationship—the kind that is difficult to terminate, and that usually finds not one but multiple avenues of financial opportunity.

If the story of the payoffs Kinney apparently made to Fat Tony *had* become public just as Steve Ross was wooing Time, Ross's supporters surely would have argued to Time executives and directors that it was ancient history (despite the fact that Kinney had been controlled by WCI until December 1978) and, in any event, that Ross had known nothing about it. When Judd Richheimer first described to me the system of payoffs, and the cash fund that he claimed was as large as $1 million a year in the late sixties (when Ross was at the head of Kinney), I asked whether such activities had not made Ross feel vulnerable. "No," he said. "He was always insulated; you can never trace it up. It takes place so many levels down—and the guy above you never wants to know exactly what you're doing."

Richheimer said that his brother Michael, who had been a vice-president of Kinney in the mid-sixties, and had been Kimmel's right hand in running parking, had been subpoenaed to testify in a government investigation of labor payoffs in the seventies. "Michael covered for the company," Richheimer said. "He said he had had four open-heart surgeries, and it had affected his memory. If he hadn't covered, he would have been dead."

Michael, who died of natural causes in 1991, had remained in touch with people in the union over the years, Richheimer said. And Michael Richheimer had discussed Katz's death with these people. "My brother said, 'Dan Katz was a fool and he got what he deserved,'" said Judd Richheimer.

Told that the FBI had investigated Katz's death and determined it a suicide—and that, as one investigator had pointed out in defense of the FBI's conclusion, mob killings are generally shots to the head—Richheimer shrugged and said, "I'm just telling you what I heard. Two in the back of the head is the signature. When they don't want it to attract so much attention, they do it other ways. The people who are meant to know, know."

8

For Ross, merging with Time Inc. would be another gloriously long reach—an extension almost as great, in its way, as in the acquisition of Warner-Seven Arts. To court the company that was Henry Luce's enduring legacy, Ross would have to span an immense cultural divide, proving, if he prevailed, that there was nothing parochial about his charm. And he would also have to do a strong selling job at home; for the environment he had created at WCI was so idyllic that few of its denizens wanted to chance its changing. His movie and record division heads, especially, worried about how the merger might affect their way of life. But in this company, of course, there was no one who—despite the most powerful misgivings—would not defer ultimately to Ross. As one division head said later, somewhat ruefully, "Steve said it would be good for me, so I trusted him. I was a loyal servant."

The real challenge was Time. And the issue there, as Ross quickly discerned, was succession—something that had proven a stumbling block in Time's discussions with other suitors. In July 1986, J. Richard Munro, Time's chairman and CEO, had named Nicholas Nicholas president, thus making him the heir apparent for Munro's job. In any proposed combination, Munro and Nicholas were adamant that, while there might be a sharing of power for a defined period, the ultimate primacy of Time Inc.—in the person of Nicholas—was the sine qua non.

Merger discussions between Time and Capital Cities/ABC were halted when it became clear that no accord could be reached on this point, among others. Also, Martin Davis, the chairman and CEO of Paramount Communications, Inc., later testified in a deposition that he had had a number of conversations with Munro about a merger of Time and Paramount, but that when Munro broached the issue of co-CEOs, and a prearranged succession plan, he had objected.

As for co-CEO relationships, Davis testified: "I pointed out from what I observed in the business world that I never saw one that worked. And I thought that in any organization, where there is always a measure of politics, all one does is engender further politics." Davis also testified, concerning Munro, "He seemed to be obsessed with who was going to succeed him, and—not who, but basically Nick Nicholas. But I did not feel it was my prerogative, or his, for that matter, to determine who was going to succeed whom. I felt very strongly, and I expressed that to him, that that was a board determination."

But with Ross—despite the fact that he had always avoided allowing a potential successor in any proximity to him, even to the point of refusing to name a number two—there was no problem. "Steve said early on, and kept saying, that he had no heir apparent, and Nick would be it," Munro told me. "That was as critical to making this deal happen as anything."

And, while others looked askance at the notion of co-CEOs, Ross warmly embraced it. He liked to remind listeners, during this period, that he was speaking from experience. As he said to me once, explaining his willingness to have a co-CEO, "Very few people have done it—but I did it! And it was one of the most wonderful experiences of my life, from 1967 until June 30, 1972, when Bill Frankel died of a heart attack." Frankel, of course, had acceded utterly to Ross, and his title of co-CEO was purely ceremonial.

From the start, Ross was dealing not only with Munro and Nicholas but also a third major player at Time, Gerald Levin—someone who would assume a cardinal role in the future, and who would appear to have been earmarked as a candidate for that role, early, by Ross. During the period of the merger discussions, Levin, Time's "chief strategist," and the behind-the-scenes orchestrator of nearly all that transpired on the part of Time, worked hand in hand with Nicholas And, in contrast to some Nicholas loyalists who were distrustful of Ross—suspecting that the dowry, Time Inc., was what Ross wanted, and that his vows to Nicholas would be short-lived—Levin was calm, serene, and unfailingly bullish on the deal.

Nicholas and Levin had not always been the collegial partners that they were during their cultivation of this merger. Indeed, their career paths at Time Inc. over the past two decades had intersected repeatedly, but always in ways that undercut, or even seemed to obviate, one of them—more often Levin. This rather dramatic history was, of course, well known to veteran Time-watchers, and one that Ross surely investigated and studied with care.

The first juncture at which Nicholas and Levin met was in 1976, at the fledgling HBO. Levin had recently persuaded Time's current chairman and chief executive officer, Andrew Heiskell, to invest $7.5 million to lease satellite time to transmit HBO's signal to cable systems. It was an idea that did not originate with Levin but one that he appropriated and lobbied for—and its application revolutionized the cable industry. However, HBO—where Levin had been chairman and CEO since 1973, when its creator, Charles Dolan, was forced out—was losing millions of dollars a year, its costs spiralling out of control. Nicholas was recognized as a deft executive, having accomplished the rapid turnaround of Time Inc.'s troubled Manhattan Cable division in the early seventies, and now, in early 1976, Munro asked him to go to HBO as its president. Nicholas refused because, he says, he would be working under Levin, and he felt he needed a free hand. But when Munro returned with the same request several months later, saying that HBO was in danger of being shut down —and promising Nicholas that he would have that free hand—Nicholas agreed. "Nick was jammed down Jerry's throat, and he hated it," one executive who worked under the two at HBO told me, "but Jerry had no choice."

It was not only territorial prerogatives that made this such an uneasy rapprochement on both sides; there was little that was kindred in the two men. Nicholas, who had joined Time Inc. immediately after graduate school in 1964, had the more typical résumé for the company (he'd attended Andover, Princeton, and Harvard Business School), but these credentials were in a sense misleading. The son of Greek immigrants, his father a career naval officer, he had attended these schools on scholarship, and regarded himself in school and, subsequently, at Time, as something of an outsider. In 1970, he had become the assistant of Time's president, James R. ("Brass Knuckles") Shepley—who was also a break from the ineffably genteel Time Inc. mold, in stark contrast, for example, to the silken Heiskell.

Nicholas's father died in 1970, the same year that he became Shepley's assistant, and several who know Nicholas well believe that he came to model himself on his boss, whom he admired intensely. Nicholas saw Shepley as someone fundamentally willing to do the hard thing, and this became a signal Nicholas trait—in style as well as substance. Often, Nicholas exhibited an abrasive edge that inspired fear and dislike among some of the people who worked under him; but Nicholas had concluded early on that it was more important to be respected than liked. "When there's something tough to do, Nick often becomes more tough, and more adversarial than necessary, as though he's steeling himself—and then he *really* does it," commented Thayer Bigelow, a long-time colleague and now a Time Warner executive.

Another close associate declared that Nicholas was critical, if not contemptuous, of the ambience of ease and privilege that vivified Time Inc. "Nick was known early on as a little brash, someone who would say things that were anti-establishment. He felt that Time Inc. was so white-shoe, slipping and sliding off three-martini lunches. He saw a cushy unreality to the place, and himself as someone whose mission was to say, 'We have to pull up our socks, tighten our belts.' "

Nicholas may have viewed himself as a reformer at Time Inc., but Levin saw Nicholas as establishment, or at least someone who could easily pass for it—and himself as the archetypal outsider. The son of a dairy man, Levin had been raised in a religious Jewish home. His mother, in fact, had entertained thoughts of his becoming a rabbi, because he was so accomplished that he was allowed, on occasion, to conduct services in their synagogue even before his bar mitzvah at age thirteen; but by the time Levin entered college, he considered the Judaic philosophy in which he had been raised too confining and parochial. At Haverford, a small Quaker college, he majored in biblical studies and became imbued with the lessons of the New Testament. He strove to cultivate humility, and deny ego; since he decided that keeping his college papers was an act of ego (did not one keep them in the hope that someday someone might read them?), he burned them, as he believed Virgil had done.

Unlike Nicholas's quite standard route to Time Inc., the path that Levin took was eclectic. After graduating from Haverford in 1960, Levin went to the University of Pennsylvania Law School; practiced law at the decidedly establishment firm of Simpson, Thacher & Bartlett; then left for the Development and Resources Corporation and, subsequently, the International Basic Economy Corporation, where he worked for David Lilienthal, the former head of the Tennessee Valley Authority. Levin has always stressed his commitment to public service as the motivation for this early career move from law to business. His first wife, however, Carol Levin, was quoted by Helen Thorpe of the *New York Observer* as saying, "I don't think he wanted to represent the seats of power, [rather] he wanted to be there."

While Nicholas for his first six years had worked in the magazine division—the heart of the company, and the only legitimate Lucean heir —Levin had entered the company in 1972 through HBO, such an incidental adjunct to Time Inc. that it was like coming in through a side door. Reasonably indifferent to his appearance, Levin cut an odd figure among the legions of trim, attractive, well-turned-out young Time Incers: he was short and unprepossessing-looking, sporting double-knit suits with ties that often jarred. And he was awed by the leadership of the company— Heiskell, Hedley Donovan (Time's editor-in-chief), and Shepley—who, while individually very different, together seemed a breed apart from most of the people Levin had known.

But with the triumph of the satellite, Levin had won an acceptance at Time Inc. that might otherwise always have eluded him. He became known as the in-house intellectual, or "resident genius," as Heiskell liked to say, and it was a role that Levin seemed to revel in—perhaps recognizing that his anomalousness at Time Inc could be not a handicap but his strongest suit.

He eschewed the more mundane exhibitions of power. He hated to— and rarely did—fire anyone. He did not seize the opportunity to claim credit for his achievements with Wall Street analysts or the media. His manner was professorial, at times verging on the oracular. Over the years, as Levin rose in the hierarchy, he would still marvel aloud at how unlikely it was that he should find himself in the aerie of corporate power. And some of his colleagues became persuaded that he did, indeed, exist on a more lofty, cerebral, even spiritual plane than they or their fellows.

At the same time, Levin was no stranger to power, particularly in its more subtle manifestations. Thayer Bigelow, who first worked with Levin at HBO in the seventies, told me that Levin is "a glutton for information. He is genuinely interested in what people are doing, from a corporate chieftain to an assistant copy editor. And then, because he has all this information, he becomes an expert on everything, and someone you rely on."

"Jerry's idea," another colleague stated simply, "is control the information, control the power."

Often, Levin, who has a prodigiously retentive memory, would exhibit his prowess—like the boy who, having memorized baseball statistics, recites them at any and every opportunity. A former Time Inc. executive recalled that upon arriving at the office in the morning, Levin would frequently remark to him, in his quiet, oblique way, " 'Well, that was quite an announcement, wasn't it?' And I'd think, 'Omygod! What did I miss?' No one, of course, read as much as Jerry did. And then he'd be so pleased that he'd caught me. I thought then that it was a way of establishing dominance. And I would say, 'Jerry, don't play "Gotcha!" ' "

As facts were power, so was language. Levin would habitually use words in conversations about business that at times seemed pleasantly surprising and evocative, at others, pretentious and highfalutin'—but they were in all cases conspicuous, setting themselves (and their utterer) apart. In a deposition he gave in 1989, he referred to Time Inc.'s "genetic predisposition" to dealing with its system of "church" and "state," and also testified that a given event had occurred "in the summer solstice." Levin was not unaware of his penchant. As he stated in the same deposition, in commenting upon notes he had written in the process of orchestrating the Time-Warner merger, "I was, as I sometimes do, trying to use a more poetic word like 'embracing' rather than what you would normally find in business notes."

Many of Levin's colleagues were awed by the force of his intellect, which for them was highlighted by his powers of expression. But one colleague who worked for Levin for years told me that sometimes he would leave Levin's office after a discussion thinking to himself, "Wow!" —and then, proceeding down the corridor, he would scratch his head and think, "Wait a minute. What did he really *say?*"

While many who worked at HBO in the late seventies credit Nicholas with its salvation, it may be that it was, more, the unlikely and unwilling couple of Nicholas and Levin that worked so extraordinarily well. Nicholas immediately fired several layers of senior management people; hired strong new executives; took a much tougher line in deals with the Hollywood movie studios that were HBO's suppliers; and made alliances with key people in the cable industry, most significantly, John Malone of Tele-Communications Inc. Levin, meanwhile, was the organization's nurturer —warm and likable, if opaque, and so genuinely interested in programming concepts ("He would engage us in what seemed like Socratic dialogues," one employee recalled) that HBO employees felt strongly supported by him. The overall result, in any event, was happy. HBO was in the black within fifteen months of Nicholas's arrival, and after that profits rose steadily.

In 1980, Andrew Heiskell recommended to the board that Munro succeed him as chief executive officer—a decision that augured the beginning of the end for the old Time Inc. Although Munro had started his career at Time on the business side of the magazine division, and had been the publisher of *Sports Illustrated* in the early seventies, it was his subsequent tenure as head of the video group that had placed him on Heiskell's short list of candidates. In the latter part of the seventies, the video group, thanks to HBO, had gone from losing several million dollars in 1975 and 1976 to becoming the largest and fastest-growing profit producer in the company, contributing nearly 50 percent of all Time Inc. earnings.

While the magazine division's earnings continued to rise in the early eighties, they were fuelled by the established magazines—*Time, Sports Illustrated,* and *People*—not the newer efforts. Over the years, Time Inc. had dabbled in many different areas—newspapers, moviemaking, forest products, broadcast-TV stations—but these had always been the poor relations, invested in only as a hedge for the magazines. (Luce had once rejected a deal to buy a movie studio, writing in a memo that if he had to invest in leisure he might consider horse and dog racing, but "would exclude the service of anesthetizing people by TV.") The core of the company, the very reason for its existence, the source of its pride and its famous "arrogance," had always been the magazines, and power within the corporation had derived from them. But now it was the video group that seemed to be lighting the way to the company's future, and its personnel—Munro, Nicholas, Levin, and others—who were occupying the executive suites on the thirty-fourth floor.

His selection of Munro, however, was a decision that Heiskell rather quickly came to regret as he watched Munro—an unaffected man who had done graduate work at Teachers College, Columbia University, and whom one might take for a teacher rather than the CEO of Time Inc.—become increasingly ineffectual in his new position. "I was surprised when Munro announced, within a month or so of his appointment, that he would retire in ten years, effectively abdicating," Heiskell said. "It was as though he stopped growing—or, more, regressed—from the day he became CEO."

The two contenders for Munro's just-vacated post, chief of the video division, were Nicholas and Levin—with Nicholas the odds-on favorite. He was credited with the turnaround of both Manhattan Cable and, far more impressively, HBO. He also had strongly advocated in the late seventies that Time Inc. should buy the other 90 percent that it did not own of the cable system, ATC. The company purchased it for about $200 million in 1978, and by the time of the Time-Warner merger in 1989, it would be valued at $7 billion. Levin, for his part, was credited with the idea of the satellite transmission and, to a degree, the success of HBO. To the surprise of many—and the chagrin of Nicholas—Munro chose Levin. It was clear that Munro was very fond of Levin personally, but Nicholas thought, too, that Munro was dazzled, and seduced, by Levin's verbal virtuosity.

When Nicholas and Levin's paths crossed again, four years later, it was an unhappy nexus for Levin. In the interim, Nicholas, as Time Inc.'s "strategy chief," had accomplished the $1 billion spin-off of Temple-Inland, Inc., a forest products division, to kudos from Wall Street, and had become Time's chief financial officer. Munro, singularly ill-equipped for the finance-driven eighties, came to rely so much on Nicholas that many saw Munro's role as primarily ceremonial ("Dick was the Queen and Nick the prime minister," commented one person). Now, Munro replaced Levin with Nicholas as video chief, and shifted Levin to the "strategy" position.

Levin, who, according to one friend, "has trouble running a business because he sees too many options," had led the company in a foray into subscription television (said to have caused a $100 million loss); and another into an experimental teletext information service (said to have had a $30 million loss). The most calamitous venture by far to occur under his aegis as video chief, however, was a deal to form Tri-Star Pictures, with partners CBS and Columbia Pictures. Time Inc. and HBO spent more than $1 billion for something that should have cost $500 million—a loss that was so embarrassing to Munro that it was hidden from Wall Street by amortizing the extra $500 million expense against the profit-and-loss statement over many years.

The Tri-Star deal, which involved HBO's providing capital for a percentage of the cost of all Columbia films, placed no cap on the amount of money HBO might have to invest. "We revised it. We had to. It was an open-ended lien on Time's treasury," recalled Francis (Fay) Vincent, then the CEO of Columbia Pictures, who has since become a close friend of Levin and praises him as having "a theological dimension to him . . . rare in a man of commerce."

Levin, in an interview in the *New York Times* about six months after assuming his post as company strategist, sounded as though he had grown disillusioned with video, where he had had his first, stunning success, but now a flock of failures. Emphasizing that much of the company's planning would now be directed to putting out new magazines, he commented: "Print is our soul and heartland and it is not as vulnerable to wide swings and sudden consumer disenchantment. There has to be a fairly simple identity that drives a company and when you get too far away from it you begin to have problems."

Nicholas, meanwhile, in taking over Levin's position at video, cut a broad swath. He fired Trigve Myrhen, the chief executive officer of ATC, under whose leadership the company had become mired in bureaucratic process. And he also fired Frank Biondi, the chief executive officer of

HBO, who with Levin bore responsibility for the Tri-Star deal, and who had been engaged in a long-time, debilitating power struggle with HBO executives Michael Fuchs and Winston Cox. Nicholas made Fuchs the chief executive of HBO, and moved Cox, an old friend, to work with Levin on strategy.

Biondi went to Munro to plead his case. Munro's door was always open; anyone with a grievance would be heard. But, as was generally true with Munro, he had only sympathy to offer. He reportedly told Biondi that he thought his firing was terrible—but that there was nothing he could do about it. At a small farewell dinner for Biondi, his wife Carol is said to have been expressing her animus for the absent Nicholas, when Levin's wife Barbara reportedly joined in with her own diatribe about Nicholas's having "screwed" Levin. Upon Levin's allegedly chiding her not to say such things about Nicholas, she is said to have retorted, "What do you mean? All you talk about at home is how much you hate him!"

In 1986, when the Time Inc. board prodded Munro to recommend his successor so that the transition upon his retiring in 1990 would be a smooth one, the consensus in the upper echelons of Time was that Nicholas and Levin were the favored contenders, though Kelso Sutton, the head of magazines, was also a candidate. Several Time executives of the period told me that they urged Munro, privately, to choose Nicholas.

Even his supporters acknowledged Nicholas's weaknesses. They believed that a conservatism had, on occasion, caused him to miss opportunities—to take a larger share of the Westinghouse Group W cable operation, for example. Furthermore, it seemed unlikely that Nicholas as a leader would ever be able to inspire the assembled troops. He had intellect, decisiveness, and sharp financial skills—but there was no magic to Nicholas. One could almost say he was anti-magic, constitutionally opposed to doing anything but the hard thing, the hard way, and allergic to what he viewed as sugarcoating, as well as to grandiloquent concepts which, as he would sometimes say, "couldn't stand the scrutiny of a sharp pencil on the back of an envelope."

Looking at the respective strengths and weaknesses of Nicholas and Levin, Munro may well have wished that he could meld them into a composite. For while Nicholas was cautious, Levin was risk-prone. While Nicholas was hard-edged and brutally candid, Levin was gentle and elliptical. And while Nicholas was somewhat bloodless, Levin was awash with free-floating enthusiasms—particularly in the area of sports and entertainment. Munro was tempted to name Levin—no one in the company, after all, referred to Nicholas as their "resident genius"—but Levin's track record, both as an operator and as a dealmaker, was wanting. (This was a point that Nicholas had not failed to make to board members, with whom he had a far better relationship than Levin did. He is said to have told them that the company needed Levin, but that Levin must never again be in a position of operating authority. According to one former Time executive, Nicholas would characteristically mask his thrust slightly. "Jerry's such a terrific guy," Nicholas would say. "It's amazing that he could have done something so *terrible* as this Columbia Pictures deal.")

One colleague who saw Levin at the board meeting where Nicholas's ascension was announced told me that while Levin rarely showed his emotions, this occasion was an exception; having learned of the decision less than twenty-four hours before, he appeared "devastated." Many in the company expected that Levin would leave, and that Nicholas, in the manner of most corporate chieftains who had just bested a long-time rival, would make sure he did.

To the contrary, however, Nicholas urged him to stay. Levin, along with several others, was removed from the board in a move to reduce the number of insiders; but, according to one person, Levin had a secret understanding with Nicholas that within a year he would be reappointed to the board, as the company's vice-chairman. Whether or not it was prearranged, this, at Nicholas's initiative, is what occurred. Munro was delighted—his composite achieved!—but having had an unhappy experience with a second-in-command foisted upon him, he had been scrupulous that the decision be Nicholas's alone. Explaining his decision to stay to a friend and colleague, Levin, characteristically, did not speak in terms of his own ambitions, but rather of a larger, mystical design. " 'First, I'm going to find what is right for this company. And once I have, I'll know my work is done, and then I will go,' " his friend recalled Levin telling him.

It was only a matter of months after Levin had begun his quest to find what was right that Steve Ross had appeared. And whatever qualms Levin, Nicholas, and Munro may have had about Ross were ultimately waylaid by desire. For the charge of Ross's excitement about the worlds they would conquer together, and the fecundity of his imagination, were irresistible—the promise of rain after a long drought. "I had thought for a long time that we needed what I always referred to as a 'transforming transaction,' " Levin told me, "because I didn't think we could build ourselves into this new world."

By the mid-eighties, Time Inc. had become a textbook case of the evolution undergone by many American companies as their leadership has passed from an inspired founder to his anointed heirs to third-generation managers, and the companies' original sense of mission and vitality has been diluted. "Time Inc. has become a well-managed organization, but it lacks the palpable passion that once inspired creative energy throughout the company," a confidential Time Inc. study, known as the Lyford Cay Strategy Report, concluded in June 1988. "The company is perceived on both Wall Street and internally as uncreative, overly cautious, investor-driven, and risk-averse," and "senior management has not communicated a galvanizing vision of the company's future growth opportunities."

Moreover, Levin was convinced that there was an urgency to Time Inc.'s predicament. The company's break-up value was then (and over the next several years would continue to be) at least double the price of its shares (in part, at least, because of the market's perception that the company was poorly managed). By 1986, the takeover speculators had begun to circle. Financial players like the Coniston Partners were accumulating Time stock, and so, according to rumor, was the arbitrageur Ivan Boesky.

Reflecting on the intensity with which Nicholas, Munro, and Levin had pursued the Time-Warner deal, Andrew Heiskell said, "In the eighties, the bottom line at Time Inc. was okay. They had a machine in hand that was making decent money, and they could squeeze it to get more. But did they start something new? No. In the end, I think it became terribly important to them that this deal get done, because it would be either yet another failure—if it didn't get done—or their great success."

This generation of manager-leaders at Time Inc. seemed almost resentful of the history that had preceded them, as though they felt that the large shadows cast by their predecessors diminished them by comparison. Referring to those predecessors—particularly Andrew Heiskell, who headed the company from 1960 to 1980—Nicholas remarked: "It was a wonderful age. If you were managing a public company, you didn't have to explain anything to anybody. People from that time have no idea what it is like today."

As soon as Nicholas became president, in the fall of 1986, he had instituted a major cost-cutting program, which included layoffs of hundreds of employees in the magazine division, as well as cutbacks in its expense account practices. In its rapt fixation on its profit margins, Time under Nicholas was no different from a multitude of blue-chip companies that had been jolted out of complacency by the pandemic restructuring of the eighties. But under Luce and his handpicked successors the company had had "twin motivations," which one former Time executive has described as "to do journalism in the public interest—and to make a buck."

The moneymaking, however, was done chiefly in the service of the journalism—not the other way around. "Luce was almost arrogant in his treatment of the business people, and many of them resented this," a former high-ranking member of Time's editorial staff recalls. It was to ensure that the editorial side would operate free from intrusion by the business side that Luce had drawn his line between a "church" and "state." At the time he reigned as editor-in-chief and CEO, he himself, of course, embodied both.

With Hedley Donovan (who succeeded Luce as editor-in-chief) and Andrew Heiskell, the practice of church and state changed slightly, mainly by virtue of the fact that there were now two people at the top instead of one. "Hedley and I discussed nearly everything," Heiskell recalled. "Church and state, after all, had to meet somewhere, even if it was in a dark corner. Hedley, as editor-in-chief, did pretty much what he pleased, but we had to discuss things and each know what the other was doing, or it would have fallen apart."

The parity that existed between the CEO and the editor-in-chief during the Heiskell-Donovan years was in large measure a function of the attitudes, and the closeness, of the two men. Donovan presided over only about 50 per cent of Time Inc., whereas Heiskell oversaw the entire company, but both were imbued with the Lucean mission. (Heiskell had been a journalist, and was widely popular with the editorial staff.) Before Donovan retired, in 1979, he decided that if the concept of church and state was to be preserved, it needed to become less personality-driven and more institutionalized. He therefore wrote what is now referred to as "the Donovan charter," a document, approved by the board, that decreed that the editor-in-chief would be responsible only to the board (of which he would be a member), not to the company's CEO, and that in editorial matters he would be the counterpart of the CEO.

Donovan was prescient. Whereas he and Heiskell had operated in friendly league, Donovan's chosen successor, Henry Grunwald, and Munro were utterly disjunctive. Grunwald, a Viennese immigrant with a formidable intellect, who was eminent on the New York social scene, intimidated and antagonized Munro. "Munro was petrified of Henry, and Henry really wasn't interested in what Munro, or others on the business side, thought," a former Time executive recalls. "He let it be a chasm. What evolved in top management was an antipathy toward the office of editor-in-chief."

During the spring of 1987, there was considerable talk among management and the outside directors about removing the editor-in-chief from the board. This was an idea generated especially by a director, Donald Perkins, who, as a member of nine corporate boards, was something of a self-proclaimed expert on corporate governance. While some believe Nicholas, too, was promoting this idea, it was Munro who urged it upon the directors. A former board member told me that Munro "saw editorial as a diversion, somewhere over there, with the editor-in-chief maybe having parity with the CEO of the magazine division." Ultimately, the board resolved to settle for a revised Donovan charter that did not include removal of the editor-in-chief; rather, it stated that the editor-in-chief should work "in close consultation" with the CEO of the magazine division, and only "when appropriate" with the CEO of Time Inc. Thus, the parity of the CEO of Time Inc. and the editor-in-chief was no more; the editor-in-chief now shared power with the CEO of the magazine division, which was merely one of the company's four operating subsidiaries.

Furthermore, while the board in the past had simply accepted Donovan's designation of Henry Grunwald as his successor, now, in Grunwald's selection of his own successor, it assumed a far more active role. There were two leading contenders for the job. One was Jason McManus, a former Rhodes Scholar, who had specialized in business reporting early in his career as *Time*'s first Common Market bureau chief; had been an excellent "Nation" editor of *Time* in the seventies and was known for his keen sensitivity to company politics. The other condender was Ray Cave, a talented journalist who, after spending much of his career at *Sports Illustrated,* had brought badly needed graphic changes to *Time* in the late seventies. Cave, however, was bristly and moody, possessed of a quick tongue and strong opinions. He was not cut from the same cloth as the corporate team players who inhabited the thirty-fourth floor, and Munro and Nicholas are said to have come to dislike him.

One former board member told me, "When Dick [Munro] thought Grunwald was leaning toward Ray Cave, he did a hatchet job on Ray with the directors. He destroyed Cave's reputation with the board." He told the board that managing editors of the various magazines "said they would quit if he was made editor-in-chief, which I know was not true. It was an unrelenting attack." This executive went so far as to say that Henry Grunwald "never had a chance to weigh the two men evenly."

Choosing the more malleable McManus was apparently seen by Nicholas and Munro as only an interim device, on the way to the full-scale demotion of the editor-in-chief, and the dismantling of Luce's anachronistic church and state. One former director recalls Munro's telling him after Munro finally agreed to allow McManus, as the new editor-in-chief, to join the board, "This can't go on. This is the last time."

By early 1987, Nicholas and Levin were unshackling the company from its Lucean past and moving it toward its future as an entertainment-oriented company. It was a future that the messianic Luce would, of course, have deplored, but once Munro had taken the helm of Time Inc., and promoted his video-group teammates Nicholas and Levin, that future was destiny. Speaking about the direction in which he and Nicholas guided the company, Levin told me, "We felt a constitutional longing. We had spun off forest products in anticipation of doing something else—it was like an unfinished symphony. Our primary experience had been generated through HBO and cable. You couldn't help but be impressed by the rate of change and the power of the medium. It had made an indelible impression, become too important a part of our frame of reference to be ignored."

In August 1987, months after Nicholas and Levin resolved to complete Time Inc.'s evolution and the meetings with Ross had begun, Levin wrote that confidential memo to Munro—from the notes Nicholas had made during his overnight stop in Zurich—which was, as it turned out, a precis of the future. Indeed, about a year after it was written, when it began to be plain within the higher echelons of Time Inc. that its proposal was destined to become reality, Nicholas complained to a colleague that Levin was taking credit for the memo, and said he wondered, briefly, whether he should assert his authorship but had decided that it didn't matter whose idea it had been—they were a team. And Levin did continue to assert that the idea of this "transforming transaction" was his—in interviews with me, and even in the course of a deposition in which he testified, about the memo, "It was my own statement of purpose and design."

The memo, in any event, declared that their "primary long-term objective" should be to bring about the consolidation of Time Inc., Warner Communications, and the Turner Broadcasting System, in which Time Inc. then owned a stake, so that "the new Time Inc." would be "an entertainment oriented communications company," and he argued, "We are already on a course where most of our asset base and expansion possibilities center on entertainment. Publishing is more limited." He went on to say that "at long last, the company would be a major motion picture producer and distributor," and added that he now saw records and music publishing (a strong division of Warner Communications) as "a significant part of the entertainment mix." Warner would make a "unique" combination with Time Inc., he said, but if that combination was "not do-able, then the only other entertainment option I think we should explore would be G&W" (Gulf & Western, which has since been renamed Paramount) As an addendum. Levin wrote: "A word of caution and reality: neither our senior management nor our Board would presently proceed to the end result I have described."

Levin told me, "At that point, it was a highly controversial idea, because there was a feeling that such a combination was not appropriate for Time Inc. We had no experience in running a movie studio, so would we be overshadowed? Why change things? Why take the risk?"

In the fall of 1987, the focus of the discussions with WCI was a joint venture that would combine Time's and WCI's cable systems, HBO, Warner Brothers Studio, and related entertainment properties, and leave aside Time's publishing division and Warner's record division—the most culturally antagonistic parts of the two companies. A joint venture of this magnitude implied, certainly in Levin's view, an eventual merger, perhaps five years hence; but it was a more gradual way of arriving at that result.

Ross, meanwhile, was continuing to underline his amenability to sharing power with Nicholas. During the summer, he had given Nicholas a copy of a *Fortune* article on an unusual but smooth-functioning arrangement at Unilever: two co-equal chairmen, two headquarters, and two sets of shareholders. It was Ross's way of suggesting something that went further than a joint venture but was still short of a full merger.

Levin, intensely aware of how much spadework remained to be done at Time before a combination of Time and Warner could be achieved, was having difficulty reining in the eager Ross. In mid-November, following an informal get-together of key Time and Warner executives, and in preparation for a Munro-Ross meeting, Levin wrote Munro another memo—one of numerous instructive memos he wrote in the course of guiding Dick Munro through this deal.

"You need to reinforce the fact that our November 4 meeting at the Helmsley Palace was a good and satisfying preliminary step in 'getting to know each other,'" he wrote. "However, we are not ready ... to want to work toward any combination now or devise any detailed structures or organizational formats. It is too early for that. For the time being, we want to remain totally flexible. .... The key here is to keep our options open with Warner, cool Steve's ardor somewhat, but maintain a deepening relationship."

As it turned out, in June 1988, after months of the Time executives' trying to fend off Ross's advances but still keep him on the hook, it was Nicholas—not Ross—who popped the question. He told Ross he wanted to skip the joint venture and go straight to a merger. It was, in fact, the more logical course: the joint venture would have created some knotty tax problems and, if the companies ultimately did merge in a stock-swap transaction, would have prohibited their doing so with a "pooling of interests"—an accounting method, permitted in stock-swap mergers, under which companies combine balance sheets without incurring taxable gains for themselves or their shareholders. This had been Ross's method of choice, from the time he had started his stock-swap mergers back in the sixties.

Given the logic of the merger, Ross's initiation of the courtship, and his relentless "ardor," it might seem surprising that it was Nicholas who ultimately proposed. But then, Ross had for years been perfecting the art of implanting *his* desire, through indirection, in someone else, so that that person would decide to become Ross's suitor; it was precisely what he had done with James Robinson and Warner-Amex. Here, similarly, he would have wanted Nicholas to feel himself the agent of this transaction —and so, in all likelihood, he simply waited for Nicholas to make his way, ineluctably, to that point.

It may have seemed to Ross an interminably long wait, for it had been roughly fifteen months since Ross, in one of his early calls on Nicholas and Munro, had walked down the block from the headquarters of Warner Communications to the Time & Life Building, bearing a booklet with charts and a text that delineated the benefits of a joint venture. But, endless as the process may have seemed to Ross, Nicholas could not have moved any sooner. Although he was in effect the company's CEO, he did not have the title, and could not deal with the board as though he did; therefore, he needed Munro's staunch commitment. And during the early months of the discussions Munro had hung back—uncertain about Time's metamorphosis into an entertainment-oriented company; feeling that he was its steward; nervous about betting the company. Nicholas had also needed time to acclimate the board to the idea of a combination with Warner. Like so many corporate board members, the outside directors of Time Inc.—many of whom had been together for well over a decade, and a couple of whom also served on each other's boards—were a largely congenial, clubby group. Some were personally close to Time's management team. Indeed, the director David Kearns, chairman and CEO of the Xerox Corporation, and a good friend of Munro's, served on the compensation committee (which reviewed the executives' contracts in this deal), as did John Opel, the retired chairman and CEO of IBM; Munro sat on the IBM board and had served on its compensation committee, and Nicholas had done the same on the board of Xerox.

It was also, however, a board composed of enough figures of note in the business community—Opel; Kearns; James Bere, the chairman and CEO of Borg-Warner; Michael Dingman, the chairman and CEO of the

Henley Group, Inc.; and others—that it took itself, and its responsibilities (and liabilities), seriously Unlike the WCI board, which was composed of Ross devotees, whom Ross dominated, many of the Time Inc. directors might heed the company's investment bankers and lawyers as much as they would Munro or Nicholas. And, because of the history of Time Inc., some of the directors seem to have felt that they were presiding over an institution as much as sitting on the board of a public company. It was, therefore—as Nicholas and, especially, Levin had long understood—a board that would require careful cultivation and persuasion. By the time the merger proposal reached the directors, the idea of a combination with WCI in a joint venture had been aired with them for more than a year.

One investment banker who had represented Time for many years was Felix Rohatyn, who, of course, had known Ross since the funeral home days; he was representing WCI, here. Rohatyn was dubious about this proposed merger ever being approved by the Time board. WCI, as he pointed out to me, was "a company made up of executives with very strong ties to each other, mainly Jewish, who would appear to be parvenus, in a glitzy business. . . . And Time is the most establishment, white-shoe company. . . ." Referring to Luce's two handpicked successors, Hedley Donovan and Andrew Heiskell—who were strongly opposed to the deal—Rohatyn said, "They represented the old guard at Time Inc. And if the board had been steeped in that kind of thinking the deal would never have worked."

At the July 1988 board meeting in which the merger was proposed, a threshold issue for the directors was what Munro later referred to as "the question of integrity"—one that had been raised in the original memo, back in August 1987, which had mentioned examining the Westchester Premier Theatre episode as part of an inquiry into Ross's past. Despite the fact that U.S. Attorney Rudolph Giuliani, in 1985, had taken the unusual step of declaring that the investigation of Ross was closed (something that was very helpful to Ross in his courtship of Time), still— probably because of the penumbra of unanswered questions that surrounded the case—it continued always to hover over him. It was, as one Ross observer expressed it, "Steve Ross's Chappaquiddick."

"One of the problems we've had in this whole transaction is that Steve is a misunderstood individual," Munro told me. "He has this aura, going back to the Westchester Theatre. But everyone looked at it; they couldn't come up with anything. So my view is, If he's not guilty, he's innocent." During July and August of 1988, Munro said, he "lived on the phone with the directors." At Levin's behest, he took copious notes of the conversations, so as not to have to rely on memory, and reviewed them with Levin. "Those notes were critical," Levin told me. "There was a high premium on being extremely precise with respect to nuances." (Munro's notes, and the notes of other participants in the deal, later became part of the public record in the courts in Delaware where most major American companies are incorporated.) In one note, Dingman was reporting to Munro about conversations in mid-1988 between James Shepley, the former president of Time Inc., and Arthur Temple, a Time Inc. director. "Shepley has been talking with Arthur and fanning the flames re: Ross," Munro wrote. "He's telling Arthur that Steve is mafia—(Remember the franchising days?)"

In reference to this written comment, Munro told me that in the early eighties Time was competing against Warner for cable franchises in various places, and often lost. "We were convinced, because we lost, that they must be doing something evil," Munro said. After losing to Warner in Pittsburgh, Time sued Warner and the city of Pittsburgh, alleging improper bidding procedures, and then settled out of court. As Munro spent more time with Ross in the spring and summer of '88, he grew convinced, he told me, that "here was a guy altogether different than anyone had imagined him to be." He went on, "I think, in all our negotiations, he never went back on anything. He was fun to be with. And we talked to a large number of people about him. They said, 'Steve Ross is one of the finest men we've ever known.' " Among those who, according to one lawyer involved in this deal, "legitimized Steve in the eyes of the people at Time" were Felix Rohatyn and Arthur Liman.

Rohatyn had given a warm endorsement of Ross to the Time board, and it carried considerable weight. Appreciative as Rohatyn was of Ross's talents, however, he was not a Ross acolyte. And while Ross had cultivated Rohatyn carefully over the years, Rohatyn had never altogether trusted him. Liman, of course, was another matter—and he was the single most influential force for Ross, with Time. Rhapsodic as always when he was speaking about Ross, Liman told me that the deal Ross created here, in its original, debt-free version, was "the greatest deal in history. . . . Every artist has to have one painting which is considered greater than all the others—for Picasso, for example, *Guernica* Well, Steve has created some wonderful paintings in his life—but this was the perfect one."

During the nearly twenty years in which Liman had been at Ross's side, through recurrent crises—Westchester Premier Theatre, Atari, Rupert Murdoch, and Herbert Siegel—Liman had not only saved Ross repeatedly, but his own stature had grown. And the more stellar his reputation, the more invaluable he became to Ross. For Liman was performing that role that Ross always loved best in his advisers: the seemingly outside person (thus lending a patina of objectivity), who is really an inside person, immeasurably loyal to Ross. It was one thing (and, of course, highly useful) to have Ken Rosen or Ed Aboodi playing this part—but Arthur Liman! It was very nearly sublime. He was so devoted to Ross as to be more cohort than counselor; but he was, at the same time—because of his public persona—the best legitimizer Ross could have had.

On "the question of integrity," the impassioned defense of Ross that Munro made to the board may have been his single greatest contribution to the deal. "As much as Nick and I tried to pull this off, Dick Munro's standing up and saying, 'Steve Ross is a righteous soul,' was critical," Levin told me. "The directors see me as an intellectual, Nick as hard-driving. But for them to hear it from Munro, who is the very symbol of integrity . . ."

One director who for a time remained unpersuaded on this and other issues was Henry (Hank) Luce III, son of the founder. After the July board meeting, Luce sent Munro a letter, quoting from his father's will ("Time Inc. is now, and is expected to continue to be, principally a journalistic enterprise and, as such, an enterprise operated in the public interest") and saying that he did not believe he could vote for the merger.

In a note on a subsequent phone conversation with Luce, Munro wrote: "He's bothered by—in addition to the point made in his letter—Ross's compensation, the 8-year contract, the ethics and foul tongues of Hollywood types, the Westchester Theatre scandal, and by employment contracts at Time Inc."

Other directors, too, were initially aghast at Ross's contract—the one Ross had fought for so tenaciously against Siegel's objections. Eventually, however, they came to accept the compensation of Ross and his key executives as the way of life in the entertainment business and, therefore, the price of doing the deal. Indeed, they seemed to reach a point where their attitude toward the financial terms of this transaction was almost laissez-faire. This was not something that went unexploited. Ultimately in this deal, Ross's stock-based plans and those of all the key Warner executives would be paid out (some of Ross's over a period of years) at the very handsome deal price. And upon the consummation of the merger the clock would be reset, with a granting of stock options equivalent to what they had had before. (This was referred to, at Warner, as "the double dip.")

One of the stock-based plans was known as the "equity-unit" plan; it included many former WCI employees, to whom it had been especially burdensome. When it began, in 1982, participants had purchased shares at their current book value, with the eventual right to resell them to the company at future book value; most took low-interest loans from the company to pay for the shares. But after Atari, the company's book value had plummeted; for years, participants—who were told they could not drop out of the plan, even after having left the company—were obligated to pay interest (in some cases, $100,000 a year, and more) on something that was underwater. In the negotiation of the Time-Warner merger, however, "book value" for these units was set, arbitrarily and really not justifiably, at the deal price—and, instantaneously, the burden became a bonanza.

"Steve was determined to make everyone whole on the equity units," said Manny Gerard, who had had to make interest payments of about $125,000 a year. "He had been telling everyone for years, 'Don't worry, I'll take care of you.' And then he was proven right—he *did* it! Most people made between $1–$10 million. My wife and I called ours, 'Operation Windfall'—and we gave away a lot of it."

Ross made it a point to be the one to tell former employees of their unexpected good fortune; he called Rafael de la Sierra, for example, to whom he had not spoken in years—and would not again. While Gerard was doubtless right that it was important to Ross to be the benefactor once more through the payout of this plan, his exacting this bounty from Time was hardly a selfless gesture. Ross is said to have received a personal payout of nearly $20 million.

The chief negotiators of the merger were Jerry Levin and Ed Aboodi. Aboodi by this time had become indispensable to Ross. He handled much of Ross's personal finances (as Solomon Weiss, who still worked for Aboodi, used to do) and advised Ross on deals, but it was really more than that: he was, essentially, the person with whom Ross did all his financial thinking. It was with Aboodi, therefore, that Ross now spent the most time at the company; in that sense—but only in that sense—he had taken Jay Emmett's place. He shared with Ross, also, a passion for secrecy and cagey maneuvering—but, lacking Ross's charm, he wore this on his sleeve. His answers to questions tended generally to be sinuous rather than straight, and this sometimes worked against him in negotiations, inasmuch as those with whom he was bartering felt, in the words of one Aboodi acquaintance, "that he would not hesitate to send them right over the edge of a cliff."

Levin apparently did not feel that way. Praising the skills of his fellow negotiator, he remarked, "Ed has an appreciation of the human being he is dealing with. Rather than try to gain leverage in an adversarial sense, he tries to assess what your needs and requirements are—not only from a business perspective but from a psychological perspective." Indeed, Ross had trained him well. And Aboodi must have quickly perceived (to his and Ross's delight) that the financial terms of this deal, from the Time standpoint, were a low priority. The extensive notes that Levin kept throughout the summer of 1988 make plain (as was also corroborated by later deposition testimony) that negotiations about price were left for last, and were seen as "almost irrelevant," as one Time director expressed it to me.

One note begins with the heading, "Munro should meet Ross alone," and goes on to say, "This is Munro's deal" and "Co-CEO succession—inappropriate for Nick to hit head-on, Munro must do it." Then comes a "Review Issues list" for Munro (whose deal it purportedly was) in his coming meeting with Ross. No. 1 is co-CEOs; no. 2, "Nick as president"; no. 3, the company's name ("Time/Warner Inc.—history and the alphabet require it"); no. 4, "central core staff"; and no. 5, exchange ratio.

What was planned was a stock-swap merger, in which every Warner share would be exchanged for some percentage of a newly issued Time Warner share. Several Time directors—most adamantly Michael Dingman —had urged that the exchange be done on a "market-to-market" valuation of the two companies' stocks, without Time's paying any premium for Warner. (In the view of another director, Arthur Temple, Time's cashing out the equity-unit plan already constituted a rather heavy premium.) "Should be market to market," Levin wrote in the memo to prepare Munro for his Ross meeting. But, he added, "we should be flexible if he agrees to no. 1"—Nicholas's succession.

Virtually all the Time directors seem to have shared management's overriding preoccupation with succession. In this they were doubtless influenced by management but also by their own sense of the specialness of Time Inc.—what director Donald Perkins referred to as its "almost spiritual value"—and therefore of their roles as its guardians.

They were, of course, not nearly so imbued with this sense as the earlier custodians of Time Inc.—people like Heiskell and Donovan, who, the directors knew, were strongly opposed to the deal, and to the notion of Time Inc.'s becoming an entertainment-oriented company. Jason McManus, on "assignment" from Levin, went to see Donovan to discuss the deal in the summer of 1988, and reported the conversation to Levin, who took notes on it. According to the notes, Donovan told McManus that Ross had had a "lifetime of bad press—something behind it"; that he did not buy "eat or be eaten," the takeover ultimatum that the Time management believed itself to face; that he thought the deal would diminish the scale of the magazines; and, finally, that his view was that "even if print is doomed—go down with the ship—strict construction of Luce."

Donald Perkins told me that the opposition of Heiskell and Donovan did not perturb him or the other directors, because "they're in the past." The directors were willing to vote for the entertainment future that Nicholas, Munro, and Levin had pointed them toward, but at the same time it was apparently important to them that they not be perceived as having presided over the demise of Time Inc. Thus, their goal and management's were fused. Perkins recalled that many of the directors were skeptical about Steve Ross's assurances that Nicholas would succeed him. Moreover, they took as instructive the experience of one of their fellow directors. In 1985, with the merger of Signal Companies and the Allied Corporation, Michael Dingman had embarked on a relationship of shared power with Allied's Edward Hennessy, whom Dingman was slated ultimately to succeed as CEO. Within months, however, Dingman was out.

"If it's just a contract, it can always be breached—as in Dingman's case," a lawyer for Time Inc. who was involved in the deal told me. Moreover, Time's outside counsel in this deal was the law firm of Cravath, Swaine & Moore—the same firm that had come to represent Herb Siegel and Chris-Craft once Siegel's relationship with Ross had deteriorated. And the Cravath lawyers were mindful of how Ross had succeeded in diluting Siegel's voting position because of a provision that had been entered into the WCI/BHC agreement at the last moment before signing. They felt that Ross was an individual with whom one could not be too careful. Thus, Time's lawyers set about constructing a plan that would make Ross's guarantee ironclad. What they wanted to do was to incorporate it into the charter of the newly merged company, through a shareholder vote; violating it would be illegal under the Delaware law governing these corporations' conduct, as distinct from merely breaching a contract, with damages paid. The lawyers drafted a four-page document, to be submitted for the shareholder vote, describing the Ross-Nicholas succession. Having designated the period from the time the merger became effective to the time of Ross's retirement as the "Transition Period," it spelled out in minute detail the rules for that period: the composition of committees, with their "Existing Time" and "New Time" directors; procedures for filling a committee vacancy and a board vacancy, and for the sale of a principal line of business All the above, including the succession provision, could be achieved only by a vote of at least a supermajority, or two thirds, of the board.

Munro sent the ironclad draft to the directors on August 4, 1988, and within a week Ross terminated the negotiations. Later, in his deposition, he explained his action by saying that he "was getting a feeling that there was some sort of maybe even paranoia by the Time board, and I didn't think that would work beneficially over the long-term pull." About Ross's unwillingness to accept a fixed point for his retirement, Munro told me, "Steve is the godfather of Warner. He built the company. It's hard to deal with stepping down."

Levin appears to have taken Ross's retreat at face value. His notes from a meeting with Aboodi in mid-August read: "If it is to happen, it will resurrect itself—no deal at this point—great missed opportunity." Groups from the two companies did meet, however, at Ross's home on September 1—a session memorialized in Levin's notes, according to which the groups continued to discuss details of the transaction, including the usual issues of succession, compensation, and core staff. The notes suggest a transaction that may be suspended but is far from dead. At the end of them, Levin wrote: "How depressed Steve was. Steve not trying to take us over."

Ross now turned his attention to an already projected friendly acquisition by Warner of Lorimar Telepictures Corporation. While it had been anticipated that this deal would close in August 1988, a lawsuit filed by Chris-Craft delayed the acquisition—and occupied Ross—through the fall. Indeed, Ross's backing away from the Time deal was, in the main, clearly a tactical maneuver. He knew that his deposition would be taken in the Chris-Craft litigation, and he would probably have to disclose the existence of the Time negotiations, if they were ongoing—something he was not yet ready to do. Furthermore, he surely was offended by that ironclad provision, and thought that by his retreating, the Time directors, realizing what was lost, would think better of their caution and extend themselves—even entreatingly—to bring him back. That, indeed, is what happened. The Chris-Craft case was resolved in early December, and within a week Jonathan O'Herron, an investment banker at Lazard Frères who, earlier, had urged the Time-Warner deal upon Munro and some of the directors at Time, and who was a long-time friend of both Ross and Time director Michael Dingman, suggested to Dingman that they have dinner with Ross. "Jonathan really played the old-fashioned role of investment banker as matchmaker in this deal," one of the lawyers for WCI commented.

Dingman had, Munro told me, "instinctively been for the deal, from the start." That might seem surprising, given Dingman's unhappy experience with Edward Hennessy. But, according to several friends, Dingman was avid for deals. ("Mike loves to make a deal, like some people love to play bridge," one said. "Life is dull without a deal.") Moreover, being a self-made entrepreneur, he was in some sense more akin to Ross than to some of his fellow board members from the corporate establishment. He did not share their misgivings about Ross. "I'm more concerned with keeping him than I am with worrying about making sure he leaves," Dingman told me. According to one of Dingman's friends, Dingman had said he believed that Time, unable to create new products, was badly in need of revitalization, and that Steve Ross—who had created a charged environment in which his people, rewarded by bonuses and incentives, produced—would be the revitalizer. Rohatyn remarked of Dingman, "Mike thought this deal would be Time's perestroika."

At the dinner with O'Herron and Ross, at Ross's home, Dingman conveyed his enthusiasm—and that of his fellow directors, too—for Ross's leadership. "Dingman told me, 'The board accepts you as co-CEO—just not for an indefinite term,' " Ross recalled. "He said, 'They need you, they want you.' "

At the end of February 1989, the deal was done. Arthur Temple, who had been opposed for reasons similar to Hank Luce's, decided that he would vote for it and immediately resign from the board. Luce, not wanting to wage a solitary battle, voted for it, too. When the vote had been taken, one director reportedly turned to another and commented: "Mafia, 12; Whiffenpoofs, 0."

Whatever the future brought for the company, the Time executives who had labored to bring this deal to fruition would be handsomely rewarded, just for having done so. They were receiving new contracts of extraordinary length, on the rationale that theirs had to equal Ross's (which by the time the deal was done would be ten years in duration, with an additional five-year term as an adviser). Munro, who had intended to retire in 1990—and had been a complacently lame duck since 1986, when he appointed Nicholas—would still retire as chairman and CEO, but would be given a new ten-year contract, to serve for the first five years as chairman of the executive committee and the next five as an adviser. In salary (with bonuses to be awarded at the board's discretion), Munro was to receive at least $7.5 million more than he would have if the deal with Warner had not occurred.

Nicholas and Levin, too, would be given newly extended contracts, now ten years in duration (with an additional five-year advisory term for Nicholas), which would guarantee Levin over $12 million and Nicholas over $16 million (figures that do not include grants of options and restricted shares, issued at the board's discretion). If any of the three lost his job owing to a change in control or a breach of his employment agreement by the company, his situation would be dramatically better than it had been prior to the deal, inasmuch as he would now receive the full value of his ten-year contract.

The exchange ratio had finally been negotiated. One of the investment bankers said he believed that Ross had requested that no investment banker be present for the negotiation—if true, an unusual stipulation for a transaction of this magnitude. The participants, in any event, were Levin and Nicholas and Ross and Aboodi (no Marquis of Queensberry rules here). The ratio this foursome arrived at was .465 shares of the new Time Warner stock for every share of Warner. O'Herron, one of Warner's investment bankers, had told Warner directors before this negotiation that anything over .40 would be "fair" and anything over .45 "a hell of a deal."

The deal was described in a press release as an acquisition of Warner by Time; but in the main the governance structure implied an acquisition of Time by Warner. Warner's general counsel and chief financial officer would assume the same roles in the new Time Warner. Gerald Levin, as vice-chairman of Time Warner, would share that post with another vice-chairman, Martin Payson, who was Warner's general counsel. The all-important compensation committee would have more Warner directors than Time directors. (The entertainment committee would, too, but that would be counterbalanced by the editorial committee, which would have a majority of Time directors.) And Warner's accounting firm, Arthur Young & Co., would become the accounting firm for Time Warner. (Subsequently, Arthur Young merged with Ernst & Whinney, Time Inc.'s accounting firm.)

The only concession that Nicholas exacted from Ross (or, at least, thought he was exacting) in exchange for all the high-level corporate positions going to WCI executives was the promise—given in a handshake from Ross—that Levin, though he was currently sharing the vice-chairmanship with Payson, would within a year become the clear "No. 3" of the organization. That way, Nicholas thought, if ever there were a power struggle with Ross, not only could he count on the directors of Time Inc. but he and Levin would make it two against one at the top.

Interestingly enough, at Ross's insistence the supermajority provisions, which in the summer-of-'88 discussions pertained not only to succession but to procedures regarding the board, the committees, and significant company transactions, had dropped away except in respect to the employment contracts of Ross, Munro, and Nicholas. Thus, in virtually all matters a simple majority of the board would suffice. The new board would be composed of twelve Time directors and twelve Warner directors. But with a Time director like Michael Dingman, and with no supermajority requirement, one could argue that Ross had already gained control.

The most important change, however, was that the ironclad provision to incorporate the succession and other governance protections into the charter with a shareholder vote was no more. This meant that the super-majority provisions on the employment contracts were mere artifacts: the contracts were only contracts; they could be breached and damages paid. The charter-incorporating provision, which would have set the succession in stone, dropped away at the very last moment of the negotiations (shades of the WCI/BHC agreement), when, according to one lawyer involved in the deal, Warner's general counsel, Martin Payson, told the negotiators for Time, "This is ridiculous. We're not doing it!"

In its place, Liman, with Levin, drafted a document that described Ross's intentions with regard to his retirement and his succession by Nicholas. That document, which was produced in the litigation, is entitled "Statement of Principles." "The merger is a true combination of two great companies," it begins. "For either company to be looked upon as any-thing but an equal partner in this transaction would sap that company of its vitality and destroy the very benefits and synergy that the combination is intended to achieve." So much for Time's claim that it was acquir-ing Warner. Regarding succession, the document goes on: "It was not a condition of the negotiations that SJR [Ross] retire at the end of five years any more than it was a condition that RM [Munro] retire at any par-ticular time. . . . When SJR resigns as co-CEO in 1994, NN [Nicholas] will become sole CEO and SJR will remain as sole Chairman of the Board of the combined companies and will continue to have an active role and provide leadership and guidance to the [Warner] businesses that he helped build."

Commenting on the fact that the document was not written in conven-tional legal language, one Time executive explained, "It tried to respect the sensibilities of Steve Ross. There's something traumatic about boil-erplate—and Steve is such a sensitive soul." As to Ross's last-minute rejection of the ironclad provision, this executive told me, "Steve's feeling was 'My word is my bond.' "

Ross had always preferred to do stock-for-stock, rather than debt-financed, acquisitions, and, in this as well as many other ways, the Time-Warner merger bore his imprimatur. It was an anomaly in this leveraged age—a healthy anomaly, Ross, Munro, and others kept stressing in the weeks that followed the March 4 announcement of the merger. In testi-mony before Congress—many of whose members were eager to do something to curb the leveraged buyout mania—Ross and Munro drove their point home: this was not a hostile takeover, not a leveraged transaction, not a bust-up-assets deal but, rather, a "grand-old-style pooling-of-interests merger."

It would give birth to a behemoth, a company with a stock market value of more than $15 billion and annual revenue exceeding $10 billion —far greater than, for example, those of Bertelsmann AG, of Germany, the world's largest media company. And, Ross and Munro argued before Congress, the new Time Warner, with its relatively debt-light balance sheet ($2.6 billion), would have not only the size but the financial flexibility necessary to compete in today's global market—a market that, they added pointedly, reaching for a congressional nerve, had recently seen a dramatic increase in foreign acquisitions of U.S. media and entertainment companies. The shoe would finally be on the other foot, as Time Warner would be primed—with its movie and television production, its direct marketing, and its record division—to take advantage of the deregulation of television markets in Western Europe, and of new markets for entertainment software in the Pacific Rim.

That was the plan—what Liman had referred to as "the perfect one" of all Ross's "wonderful paintings." But it was thrown into disarray when, on June 7, two weeks before Time and Warner shareholders were scheduled to vote on the merger, Paramount Communications, Inc. threatened to foil the deal by making a $10.7 billion cash tender offer for Time, at $175 dollars a share. In the face of Paramount's hostile offer, the proposed merger of Time and WCI was reconstituted as a $14 billion bid of cash and securities for Warner by Time. Thus, the deal was radically altered, in a variety of ways. It had now become the very kind of leveraged transaction that both Ross and Munro had deplored in their speeches before Congress, with a long-term debt not of $2.6 billion but $16 billion. Because it was no longer a pooling-of-interests transaction, it would incur an enormous amount of goodwill, which would have to be amortized for many years, undermining the company's earnings.

WCI shareholders would become richer, inasmuch as the price of WCI shares went from an estimated $50 to $55 per share (based on the price at which Time stock was trading) in the prior stock-swap deal, to what Time said would be about $70. (More than half of the WCI shares would be purchased for $70 in cash, and the rest exchanged for a complicated package of securities, in the transaction's "back end.")

And, finally, there was no longer any confusion about who was acquiring whom: WCI was incontrovertibly being acquired by Time.

But in one amazing way the deal did not change. The governance provisions, which—except for Nicholas's purported succession—implied the acquisition of Time by WCI, remained untouched. The Time-Warner deal may well signal the first time in corporate history that one company has acquired another and put in place a governance structure suggesting that the opposite occurred.

Once Paramount had made its bid, however, Time was at WCI's mercy. If it couldn't achieve the WCI transaction, then the managers' worst nightmare—that Time would be taken over and they would be thrown out, either by Paramount or by some higher bidder—would come true. And, even harder to bear, they would have brought it upon themselves, through the very actions they had undertaken in large measure to avoid it.

In theory, Time and WCI could have pursued their stock-for-stock transaction even in the face of the Paramount bid. But that merger required a shareholder vote—scheduled for two weeks from the time Paramount made its offer—while a cash tender offer did not. And, in general, the Time shareholders (many of whom had long been unhappy with the management of Time, and had become even more unhappy at the dilution of their shares in the rich deal given Warner) would not vote for this deal now. It offered them no cash—only some vague hope for future stock appreciation through the much-touted but highly dubious alchemy of synergy—while Paramount was offering them $175 dollars a share (ultimately sweetened to $200) for shares that, in 1988, had traded at prices as low as $79. One lawyer on the Time-Warner team told me, "We knew we wouldn't get the vote—or, as I guess we said publicly, it was 'problematic.'"

When the Time-Warner team decided to skirt this roadblock by changing the form of the transaction from a stock-for-stock merger to a cash tender offer, which would not require a vote, their motivation was utterly transparent; and what was in effect a withdrawal of the vote became, in the view of lawyers involved on both sides of the Paramount litigation, the most difficult issue to defend, and one that could conceivably have caused the Delaware courts to rule differently.

In Delaware Chancery Court, where Paramount sued to obtain an injunction restraining Time from buying Warner shares, Paramount argued, mainly, that Time had put itself up for sale in the original merger agreement, and therefore it was the responsibility of the Time directors to act to maximize immediate share value, essentially by auction.

Even if that was not the case, however—and Delaware Chancellor William Allen found that it was not—Paramount argued that Time's tender offer for Warner was a defensive, unreasonable response to Paramount's tender offer, and that the shareholders could not lawfully be deprived of the right to choose between the Paramount and Warner alternatives. While Chancellor Allen agreed that the Time tender offer was defensive, he found that where a board "continues to manage the corporation for long-term profit pursuant to a pre-existing business plan that itself is not primarily a control device or scheme, the corporation has a legally cognizable interest in achieving that plan." He found Time's actions "reasonable in relation to the specific threat posed to the Warner merger by the Paramount offer."

Chancellor Allen, who had earlier written decisions that expanded shareholders' rights—particularly shareholders' right to a choice between alternatives—had been feared by the Time and Warner lawyers. Once he had decided in their favor, however, most felt quite confident that the Delaware Supreme Court would affirm his decision. Still, one of the Supreme Court justices, Andrew Moore, was known to be especially angered by managements and directors who he felt had manipulated matters to their personal advantage. "As we were walking into the State Supreme Court," a lawyer on the Time-Warner team recalled, "one of the other litigators said to me, 'I don't know—I'm worried. Will Moore feel there have been corporate shenanigans?' "

This had been the theme of Paramount's briefs: that Time's management and directors had "abdicated their responsibilities to the Time shareholders in favor of the 'Time Culture' "—a phrase, "created by management and adopted by the directors," that "appears to involve little more than the preservation and enhancement of Time senior management positions" and "permeates every aspect of this case."

Time had therefore been forced to defend the absolute primacy given to Nicholas's succession, from the earliest conversations that management had had about this deal, and also others, through the negotiations with WCI, in which everything, always, had been negotiable but this. It was not enough for the directors to say that they had not wanted to preside over the demise of Time Inc., or that they had felt to some degree entrusted with the preservation of a journalistic institution and that they had hope that Nicholas would somehow manage to preserve, in the context of this new entertainment giant, whatever had ineffably made Time Inc. Time Inc. That appears to have been how some of them, at least, felt. But it was a fuzzy sort of concept, particularly in contrast with their clearly delineated responsibility, as fiduciaries for Time's shareholders, to guard against management's entrenching itself (with ten-year contracts) to those shareholders' disadvantage.

What Time's management and directors now testified was that it was indeed vital for Time management to be the successor, because the Time culture—which they said was largely defined by editorial integrity, protected by the unique structure of "church" and "state"—had to be pre-served. And this on account not merely of high-minded principle (though there was an abundance of that voiced) but of the financial health of the enterprise (and, consequently, the shareholders' interests).

Thus, church and state, that "antiquated" concept which during the tenure of Munro and Nicholas had been maligned, attacked, and dimin-ished, and had come within a hairsbreadth of being dismantled utterly (with Munro's attempt to remove the editor-in-chief from the board), now became the rallying cry, the banner for the fight. In a letter to Martin Davis, Paramount's CEO, Munro wrote: "We cannot and will not ignore the public interest. The journalistic integrity of our publications—the independence of their editorial voice—isn't window-dressing. It's the essence of who we are and what we do . . . and we're determined to preserve it." And in his deposition, Munro elaborated on this point. "I think because of the nature of the environment within our editorial ranks, i.e., our separation of church and state, that we are able to employ the finest journalists, produce the finest magazines and therefore return the most profits to the shareholders," he testified. "So I think we do take that quite seriously and I guess our feeling was that Gulf & Western [Para-mount] might not be terribly sensitive to that."

Chancellor Allen was not impervious to the possibility that what had been dressed up as a commitment to protecting Time's editorial integrity (and, thereby, its economic viability) was really something else. "It is noteworthy . . . that Time's magazine business contributes about 40% to its gross income and will contribute about 20–25% of the revenue of a merged Time-Warner," he wrote. The decision went on:

One is entitled to be suspicious, therefore, that some other motivation than protecting the journalistic integrity of *Time* and *People* Magazines may be at work in the insistence on assuring the integrity of the journalism for financial reasons. Not only did magazines not provide the dominant part of the income of the merged entity, but Time was not proposing to merge with a firm to whom the importance of expressive freedom is presumably unknown. How great a threat to 20% of the combined gross income did Warner represent? Yet maintaining a Time culture—all the outside directors except [Arthur] Temple agree—was the first and central requirement and could only be assured by securing the top job ultimately for Mr. Nicholas.

There may be at work here a force more subtle than a desire to main-tain a title or office in order to assure continued salary and perquisites. Many people commit a huge portion of their lives to a single large-scale business organization. They derive their identity in part from that organization and feel that they contribute to the identity of the firm. The mission of the firm is not seen by those involved with it as wholly economic, nor the continued existence of its distinctive identity as a matter of indifference.

It is doubtless true that Munro, besides being delighted to have a new contract that would earn him millions of dollars, cared deeply about Time Inc. and wanted to do the right thing by the company. It is doubtless true also that Nicholas, besides being pleased by his new contract, believed in his heart that he, and he alone, was qualified to lead Time into a stronger future—and, similarly, that Levin, besides being gratified at having resurrected his career and having achieved a new contract, loved Time Inc. and saw himself as the keeper of the flame.

That most people have mixed motivations but believe, often passionately, that their intentions are good ought not to cloud the picture. The deal that Time's managers were able to strike was not solely seigneurial, but it was seigneurial; it was not solely self-interested, but it was self-interested; and it was not solely venal, but it was venal. In the end, what was most remarkable about this mammoth struggle played out among three public companies, representing over $20 billion in market capitalization, was that Time's managers were able to preserve the exercise of their intensely personal preferences against all intrusions by another bidder, and even by their own shareholders, judicial scrutiny notwithstanding. Thus, those shareholders, whose stocks had been trading at about $105 before the deal became public, were denied the right to choose between the company's long-range promises and the cash offer of $200 a share (which if a contest had been allowed by the courts would in the view of some Time shareholders have gone as high as $225 or even $250). And the Delaware decision, moreover, was widely hailed in corporate quarters as a reaffirmation of the rights of directors to manage companies, particularly in carrying out strategies for the long term.

Ross had won. Even Time Inc., that bastion of privilege, had yielded to him. Eddie Rosenthal, long since retired but still a director emeritus of the company, was both proud (from Riverside funeral home to Time Inc.!) and incredulous. "To me, this was the most impossible deal in the whole world," Rosenthal declared. "Henry Luce must be turning in his grave." Apart from the taste of triumph, however, what Ross had really won was another question. Indeed, because of Paramount's intervention and the debt that the merged company had incurred (a singularly unlucky thing to have happened to someone as lucky as Ross), he found himself in a situation that was arguably more challenge than opportunity.

The debtload, of course, limited his options, and compelled him to turn immediately to devising some means of paying it down. But the changed structure of the deal had also fuelled other resentments, regarding comparative compensation at the new Time Warner—which was vastly unequal, with WCI paying its executives at entertainment-industry levels heretofore unimagined at Time. Moreover, while Time's troops had lost a chance to sell their stock at $200 a share, thus garnering nothing, and watched the company's generals who blocked that offer profit mightily, their new colleagues at WCI had, of course, been cashed out at a munificent price. At the very apex of this much-resented profiteering was Ross, who was garnering $193 million from the payout of his stock-based plans. Several of his key corporate executives were receiving about $20 million each, and a few of his division heads several times that. And then, of course, because of the "double dip," they were being given new grants of stock options.

From the standpoint of the Time executives—who, even decades after Luce, still inhabited a remarkably genteel, upper-class kind of world—it was one thing to have to merge for compelling business reasons with people whom they found rather déclassé. But it was quite another to recognize that those people—after having been acquired, at full price— had the upper hand in terms of both money and power. It was the kind of recognition that tended to inflame already existing prejudices. And it was precisely that view—essentially, that Time paid WCI to be taken over —which gained currency at Time in the days after the merger. An in-house cartoon pictured Ross at his desk, grinning broadly and saying, "I got mine—and yours, too!" One of Ross's division heads recalled Time Warner's first get-together, held at Time's traditional watering hole, Lyford Cay in the Bahamas. "The clash of cultures was so evident," he remarked. "There we were—some of us never went to college at all, or, if we did, not to the Ivy League. And there they were—these WASP, blueblood, aristocratic guys—who went to Ivy League schools and had Roman numerals after their names. They were nice enough. But then, those people are always nice, no matter what they're thinking."

And, even before the deal was final, the seeds of an internecine feud had been sown between HBO's chairman, Michael Fuchs, and Warner Bros.' CEO, Robert Daly, and its president, Terry Semel. Fuchs had wanted for some time to begin making movies not only for pay TV but for theatrical release. In the summer of 1988, when the deal was being negotiated,

Ross, Nicholas, and Fuchs had met in Los Angeles with Daly and Semel. Fuchs had argued that HBO should have a comedy label at the studio, and should start making movies—perhaps four or five a year in the beginning—for theatrical release. Daly and Semel were vehemently opposed. Daly and Semel won. As one Time executive, listing the divisions of Time and Warner, commented: "Publishing and records are off by themselves. The cable divisions fit together like an Erector Set. HBO and Warner Bros. are the one area where there is actual potential for synergy, and instead what you have is an ego clash."

Calming such tempests, and melding these disparate parts into a coherent whole, would be a challenge as large as the debt burden for Ross. In a sense, though, there was no task to which he was better suited; for, at its heart, it was about understanding people and what motivated them, and then using those perceptions to manipulate them according to his design. It was, essentially, how he had built WCI, and it was certainly how he had won Time. For the Time-Warner deal, in the end, stood not as a testament to any model of corporate governance but, rather, to the triumph of personality. As one Time Inc. director told me after he met Ross, "Steve makes people feel like he sees things their way—it's his strength." Referring to Paramount's effort, he added, "If Martin Davis could have done it, he would have had Time."

Here, however, Ross had committed himself to a form of shared power, as co-CEO, so his moves would have to be even more subtle and adroit than when he had held supreme sway at WCI. And, in addition to problems of ego and personality clashes, there were a host of other new issues to be dealt with—not least of which was whether Time's or WCI's culture would prevail. Time was institutional, accustomed to corporate governance, while WCI was entrepreneurial, loose, free-wheeling, and, of course, at the corporate level, utterly controlled by Ross. "Ed Aboodi and Arthur Liman serve and service Steve Ross in a personal way," a Time executive told me. "They've done a good job of handling that, but obviously a system where someone is so personally dominant is not a system of checks and balances." This executive acknowledged that Ross expected Time to become more like WCI, and that Ross believed the Time board leaned too heavily on its advisers—investment bankers and lawyers (who, for example, came up with the charter provision that Ross defeated)—instead of taking direction from a strong CEO. "But the Time Inc. side of management will be running the board more than Steve will," this executive told me. "Even though he's sixty-two years old, and very wise, Steve Ross is going to be exposed to a whole round of experience he hasn't had. He is not used to a board he doesn't control. But that was the trade-off he made here. A very significant one."

That remained to be seen. In the pre-merger history of the deal, there had been no evidence that Time could wrest anything from Ross that he did not want to give. He gave Nick Nicholas the position of co-CEO and the promise of succession—but refused, of course, to incorporate that provision in the charter. Had Nicholas been closer to his own mold and therefore a more likely candidate, Ross might not have been so willing to make his promises. As his old friend Joe Lehman had pointed out, Ross in all his acquisitions always made certain that he was not joining league with anyone who might successfully challenge him; that had been true in the sixties, and it still was.

In some ways reminiscent of the Ross-Siegel match, Ross and Nicholas were a study in contrasts. Ross dwarfed Nicholas in stature, but it was more his outsized presence that made Nicholas—who could be remote, awkward, and stolid—seem exaggeratedly so. Ross, of course, had made his key people multimillionaires, and they were devoutly loyal; indeed, a cult of personality had grown up around him. Nicholas was surrounded by executives who made prosaic incomes, and at least some of whom were envious of the deal he had cut for himself and feared him more than they liked him.

Ross was virtually incapable of firing anyone, and had had others do it for him in the aftermath of Atari; but Nicholas did it readily when he felt it was required, and—in the view of those who had felt his cut—cold-bloodedly. Ross's lifestyle, supported by the corporate treasury, led even his friend Liman to remark that Ross was "the last great pasha of American business." Nicholas's attitude toward such exploitation of corporate assets was, probably, even more straitlaced than Siegel's. And while Ross's time-worn credo was that it is sins of omission, not commission, that kill you in business, and he therefore wanted his people to be unafraid of error and comforted by his presence ("You have to be solid, you have to be a rock, you have to be a father—you have to encourage them to make mistakes, and they will, because they know you're there," Ross declared), Nicholas was faulted by his critics for those very sins of omission.

Ross's credo had become the cornerstone of the Warner Brothers Studio. "Look at the people who have succeeded in the movie business in the last twenty years—Steve Ross, Charlie Bluhdorn [the former chairman and CEO of Gulf & Western], Lew Wasserman [the chairman and CEO of MCA]," Robert Daly said, when I interviewed him shortly after the merger. "What did those three have? The intelligence and the financing and the guts required to stay at the table and play. Everyone else with limited financing and limited guts has failed."

This was his own chief concern about the merger, added Daly, who, until Nicholas appeared, was believed by some at Warner to be Ross's likely heir. "We kept asking, Would anything change that would affect the guts to stay at the table?" In the end, Ross had persuaded Daly and Semel that nothing would change. They would continue to have the autonomy they were accustomed to: they, and only they, would decide what movies would be made. And their bonuses would continue to be awarded at Ross's sole discretion.

But the peace that Daly and Semel made with the merger was, in effect, conditional upon Steve Ross's continuing in control. In this, they were not alone at Warner. One Warner associate remarked, on being asked about Nicholas's purported succession as sole CEO in five years, "Five years is a long time. In five years, Nicholas may not even be in the company."

Ross was, of course, extremely supportive of Nicholas publicly. When I pressed Ross about his view of Nicholas as his successor, he told me, "Nick is good—he's competent, he's hands-off. Give him a chance. And," he added, "he's had a hard time. He's been in a no-man's-land, because he was not, formally, CEO. And he's had a board that's always remembering Luce. I will shield him from the board."

Among his own people, however, Ross was apparently sending out rather different signals. Robert Pittman, a Ross favorite who had run MTV before WCI sold it to Viacom and who returned to the company in 1989 after a hiatus, recalled much later that he and Ross had been in Acapulco in March 1989, shortly after the merger had been announced, and they were discussing Nicholas as his successor. "Steve was *worried*. I mean, he wasn't plotting, or anything, but we were talking, and he was saying, 'You know, I'm just worried about Nick—' "

Moreover, Cy O'Neil later recalled something Ed Aboodi had said to him at the time of the merger. Aboodi, he noted, was notoriously circumspect, and it was difficult to elicit any information from him that he did not want to give. But he had made a point of remarking to O'Neil that "the person at Time who really understands this merger, who really gets it, is Jerry Levin."

One of the more remarkable components of this remarkable deal was the trust that Nicholas appeared to place in Ross's protestations. Unless, of course, he hadn't. Nicholas, who was fifty, apparently decided that the mortality tables were on his side. As the deal was entering the later stages of negotiation, Nicholas held a meeting with a group of high-level executives, many of whom had been expressing to him their skepticism about Ross's promise that Nicholas would succeed him. Nicholas is said to have told the group not to worry, because Ross was sixty-two years old and in poor health. Indeed, Nicholas had been told (and communicated this information to Munro and Levin) that Ross had had a bout with prostate cancer in the mid-eighties—something that had never been publicly disclosed, and was known only by a handful of people apart from Ross's family and closest associates. Moreover, Nicholas had reportedly been told that Ross's prognosis was poor: the cancer was likely to recur within the next few years, and he would not survive.

Ross, of course, was mortal. But he was also the quintessential survivor, and to bet against him—particularly at this moment, when he had just assumed dominion over the largest media-entertainment company in the world, which had given him an enormous charge of excitement—seemed high-risk. Ross, for his part, was confident of the future. He had no thought of retiring, or even receding. "I will be there," he declared, shortly after the merger. "I will be there as co-CEO for five years, and then I will be there as chairman of the board and Nick will be the CEO. I don't want the day-to-day responsibilities. I want to plan. I want to dream. But I will be there."

Anything else, for Ross, was unthinkable; he had not scaled this peak only to descend. "It is a remarkable thing for him, to be co-CEO of this company," Levin said, a trifle wistfully, as the deal was about to be consummated. "There is only one Time Inc."

Ross couldn't have agreed more. "Time," he said warmly, "has such pizzazz."

# 9

In May 1990, several months after the closing of the Time-Warner deal, Dick Munro retired, on schedule, as he had announced he would ten years earlier—though with at least $7.5 million more than if the merger had not taken place. He had had only a brief experience as co-chairman with Ross in the new Time Warner, but he told friends that it was enough to know that it was not for him. Ross's marathon meetings, which typically continued for many hours, drove him to distraction. During their courtship, Munro had found Ross "fun to be with," as he told me at the time, but being in business with him was a different story. One director told me that Munro had recounted a trip that he and Ross had taken to Los Angeles, on a Warner corporate jet. Throughout the six-hour flight, Ross talked deals to him, non-stop, which Munro found exhausting; then, upon arriving at the Beverly Hills Hotel, Ross had turned to the bleary-eyed Munro and said, "Let's just order some Chinese food and keep going!" Munro told one colleague that the happiest day of his life was the day he retired.

Munro and his wife decided to host two farewell parties at their home in New Canaan, Connecticut—the first night, for all their friends from the old Time Inc., drawn from all levels of the company; and the second, for the more senior corporate executives of the new Time Warner. The first night went as planned (except for a speech by Nicholas during which he made an extemporaneous attack on Munro's predecessors, particularly Heiskell, that many thought gratuitous and almost bewilderingly inappropriate). By mid-afternoon of the second day, however, so many of the executives from the old Warner side had said that they couldn't come (because of sudden, urgent meetings) that the Munros cancelled the dinner. They invited some neighborhood friends over and gave the rest of the huge catered spread to organizations for the homeless. "Dick knew then that he was history," one former Time executive commented.

In a culture as intensely familial as WCI's, such behavior might be deemed especially surprising, even aberrant. But Dick Munro was not family; and, with the merger achieved, there was no longer any need to pretend that he ever would be. To those on the Time side, however, this rude rebuff was further confirmation of what they already perceived—their subordination and their negligibility in this new world. After the fiasco of Munro's farewell party, which added insult to injury, Nicholas reportedly remarked to a colleague from the old Time Inc., "They just don't conduct themselves the way we do."

That was one of the few times that Nicholas associates recall his making a critical comment about Warner in the early months of the merger. In public, Nicholas gave every appearance of having resigned himself to his role as Ross's subordinate; the only indication of impatience occurred in private conversation when he is said to have commented, on occasion, "You know, Steve is not a well man."

Nicholas had never been especially well liked by the troops at Time Inc., but he had been generally perceived as a strong, decisive executive, and, popular or not, he was now their surrogate; so many disheartened Time employees were waiting eagerly for Nicholas to start laying claim to his, and their, territory. Instead, they found an even more remote and relatively passive Nicholas, apparently unwilling to fight for them. As one executive from the Time side recalled, "The Time people kept looking around and saying to each other, 'Where is Nick?' "

Nicholas had not become infatuated with Hollywood, as some speculated, or seduced by the lavish new perquisites of Time Warner corporate life. He had not fallen under Ross's spell  Rather, what he was attempting to do was to find a means of coexistence that would enable him ultimately to reap the benefits of the bargain he had struck. As one person who had been close to both companies, but especially Warner, for many years, told me, "After the merger, I gave Nick one piece of advice. I said, 'Keep your head down, don't make waves—and in five years you'll be the head of the largest media-entertainment company in the world.' "

Though he probably did not realize it at the time, Nicholas was faced with a Hobson's choice; for, in accepting Ross's sovereignty and repressing his own instincts in order to survive, he was yielding not only primacy but that which made Nicholas, Nicholas. And as he became a paler, more tentative version of himself, he began to alienate some of his constituencies.

The ally whose loss would perhaps be the most damaging was Michael Fuchs, CEO of HBO. Fuchs, whom Nicholas had elevated to that post when he had fired Biondi, had been a Nicholas stalwart; in the past, he would often say that he had been Nicholas's "campaign manager" (lobbying Munro, and lobbying others to do the same) when Nicholas was jousting with Levin for the presidency of Time Inc.

The merger, however, was a blow to Fuchs; he would have preferred that Time Inc. make its way into the world of entertainment by expansion through HBO. And the first rift between Nicholas and him occurred in the summer of 1988, before the deal had been consummated, when the two men met with Ross and Warner Bros.' Bob Daly and Terry Semel, who had rejected out of hand Fuchs's proposal that HBO start making a limited number of movies a year for theatrical release. Ross, as always, supported his executives—but Nicholas, to Fuchs's dismay, did not support him. "Michael is very loyal," commented one of his colleagues, "but he demands extreme loyalty in return."

In October 1989, after the battle fought by Time and Warner against Paramount had been won and the merger agreement set, Fuchs and Levin, who had been friends since Fuchs had joined HBO in the late seventies, went to dinner at New York's Plaza Athenee. There, Fuchs is said to have told Levin that Nicholas would never make it with Ross but that he, Levin, could; that if Levin were to supplant Nicholas, then he would end up leading the company when Ross retired; and that Fuchs would back Levin in that bid for power (shared power, really, inasmuch as Fuchs in this scenario would someday become Levin's partner and, perhaps, successor). Levin was said to have been characteristically enigmatic.

While this was almost certainly the first solicitation to mount a coup against Nicholas that Levin had received, its underlying premise—that there would be no conjugation between Nicholas and Ross, and that Nicholas was unlikely ever to achieve his ascension—was practically dictum on the Warner side (Ross had surely communicated his "worry" about Nicholas to others besides Bob Pittman), as well as among many outside observers of the match. Levin, who is both astute in his observations of people and extraordinarily farsighted, focusing always on the long term, should have been the first to apprehend the enormous likelihood of Nicholas's being subverted; he had, after all, been studying Ross and the Warner environment for over two years. Friends, in any event, pointed the obvious out to him. As Fay Vincent commented, "I told Jerry that co-CEOs would not work, and that Steve Ross would prevail."

And when, in an interview with Levin in 1989, I asked him about the notion that Ross might be looking at him, not Nicholas, as his more likely successor, Levin replied: "I have a missionary zeal that relates to this company, and therefore I am committed to bridging some gap in communication and style—and you don't have to be CEO or co-CEO to have an impact."

During 1990, the relationship between Fuchs and Nicholas continued to deteriorate. Fuchs, warring with Daly and Semel over the amount HBO would pay for Warner Brothers movies (he thought it should be less than it was before the merger), was furious that Nicholas did not intervene and force them to agree to Fuchs's terms. Worse, Fuchs apparently felt that HBO, and he, had been powerfully diminished by the merger— becoming a smaller and far less important part of the whole, much further removed from the decision-making process of the parent company.

In the fall of 1990, there were even reports in the press that Pittman, a contemporary of Fuchs, might be slated to take over Fuchs's job. (Pittman had returned to the company in 1989 in an indeterminate position. He was widely seen within the company as a shameless self-promoter— someone whose claim to fame was that he had started MTV, when in fact it had been started by John Lack and Jack Schneider, and Pittman had developed it—and wherever Ross tried to place him in the company, he met opposition. Eventually Pittman was put in charge of Time Warner's venture in Six Flags amusement park.)

Fuchs reportedly felt that throughout this trying period, Nicholas gave him no support. And in early November 1990, at a meeting with about a dozen staff people at HBO, Fuchs exploded at Nicholas, lambasting him for not supporting the division. Several days later, he wrote Nicholas a note of apology. But later that month, at a company retreat in La Quinta, near Palm Springs, Fuchs, during a late-night walk with a close colleague from the old Time side, discussed taking steps to try to bring about the ouster of Nicholas and the promotion of Levin.

While Nicholas was losing an ally, Levin was winning a powerful new one in the WCI camp in Oded Aboodi. The groundwork for this relationship had been lain during the pre-merger period, when Levin and Aboodi, as chief negotiators for Time and Warner, respectively, spent long hours together, frequently poring over configurations of the deal until midnight. And, of course, it was Aboodi who had told Cy O'Neil that it was Levin (and, by implication, not Nicholas) who really understood the full ramifications of the merger.

Ed Aboodi, probably more than any other individual, was conspicuous in the merged company as a creation of the WCI environment—someone whose very existence was emblematic of Ross's sovereign and idiosyncratic ways. He was Ross's closest associate and most trusted adviser, an executor of his will, and, in fact, the only person familiar with Ross's personal financial dealings. Some people, pointing out that Aboodi was involved in every significant financial transaction at the company, suggested that he was functioning, in effect, as its chief financial officer. To say that, however, was to minimize his role. In fact, there is in the lexicon of conventional corporate life no title that adequately conveys what Aboodi was doing; the descriptive term that comes closest is *eminence grise,* but many, more pejoratively, called him "Ross's Rasputin."

Aboodi referred to himself as a "non-exclusive employee" of Time Warner, meaning that his agreement with Ross permitted him to work for others as well—though the overwhelming majority of his time leading up to and following the merger appeared to have been spent on Time Warner business. His investment and tax firms occupied rent-free office space in the Time Warner headquarters, and Aboodi received a salary and benefits from Time Warner.

Because he was not an executive, however, Aboodi was free of any corporate accountability. What he was paid for his work on the numerous transactions he was involved in on behalf of Time Warner was never disclosed either in public filings or to the board (the Time-Warner merger was an exception, since his fee there—$8 million, plus the management of a $150 million investment fund—had to be disclosed, along with the fees of other advisers). Another advantage of Aboodi's technically separate status was, of course, that he was able to employ Solomon Weiss, for Ross.

With Ross's backing, Aboodi had also started a bank—a sideline he could not have undertaken were he an executive of Time Warner. He was chairman and president of the Berkshire Bank, a small commercial institution in New York City, opened in 1989; its purpose, according to Ralph Peterson, the treasurer of Warner Brothers, was "that it would lend to people who would invest in his deals." This notion—of controlling a bank that would lend to his projects—was one that had been attractive to Steve Ross always. Back in 1969, Kinney had acquired a New Jersey bank, Hackensack Trust (renamed Garden State National Bank); but, because of a change in the banking laws, WCI was forced to sell the bank in 1980.

Aboodi began to organize Berkshire in 1988, in concert with Susan

Fisher and Robert Greenwood. Greenwood had had a private banking relationship with Ross and other WCI executives (conducted mainly through Solomon Weiss) dating back to at least the early seventies, at Manufacturers Hanover. In the early eighties, Greenwood had linked up with Fisher, who was also working at Manufacturers Hanover, and together they had moved, as a team, from Chemical Bank, to Marine Midland, to Manufacturers & Traders, and thence to Berkshire, within roughly six years. This in itself was anomalous in the world of private banking, an area where stability and long-term relationships are paramount and moves to different banks relatively infrequent And they brought along Aboodi and Ross as lucrative clients—and, through them, many of the WCI extended family—as they travelled from bank to bank.

As chief operators of Berkshire, Fisher and Greenwood were a curious, if not bizarre, choice for someone as keen as Aboodi to make. They had abandoned at least two of the banks they'd worked in during the eighties under duress—leaving many millions of bad loans behind them. One of the banks, an officer told me, has suffered "$20 million in charge-offs [unrecoverable loans], and the meter is still running." Furthermore, Aboodi is said to have been warned, explicitly, about their malfeasance by several people—including an officer of one of the banks from which they had been fired.

Fisher, whose talent was marketing ("She brought us the good, the bad, and the awful," an executive of one bank where she had worked said), and Greenwood, trained in credit, were to be the president and chief operating officer, respectively, of Berkshire, according to the application that they submitted to the New York State Banking Department in 1988. One person at the Department told me, however, that because of Fisher and Greenwood's track record, "we insisted that they not occupy those positions," so James Carey was brought in as president and CEO. Fisher became a senior vice-president in charge of business development, and Greenwood a senior vice-president in charge of account management.

Berkshire was capitalized with about $7 million. Aboodi, its largest single shareholder, owned nearly 10 percent of the stock; Ross, too, was a substantial investor, as was Warner Music CEO Robert Morgado, an Aboodi ally and a director of this bank. And many of the other investors came from the Warner family—both current and former employees. Some, however, resisted the pressure to join the group; Peterson of Warner Bros., for example, said he declined because he didn't feel comfortable with Fisher and Greenwood.

By mid-1992, three years after opening, the bank had suffered continuous large losses ($2,369,000, for 1991, after a loss of $1,127,000 for 1990); its management had reportedly tried to sell it, without success. Many of the loans Berkshire made were, according to one investor, to "very big-time players in real estate." (At least one of those troubled loans, this investor added, was to Arthur Emil, a New York developer who was a general partner, along with Aboodi, in the Palmer Square development in Princeton, New Jersey—a property on which the Bank of New York, the major lender, had foreclosed.)

James Carey, Berkshire's president, resigned in mid-1991, and Fisher and Greenwood resigned in September of that year; Greenwood's resignation (which prompted Fisher's, since they had now married) was said to have been brought about as a result of an FDIC investigation. According to one person, Greenwood had made loans to a number of people who were, in fact, substitutes for a single individual (thus enabling that individual to evade the lending limit).

Aboodi assumed Carey's position while a search was undertaken for a president and senior lending officer, but it was Aboodi's twenty-six-year-old son, David, a vice-president, who was actually charged with running the bank day to day. (David Aboodi, who was active in the stock market, trading for the Aboodi family account, was under investigation by the Securities and Exchange Commission for having traded Time Warner stock at a propitious moment, and thus possibly having violated the securities laws on insider trading. This investigation, which began in early 1992—and is said to be exploring, as well, the possible role of Ed Aboodi in the trade carried out by his son—is still ongoing.) In the latter part of 1992, the bank finalized a "Memorandum of Understanding," which is a confidential censure and prescription for remedial action, issued by the FDIC and the New York State Banking Department.

Some members of the WCI extended family invested in both of Aboodi's failed projects in this period—Berkshire Bank and also Palmer Square—and it was they who felt especially benighted. Several told me that they invested on the strength of their understanding that Aboodi was going to be heavily involved in both entities, particularly the bank, and that they had no idea he would be fully engaged at Time Warner. "He's the chairman of the bank, and he's never there," said one investor. "He's always in Japan, or France, for these Time Warner deals."

This person described the frustration, echoed by others, of attempting to obtain information from Aboodi about their investments. "Ed has a very Middle Eastern mentality, secretive by definition. He understands that the law requires disclosure, but he will only report what he feels he really has to. He has a familial style—taking in only members of the

Warner extended family—and he is the paterfamilias. He is *very* close to the vest, so you never know what he is thinking, and since he is the paterfamilias, you're only supposed to follow him, not to question him. He is a terrible manager—he never delegates. Once again, he is the paterfamilias, so the ultimate decision is always his."

This investor added that Aboodi had become close to unreachable. "At the end of a day he must have dozens of unreturned calls—and then, when you finally do get him, he is all smiles, as though there is nothing wrong. You know, when things go badly, and when they can't get answers, people get angry. And, today, there are a lot of angry people out there.

"But Ed has only one master," this person continued, "and that is Steve. He is Steve's instrument, his factotem, his alter ego. I must say, if I were a director of Time Warner, I would want to know, who is this Aboodi? What are the company's relationships with him? How much is he being paid? What decisions is he making?"

The Time executives who worked to bring about the merger may not have apprehended the pervasiveness of Aboodi's power, but they were aware of its unorthodox nature. One, indeed, had commented to me that the system whereby Aboodi and Liman served Ross so personally, as though he *were* the company—and maintained with him relationships that were exempt from the scrutiny of the board—would have to change, yielding to Time's system of more formal corporate governance.

In the event, however, Aboodi's role had only grown in significance, and had gone unquestioned by the merged Time Warner board. One director, who told me that he and his fellows had no idea, for example, about what Aboodi was paid and had never inquired, explained their reticence this way. "Steve is always extolling the virtues of Ed. He will say, 'Ed labored beyond the call of duty' on this or that deal. So I would say that the directors keep quiet for political reasons—they understand the importance of Aboodi to Steve."

From the start, Aboodi and Nicholas were like oil and water—the one so sinuous and secretive, the other corporate and blunt. At one point, in early 1991, Nicholas clashed openly with Aboodi, questioning the propriety of his role at the company. Aboodi is said to have threatened, briefly, to quit, reportedly saying that his "feelings were hurt, to think that Nick did not trust him."

Levin, however, cleaved to Aboodi. Almost immediately, they began to work together on what Ross dubbed his "strategic alliances"—partnerships with companies in Europe and Asia that would expand Time Warner's global reach. Lacking financial skills himself, Levin now came to rely on Aboodi's as, earlier, he had on Nicholas's. Even more, he became mesmerized by the way Aboodi and Ross would conjure up deals together; what he had experienced at Time Inc. seemed sophomoric, and he is said to have felt that he had finally joined the major league. The bond between him and Aboodi intensified in what appeared, to others, to be a mutual admiration. As a Time Warner executive told me at this time, echoing a view shared by many others in the upper reaches of the company, "Jerry and Ed are like brothers."

In January 1991, Jerry Levin and Ed Aboodi came to Nicholas's office and proposed that Levin be made chief operating officer, or COO, of Time Warner. They were suggesting not only that Nicholas be relieved of that position—since, as they pointed out, he had more than enough to occupy himself as co-CEO and this would, in a sense, ratify his parity with Ross, making him seem less of a "junior partner"—but also that the dual reporting structure that had been put in place at the time of the merger be revised. In the existing system, all Time Inc. divisions reported to Nicholas, and all Warner divisions to Ross. But, they continued, it would make more sense operationally—and also be more "symbolic" of the two companies' union—if all divisions reported to one person, namely, Levin.

Nicholas, who had been COO for nearly five years and was eager to devote himself more fully to being co-CEO, welcomed the idea. It would make Levin the clear number-three person in the organization, a promise that Nicholas had, of course, exacted from Ross at the time of the merger. Since he had been including Levin in all his meetings, Levin would be well prepared; and while Nicholas had long considered Levin weak as an operator (as video chief and, before that, at HBO), those experiences had occurred a number of years before, and Nicholas thought Levin was now better equipped for such responsibility. However, he told Levin and Aboodi that he doubted Ross would agree to it, since Ross and his Warner division heads—particularly Robert Daly of Warner Brothers—jealously guarded their reporting relationship. The three then walked down the corridor to Ross's office, where Ross, upon hearing the proposition, immediately and enthusiastically endorsed it. This took Nicholas by surprise —but, had he known Ross better, he would have realized that the proposal had almost certainly come from him.

With that move, the stage was set for the eventual excision of Nicholas, and his replacement with Levin. It allowed Levin access he had not previously had to Warner division heads, with whom he now set about building rapport. It also caused Nicholas to be somewhat less in touch with the businesses, including those on the Time side, and to lean even more heavily on Levin—who had a thirst for information that now, more than ever, could not be slaked. Nicholas, who apparently still believed that he and Levin were functioning as the team that he had envisioned at the time of the merger ("Jerry and I" had become, for him, almost a figure of speech) is said to have commented to one colleague: "Jerry is my right arm and my left arm."

When I interviewed Nicholas in 1989, he had responded to my raising the possibility of conflict between him and Ross as co-CEOs by saying, "I'm basically an operating person. I have dealmaking skills but not Steve Ross's [dealmaking] skills. We're not going to collide a lot." Now, after little more than a year of life in the merged companies, Nicholas was increasingly intent on using *his* dealmaking skills to move the company in the direction in which he, as co-C.E.O., thought it should be going— and he was, therefore, content to cede the operating duties to Levin.

Perhaps, if the merger had been consummated in the form in which it was conceived, as a stock-for-stock combination—rather than the cash buyout, encumbering the merged company with $16 billion of debt—the tensions which began to fester between Ross and Nicholas would not have been so extreme. But the need to unburden the balance sheet of that huge debtload worked as a catalyst, bringing to the fore those predispositions—in Ross, as a founder, and in Nicholas, as a manager— that were most stereotypical, and diametrically opposed.

Nicholas wanted to reduce the debt by selling assets. It is a classical strategy (even dubbed, in business textbooks, the "weed the garden" approach), one that was ritually employed in the buyouts that transfigured the eighties. By mid-1990, Nicholas had drawn up a list of what he considered peripheral assets—so peripheral that once they were sold, he told Ross, Ross would not notice they were gone. On this list were cable systems, in non-strategic areas, which Nicholas calculated would bring about $3 billion; music publishing (Warner Chappell, which WCI had acquired in 1987), about $1 billion; and a miscellany of other items, including Hasbro stock, which would bring another $1 billion.

Ross, of course, was constitutionally not a seller. He had sold heavily in the early eighties, but that had been under the threat of bankruptcy and, additionally, the prod of Herb Siegel. "Founders are notorious for not being able to sell assets," Nicholas told me. "Each asset is like a child. Managers, on the other hand, are not sentimental. They sell assets if necessary. They don't think in such grandiose ways."

Ross had a different plan: the "strategic alliances," which he insisted were not primarily a vehicle for raising capital, but rather constructs vital to Time Warner's realizing its potential as a global force. Ross was a vocal critic of the sale of Columbia Pictures to Sony, and, subsequently, of MCA to Matsushita; the same benefits (of a software-hardware alliance, and expanded access to the Asian marketplace) he believed could be obtained by selling minority interests—while maintaining American ownership and control.

Ross articulated his general view of this global corporation of the future—not "a huge monolith, but rather a parent of many smaller companies" (which would "operate autonomously... and... retain the national identity and cultural identity of the country in which it operates") —at the Edinburgh International Television Festival in August 1990, where he was the keynote speaker. (To highlight his perspective, the 1990 Time Warner annual report was printed in six languages.)

Nicholas liked the idea of setting up small local companies in Asia and Europe to operate as joint ventures; but he was strongly opposed to selling even a minority interest in Time Warner's sterling assets as a means of raising capital. As he saw it, "I wanted to sell the weeds—and Steve was selling the roses." According to a couple of Time Warner advisers, Nicholas was also leery of Japanese partners, fearful, as one adviser expressed it, "of letting the Japanese get their nose under the tent."

By early 1991, Ross, Aboodi, Levin, and others at Time Warner had devoted more than a year to pursuing a strategic alliance in what must have seemed, increasingly, a quixotic quest. While it was true that C. Itoh (a Japanese trading company which has since changed its name to Itochu) had approached them in early 1990, since then Time Warner executives or their agents had approached more than twenty companies, including Canal-Plus, Bertelsmann, Siemens, Allianz, Unilever, Générale des Eaux, Societé Générale, Toshiba, Hitachi, Nippon Life, Matsushita, and even the Sultan of Brunei.

Meanwhile, Nicholas—blocked from pursuing his chosen strategy, and essentially hamstrung—began to chafe at Ross's dominion. Ross had always presided over WCI, but earlier the atmospherics of his reign had been different, rife as the place was with levity and a strong sense of camaraderie. In the last several years, with the enormous expansion of Ross's kingdom, and his concomitant wealth and power, he is said to have grown more isolated and imperial, surrounded at the corporate level by a handful of people who try to anticipate his every wish and who rarely, if ever, contradicted him.

Within this insular world, everything—even the dictates of time— seemed to yield to him. Nicholas would later recall that executives would wait in their offices for a summons to a meeting with Ross, which, once it finally began, would usually continue for hours; and he, Nicholas, typically was the only one who might say that he had to leave to keep another appointment. The rest generally stayed for the duration, and appointments were foregone (Levin, on one occasion, kept his lunch date waiting for well over an hour because he found it impossible to tell Ross that he had an engagement).

Even when Nicholas was on his best behavior, his very existence as a co-CEO apparently taxed Ross's patience. One Time Warner executive commented that "Arthur [Liman] and Ed [Aboodi] told me how agonizing it was for Steve to have to sit in meetings and look to Nicholas, to make sure he was in accord, when for all these years he was so used to just making his decisions"—and he snapped his fingers, "like that."

Ross's seigneurial prerogatives embraced things large and small. Although at Time Inc., as at most major American corporations, the annual meeting was held at roughly the same time each year, at Warner historically—and now, at Time Warner—it was scheduled at Ross's discretion. Nicholas did not consider this an issue of great moment, but he did believe that it was something that "set a tone." Moreover, it must have seemed to Nicholas a relatively innocuous area in which to exercise his will. He spoke to Levin, who agreed with him, according to Nicholas; but several days later, Nicholas says, Levin told him that he thought they "should do it Steve's way." As one colleague of Nicholas and Levin remarked to me, "I was in a lot of meetings with Nick and Jerry where Jerry said, 'I agree with you, Nick'—but what he said to Steve, I have no idea."

The summer and fall of 1991 were Time Warner's—and, especially, Steve Ross's—crucible, for to many enraged shareholders he had become the personification of all that was wrong with the company. The crisis began with the announcement of the ill-conceived "rights" offering in June. With the resurgence in the equity markets in the spring, Ross and his colleagues had become enamored of the idea of raising capital in the public markets. Because they wanted to raise an extraordinarily high amount—about $3.5 billion, the largest stock offering in Wall Street history—they had chosen a "rights" offering (unusual in the United States, even in its plainest form), and added to it a complicated, coercive twist. Existing shareholders, in order not to have their ownership percentage diluted, would have to subscribe to the offer; but since the price of the shares would depend (in a sliding scale) upon the ultimate level of subscription, the subscribers did not know what price they would pay for the shares they were promising to buy.

Shareholders' reaction was scathing; within days of the offering's announcement, Time Warner's outstanding shares had lost about 22 percent of their market value (or, $1.5 billion). And, while the offering price range had reflected a tantalizing discount to the price of Time Warner stock where it was trading before the announcement, once it had plummeted, shareholders felt forced to buy in order not to be diluted, and at prices that were not yet known—but that now seemed likely to be above the market price.

The shareholder rebellion, moreover, was as foreseeable as it was violent. The investment banking firm of Goldman, Sachs declined to participate in the offering, and Felix Rohatyn of Lazard Frères reportedly agreed to do so only out of deference to his nearly thirty-year-long relationship with Ross and the company, on the promise from Arthur Liman that he would convey Rohatyn's negative assessment to the board (something which, according to the recollection of several directors, Liman did obliquely, in passing). Other investment bankers involved in the deal also are said to have warned that this structure was not their first choice—although, if the company were insistent on raising over $3 billion, it was probably the only alternative.

According to several Time Warner advisers, the person Ross most heeded, as usual, was Aboodi. While the intensely complex structure of this offering appears to have been devised at Merrill Lynch, many outside the company who know Aboodi refuse to believe that it was not, at least to some degree, his handiwork—and some referred to it, at the time, as "an Aboodi special." Aboodi is famous for his penchant for financial intricacy ("Give me long enough, and I can make any deal complicated," he will often say, half-joking). It was, of course, a penchant or, more, passion, that he and Ross shared, and that probably accounted in large measure for their closeness; when it came to financial design, they, and they alone, spoke the same tongue. And, as one adviser told me, recalling the private meetings held at the company on the subject of the rights offering, of which Aboodi was strong supporter if not part-author, "the remarkable thing was to see how belligerent Levin was, in support of this structure and of Aboodi."

In the midst of the public maelstrom created by the rights offering came press articles proclaiming that Ross's compensation for 1990 was $78.2 million. As Ross repeatedly pointed out, $74.9 million of that represented a one-time payout for his interest in Warner, from the merger (he would receive an additional $121.1 million over the next several years). Ross defended his bounty as a founder's due.

Critics, however, argued that Ross had never owned more than 1 or 2 percent of Warner Communications or its predecessor companies, thereby never having exposed himself to downside risk; and that he captured all the upside by virtue of his 1987 WCI contract—the one Herb

Siegel had fought against—which was, of course, a dense, multi-faceted farrago of stock options, deferred compensation, bonuses, and posthumous provisions, and guaranteed him about $14 million a year over a decade. In the merger, Levin and Aboodi had negotiated Ross's Warner payout according to the terms of this contract, and then, the contract's renewal, with the granting of 1.8 million stock options in Time Warner.

Ross was pictured as avarice incarnate. His allies from WCI in the seventies told me that while the Ross they knew had loved money and, toward the end of that decade, especially, had lived in majestic style, venality had by no means been his defining characteristic. Several—perhaps out of their affection for Ross, like the parent who attributes their errant child's behavior to the influence of the child's friend—blamed Aboodi, arguing that a good adviser would rein Ross in and persuade him that whatever is patently excessive carries its own retribution. Instead, these friends believed, Aboodi and Ross—with their congenital secrecy and love of legerdemain—fuelled each other's more negative traits.

For many months, Ross and other Time Warner executives had been talking to analysts and the press about "strategic alliances" and suggesting, in general terms, that one would soon be realized. Even before the rights offering, shareholders were angry. Paramount Communications, of course, had bid $200 a share for Time Inc., and the Time Inc. board had rejected that offer as inadequate, their investment bankers declaring that Time Warner stock would quickly rise over $200 a share, and by 1993 would be trading at $302–$380; but the stock had been in the doldrums, trading between $66 and $125 through 1990 and the first half of 1991. Now, added to the bombardment over the coercive rights offering and Ross's gargantuan compensation came articles claiming that there was no reason to believe Time Warner executives when they spoke about a coming deal with an Asian or European partner, since they had no credibility.

In the road show to promote the rights offering, Ross was characteristically voluble about his vision of the future of Time Warner and its global partnerships. But Nicholas, appearing with Ross, began to distance himself. As he said on one occasion, "I am in accord with Steve on his philosophy, but I'm from the Yogi Berra school—when we have a deal, we'll tell you."

Nicholas must have been rankling at taking the heat for events over which he had so little say. He had endorsed the rights offering—but only because, at that point, he felt there was no alternative. Ross would not agree to sell assets; no deal had yet come to fruition; and capital had to be raised. Indeed, given the ratios stipulated in the covenants on Time Warner's bank loans, if the company did not find a way of reducing the debt by the end of 1992, it would be in violation of those covenants. The worse things got, in the summer of 1991, the more Nicholas must have thought that—had he been able to do things his way—all this public outcry, and the concomitant damage to the company's image and finances, could have been averted.

Some Warner division heads would later say that they noted the schism between Ross and Nicholas at this time. "Just my impression from reading articles about the rights offering, I got the sense that it was all Steve's doing—they weren't standing shoulder to shoulder," commented Terry Semel of Warner Bros.

"Once you say, 'I told him not to do it,' that's the beginning of the end of a partnership," Robert Daly said, adding that he and Semel spoke from their own experience; they have been partners at the helm of Warner Bros. for eleven years—an unusually long union, and tenure, in Hollywood. "Two good partners would never find a way for one of them to take the rap more than the other. They would close the ranks."

By early July, it seemed increasingly likely that the Securities and Exchange Commission would withhold its approval of the rights offering (as it ultimately did) because of the lack of disclosure of what, in the end, investors would pay for their shares. Nicholas (who by this time believed that Ross would almost reflexively reject any alternative that he proposed) contacted an investment banker at Salomon Brothers and asked if the firm could lead an underwriting for a "plain vanilla," fixed-price rights offering that would raise $2–$3 billion—and, if they thought they could, to propose the deal to Ross. That revised issue, which offered the stock at $80 a share, a healthy discount to the stock's trading price, was successfully completed in early August, raising $2.76 billion.

With the offering finally accomplished, Ross and his lieutenants immediately turned to their hoped-for strategic alliance with Itochu and Toshiba—a deal that had been in discussion, sporadically, since early 1990. And it was the news, in mid-August 1991, that this deal appeared to be coming to fruition that finally destroyed even the semblance of a working partnership between Ross and Nicholas.

Nicholas, long opposed to what he thought of as "selling the roses," had come to believe that, after all this time, there was little likelihood of the prospective Japanese partners coming up with the $2 billion Time Warner wanted. Since at least the start of 1991, that was the amount Time Warner executives had been telling the board that they planned to garner from such a deal. According to Nicholas, the two sides had not been able to come to terms in the spring of 1991 because Itochu and Toshiba were only willing to invest $500 million each, or a combined $1 billion.

Now, however, in August, Nicholas learned that that was the amount of the deal that was brewing. A subsidiary, Time Warner Entertainment, was to be created, into which would eventually be put (with the addition of other partners) up to 50 percent of Time Warner Cable, Warner Brothers, and HBO. Itochu and Toshiba, for their combined $1 billion, would own 12.5 percent of those divisions. There was also to be a local company in Japan, TWE Japan, which would be owned fifty-fifty by Time Warner and by their Japanese partners.

Nicholas went to talk to Levin. He was contemptuous of the $1 billion; he believed he could have raised it by selling the most incidental assets. He hated losing a percentage of the upside of Time Warner's "crown jewels." He was worried about the issue of control, and in this he was not alone; Bob Daly and Terry Semel, too, were adamant that Warner Bros. not give up control of its marketing and distribution in Japan (they would ultimately become satisfied that it would not be doing so). He believed in the idea of local partnerships, or joint ventures, around the world—such as HBO Ole, in Venezuela; HBO Singapore; a Time Warner Cable joint venture in Sweden; and one in Hungary, all recently formed. But none of these involved the foreign partner putting up capital for an equity stake in Time Warner.

And he didn't buy the argument that these foreign partners' owning equity stakes would accelerate the growth and profitability of Time Warner; to him, the downside was clear, while the upside (from such benefits as a hardware-software alliance, for example, though no specific application of technology was agreed upon) was fuzzy at best. There was, furthermore, no business plan, no mutually agreed upon set of expectations, which to Nicholas's way of thinking was a recipe for disaster in a joint venture. Jerry Levin, Nicholas would later recall, said that he agreed with him.

Within the next couple of days, Nicholas says, he encountered Aboodi in Levin's office and questioned him about why he was going forward in negotiating a deal for only $1 billion—to which he, Nicholas, was opposed. Aboodi was noncommittal. Nicholas then began to berate him, in a raised and furious voice: Did he work for Time Warner, as he was paid to do? Or did he work for Steve Ross?

After that, Nicholas seemed impelled, headlong, on a collision course. He hired Cravath, Swaine & Moore, Time Inc.'s historic outside counsel, to examine the papers on the Toshiba-Itochu transaction. (Liman's firm, Paul, Weiss, had been engaged to work on this deal; although at the time of the merger, management indicated that the two law firms would share equally, Paul, Weiss had received about three times as much business from Time Warner as Cravath.) And he talked to Cravath senior partner Samuel Butler about his opposition to the deal and his willingness, if necessary, to challenge Ross. Butler advised him, repeatedly, to make a list of the directors and count those whom he considered certain support-ers; Levin, despite whatever he had said to Nicholas earlier about concur-ring with him, would clearly not be one.

Liman came to see Nicholas, and said that Ross wanted to bring the matter before the board; to which Nicholas replied that if Ross did, he would lose. It may have been mere bravado, though Nicholas would insist later that he believed at the time that if he laid out for the directors his strategy for dealing with the balance sheet (something he had never done), his would be the more likely winner. However improbable this seems—after all, it was because of Ross, the progenitor with the fecund imagination, that many of the Time directors voted for the deal in the first place—it never reached that point. Nicholas spoke to Dick Munro, who called Time Warner director Donald Perkins, who, in turn, called Nicho-las; but Nicholas did not speak with any other directors.

Instead, when Ross came to see him, Nicholas agreed that they should try to resolve their differences rather than asking the board to do it for them; and that he would attend a presentation on the deal, made to him by all those working on it. Held several days later, it was a very un-Warner-like meeting: a carefully prepared, well-organized, ostensibly democratic process, after which all involved, having heard the pros and cons, cast their votes. Nicholas, along with everyone else, voted for the deal.

Asked about his having thrown down the gauntlet, only to retrieve it, Nicholas said, "I couldn't be a yes-man. But I was trying, still, to be a team player. I thought that I would continue, do my best to contain the damage —and that time was on my side."

Nicholas had retreated, but on the WCI side the breach was set in stone. As one Time Warner executive commented, referring to the presentation on the Toshiba-Itochu deal made to Nicholas, "That was when a bunch of us knew the world was going to change." And, through the fall of 1991, a persistent, well-cultivated strain of anti-Nicholas sentiment did indeed begin to spread through the upper levels of Time Warner.

Nicholas, increasingly isolated and unaware of what was being mar-shalled against him, was the victim of the corporate structure to which he earlier had acquiesced—one wholly comprised of Warner loyalists, with Levin the single other Time person. Nicholas continued to believe, as he had from the start, that Levin and he were a team, and refused even to entertain any doubts on that score; when one executive from the Time side came to see Nicholas in the early fall to suggest that Levin might be less than trustworthy, Nicholas dismissed the notion out of hand.

While the ending was apparently known to Ross, Aboodi, Levin, and a handful of others, the rest of the script, of the undoing of Nicholas, remained to be written. Some thought was reportedly given to dispatching him soon after the confrontation on the Toshiba-Itochu deal, but the moment was quickly seen to be wrong, coming after the summer's calamitous publicity triggered by the rights offering. In lieu of precipitous action, then, a plot line was given time to develop. And Nicholas, being Nicholas, played unwittingly into the hands of what one person referred to as "the Steve forces," who were planning his demise.

His most self-damaging moment occurred at the Time Warner annual meeting, in late September. For Ross, especially, the meeting was gruelling; he was delivering his much-prepared defense of his $78 million payout, against a backdrop of pickets, fired employees, and union spokesmen, all protesting the layoff of six hundred employees at the magazine division announced just the week before. Into this melee came Nicholas, and, in response to a question about future layoffs at the publishing division, he said, in his signature overtoughened way, that cost control "must be a way of life for any business that wishes to survive in the global marketplace."

Old Warner hands were aghast, feeling that this was a time for palliatives, not more bitter pills—and knowing that Nicholas's response was one that (no matter its truth) Ross would deplore; he and Nicholas, standing at their respective podiums, had never seemed more flagrantly out of sync. Indeed, after the meeting, Ross complained to me about Nicholas's handling of other questions as well, saying that he'd written notes to Nicholas that Nicholas had ignored. "It's hard. If you're not used to these meetings, if you haven't been doing them for years . . ." Ross trailed off. It was, however, extraordinary for Ross to be so openly critical of a fellow executive, let alone his co-CEO, and indicative of how numbered Nicholas's days were.

An attempt Nicholas had made, the previous July, to find a capital-raising alternative to the strategic alliance also was now transmuted into useful propaganda. He had wanted to create a joint venture combining Warner Music with MCA Music; since Warner Music was much larger, Time Warner in the capitalization of this entity would receive roughly $3–$4 billion in cash. According to Nicholas, Ross had said he liked the idea, but urged that it be kept secret (Levin and Aboodi were the only others at this meeting), and that someone from outside the company make the approach to MCA. This was classic, circuitous Ross. Feelers were extended but nothing more occurred. In the fall, however, Robert Morgado—the highly political, powerful chairman of the Warner Music Group, close to Ross and Aboodi—learned from within the company, as he would later say, that Nicholas had "talked to an investment banker outside about selling the music business."

Had he spoken to Nicholas about it, he presumably would have heard that it was a proposed joint venture, not a sale of the music business, and that it was Ross who had urged it be kept secret. But Morgado says he chose not to dignify the proposition by bringing it up with Nicholas. "I never thought, for a minute, that this company would do something so audaciously stupid," Morgado told me.

Other initiatives that Nicholas undertook, characteristically counter-cultural in this Warner-dominated company, served to broaden and strengthen the opposition to him. Long known as "Nick the Knife" for his cost-cutting zeal at Time Inc., Nicholas had been eager to begin scaling back the notoriously luxurious WCI lifestyle, particularly at the corporate level (with, for example, its seven planes), where the expenses were the most egregious. This must have awakened in Ross bitter memories of Herb Siegel; Nicholas's overtures to Ross on this subject, in any event, had always been rebuffed. Now, however, shortly after Labor Day, Nicholas showed Ross the preliminary budget numbers for 1992 and, much to Nicholas's surprise, Ross said, " 'I think we have to cut,' " as Nicholas later recalled.

Ross said that it was important that the cost cutting be perceived as something they were both endorsing, Nicholas continued, and that Morgado, who had done cost cutting at WCI in the early eighties following the Atari debacle, should work on it with Philip Lochner, the former general counsel of Time Inc. who had recently returned to the company after a stint at the SEC. Just as with the music joint-venture idea, nothing actually was done on the cost cutting; but word was soon travelling through the company that Nicholas intended to cut back drastically on the perquisites that had long been staples of life at Warner, and that he was focusing not only on corporate but the divisions as well, particularly the Hollywood studio.

During this time, Nicholas also gave some thought to corporate governance—which had lately become the focus of increasingly powerful shareholders' rights groups—and, as always, he aired his thoughts with Jerry Levin. Among other issues, he believed that the board, with twenty-four directors, was far too large, and that it had too many insiders (excluding Ross and Nicholas, there were six). According to one director from the WCI side, Levin used this information to further inflame Ross. This director told me that "Jerry said to Steve, 'This is Nick, consolidating his position.' It was another trigger." By the late fall, people like Time Warner vice-chairman Martin Payson, who had been Warner's general counsel for nearly two decades, and Time Warner's chief financial officer, Bert Wasserman, thought that Nicholas wanted to remove them from the board, and, perhaps, their jobs.

Wasserman may have felt that Nicholas had targeted him especially. In October, while Ross was in Japan negotiating the Toshiba-Itochu deal, Nicholas, scanning the *Wall Street Journal*'s listing of insiders' stock purchases, read that Wasserman had sold Time Warner stock (it was more-over, just a few days before quarterly earnings would be released—a blackout period for insiders). Aghast, he contacted Ross and the company's general counsel, Peter Haje, who had joined the company from Paul, Weiss. After an inquiry conducted by Haje, it was determined that Wasserman had committed a careless error in having failed to check with Haje before selling the stock; he was said to be embarrassed and contrite. But it was an extraordinary lapse for a chief financial officer.

In late November, Ross was diagnosed once again as having prostate cancer, and he began to undergo chemotherapy. With his illness—and the fact that it was a recurrence—came an even greater sense of urgency about resolving Nicholas's fate (one division head, who had expected Nicholas's ouster earlier, said he was "annoyed" when it had not yet been accomplished by Christmas). Should Nicholas by this accident of fate achieve the succession that was, contractually, his, the scenario was both easy and, to Ross loyalists, alarming to envisage: costs would be cut and the lifestyle radically altered; the Toshiba-Itochu deal would be cancelled; assets sold to pay down the debt; insiders removed from the board, and many of the Warner family retired. As for the company's advisers, Aboodi would be dispatched, and Liman's role radically reduced, with Cravath getting as much work as Paul, Weiss or, more likely, the lion's share.

This was probably the first time that the Ross devotees considered that Nicholas might actually run the company. Before this—even before he had had the unforgivable temerity to challenge Ross—he had been seen, more, as someone who served at Ross's forbearance. One former WCI director recalled a meeting held with Liman shortly before the Time-Warner merger, at which he had asked Liman what would happen if Ross and Nicholas did not get along as co-CEOs. "Arthur said—dismissively, you know, as though it was almost too obvious to bother answering—'We'll fire him.'"

• • •

By mid-January 1992, the plan was in place. Levin is said to have called Viacom CEO Frank Biondi, fired by Nicholas and his long-time adversary, but someone with whom Levin had remained close since their HBO days, and said, "'Just sit tight for a few weeks—something good is about to happen for us all.'" At about this time, Martin Lipton, of Wachtell, Lipton, Rosen & Katz, was hired to represent the company vis-à-vis Nicholas. Since Liman would be one of the players in the unseating of Nicholas, he perhaps felt that if he were also counsel to the company he would be wearing too many hats.

And, on the evening of January 25, on an HBO cruise for affiliates, Michael Fuchs—who had recently renegotiated his contract with Levin, winning terms that gave him parity with Daly and Semel of Warner Brothers, making him one of the three highest-paid executives in the company —reportedly talked to Dick Munro, urging him to rethink the issue of succession because Nick Nicholas was the wrong one. ("Jerry knew that Michael was doing this. It was something that Jerry couldn't broach with Munro himself, because he was the beneficiary," one of their colleagues explained.) After their discussion, Munro is said to have confided in a friend, "Nick has gotten himself into a real mess."

As the action began to unfold, on Sunday, February 16, Nicholas, oblivious, was on a long-scheduled family holiday in Vail, Colorado—a vacation that he always took at this time each year. Levin paid a three-hour visit to Munro at his home in Connecticut; Munro is said to have protested later that for the first hour he had no idea what Levin, even more opaque than usual, was talking about. Eventually, though, he got the message. Munro called former Time director Donald Perkins. He did not call Nicholas (according to Liman, directors were told that Nicholas was not being called—with the directive, implicit, that they not call him). And the next morning, although Munro is said to have known that the matter of Nicholas's resignation would be resolved that week, he left for the French Alps to watch the Winter Olympics.

Stunning as Munro's virtual evanescence might seem, it was consistent with his past performance that he would make no move to oppose what was already in motion. And, while having Munro's blessing no doubt made it easier for Levin (he is said to have likened it to Jacob's seeking of Isaac's blessing), it was by no means a requisite. Excluding Ross, Levin, and Nicholas (who would not be voting), there were eleven Warner directors to nine Time directors. Nicholas had lost two strong supporters on the board in recent months: David Kearns, who had resigned in the fall when he became Assistant Secretary of Education; and James Bere, probably Nicholas's staunchest ally, who died in early January, days before the plan began to be set in motion. Furthermore, Michael Dingman, the former Time director, was thought by many close to the situation to have been a Ross loyalist since the time of the merger.

And while some other Time directors besides Dingman might have been sufficiently independent of their origins to, say, have voted for Ross, not Nicholas, on the issue of the strategic alliance, it is unimaginable that a WCI director would not have supported Ross here. Liman called the WCI directors on Sunday, February 16, to, as one put it, "warm us up," and then Ross called them. When I asked one of them how Liman had persuaded him that this was the right course, he replied, "It wasn't a call to persuade. It was, 'This is what Steve wants and you go along with it.' It was a done deal. And then Steve called, and he said, 'These have been the worst two years of my life. I can't stand it any more with this guy.' He also said the Time directors were on board. I found out later they'd only talked to one, or maybe two, by that time."

While Levin was charged with handling most of the Time side, Ross called Henry Luce III. "Steve talked about the Japanese deal," Hank Luce recalled. "He said Nick delayed the deal by objecting to aspects of it for some weeks and that jeopardized it. The rest was softer. Stuff about his work habits—the statement that he never took a phone call after 6:00 P.M. has to be false. About his not having a constituency—he stayed at his desk, reading position papers instead of buttering people up, taking them out to dinner. And the criticism that he was bogged down in trivia of corporate governance instead of focusing on strategic policies—in my view, a bum rap. I told Steve that I thought it shouldn't be voted on in the board without a general discussion, and that I didn't think phone calls were a substitute for that discussion."

Don Perkins, well known as a stickler for governance, flew in from Chicago to see Ross, who was at home and in one of his active periods between chemotherapy treatments. Beverly Sills also paid Ross a visit; according to another director, "they wanted Beverly to work over Ed Finkelstein [a former Time director and now former chairman and CEO of Macy's], because she's on his board." Those Time directors who were apparently considered the most likely to inform Nicholas of what was afoot—Matina Horner, Jason McManus, and Richard Parsons—were not called until late Wednesday, by which time Nicholas had been told.

Telling Nicholas had not been a sought-after job. Late Tuesday, Levin went to Cravath to inform Sam Butler (who, having known nothing—in contrast to Liman, his theoretical co-outside counsel—was shocked) and also to ask him to call Nicholas. Butler declined. It was apparently a call that neither Ross, nor Levin, nor Liman wanted to make. (Referring to Ross's well-known aversion to confrontation, Liman told me: "We were afraid for Steve to call, afraid he'd say, 'Okay, I know, it's hurting you and your family, I'll resign.' ") In the end, Perkins did it. "Are you sitting down, Nick?" he began.

According to Nicholas's wife, Lyn, Perkins's news plunged Nicholas into such a clinical state of shock that he was "in no condition to fight. And there was no time to recover, and prepare—the board meeting was the next day." Moreover, directors whom he called told him it was over; one director, whom Nicholas considered an ally, counselled him to protect his family by not fighting and by concentrating on his contract.

At the meeting the next day, which was conducted by Martin Payson, there was no discussion of the reasons for Nicholas's termination. Many of the directors participated by telephone, including Munro, from France. Ross, by phone, said little, other than that he expected to be back in the spring; Lipton was at his side, at home, in case anything unforeseen occurred. Aboodi was present, as he usually was at board meetings ("Since Steve has been sick, especially, some directors wonder, does Aboodi have a tape recorder?" one director commented). While Aboodi, ostensibly having no authority in the company, obviously could not be involved in this event's execution, he had been deeply involved in its strategizing, a Time Warner executive told me. (In an article in the *Los Angeles Times* the next day, however, Aboodi would be quoted as saying that this event had "caught me completely by surprise.")

Nicholas, through his lawyer, insisted that the board demand his resignation; according to the documents Lipton had prepared, Nicholas would have been tendering it voluntarily, and there might then have been some question about what was due him, according to the terms of the fifteen-year contract he had received at the time of the merger. However likely Nicholas's demise may have been from the outset, shareholders were now paying dearly for it. Ultimately, he would receive not only a lump-sum payment of $15,750,000 but a continuation of salary and benefits until 1999, which would prolong the life of his hundreds of thousands of option shares; depending upon the performance of Time Warner stock, those could be worth more than $45 million.

The only director who did not vote in favor of requesting Nicholas's resignation was Hank Luce; the vote on Levin's promotion to co-CEO, however, was unanimous. (Interestingly enough, no contractual provision was made for Levin's succession, and while one may argue that that provision did Nicholas little good, its absence, in Levin's case, was notable.)

At the close of the meeting, Perkins, reportedly seeming close to tears, is said to have declared that the next board meeting would have to be devoted to the subject of governance; that management could not continue to keep directors in the dark, as they had been doing. He reportedly added that he had been apprised of the rift between Nicholas and Ross in his conversation with Nicholas, in August, but that he was amazed to learn that his fellow outside directors knew nothing. (The next board meeting, in March, would be devoted to the unveiling of the new *Time* magazine format; no discussion of Nicholas or governance would take place.)

During the next few days, Time Warner's press machine, organized by the outside consultant Gershon Kekst, moved into high gear, successfully portraying the shift as a healthy one for the company. Wall Street agreed, with Time Warner stock moving up several points upon the news. In numerous articles, Nicholas was portrayed as an incompetent and friendless executive, charged by a host of unnamed Time Warner executives with a panoply of wrongs and failings—ranging from his having cost the company $100–$200 million by delaying the Toshiba-Itochu deal (there is no evidence of this), to his having wanted to sell the record business, to his having "grown smaller while the job grew larger," to his having been a "bean-counter" in contrast to Levin, who, like Ross, was a "visionary."

Interestingly, he was alleged both to have tried to seize control, "like Alexander Haig," when Ross was taken ill (Nicholas apparently responded to a query about Ross's health from one institutional shareholder by saying, "Jerry and I are running the company") and also not to have taken the helm decisively at that time. According to one person, Levin said that certain directors had been grumbling about Nicholas's failure to assume control. James Bere's name was floated, in this regard, by several people, but Bere could shed no light on what his complaints might have been, of course, since he had just died.

As Nicholas reportedly said over and over again to one friend on the Wednesday night that he learned of his firing, "If the directors thought I should have taken charge more, why didn't anyone tell me? I would have done it. Why didn't Jerry tell me?"

About a month after the firing, I interviewed Arthur Liman in his office at Paul, Weiss. While it was true that Liman's relationship with Steve Ross, over the past twenty years or so, was one from which both Liman and Paul, Weiss had profited regally, that relationship seemed to be defined most by the emotional attachment Liman felt to Ross; the legal role he played seemed, more, in the service of that. It was, of course, Liman who had done the most to establish the comfort level of Munro, and the Time Inc. outside directors, with Ross and WCI. On the wall of Liman's conference room there hung a framed photograph of Ross, Munro, and Nicholas. Munro wrote, "Without you, the Time-Warner merger never would have happened," and Nicholas, for his part, added, "You led us through the wilderness."

Liman seemed well satisfied with the process that had culminated in Nicholas's removal. "I think this was handled with a great deal of sensitivity and grace," he told me. He acknowledged that, in its aftermath, some directors were unhappy. (Indeed, one Time Warner adviser had told me that many were left "with a bad taste in their mouths," and fearful that now, at a time when outside directors have been assuming increasingly activist roles, the directors would be criticized as rubber-stamp and retrograde. On a more personal level, Munro was said to be wracked with guilt and also confusion, wondering aloud whether he had been "used." And John Opel, the reserved former chairman of IBM, informed the company that he did not intend to stand for reelection.)

"Directors will always feel they should have more participation," Liman declared, "but once the issue surfaces with directors, it becomes political, even Machiavellian. You're inviting lobbying, appeals for support. It's hard for me to imagine how they could have been in at an earlier stage without a sloppier ending."

Liman emphasized repeatedly that this event had been "not about Steve versus Nick, but Nick versus Jerry. . . . One of the things that was critical from the first moment was that this not be perceived as a Warner takeover—it was just the opposite! Because if Steve got hit by a truck and Nick couldn't make it [as CEO], then maybe some other candidate would come in, from the Warner side. But this way, it assured Time succession. That was important to the Time directors."

Levin was, indeed, indispensable to the execution of Nicholas, if it were to be tastefully done. Only Levin could make it seem not to be the "Warner takeover" that had been predicted from the outset. And only Levin could go so far as to suggest that what had occurred was not about the sovereignty of Ross, and not about his own betrayal and opportunism, but about the salvation of Time Inc. Just as he (along with Nicholas and Munro) had wrapped himself in the cloak of the Time Inc. culture before the Delaware courts in the summer of 1989 to defend Time Inc.'s rejection of Paramount Communication's bid, so now he donned that versatile garment again.

In the days immediately following Nicholas's firing, Levin—emotional, fervent, referring to his "messianic zeal" for Time Inc. and his desire to speak "from the heart," to give people "the unvarnished Levin"—held a series of meetings, from morning to night, with the various magazines' staffs. His message was unmistakable: with Nicholas gone, a new day was dawning in the Time-Life Building.

Levin was well aware that the journalists at Time Inc. had been badly dispirited by the merger, feeling that they were working for a diminished product, a relatively peripheral part of the whole that might well be sold; and that the layoffs had only added to the generalized depression and insecurity. Standing before these groups, Levin swore that "journalism is at the core of Time Warner," and said that "if there have been problems in the past, now is the time to correct them." He had come to the realization that such a correction (by the excision of Nicholas) was required, he said, during "a walk in the woods," over Christmas. And he was assuming this role, in many ways difficult for him, because of the company's need for "strong symbolic leadership," not "because I have a large ego; I don't."

In a not-so-oblique reference to the just-departed, Levin declared: "I don't think our orientation should be that layoffs are a way of life." He reiterated what had been said at other times since the merger, namely, that the magazines would not be sold. And he urged everyone to put aside "concern about political agendas" and to feel "trust . . . respect . . . and, finally, love—in the unconditional sense. Agape, I think it's called."

Levin's audiences were generally responsive to this almost evangelical appeal, apparently willing in the hope of redemption to overlook at least one decidedly discordant note. For if the journalists by and large believed that the merger had caused, or dramatically accelerated, the general diminishment of their station (a belief that had led many to vilify Nicholas, and now to celebrate his demise), it was ironic that the person standing before them as their self-proclaimed saviour was the same person who, on the Time side, had worked hardest to bring the merger about; was profiting richly from it; and had now maneuvered himself into a position that never would have been his had the merger not occurred.

It may be that Levin's greatest gift, even greater than his much-celebrated farsightedness, was his power of persuasion. It was not so much his verbal facility—that could seem showy and overdone—as the way his words, at times, seemed to emanate from some deep inner core of conviction. "There is this force to what Jerry says—in the sense of Luke Skywalker, 'May the force be with you,' " commented Thomas Kessenger, the president of Haverford College, where Levin was chairman of the board of trustees.

Some friends, however, suggested that the precursor to Levin's ability to persuade others was an equally prodigious capacity for self-persuasion —of the rightness and, often, moral grounding, of whatever position he happened to be taking. A long-time friend and colleague who, like many others, saw the magazines as the most separable division of Time Warner —the one least related to the entertainment whole, the one that the powerbrokers in the rest of the company tended to disparage—predicted that within a few more years Levin would again be addressing employees in the Time-Life Building, declaring with that same "messianic zeal" that it had finally become clear to him that only by their being spun off would the magazines be enabled, at long last, to achieve their manifest destiny.

Such a scenario was not altogether implausible since, in the end, the consummate beauty of the part Levin played in the firing of Nicholas was that, wrapped as he was in the cloak of Time Inc., that garb was essentially camouflage. For while Levin at those meetings with the journalists said he regarded himself as a "Time Warner person," and urged them to do the same, some who knew him well in the company wondered whether he would not more aptly be described, by this time, as "a Warner person."

He had, after all, found his closest relationship at the company with Oded Aboodi, a walking paradigm of the freewheeling WCI way of life, and he had discarded Time Inc.'s institutional mores, with its notions of corporate governance, like so many outgrown articles of clothing. When the board asked both Levin and Nicholas to reconsider their bonus increases for 1991, Nicholas agreed, though he retracted that agreement after he was fired. But Levin is said to have declared—in an expression of entitlement worthy of his most seigneurial WCI colleagues—that he was "offended," and he refused (he received, as requested, $1,750,000, in addition to his salary and deferred compensation of $1,050,000, and option grants). He had from the start been keenly solicitous of Ross, making his obeisances with perhaps even a greater eagerness than his more seasoned WCI colleagues. Indeed, he seemed like nothing so much as a supplicant asking and assaying to join the WCI family.

And his apostasy had served him well. As director Michael Dingman told a friend, "Steve just wanted Jerry in there because he wants someone who will do what he tells him to."

Were Ross to return, he and Levin would make more congenial co-CEOs than Ross and Nicholas ever could have. Each was passionate about the entertainment business and had an affinity for what he saw as the big picture (Ross, for his part, rhapsodizing about "dreams," and Levin about "the force of ideas"). They rivalled each other in their excitement about the future of cable; Ross was said to have made about 15 trips, and Levin perhaps 25, to the Time Warner Cable facility in Queens, which operated the world's first 150-channel, two-way interactive cable system. Probably the strongest trait they shared, however, was resilience: Ross had come back, repeatedly, when he had been counted out, and Levin, too, had survived repeated setbacks and failures, only to triumph ultimately over his erstwhile partner, ending a rivalry that had lasted nearly twenty years.

So, with this, the two quintessential survivors were joined. If not for Ross's illness, however, there would have been no contest; Levin had met more than his match. As one adviser to the company commented, "It is ironic that having done all this, Jerry now finds himself in the position that Nick was in—waiting for Steve to die."

There were some directors and advisers who theorized together after Nicholas's firing. that perhaps he welcomed the event (albeit subconsciously) because he had been trapped, increasingly powerless, in such a daunting endgame. Whatever the benefits of freedom, Nicholas for his part deplored the way in which it was done. "A truly independent board," he told me, "would at least have tried to establish some kind of fact base. They would not have done something like this, without even really knowing why they were doing it."

Nicholas, of course, could be faulted for not having returned from Vail for the meeting to force the directors to confront him. He faulted himself, particularly, for not having continued what he had started the August before, to bring the issue of the Toshiba-Itochu deal before the board. Then, he would have been not just opposing that deal but advocating his strategy for the company, as opposed to Ross's—something that he never did. "If I had lost, I wouldn't have liked it, one bit. But at least then it would have been about issues and substance, not ego and power."

In the aftermath, Nicholas puzzled over how he could have been so blind. At Time Inc., after all, he was known for his political acumen. But, he reasoned, when he moved from the Time-Life Building to the thirty-fourth floor at Time Warner, it was "as though I had arrived on a new planet. If you landed on Mars, would your political instincts be relevant? In the culture in which I grew up—with Shepley, Heiskell, Donovan, and Grunwald—it was inconceivable that such a thing could happen."

Levin, of course, came from that culture too, which is perhaps why Nicholas never suspected him. Nicholas claimed that Levin never appeared to be anything but his ally Once, about a year earlier, Nicholas recalled, "Jerry said, quite spontaneously, in the middle of a conversation about something else, 'You know, I have completely accepted you as CEO.' "

Levin, meanwhile, was diligently priming himself for his own hoped-for assumption of that role. In a speech in May 1992 before the Time-Life

Alumni Society, in which he remarked that giving speeches was difficult for him and that "for most individuals . . . it's an assertion of ego, which I also find difficult to do," he commented that he believed it vital that a CEO stand for articulated principles. Among his, he enumerated "management as a humanist art," the importance of ideas, and morality and integrity (which, he said, Munro had stood for, and he now would).

And, in an aside, Levin—expressing his perennial bewilderment at finding himself, somehow, in ever higher and more powerful positions —added, "I've been somewhat of a student of the way corporations are run, and I never *dreamed* I'd be an active participant."

10

There had been only rare occasions in Steve Ross's life when he'd focused all his intensity on something but been unable to bend it to his will—as, for example, in his struggle to restore Ken Rosen. Generally, when he concentrated and *fought,* he prevailed. He proceeded from an innate optimism, a belief in his powers, and a consequent conviction that what others might deem impossible would prove to be doable; indeed, it was the kind of spirit that informed the old movies of the thirties and forties, which he had grown up on, and of which he became such a devotee in later years.

It was an ideal credo for a freewheeling entrepreneur, out to build an empire from scratch, and it had served Ross well. In the space of thirty years, he had done just that. And when Paramount's bid so fundamentally changed the construct Ross had conceived, he had adjusted, immediately —and turned to the job of making it right. It was ironic, however, that the Time-Warner merger—his consummate ambition realized—at once plunged him into the very situation he had tried diligently to avoid through most of his business career.

Ross had generally guarded against becoming overleveraged because it would limit his options and lessen his control. "We have to control our destiny," he had declared, in his habitual refrain, and that maxim defined his approach to many situations in his business life. It was reflected in the importance he attached to distribution, and also to being of sufficient size in all key businesses; in the way he dealt with Herb Siegel; and in his attitude toward debt. Long before the Atari debacle, this had been his catechism. That experience—during which the banks held a gun to his head—had only deepened his instinctive antipathy for incurring a large amount of debt. And that was the only other time, prior to the Time-Warner merger, that he had been so burdened.

When Ross fought his way back from the brink of Atari and the crushing debtload of that period, however, he had not been able to follow his instincts untrammeled, because he had had Siegel reining him in. Thus, in order to purchase the whole of Warner-Amex, he had sold MTV and Nickelodeon. But for Siegel, Ross would have not sold them and would, instead, have borrowed in order to buy. For as much as he disliked debt, he disliked selling favored assets more. Eventually, as MTV and Nickelodeon grew astronomically in value, Ross felt validated; his instincts had been right. Years later, those sales seemed, still, to grate. "I never wanted to sell them," Ross told me, in late 1989. "Siegel never understood software. He owned TV stations, had franchises—that's different. Siegel's problem was, we *made* more money than he did in revenues.

"I'm not a seller," Ross stated emphatically. "We're builders."

Ross, therefore, had set out to solve the problem of Time Warner's $16 billion debt with his congenital optimism and an approach that had performed well for him in the past. He would *not* sell—Nicholas's wanting to must have been another irritating reminder of Siegel, but Nicholas, as became clear, did not have the power or the will ultimately to challenge Ross—and he would instead take the joint-venture route. He had done it with American Express, and from his standpoint it had worked like a charm; a partner (of a separate entity, not the parent company) had contributed 50 percent of the capital, but he had maintained control.

That, surely, was the paradigm that Ross had wanted to recreate—but now at a more elevated level, and renamed (because of its global context) a "strategic alliance." American Express had been something of a reach for upstart WCI in the late seventies; now there was no partner in the world too grand for Time Warner. And Ross had set about his courtships even before the deal was done.

He was in Paris for the celebration of the bicentennial of Bastille Day, July 14, 1989—the very day that Chancellor William Allen, of the Delaware Chancery Court, handed down his decision refusing to grant Paramount's requested injunction, and thus paving the way for the Time-Warner transaction (Paramount would appeal to the Delaware Supreme Court, but once Allen had decided, Ross and his allies were confident).

It may well have been the ultimate moment of celebration in Ross's life. He and Courtney were staying at the Ritz, as was their custom, with an entourage that included William vanden Heuvel and Quincy Jones. The G7 was meeting in Paris, and many heads of state were staying at the Ritz; Ross, said vanden Heuvel, "was treated like a head of state." Jones, who was co-producer of the Bicentennial parade—which included fireworks, dancers, and performances by the Florida A&M band and James Brown—would later recall Ross's "walking down the Champs-Elysées as though the whole celebration was for [his] victory."

But Ross, characteristically, was not *only* celebrating. "Steve was meeting in Paris with [Giovanni] Agnelli and also François Dalle," vanden Heuvel recalled. Giovanni Agnelli was chairman of Fiat and Dalle was the vice-president of Nestlé. "He saw that debt as the enemy, and ever since [Martin] Davis had come in in June," precipitating the assumption of debt, "Steve had been figuring out how to reduce it. His idea was to get three or four major entities who would be helpful to Time Warner, and motivate them to help by their having a major stake. He wanted to have major leaders of the industrial world as his partners.

"Steve felt, if you had Nestlé, Agnelli, and Toshiba (or someone like that) in the Far East, it would be great. He knew if the Street saw the debt under control, the price of the stock would rise. The problem, though, from [these prospective partners'] point of view, was asking them to put a major block of money into something where they didn't have any say. What he was offering them was a front-row seat in the telecommunications world."

It may be, however, that in this latest stretch of the ascent that had composed his life, Ross's reach had finally exceeded his grasp. For what began now, following his greatest triumph, was a period in which the gambits, strategies, and personal proclivities that had meshed and worked so brilliantly for Ross in the past did not seem to work any more.

His experience with the French pay-television company Canal-Plus was illustrative. Warner Bros. had been an active supplier of movies to Canal-Plus (which also owned major stakes in pay channels in a number of other European and African countries and had become the largest buyer of American film rights in Continental Europe), and now, Canal-Plus was becoming involved in large film co-production deals. Ross had known the company's venerable chairman, André Rousselet (a close confidant of President François Mitterrand, and his former chief of staff), and its CEO, Pierre Lescure, for several years. They would have made very attractive European partners.

Some of the relationship-building groundwork, moreover, had already been laid. By the late eighties, WCI had become almost an honorary

French citizen. It had been a generous contributor to a number of French cultural causes, including the Opéra Bastille. And, in the midst of all this beneficence, Ross had even succeeded in making a friend of Jack Lang, the iconoclastic Minister of Culture who, after taking office in 1981, was famous for having called for a crusade against the "cultural imperialism" of the United States—"this financial and intellectual imperialism that no longer grabs territory, or rarely, but grabs consciousness, ways of thinking, ways of living."

Commenting on the friendship that had developed between Ross and Lang, Lescure said, "Lang was not fighting the Americans, he was fighting to protect French culture, and Steve was one of the first to understand that. He knew that if you wanted to be involved in this new market, you would have to share a lot [in co-production]. There was one American distributor—whom I will not name—who said, 'Our products are the best. You have to buy them. You don't have anything to compare.' Steve would never have said that."

As Rousselet expressed it, "Steve Ross is one of those Americans whom we feel to be sincere about French cultural institutions."

Lescure found Ross's personal style appealing, as well. "When I went to his office for the first time, there was Art Deco furniture that you could sell at auction. On the wall were de Koonings. Each piece was his personal choice. He saw in my eyes that I liked this. If you are in the entertainment business, it is impossible not to have an aesthetic point of view."

He also seemed to consider Ross something of an original—a surprising character to encounter as chairman of one of the world's largest corporations. He recalled two incidents that had convinced him of Ross's anomalousness. The first occurred at the opening of the Opéra Bastille. "The G7 was meeting in Paris, [President] Bush was here, and the police, for security, asked that everyone arrive very early at the opera. I convinced my girlfriend to be on time, for the first time," recalled Lescure, who was then seeing the actress Catherine Deneuve. "We arrived, we were shown to our seats in the balcony, and we are in an empty hall. We were the *first*. She said, 'This is the last time.'

"After ten minutes, another couple came—it was Steve and Courtney. After that, the African ambassadors came. Ten meters from where we were there was a special balcony for the photographers. One of them had a zoom lens, and he saw Steve was wearing a Batman pin in his lapel. He said, 'Aha! Batman!' Steve reached into his pocket—he had his pockets full of them!—and he started handing out these pins to the photographers. Then the African ambassadors said, 'Please, could we have one?' Steve was standing on the balcony, handing out pins to everyone.

"Another time, Steve was here, with Jerry Levin and Ed Aboodi, talking to me and André and others, and he was explaining to us the picture he has of Time Warner in the year 2001—interactive cable, music, etc.—all amazing. And at the end, he turned to Rousselet (who is *so* French) and said, 'Time Warner will be present in so many ways in the daily lives of American people and people around the world—and to be present in the daily life means many things.' With that, he opens a big bag—and brings out a Bugs Bunny T-shirt!

"In France, it would be so unusual for a chairman to be so involved in the product," Lescure continued. "Usually, the chairman will be good at the financial side, a good manager—but ask him about programming and it is another planet. They may not know what kind of programming they have."

As Lescure described his and Rousselet's relationship with Ross, it all sounded very familiar: Ross had been adroit, savvy, charming—and singular enough to cause them to remark upon it. In the end, however, despite all Ross's romancing, and despite their being eager to do business with Time Warner on individual projects, they rejected his advances for the strategic alliance. Rousselet, for his part, said that the "investment required was too great," and also expressed a general, amused skepticism. "He is a great seducer, and he has a wonderful smile—even if one should not believe everything he says," he said of Ross, smiling himself.

Asked if he had anything specific in mind, Rousselet responded, "It's a general behavior, a deviousness. In France, we say, If you listen to people who flatter you, you're in trouble. But," he added, wryly, "I am naive enough to believe that I am special."

Lescure explained their lack of interest by saying, "We are not a bank. By which I mean, if we put the money in an investment, we want to be involved. And what participation would we have here in what was going on there? We would have been a passive investor—and, yes, that was what Steve Ross wanted."

The assets that Ross was going to put into this joint venture—Time Warner's cable, its movie studio, and HBO, the same configuration that he had initially drawn when he was contemplating forming a joint venture with Time Inc.—were of course powerful and attractive ones. But they were being offered on his terms. And what Ross, the world-class salesman, was really selling here was himself—the chance to come along for the ride with someone who had proven in the past that he could see into the future, and was confident he still could.

It was precisely this, however, that Lescure was not buying. "I think that ten, twenty years ago, he had a real capacity to look into the future.

When he saw cable, and it was in its infancy. But, the things he talks about today," Lescure continued, referring to the presentation Ross had made to them about Time Warner in the year 2001, "are more evident. He sees generally. But he cannot say, invest *here*. It will be for the people around him to do that."

And so it had gone, for Ross. He had scoured the world for buyers and in the end, after two years' gruelling effort, had succeeded in sharing only Toshiba and Itochu—for a disappointing $1 billion.

It had been a punishing period. Ross told those close to him that he did not understand the attacks on him in the press—for the coercive rights offering, for his $78 million payout—and apparently there was no one in his small circle who either was not similarly myopic or who dared explain to him how such things were fairly perceived. He had been enraged by remarks David Geffen made about him in *Forbes,* after Geffen had sold his record company to MCA and had then made two thirds of a billion dollars when Matsushita acquired MCA. Geffen—the only person Ross had backed to turn on him publicly—was quoted as saying, "His [Ross's] biggest get-off is when he can sit there after a deal is made and say how he took someone to the cleaners."

Geffen's statement was true as far as it went—although he omitted that the art of it, of course, was to take someone to the cleaners but do it so brilliantly that that person did not know it and went away happy. What Geffen had done, in any event, was viewed by Ross and his most ardent supporters as a kind of sacrilege, attempted patricide. The pact, however implicit, was that Ross supported you and cared for you, he would bolster you when you faltered, he would always be there, he would be the idealized father you never had; and you, in turn, simply had to do your best at the thing you loved and give him your undying fealty. Fealty meant ascribing to the legend: Ross was good, he was honest, he was fair, and he was loyal to death. Geffen had dared to make a very small rent in the veil.

The two men had had a long and complicated relationship. While Geffen, years later, would say that Ross had always taken advantage of him in the deals they struck, the prevalent view in the upper strata of WCI was that David Geffen did better in his negotiations with Ross than anyone else in the company did; that, as several said, he "had Steve's number."

Who got the best of whom, in their earlier years, may be debatable; but there is no question about who achieved it in the final deal they made, in 1985, when Ross signed a deal with Geffen that gave Geffen 100 percent of his company by 1990. Mo Ostin had refused to make that deal with Geffen, but Ross—rather than giving Geffen an advance of $5 million a year—had done so. Then, as the end of the contract period approached, MCA had outbid him for Geffen's company, paying $600 million—all of which went to Geffen. While it did not have the magnitude of the swing that took place after Ross's sale of the Uris properties to Olympia & York, this deal still stood in the history of Ross's dealmaking as one of the worst.

The sting of having been so bested was enhanced by Geffen's public criticism, which, to Ross, was a personal violation. According to some who knew both men well, Geffen's hostility was triggered by Ross's having failed to tell him about the pending Time-Warner merger. Ross had intended to tell him just before the official announcement, but then news had leaked, so it became public before Geffen was informed. "Part of David's great talent has always been that he keeps his ear to the ground, he hears the buzz, and then he swoops," one former WCI executive said. "He *has* to be in the middle of the action; his resource is news. So not to be in the middle of the Time-Warner action was such an *embarrassment.* He felt abashed with his friends."

Though it was far less critical, Geffen was also angered, at the time of the merger, by his discovery that Streisand, Eastwood, and Spielberg had received options shortly beforehand when he had not. (It was not the options per se that mattered, but the fact that Ross had given them to others and not to him.) These options, however, were only a fraction of a total of about 133,000 options (some of which had gone to employees, as well). Geffen was apparently unaware of the batches of 100,000 and 200,000 options that Streisand and Eastwood, and Spielberg, respectively, had received in 1988.

During this period, Steven Spielberg commiserated with Ross. "It made him so unhappy, the bad PR in the last couple of years," Spielberg recalled. "I had a similar experience—people don't see my movies, they see my success, they think of how much money I make. He used to say that people don't understand. They want to knock the statue off the pedestal. They want to kill Steve Ross and *be* Steve Ross."

Ross had driven himself to close the Toshiba-Itochu deal. Ever since his surgery for prostate cancer in 1985, he had undergone periodic blood tests. In the summer of 1991, there was a suspicious elevation; he had, however, undergone no further tests but had continued on his arduous schedule. In the fall he'd flown to Japan for a meeting on the Toshiba deal, then back to Long Island for Spielberg's wedding, then immediately, to Paris. Daly, who was in Paris with him, would recall that Ross was occupying the suite above his room and he heard him pacing all night long.

"He was getting faxes all night from Aboodi, who was in Japan," Daly said. "He had a fever on that trip, he was drenched with sweat. I said, 'Steve, you are going to kill yourself!' But, you know, when he was working a deal, you could not have a conversation with Steve. He'd drag you into a meeting and get out his yellow pads—everything in longhand—and when the meeting was over, you felt like he'd siphoned everything from you. There was nothing left."

In late October 1991, with the Toshiba deal finally in place—but that only one piece of the puzzle—Ross was forced to take to his bed, suffering severe back pain. And when he learned, at the end of the month, that his tumor was back and that there was nothing much to be done, he is said to have declared, in effect, "What a time for this to happen . . ."

As chairman and co-CEO of a public company, Ross, of course, had a responsibility to disclose the gravity of his condition. But he dealt with the issue of his mortality as he had with other sticky problems in the course of his business life; he preserved his deniability. His doctors at Memorial Sloan-Kettering decided on a regimen of radiation and chemotherapy, but even if it were successful, the therapy was expected to grant him only six months, perhaps a year. Family members were given this prognosis, but Ross, who must have grasped his situation, is said never to have asked the direct question of his doctors at Sloan-Kettering.

In any event, on November 26 he put out a two-sentence press release, which said that he was beginning therapy for prostatic cancer. "My physicians are optimistic and I am maintaining my normal work schedule," Ross said.

One family member commented later on the consistently positive message that continued to be put forth over the coming months. It wasn't true—but, after all, he wasn't the President of the United States." Such relativism, however, only serves to obscure the issue, which was Ross's accountability. He had long behaved not as an employee of a company owned by public shareholders to whom he was accountable but, rather, as though that company were his private fiefdom; and he continued to do so in this instance. There was some concern at Time Warner about incurring SEC liability under full-disclosure regulations, particularly as the months wore on and suspicions about his deterioration grew. Nicholas and Levin, among others, knew that Ross's cancer was a recurrence; that, given that fact and his age, it was probably hopeless; and that this was said to be his doctors' view. Although some say that Liman knew the prognosis was poor, he professed in a letter to this author to have been given encouraging reports directly by Ross's doctor. In any event, Liman persisted in giving upbeat reports on Ross's progress.

Furthermore, while illusory reports of Ross's prognosis were circulating, something no less critical than the question of who would lead the company into the future was being decided. For, prior to the directors' voting to fire Nicholas, Ross had explicitly assured them that he expected to be back in the spring; so that they were led to believe (if indeed the directors believed Ross) that they were choosing, in effect, not between Nicholas and Levin, but between Nicholas and Ross. Had they known the truth about Ross's prognosis, it is altogether possible that they would, still, have chosen Levin; but certainly the choice would have been harder, and more debated. In any event, they ought not to have made so momentous a decision on a false assumption.

As Ross underwent intensive chemotherapy, his family gathered around him. There had been years of relative disconnectedness between him and his grown children, Mark and Toni, both of whom had suffered from his sporadic bursts of attention as they were growing up. "I had a Warner brother," said Mark Ross. Speaking of his father, he added, "There was no balance in his life. There were times when it was hard to distinguish between family members and associates."

Toni Ross said, "My father was very intense. When he was present, he was very present. But then he was absent—I felt there was a tremendous absence.

"We *were* close," she continued, "but I didn't realize it for a long time. Growing up, it was very hard. I would think, Why do I have to share my father with all these people? There were all these people who felt like he was *their* father—but he was *my* father I didn't understand why there had to be all these other people; and for a long time, I felt like there was less, even, for us than for others." Before her father became ill, however, she had finally achieved a sense of resolution; she accepted that he was who he was, and realized that she "adored" him.

Shortly before his cancer returned, Ross, too, had begun to say he wanted to spend more time with his family. In June 1991, he had gone on a two-week trip with Mark—just the two of them, the first time they had gone away alone since Mark was nine or ten—and he had let Mark plan it all. (As Toni pointed out, for her father, first, to have taken more than a day, and, second, to have let someone else plan the itinerary, was "groundbreaking.")

They had travelled through the Bordeaux region, visiting châteaux and buying their favorite wines (this had become a hobby of Ross's—Jack Lang said it was an interest they shared, and that Ross, in fact, had called him during this trip, extolling the splendors of these French wines). And they had wound up in Paris, where Ross introduced his son to Lang, and they met Mark's wife, who was pregnant. The usual Ross scene ensued. "He brought us to the toy store he loved, to the children's clothes store he loved. He took me to his Paris tailor. And he bought me Charvet ties

—you know, the ones with the stripe he always wore—two, in every color," said Mark Ross.

Once Ross became ill, both children were with him much of the time. Neither had had any relationship with Courtney Ross for a number of years, and this did not change with Ross's illness. Courtney had departed in September 1991 for a trip around the world, taking their daughter Nicole, then eight years old, and an entourage that comprised a school that Courtney had started.

Ross was putting the best face on this trip when I interviewed him in the fall of 1991; he volunteered, rather too hurriedly, that it was a great opportunity for Nicole, and that he would be travelling to meet them at various junctures. (He did, in fact, meet them in Tokyo in late September, where, according to an item in *Newsday,* they checked into the posh Hotel Seiyo Ginza with over two hundred pieces of luggage.) Friends of Ross insisted, however, that Courtney's trip was a de facto separation, although Courtney (through her lawyer) and Liman later vehemently denied it.

Courtney Ross and her entourage were in Hong Kong when, in November of 1991, she learned of Ross's diagnosis, and she returned immediately. From that time on, she took charge of Ross's life. She coordinated his medical care—pressing his doctors to do more, refusing to give up, seeking advice from other parts of the world, bringing in doctors from China. She, alone, with Carmen Ferragano, who remained always at his side, controlled access to him. And she continued to maintain, publicly, that he was improving.

She may well have done this because she knew it was what Ross wanted, and also because she believed that in fostering a widespread illusion she was also preserving some degree of hope for him. However, it was true, too, that in so doing, she was preserving Ross's power within the company as long as possible. And she had not previously seemed disinterested in that power, or averse to capitalizing on it for her own ends on occasion.

The person that some of Ross's long-time associates recalled from her days at Jungle Habitat—someone who treated others condescendingly, and used Ross's intercession to accomplish what she wanted—had changed over the years only in degree. Acquaintances said that after she married Ross, Courtney seemed intent on proving herself in some creative venue—though, some thought, without being willing to start at what was the relatively low level of her experience and work her way up. She toyed with the idea of becoming an interior designer—she decorated Spielberg's and Ross's homes, and Ross's office—but did not pursue it. She had produced the film on Willem de Kooning built around a series of interviews that she conducted, mainly with the artist and his wife Elaine (Courtney had asked Dustin Hoffman to narrate it, and he had done so). And, by the late eighties, she had decided that she wanted to produce movies.

She apparently learned that Hoffman was thinking of making a movie of a particular novel. According to Hoffman, Steve Ross contacted him, suggesting that Courtney be the executive producer of that movie, and in the course of their conversations, negotiated a three-year, non-exclusive deal between Hoffman and Warner Bros. As it turned out, Hoffman did not make a movie of the book; nor did any of his other projects come to fruition in the three-year period. He thought that Daly and Semel were unhappy at Ross's having interfered and made this deal, he added, inasmuch as it had been expensive for the studio and, despite his best efforts, had not been productive. Hoffman also believed that Ross had been intent on the deal because he wanted Courtney to become the producer.

Courtney Ross did produce *Listen Up,* a documentary about Quincy Jones, which opened in the summer of 1990. It was, of course, inappropriate that the chairman's wife should be producing a film, and one, moreover, that could probably have been predicted from the outset to achieve little commercial success. Bob Daly is said to have attempted to justify the situation by reasoning that its subject, Jones, was a member of the Warner family and therefore, if it were going to be made, it should be made there.

While others at the company were sensitive to the conflict of interest, and to the importance of not according this film special treatment, Courtney Ross did not seem to share their concern. According to many close to the company, she was uninhibitedly herself—perfectionist, demanding, high-handed, detail-obsessed—her behavior not unlike that of the stars whom, with Ross, she cultivated. She was reportedly irate at what she deemed the studio's failure to promote the film properly, and some employees who incurred her displeasure are said to have felt that their jobs were threatened.

Under her direction, the film became "the centerpiece of the industry of *Listen Up,*" as one Warner Bros. executive said; there was a book, a CD, a tape, and merchandise, such as cups and T-shirts. A charitable foundation ("Listen Up" Foundation) was started. Several premieres were held. In the end, the studio was estimated by one executive at the company to have spent as much as $15 million on the film.

In the first six months or so of Ross's illness, when Ross, Courtney, Liman, and others continued to predict his imminent return to work (first it was February or March; then May; then June), Courtney was attempting to consolidate some power of her own at the company. She wanted to become Time Warner's representative in China—an agent of sorts, receiving a commission on all Time Warner products sold in that country—and had been working on this project for some time with the knowledge of Time Warner management.

She had discussed a version of this idea with Nick Nicholas before he was fired; then, she continued with Levin. Courtney Ross, through her lawyer, would later say that she had worked on this China project for many months and was "explicitly promised a contract providing fair compensation for her efforts in the company's behalf" by both Nicholas and Levin. However, Nicholas would later say that he had not promised her a contract. Levin, of course, is famously oblique; and if Courtney Ross misinterpreted his responses, she would hardly be the first to have done so.

In any event, Levin is said by a company colleague to have expressed irritation at the very notion that Courtney, the wife of the chairman who had just received such a huge payout, should be putting forth this idea. He is said to have further expressed his indignation at the fact that when a meeting was held to discuss Courtney's proposed project (something that, he told his colleague, he had done as a courtesy), she brought to represent her a lawyer, Bertram Fields. Courtney claims that Levin also brought his general counsel, Peter Haje, to the meeting. The contract, in any event, never materialized. One long-time adviser to the company remarked, "What Courtney was proposing was unthinkable, even for *this* board."

One proposal of hers that did succeed was her desire that she, and also her lawyer, Fields, be appointed co-executors of Ross's will. The existing co-executors were Arthur Liman and Ed Aboodi; now, with these additions, there were four. Other changes were made in the will during this period, too, which were said to benefit Ross's three children. According to one person, a "charitable trust" that had been included in the will was eliminated; it was said that Ross had concluded he had given away enough in his lifetime.

In early June 1992, Ross was promising that he would be back to work in time for the annual meeting, which was to be held in Los Angeles in July. It must have been something he wanted so much that he, and perhaps those around him, thought he could achieve it by sheer force of will. His last annual meeting, presided over by him and Nicholas jointly the previous September, had surely been the worst of his career—fired employees had picketed at the entrance, and he had tried to defend his compensation to a partly hostile audience. Even putting those issues aside, Ross—who considered these meetings his metier—had found it lacking. "I went into hibernation for ten days, preparing," Ross had told me ruefully, shortly after the meeting. "Where were the good questions? Where were the by-law questions?" Now, it must have been difficult to accept that that sorry event—after a career of masterfully orchestrated, superb performances—should have been his finale.

But it was. Later in June, Ross announced that he was undergoing renewed chemotherapy and taking a temporary leave of absence so as to concentrate fully on his recovery (before this, he had been in frequent touch with his associates by telephone). The meeting, which thus became Jerry Levin's debut, was a raucous affair, at which police officers demonstrated and attacked Levin, personally, for his defense of Ice-T's song "Cop Killer," on a Sire/Warner Bros. album.

Levin had written a *Wall Street Journal* Op-Ed article defending Time Warner's support of the song on First Amendment grounds—an argument that was specious, since judgments about what to publish, record, or film are made constantly at Time Warner and other companies, and a negative decision cannot be equated with censorship. Ross was said to have been unhappy with Levin's handling of the issue, and to have thought that it was wrong to put the company on the line by raising it to such a broad issue of principle, as his article did; that Levin should rather have found a way to push the issue down to the divisional level. In any case, by early 1993 the company had dropped its association with Ice-T.

Courtney Ross, escorted by Steven Spielberg, came to the July meeting in Los Angeles in Ross's stead. She conveyed his thanks to all of Time Warner's extended family—colleagues, artists, and shareholders—for the "fantastic" success of the company, and she spoke of his eagerness to return. She was given a warm reception, but it was more for the ailing Ross—to whom so many on the Warner side, at least, were as devoted as though he were family.

It was difficult to find any constituency for Courtney Ross among the legions of Steve Ross's fans and friends. It seemed that what so many had earlier experienced as the Ross magic had begun to falter not only in his professional life (as with Lescure and Rousselet, and all the others who had spurned his advances for a "strategic alliance") but also, more fundamentally, in Ross himself. To the extent that many Ross loyalists felt that Ross had changed in the last decade—growing more venal, celebrity-oriented, imperial, isolated, and outrageous in his excesses—they tended, rightly or not, to affix a good deal of the blame on Courtney, who had been with him through those years.

In truth, the two were so alike in their love of luxury that it is difficult to distinguish the influence of one on the other; and it is probably true, too, that the cupidity of each only potentiated that of the other. It would be difficult to assert, for example, that buying a castle, Olmeta, in Todi, Italy—actually an entire peasant village, plus an additional 240 surrounding acres—was something that Courtney wanted but Ross did not; he, too, had grown fond of Italy, and he told me that he wanted Nicole to become bilingual. Courtney Ross, for her part, explained the allure of this particular, rustic locale to a *Wall Street Journal* reporter by saying, "What my husband and I found so charming about it is that, as [our architect] put it, it's so poor." (She later explained, through her lawyer, that what her architect and she meant to say was that its charm lay not in its being poor but in its being "rustic"—"not a posh villa but a rough-hewn, country place.")

Certain flourishes, however, did seem to carry Courtney's stamp. After Spielberg, Geffen, Quincy Jones, and Michael Jackson had spent a weekend in East Hampton with the Rosses in 1985, Courtney sent each guest a memento: a five-volume set of hand-painted books, each an original edition, with photos of the weekend and an accompanying text, written in an elegant calligraphy as a fairytale, featuring a duke, a prince, and a king. The Rosses' Christmas card, each year, was, of course, oversized; its cover a drawing by Nicole, and inside, a message written by Nicole about her family's contributions to poor families in East Hampton. Courtney was fond of animals; in addition to the King Charles spaniels, there was a miniature pony, a goat, and a burro, among others.

Then there was the school that Courtney had started a couple of years ago. It was said to consist of a handful of little girls Nicole's age, and its premise seemed to be that the world was their classroom. Thus, if they were studying archeology, they would go to Egypt on a dig; if they were studying Chinese culture, they would go to China. In early 1993, they went to Paris to see the Egyptian artifacts on view at the Louvre in preparation for a planned trip to Egypt. On that trip to Paris, according to several people, they chartered a private jet and stayed at the Ritz.

The cock-eyed nature of such phenomena makes their etiology difficult to fathom. Was it the enactment of a childhood fantasy, growing up in Bryan, Texas, of how one would live if one were a princess—or if one became what Gloria Sale wanted her daughter to be? While there was a self-conscious effort to remember, in the midst of all this opulence, that the world is a variegated place (the reference to the poor in the Christmas card, the inclusion of at least one black child in the school), still the effect was to create a realm so insular, so privileged, and so rarefied as to be, perhaps, unique. *That* would have pleased Ross. But it is difficult to believe that someone as astute as he did not realize that something, here, had gone terrible awry.

However bent Ross had been on creating a life imbued with elements of fantasy, and however sovereign his style had become, still he had not evinced an hauteur, not treated people in menial positions as though they were less than he. In this sense, at least, he never became grandiose; he allowed people their dignity; he remembered who he was. And whatever he did was so animated with warmth and originality that people who knew him well tended either to admire his excesses or to forgive them —but not to recoil from them.

Courtney Ross, however, had treated people in a high-handed way when she had not been in any real position to do so; once she obtained the position, that trait apparently became amplified. But in the past, Steve Ross had always been there to smooth over hurt feelings and generally leaven the atmosphere. Courtney was apparently capable of being quite generous with long-time staff members, who she felt were devoted to her; but even one of these acknowledged that it took a long time to get used to Courtney Ross's perfectionist ways, that those who had relatively brief exposure to her often found the experience a misery, and that while Courtney was difficult at best, Ross was someone who was unfailingly kind to those who worked for him, and was loved by some of them.

Desmond Atholl, who worked for many years as a majordomo before he turned to writing books, was hired by the Rosses several years ago to cater a party for Nicole Ross's birthday. "There was a dinner party the night before the big party for Nicole, and Steve Ross was very pleased with it, and in a very happy mood—he said, 'I know this is going to be a wonderful weekend. You and your staff go in the kitchen and get out the Dom Perignon. I want all of you to have a lovely time!' " Atholl recalled.

"The next day, I heard Courtney saying to the cook, 'How *dare* they drink our champagne! And tell me, did they eat our caviar, too?' We had been *invited* to do so. Steve Ross had been so charming. He treated us like human beings. He treated everyone with respect." By contrast, he felt that Courtney wanted people to kowtow to her. "When I met her, I chatted with her like a regular human being." Atholl suspected that Courtney did not like that, that she wanted her staff to grovel.

On the 172-foot yacht *Papa's Place*, which the Rosses had chartered for the summer of 1992, Ross was so ill that his countervailing influence was largely lost, and Courtney was more in command. (When Ross chartered a yacht, at least part of the expense was borne by Time Warner, one former Ross associate said; if stars, or studio or record executives, visited, some of the cost was said to be charged to the appropriate division's overhead.) And, with Courtney setting the tone, the boat soon became a troubled, unhappy place for its crew. A person on board who had ample exposure to Courtney commented, "To say that she was imperious, high-handed, and arrogant would be a gentle, kind way to describe her."

Another crew member explained that "the crew's first indication of what a nightmare this charter was going to be came before it even began, when [the Rosses' majordomo] was on the phone eight times in the space of a couple hours—insisting that they had to know the measurements for the beds, because the Rosses *had* to have new sheets. (We'd never heard of that before—this yacht had luxury sheets, I can assure you.) The captain wasn't there so we didn't have the key to go down and measure the beds. But [the majordomo] could not accept that. He kept calling. It seemed like his job was to accomplish the impossible."

Next, Courtney ordered certain changes in the ship's interior—starting with removing paintings from the walls, including those that were permanently affixed. (Courtney Ross would later say, through her lawyer, that she had done this because Steve Ross wanted to be surrounded in this, his temporary home, by the paintings he loved.) After complying with some of her demands, the captain finally balked—which enraged Courtney. Yet another crew member commented, "People don't generally expect to redecorate a ship when they don't own it."

The Rosses brought their own sizable house staff, for which there was insufficient accommodation, on board—something that was unusual, too, and that led to further tensions. Their imperious majordomo—someone who, according to one person, "had a flair for making the staff members' lives miserable"—soon won the enmity of the ship's crew as well. The crew was told not to address Courtney Ross; any questions for her were to be relayed to the majordomo (a practice, Courtney explained through her lawyer, which was instigated by the majordomo).

Courtney Ross seemed to crew members someone who was accustomed to having her every whim satisfied, willy-nilly—with seemingly little regard, they thought, for those who were expected to do so. They noted that her manicurist, having been summoned, would arrive on the boat and then be kept waiting, often for many hours. When Courtney, whose parents owned the Coca-Cola bottling franchise, discovered that there was Pepsi on the boat, she is said by one crew member to have ordered that all the Pepsi be removed from the ship. A crew member said that Courtney Ross requested that when her daughter, Nicole, was served, only Baccarat crystal be used—a practice, however, that could not be accommodated because there was no Baccarat on the ship. (Courtney Ross, again through her lawyer, denied that Nicole drank out of Baccarat.)

The crew were further alienated when they received their tips after the first month, which were much less than they were accustomed to. Some crew members were convinced that the meagerness of the tips reflected Courtney's anger at their being insufficiently servile. "We were crew members on a ship, we weren't servants. Courtney couldn't get us to cross that line—and she really wanted to," one commented. By August, the crew had become so demoralized that several of them quit. But even one who quit because of finding the Ross contingent insupportable emphasized how striking it was that Ross, despite being so seriously ill—and in contrast to those around him, particularly his wife—was generally kind and considerate.

Many from Ross's past, fearing by this summer that he was dying, wanted to see him—among them, Roger Smith, Bob Tisch, Rafael de la Sierra, Amanda Burden. Carmen Ferragano would thank them, and tell them that Ross would want to see them, too, but not just then; that he was doing better; and, in many instances, she would suggest that they write him a note instead. Notes came by the hundreds. Ross's first wife, Carol, was one of the few from his more distant past who was allowed to see him, even when he was in the hospital, very ill; and one day in midsummer, she, her husband, Arthur Maslow, and much of the Rosenthal clan came to spend a day on *Papa's Place*. And they departed with duffel bags bulging with Warner memorabilia: a Ross trademark (for years, Ross had delighted in handing out Warner Bros. merchandise—sweatshirts, caps, T-shirts—at annual meetings and, it seemed, every other opportunity. Whenever his ship docked, he would go ashore laden with goods— as one friend commented, "Every waiter in St. Tropez was wearing his stuff").

Ed Rosenthal had died in May 1991, at the age of eighty-seven. By way of tribute, all his children and grandchildren spoke at his funeral—even those who shied terribly from such public performances. After the service, when Doris Rosenthal was receiving people at home, Ross had knelt down next to her chair, handed her a single rose, and, with tears in his eyes, told her, "I loved him so much."

That had surprised her; for after Ross's divorce from Carol, he had grown increasingly distant from the Rosenthals. He would send flowers on special occasions, but with a note written by one of his secretaries. Doris would tell her family that if he didn't have time to write the note himself, he shouldn't send the flowers. The Rosenthals remained very close to Solomon Weiss, and they held it against Ross that, after Weiss's conviction, Ross would never see him, except in a large gathering. And when Ed Rosenthal had become ill with leukemia, it was mainly Carmen Ferragano, not Ross, who called to see how he was doing. In the end,

Doris and Ed Rosenthal felt that Ross over the years did not behave appropriately toward the man who had given him his big chance—without which, arguably, Ross might simply have become the best salesman in the garment district. According to one member of the Rosenthal family, Edward Rosenthal believed that Ross was a "user."

That was not to suggest that there was not the usual example of spontaneous personal generosity on Ross's part, which caught people offguard and tended to soften, or at least faintly complicate, an otherwise harsh judgment. The year before Ross had become ill, the son of Peter Rosenthal (Ross's former brother-in-law), a college freshman who had not seen Ross since he was a small child, wanted to meet the now-legendary figure who had been his uncle. It was during the time when Ross was under siege, vilified in the press for his payout, struggling to achieve a strategic alliance.

Nonetheless, Ross had agreed, and the youth had come to his office, expecting a fifteen-minute audience. To his amazement, Ross spent a couple of hours with him. And Ross had of course not talked about himself but wanted to know what the young Rosenthal thought about so many things; he had been interested in *him*. Rosenthal came away telling his family that it was an afternoon he would never forget.

When Ross was very ill, in the hospital, the only one of all the stars who had formed his social circle over the last decade whom he saw was Steven Spielberg. In fact, Spielberg was the only non-family person, other than Ferragano, who was with Ross during these periods. To a degree, Spielberg had taken over the role of Jay Emmett as best friend; however, because of the difference in age, Ross's relationship to Spielberg was more that of a father to a son. Spielberg would often characterize their relationship that way—which may have incited certain proprietary emotions in Ross's children, and also raised the question of where, in this picture, Spielberg's own father fit.

When I asked Spielberg whether his father was still alive, he said, "Yes. And I was very conflicted. Because Steve was very much what I wish my father was." (Spielberg's father is an electrical engineer who once was quoted in a *Wall Street Journal* article saying, of his son's movies, "I didn't care for *Indiana Jones* and I hated *1941*. When I told him, he said, 'Don't talk to me, Dad.' ")

"Steve was very parental," Spielberg added. "He probably parented us more than he did his own kids."

What Spielberg afforded Ross, one can only guess; certainly it must have been not only the value Ross had garnered from the relationship in his business life but emotional sustenance as well. And, if one posits Ross's attachments to Steven Spielberg and Amanda Burden as among the more powerful ones he formed in his life, they have a similarly ideational quality: Ross would have seen Burden as the luminous embodiment of class (enhanced by the connection to Paley); Spielberg, as the embodiment of creative talent, in an area Ross understood and loved.

Spielberg, like many others before him, basked in the glow of Ross's attention, thrived in it, came to depend on it and to find life more vivid in his presence. All that set Spielberg apart from his predecessors was that he got more of Ross's attention, over a longer period, than most did. In the time before Ross became ill, Spielberg recalled, "we spent months sitting in his backyard under the sun. I'd be reading scripts, he'd be on the phone, talking to Ed Aboodi, or scribbling on a yellow pad. Sometimes, I'd be talking to him about where to go to dinner, and I could see he'd be lost. He'd be structuring something, running numbers in his head, he'd drift. He'd try to pay attention—but instead of looking into my eyes, he'd be looking at my left ear. I'd know he was someplace else.

"But whenever I would be talking about things important to me, of a personal nature, he'd focus. He'd put the pad down, hold his hand up to the houseman, Jerry, to signal no phone calls, and he'd look at me intensely. He'd be *into* what I was telling him about my personal problems. The phone messages would pile up. We would talk for hours. I completely opened my life to him. I never had, to anyone, before—not to my parents, not to my siblings, not to my girlfriend. And not to a psychiatrist —I didn't have one."

Ross, however, had not confided similarly in Spielberg. "He never told me his feelings about his kids, about Courtney. He got more from giving than getting. The way actors give every last drop to the public, Steve in that sense wrung himself dry . . . He was a giver."

"It was the first time I really had someone in my life who cared about me, as opposed to what I could do for them," Spielberg added. And on this point—that Ross had had no agenda, in their friendship—Spielberg was adamant. He acknowledged that there were many things Ross did which had "a kickback effect"; but, he insisted, "I think he really looked upon me as a friend—without an agenda. That was rare in his life, so I think it represented a little bit of a vacation."

Like Ross, he had always been "a workaholic," Spielberg continued. Ross played as hard as he worked, of course; that was what had initially drawn Spielberg and so many others to him—a style that bespoke a talent, or, more, an insatiable appetite for life. But that was what Ross was —appetitive, at work or play, and never fulfilled. Ross, in any event, had pushed Spielberg to pause and take satisfaction from a completed work, to enjoy more of life's day-to-day pleasures, to open himself to friendship.

to become a father. "Steve didn't practice what he preached," Spielberg acknowledged. "He never looked back, or even looked into himself. But he would alway encourage me to take more pleasure, and *not* to style my life that way."

Spielberg said he had tried hard to find ways that he could "give back" to Ross. It was not easy. He had rented a house in the Virgin Islands and tried to entertain him, Ross-style, but Ross had taken over the daily itinerary—deep-sea diving here, dinner there ("It gave him happiness to be in control of the pleasure cruise"). One thing that Spielberg had been able to do for him was to speak at the WCI annual meeting in 1987, where Ross had finally claimed victory in his struggle with Herb Siegel. And once Ross was ill, Spielberg said, he had been "part of his rehabilitation.

"I said, 'You've got one thing on your side. You've got luck'—he was the luckiest man I've ever known. 'You've got to think of your own body as a deal. You can't realize your dreams until your health is better. You have to work as hard on yourself as on Time Warner, or on the TWE deal with Toshiba—and then you'll get well. You owe this to Courtney and Nicole and Toni and Mark and to me.'" They had spent a lot of time, Spielberg continued, talking about what they would do when Ross got better. They would buy a yacht together (Ross's solution for the insubordinate crew—and they did in fact make plans to purchase one for $11 million), and Ross would spend more time with his children.

During this period of his illness, Ross had "some crashingly low moments," Spielberg added; but the task he set himself was to get Ross to smile. "I got him to smile almost every time I saw him—and I'm not a funny guy. One time he had just come out of a chemo session, he was not feeling well at all, sitting all bundled up on the deck. I was fishing—and it reminded Steve of when I had been fishing a year earlier. The captain had been standing behind me. I cast—and hooked his leg! The hook went right into his thigh. Steve was *apoplectic* with laughter. He laughed for an hour and a half. So, now, as I was starting to cast, I heard this laughter—Steve was pointing at me, and at the hook—and gesturing to people to back off. I thought, Thank God I hooked the captain a year ago!"

Spielberg was happy to be the source of Ross's amusement, through his awkwardness or his credulity. "He loved to play practical jokes on me. I fell for it every time. He used to say, 'How could someone so successful be so gullible?' Steve *never* fell for it—you couldn't put anything over on him."

Ross continued, during his illness, to be the irrepressible prankster he'd been all his life. Spielberg recalled visiting him in the hospital in

Southampton, where Ross was receiving a transfusion. "I was trying to get him to smile. I told him I'd read that three people had died from eating Louisiana oysters and I had had oysters for lunch—how did I know whether they were Long Island or Louisiana oysters? He shrugged, as if to say, you never know. The doctor came in to examine him, and Courtney and I went out. All of a sudden, the doctor came rushing out. I said, 'What's the matter?' He said, 'We've got sixty people in the hospital who ate oysters earlier today—a whole floor of critically ill people.' I thought, That's it! And then I heard Steve laughing . . ."

With Ross, the set-ups never stopped. They had always run the gamut from the wholly benign to the most Machiavellian: some, he had enacted for the sheer fun of it; some, to make himself more interesting or accomplished in others' eyes; some, in deadly earnest, to achieve a business goal. And sometimes, in all this tireless orchestrating, there was an overlap.

The Cleveland Browns gambit had apparently started as an outright joke, then perhaps become a bit of a prank (Ross's saying it in front of the credulous, while rolling his eyes at a knowing friend), and then it was something he fully adopted. His daughter Toni said, "I grew up believing that my father played tight end for the Cleveland Browns, that he broke his arm playing and he had to give it up." He had told her that there had been some small articles about him, but he'd destroyed them, because he'd loved it so and then he couldn't play any more. When she learned, much later, that it wasn't true, she said, she had not discussed it with him. "He would have been embarrassed." She added that she thought "people made too much of that—as though it meant that everything was a lie."

It was with Burden that Ross had carried his self-embellishing to its most fanciful extremes, with his suggestion that he had not only played for the Cleveland Browns but was also, secretly, a hit songwriter and, further, connected to the government in some mysterious way. But later, too, as he increasingly kept company with people whose talent he admired, he apparently felt the need, on occasion, for a touch of gloss.

In the summer of 1989, when Dustin Hoffman was performing *The Merchant of Venice* in London, Ross had flown over to see the play and chartered the *Klementine,* his favorite yacht (for which *Papa's Place* would be just a substitute). Hoffman and his family joined Ross on board. He and Ross were sitting on deck on a Sunday morning, Hoffman recalled, and he was laboring over the *Sunday Times* crossword puzzle. Suddenly, Ross—with a small, giveaway grin—said, in his kidding way, "What word are you having trouble with?"

Hoffman passed it over to him—thinking, however, that Ross, while a numbers wizard, was no wordsmith, and that his interest was surprising. In ten or fifteen minutes, Ross had completed most, if not all, of the puzzle. Hoffman was agape—and, years later, was still bewildered. How Ross performed this feat remains a mystery; but that he could not have done it without machination seems almost certain. He is said to have been such a poor speller that he was frustrated even by commonplace crossword puzzles—let alone the *Sunday Times*.

Hoffman had received the full measure of the Ross treatment. "He called and said, 'Listen, I've chartered this boat, Courtney and I can't use it for two weeks, it's in the Mediterranean, the captain will take you wherever you want to go—do you think you could use it?' It was a 160-foot yacht, with ten in crew. We invited Barry Levinson. It was the best vacation we ever had," Hoffman added.

On another occasion, they were walking down a street in Paris, when two very expensive pieces of sculpture in a shop window—a Roman bust and a woman's torso—caught Hoffman's eye. After some debate, he and his wife decided to buy the torso. Ross said that Courtney would make sure it was authentic. Some time later, Ross called to say that it was, indeed, authentic—but would Hoffman do him a favor? Courtney loved it, and he wanted to surprise her with it. Hoffman assented. Then, Ross sent him the Roman bust as a gift.

Once, when Hoffman called Ross to ask his help in raising money for a young girl who needed a bone-marrow transplant, Ross had contributed $1 million (Hoffman did not know if it was from the company or from Ross personally), and had also hosted a meeting, at his office, to which he invited potential contributors. "One pledged $25,000, another $50,000 —these were multimillionaires!—and then, with some of them, the money never came. Only when you try to raise money from the rich do you realize how difficult it is," Hoffman said. "*Nobody* gave like Steve Ross."

When Ross became ill, Hoffman called a few times and left messages, but the two did not speak. Then, in September 1992, he got a message from Carmen Ferragano that Ross wanted $150,000 for Bill Clinton's campaign. Ross also sent a one-minute videotaped excerpt of Dan Quayle, at the Republican National Convention, raising his arm in what looked something like a Nazi salute. Ross had not been an early Clinton supporter, but by the summer he had become an aggressive fund-raiser and contributor.

Hoffman, however, was in a dilemma. He and his wife had been discussing how "obscene" they thought it was that it cost a couple hundred million dollars to run for President, and they did not want to contribute so substantially to a process that they thought was wrong. Finally, they had decided that Hoffman would call and tell Ross that he would give to whatever charity Ross named, but not this. Hoffman, however, procrastinated. Then, in late September, Ross called. His voice sounding hoarse and raspy, he said, "I think of you as a friend and I'm just hurt that you didn't call." Hoffman explained what he had been wrestling with, and Ross said, "Yes, but did you get my tape? He looks like a Nazi, we can't let those guys in again." Hoffman continued to try to explain; and Ross broke in, Hoffman recalled, saying, "Forget it. I would never want you to do anything against your principles. I just want us to be friends."

It was a painful, disjunctive episode, that probably bespoke, among other things, the limits of their friendship. Much as Ross had tried to draw Hoffman into his inner circle of stars, Hoffman did not become smitten in the way that others did, and did not feel that Ross and he were close. There had been one or two occasions on which Hoffman thought that Ross had let down his guard; but mainly Ross had been, for all his charm, inaccessible. Hoffman was quick to point out, though, that Ross did have qualities that he liked. "I never saw him hurt anybody. I never saw him mean. I never saw him unkind. If I were playing him"—Hoffman paused, and then continued—"this was a man who never *sat* in a chair, but the chair was like the starter's blocks for a runner—'Can I get you anything, let me get you . . .'

"And I think it was genuine. If he had not become so successful, this monolith, I can see him with the guys (he was a man's man, I guess they call it) in a working-class bar, and he's saying, 'I'll get it, I'll get it! Charlie, what do you want, I'm getting it!'

"He could have been a maître d'," Hoffman continued. "He'd be kind to the help, the one who always had his eye on the tables to make sure everything was just right, who if something broke would be there, cleaning it up himself . . .

"If he was anything, he was that. There was a magnet in him, that way. He was anticipatory." Hoffman paused, then went on, "The critics would say that it was all for a purpose—and it may be that it came to be used that way. But I think that he started out like that. I don't see him being so different if he had not become successful. He would still have been that way—and he would still have been ill at ease in life." Referring to the tumult with which Ross surrounded himself, he added, "I never saw him in repose."

On September 19, Ross turned sixty-five. Finding a great gift for Ross was no mean challenge; he was an avid and tireless consumer, and there was little he spared himself. Spielberg—who, of course, had received wonderful presents from Ross, and who had struggled through many a Christmas and Ross birthday—felt he succeeded this time. He bought Ross a turn-of-the-century Victrola, and Ross loved it. "I was finally able to give him something that he was *effusive* about," Spielberg recalled. He also made a small film for Ross, based on Ross's all-time favorite, *It's a Wonderful Life*

Just as George Bailey, so overcome with despair that he is about to throw himself off a bridge, is through the devices of an angel shown what the world would have been like if he had not lived, so Spielberg set out to show the world as it would have been had Ross not lived. "I dreamt this up when we were in Hawaii, filming *Jurassic Park,*" Spielberg said. "We had Bob Daly and Terry Semel as hobos, looking for food in trashcans. Clint Eastwood, instead of being the legend, was a stuntman, an extra. (Joel Silver shoots him—and actually kills him.) Quincy was Clarence, the angel. Chevy Chase was God.

"I was in a mental institution, totally enclosed in a straitjacket, just my fingers free," Spielberg continued, and—like the mountain in *Close Encounters,* "I was putting together in shaving foam the face of E.T. and not quite knowing what I was trying to express. I said, 'He came to me . . . he came to me . . . he was a six feet three E.T.!' "

In late October 1992, Ross travelled to Los Angeles to undergo surgery. It was performed by Dr. Donald Skinner, at USC's Kenneth J. Norris, Jr., Cancer Hospital. His doctors at Memorial Sloan-Kettering had warned that the operation was futile, family members said; but Dr. Skinner was holding out the possibility of long-term survival, with a good quality of life, while Ross's other doctors had virtually nothing left to offer. Besides, it appeared to his family that he was dying; he had not been able to eat or drink in months and they felt, as did he, that this was at least a chance.

After a radical ten-and-a-half-hour operation, Dr. Skinner proclaimed it a success. He told the family that he had been able to remove the tumor, and that some remaining lymph nodes could be treated with chemotherapy once Ross had regained his strength. It seemed almost a miracle. For the first time since Ross's cancer had been diagnosed as having returned, a year earlier, the optimistic reports that the family made public were ones that they believed.

Before Ross left for California in October, Hugh Culverhouse, a Time Warner director, had come to see him to discuss reducing the size of the company's board. With the merger, the two twelve-member boards had combined. In the fall of 1991, of course, Nicholas had begun talking to

Levin about the need to reduce the size of the board, and also the number of insiders. After Nicholas was fired, the issue had continued to percolate. The giant California Public Employees Retirement System (Calpers) pension fund had warned that if no action were taken, it would file a shareholder proposal for a by-law amendment, to be voted on at the next Time Warner annual meeting, which would require the elimination of most of the insiders. Moreover, the sequence of controversial episodes—the coercive rights offering, the firing of Nicholas, the Ice-T imbroglio—had not augmented the board's reputation for judgment, integrity, or deftness. And there was a general recognition, even among board members, that they needed some new outside directors with stature to lend.

In September, Levin had assigned Hugh Culverhouse and Dick Munro to explore the issue of reducing the board, and to make recommendations. An associate of Levin's explained that in choosing Culverhouse, from the WCI side, and Munro, from Time, "Jerry was looking for people who had symbolic value in the company."

It was true that Munro had been Time Inc.'s chairman and CEO (albeit a hapless one), but he was an odd choice inasmuch as he could, himself, be considered an insider. In addition to his former role at the company, he was chairman of the Executive Committee, a position which provided him compensation of $1 million in 1992. In only one respect, however, was he a perfect choice: he was the person on the board to whom Jerry Levin was closest, and upon whom Levin could rely to take direction. That was how they had worked together in the past—Levin had guided him through the creation of the merger, constantly debriefing him and telling him what to say. And they had in a sense sealed their collaboration in the firing of Nicholas, when Levin had sought, and obtained, Munro's blessing.

Moreover—as would soon become generally apparent—Munro by this time had become a man with a grudge. He knew that many of his old Time Inc. colleagues derided him for having betrayed their company in the merger (and profited handsomely himself), while his Warner colleagues, on the other hand, were dismissive of him (they had not even shown up at his farewell party); and, after Nicholas's firing, both sides considered him weak, as well. In carrying out this assignment, however, Munro might have the chance to show the Warner folk he was no patsy after all, and to vindicate himself, somewhat, with Time.

Culverhouse was a relative latecomer to the WCI board, and if he symbolized anything there, it was opportunism. He had joined the board as one of Herb Siegel's directors; Ross had courted him (there had been easy rapport, with Culverhouse owning a football team, the Tampa Bay

Buccaneers); and, ultimately, when Siegel sued the company in its acquisition of Lorimar, Culverhouse (after first assuring Siegel he was with him) had sided with Ross. Ross had rewarded him with a seat on the Time Warner board. Ross, of course, was wise enough to know that one who has betrayed once may well do it again. A friend of Ross's recalled that sometime in the last couple of years someone had remarked to Ross that "Culverhouse is a snake," and Ross had replied, "Yes, but he's *our* snake"—and added, "but don't fall asleep in the grass."

Why Ross did not heed his own warning is not clear. But he was, of course, very ill; besides he could not have imagined that any action would be taken without his blessing. A Levin associate, describing what he believed transpired when Culverhouse met with Ross, said, "Steve is said to have made general comments about how he understood the board had to be downsized and some insiders had to go. But he may well have said, 'Let's wait until I get back.' "

Considerable attention was paid to process. Indeed, it was somewhat reminiscent of the handiwork that Levin, Nicholas, and Munro had exhibited in bringing about the merger. There, a consensus had been built in the Lyford Cay task force, which had reached the conclusion, favoring such a merger, that the three top executives had always known it would; and then Munro and Nicholas had travelled around, discussing the report with directors, building support. Now, Munro again made his congenial rounds, interviewing directors, reporting back to Levin, interviewing more, and building a consensus. Thus prodded, the directors generally agreed that an ideal size for the board would be about fifteen directors, including a few new ones.

Traditionally, a dinner attended by all the directors had been held the night before a Time Warner board meeting; under Levin's aegis, the insiders (except for himself and Munro) were excluded from these dinners. And it was at one of these dinner meetings that all the directors were asked to give their proxy, essentially—agreeing that whoever was asked to resign would do so. This, of course, would serve to diminish the chance of any large-scale resistance. The insiders, however, were never asked; nor, apparently, were they aware at the time that such an action had taken place.

While the outside directors did make the requested pledge, there was apparently a general expectation that Culverhouse and Munro would be reporting back to the board and their recommendations discussed at a meeting—as, indeed, would seem only normal. Perhaps it was Culverhouse, however, who recalled a process from his days on the old WCI board whereby the special committee comprised of Troubh and

Buttenweiser had been given sole authority to make the determination about the Armstrong Report. There, however, that unusual authority had been explicitly ratified by the full board.

In early December, Munro and Culverhouse met with Dale Hanson, of Calpers. Hanson had already made Calpers' position plain: if there were no board changes by the end of the year, Calpers would be filing its proposal for a by-law amendment. That deadline, however, hardly carried the force of an ultimatum; if changes were made after the end of the year but before the annual meeting, the proposal would simply be moot. Describing their meeting, Hanson said, "We had an indication of where they were going, but we didn't go 'yea' and 'nay' on individual directors. Munro raised the question of whether we thought he should continue [as an insider]. I said, 'You've got to have a carry-over from *Time* magazine!'

"While they didn't say *exactly* when, we knew that the change was coming in the very, very near future," he added.

That, however, was a well-kept secret. As had been true in the firing of Nick Nicholas, a premium was placed on timing and surprise here. Like Nicholas, the targeted directors were stunned, on the Monday of the last week before the Christmas holidays, when Munro and Culverhouse began to place their calls. And, as in Nicholas's case, too, there was to be no full boardroom discussion; they were demanding the directors' immediate resignations.

In the coup against Nicholas, Levin had acted as Ross's agent, and Ross had remained aloof; now, Munro played that part for Levin. According to a couple of people involved, Munro did it with toughness, if not belligerence—lacing his speech with expletives as he encountered resistance from former WCI directors. One person, who noted that Dick Munro appeared to be enjoying his task, recalled that over the last year or so, when Ross was not around, Munro had remarked to other directors, "We *bought* this goddam company! And I've taken all this shit!" From Munro's standpoint, at least, this was the revenge of Time Inc.

From the Time side, outside directors Michael Dingman and Matina Horner, and *Time*'s editor-in-chief Jason McManus had been chosen to resign. It was almost too richly ironic that Munro, who years earlier had made it his goal to remove the editor-in-chief from the board of Time Inc., should now finally succeed in doing so—and should even justify retaining his own position on the board, in the words of Dale Hanson, the monitor of corporate governance, as the "carry-over from *Time* magazine"!

McManus, unsurprisingly, went quietly—expressing the view that he could better perform his editorial duties since he would no longer have to recuse himself, as he had, from many stories. There was no attendant hue and cry. The construct of church and state that Luce had put in place had become so incontrovertibly altered, and the position of editor-in-chief during McManus's tenure so diminished, that it no longer seemed to make any difference whether he occupied a board seat or not.

From the WCI side, directors whose resignations were demanded (in addition to Deane Johnson and Allan Ecker, who had earlier announced they intended to resign) were insiders Martin Payson, vice-chairman of Time Warner, and Bert Wasserman, its long-time CFO; and outside directors Willian vanden Heuvel and Benjamin Holloway. For Payson, especially, it was a bitter comeuppance; he had feared that Nicholas would do this very thing to him, and he had lent critical assistance to Levin in the execution of Nicholas. It was a very rude break with the past for these directors—coming as they did from the Warner family, where directors rather than leaving the board in their advanced years often became directors emeriti, where employees were, as a rule, not fired but shifted to other positions—where safeguarding individuals' dignity was, generally, a company priority.

This process offended and angered virtually all the designated directors on the Time side as well, however; and several agreed that if it were to be carried out so summarily by this "committee," then those two, Munro and Culverhouse, might at least have gained a measure of credibility if they had included themselves as resignees. But the only directors sufficiently enraged to threaten a counterattack were, predictably, those Ross loyalists who had felt their lives bound up in WCI—Payson, Wasserman, and to a lesser degree vanden Heuvel.

In late November, the board had requested a letter from Ross's Los Angeles doctor stating his prognosis. That letter reportedly stated that the operation had been a success; that Ross would be back in touch by mid-January 1993; that he would eventually be able to resume some level of participation, but never his full-time duties. Indeed, in mid-December, executive vice-president Geoffrey Holmes told a group of analysts that Ross would be returning.

Since his surgery, Ross had been incommunicado; he saw only his family and Ferragano. Now, Payson, Wasserman, and vanden Heuvel—supported by Arthur Liman, who allied himself with them—demanded the obvious of Levin: Why couldn't it wait a matter of weeks, until Ross could offer his view? Not that his view would be decisive, they said, but he should be given the opportunity to be heard. Levin is said to have responded that it would be a terrible thing with which to confront Ross, in his weakened condition.

It was not much of an answer, but Levin could not give what was surely the real answer: that it couldn't wait precisely *because* Ross might soon be back in touch and the plan would be stymied, or compromised; because this was the ideal moment. Levin may not have believed the sanguine, long-term forecast of Ross's California doctors; he may have ascribed to the Memorial Sloan-Kettering view, that it was hopeless; but he had no reason not to believe, at least, that Ross's California doctors had succeeded in prolonging his survival. And, as long as Ross lived—and still controlled the board—Levin's own future was not altogether secure.

That Ross had ever truly countenanced an heir apparent was something that Levin is said to have questioned. It was clear that Ross had, in effect, had his fingers crossed when he told Nicholas he was his chosen successor. Ross is said to have kissed Levin on the cheek and told him he loved him when he sent him to carry out the execution of Nicholas; but Levin had to wonder whether that meant that Ross had really accepted him not only as a member of the Warner family but as his successor—or, rather, were his fingers crossed again? Plainly, Ross preferred Levin to Nicholas, but what if Ross were merely using Levin to provide an essential interregnum? One could not *read* Ross; Levin could not know.

While this dilemma was most critical to Levin, others were pondering it as well. Through the latter part of 1992, there was frequent press speculation that Levin was not sufficiently dynamic to lead an entertainment company like Time Warner, and that Ross might prefer to see his creation in the hands of Barry Diller, the former chairman of News Corp.'s Fox Inc., or Michael Ovitz, the chairman of Creative Artists Agency. The reports achieved such currency that Diller wrote Levin a letter saying that he did not want his job. Ovitz did not. Interestingly enough, John Calley, the former president of Warner Bros., had urged Ross in 1980 or so to hire Ovitz as his number two; the two men had talked, but nothing materialized. In September, Ovitz requested a meeting with Ross, and flew to East Hampton to visit him; a client of Ovitz's was interested in making a major investment in the company.

Even if Ross was not musing about a stronger successor, and should die with Levin in place, Levin still could not feel completely secure with a board that was, mainly, Ross's. If Levin were to stumble and a challenger appeared, how faithful would they be to him? It was simple arithmetic. By the winter of 1992, the board had twenty-one directors (it had lost a few through attrition): twelve from WCI and nine from Time.

But if Levin were to succeed in reconstituting the board according to his design, it would have six Time directors (including Levin), and six

WCI directors (including Ross); Levin would then add several new ones. Moreover, while there was an apparent equality in his design—six and six at present—when Ross died, the majority would become Levin's. And, even before Ross died, it really *was* Levin's—because Culverhouse had already crossed over. As one of Levin's associates later said, there was no other director on the WCI side who would conceivably have participated in this action, at this time, in this way.

Faced with Levin's implacability, Liman reportedly discussed with Courtney Ross and Carmen Ferragano the possibility of broaching it with Ross. By Wednesday of that week, December 16, Ross began to suffer heart trouble and also contracted pneumonia. It was impossible to have a discussion. Finally, in a meeting with Levin, Liman is said to have berated him loudly, insisting that there was no reason not to wait.

In so doing, Arthur Liman appeared to put at risk even his own continued representation of his firm's largest client. That Liman should have done something that others would later term "suicidal" was, however, not surprising. Liman was so devoted to Ross that he had always been willing to do virtually anything for him; now, at this moment, he even seemed to sacrifice his own interests to that end. Levin reportedly cut him short, demanding hotly, "Who are you representing, Arthur—Steve or the company?"

Levin recounted this exchange to several people; it was apparently a line he was proud of. It was, in fact, a verbatim echo of what Nicholas had said, in *his* angry exchange with Ross's other arch-protector, Ed Aboodi (who, unlike Liman, did not ally himself with the Ross loyalists but remained docile *vis-à-vis* Levin during this struggle). For his insubordination, Nicholas had been dispatched. Levin, by contrast, had been all humility until this moment, when the power at long last was within his grasp—and then he, too, uttered these words. In Ross's kingdom, they had been incendiary and treasonous words: Steve *was* the company. By their utterance, Levin gave notice that the kingdom was now his.

On Friday, while the battle was raging in New York—and Payson, Wasserman, and vanden Heuvel were refusing to resign without Ross being given a chance to express his views—Ross, very weak, was watching *The Godfather* and then *The Godfather Part II* with his son. Both Toni and Mark Ross had spent weeks in California, remaining in Ross's hospital room, after his operation; then, in mid-December, they had returned to New York. But when Ross worsened on Wednesday of this week, Mark had flown out. By Saturday, he was told his father was not in any danger, and that he should go home; Toni was planning to come on Sunday. There with Ross, at that point, were Courtney Ross, their daughter Nicole, and Carmen Ferragano.

Shortly after Mark arrived in New York early on Saturday evening, he received a call saying that Ross's doctor had determined that something was amiss, and that he had to operate to see what the source of the trouble was. Late that evening, Ross's doctor called and told Mark that he had done so; that the cancer, now, was everywhere; and that his recommendation was not to wake him up.

A couple of hours later, Ross died. As the calls went out in the early hours of that Sunday morning, December 20, friends were told that he had been operated on, and died. One family member said, "Courtney felt it was the right decision. I believe that it was, too. Although I also think it was one that Steve—if he had had to make it himself—could not have made."

He could not have, one guesses, because the Ross credo was that you never give up, you fight and *win,* against all odds. And those who believed in the living legend he created had continued over the past year to view him, at least in some inchoate way, as invincible—even as he receded before their eyes. Toni Ross said that when it finally came, her father's death "stunned" her.

She had listened to the doctors, struggled with the hopeless prognosis, and spent most days with Ross, once he became ill. There were times when she seemed to accept, emotionally, that he was indeed dying— once, a friend recalled, she had begun to weep in a phone conversation, and had said that she knew she was never going to dance with her father again. Still, in the end, she realized that acceptance had eluded her, and not because of unresolved angers, or things left unsaid, or needs unmet: the hard road, generally, that their earlier relationship had been. It was, rather, that the force of his persona overwhelmed everything her mind had processed.

"I didn't believe my father could die," she said.


On the afternoon of Sunday, December 20, the Time Warner board held a meeting by phone. The previous day, the board crisis had finally been resolved. Wasserman, who had declared his intransigence, backed down —deciding that, more than anything, he wanted to remain with the company, continuing his role as CFO. So he agreed to resign as a director before the 1993 annual meeting. Martin Payson had been given that option of remaining in his position, as vice-chairman, initially; but he had been so emotional and angry that he was told to quit or be fired. Now, without Wasserman as an ally, he decided it was time to give up the fight; so he resigned, after negotiating a settlement said ·to total roughly $9 million. Having lost his troops, William vanden Heuvel was still refusing to tender his resignation, but it was immaterial since his term would expire before the next annual meeting and he would not be renominated. All this had fallen into place for Levin, before he or any of the others knew Ross was about to die.

But then Ross *had* died. And timing, which Levin had employed so deftly in both the strike against Nicholas and this one, suddenly turned and bit him. That Steve Ross's death should coincide precisely with the consummation of Levin's reordering of the board was a piece of singularly bad luck for Levin. On the day of Ross's death, Levin was forced to put out a press release entitled "Time Warner Reports Changes on Board of Directors."

However awkward the situation, it did not, incredibly enough, inhibit Levin from making one additional move to shore up his power. During the telephonic board meeting, director Donald Perkins spoke up. It was Perkins, the avatar of corporate governance, who—after Nicholas's firing —had made his emotional plea that the board adhere to a higher standard of conduct in the future, and that management not continue to keep directors in the dark; and he had continued during the year to remind his fellow directors of the governance standard to which they should aspire. In this coup, he was apparently in the loop; several directors said that they believed that he had planned the move, along with Levin, Munro, and Culverhouse.

Now, Perkins told his fellow directors that he had been informed by two company executives that a *New York Times* reporter, Geraldine Fabrikant, had asked whether Levin was going to be immediately named chairman, in Ross's place; and that she had also expressed the view that if he were not, it might be read by the Street as an expression of the board's lack of confidence in Levin. Therefore, Perkins was suggesting that they name Levin chairman.

At this, director Ray Troubh fairly shouted, "Steve has not been dead twelve hours!"

Troubh went on to say that he supported Levin, but that his being made chairman was something that should be done in due course. Were they in all seriousness suggesting that the company should make such a major move based on a reporter's statement? The idea was put aside.

At the next board meeting, however, in January 1993, Levin was made chairman. Fay Vincent, the former baseball commissioner and former CEO of Columbia Pictures, attended the meeting as Levin's first nominee to join the board. Vincent is one of the very few whom Levin apparently trusts; he was, reportedly, Levin's confidant in the step-by-step process that led to the dispatching of Nicholas.

Vanden Heuvel, whose presence was unwelcome, read a peroration he had written in memory of Ross; it was as flowery and emotional as those he had delivered when Ross was alive. Herb Siegel and many others had been cynical about the role vanden Heuvel had played *vis-à-vis* Ross —but there was nothing to be gained any longer, and yet, here he was, insisting on the chance to be Ross's most ardent boardroom booster one more time. It was reportedly met with uncomfortable silence.

This time, vanden Heuvel did not have to defend Ross's compensation —although it did, appropriately enough, furnish a small postscript after his death. An article in the *Wall Street Journal* estimated that, according to Ross's contract, Time Warner would be making payments of at least $300 million to his estate—from death benefits and from Ross's options plan. Moreover, two aspects were deemed unusual, if not unique: the death benefits would continue for three years; and, most strikingly, the period in which Ross's heirs might choose to exercise the options was not the usual one year, but nine years. That was critical. For while Ross's package of options on 7.2 million shares (after the stock split) of Time Warner stock were underwater at the time of his death (the stock was trading below the strike price of $37.50), a stock price rise of 10 percent to 12 percent a year would result, in nine years, in the options having a value of $220 to $325 million. These provisions had been put in place at the time of the merger.

While Gerald Levin surely harbors no ambitions to rival Ross in his compensation, he may in his hoarding of power. Levin was now chairman and CEO, and he was also retaining the title of president. In an interview with a house organ, in response to a question about whether he intended to name a chief operating officer or president, Levin replied: "I don't believe there's a need for traditional structures like a chief operating officer, in the way that's normally understood. . . . I'm not looking for layers of management or outmoded forms of support."

In not deigning to name a number two, then, Levin was not so dissimilar from his predecessor. However, while no one had been more jealous of power than Steve Ross, he had managed over three decades to wield it in a way that rarely left blood on the floor, or made mortal enemies. He was able to do that largely because he was at the fulcrum of something that was of his own creation.

Not so Levin. He was a corporate manager, who had made his way through the ranks. To reach this apex, he had had to overcome Nick Nicholas; and he had had to wrest control, in the end, from Ross and his allies. And these moves, for all his effort to cloak them—in Nicholas's case, in the garb of Time Inc., and in Ross's case, in corporate governance —were naked graspings of power. One cannot claim a victory for corporate governance in a coup.

Levin had made it to this point by himself, and so he intended to remain. After the merger, he and Nicholas had moved over to 75 Rockefeller Plaza, to occupy newly designed offices on the twenty-ninth floor, with Ross. After Nicholas's firing, his office had been made into a conference room. Now, Levin announced that Ross's office would be made into a new boardroom—not, as some in the company had assumed, into several smaller offices. Thus, in a building cramped for space, Levin, the first chairman, CEO, and president of Time Warner, would occupy the twenty-ninth floor alone.

Ross's memorial service was held at Carnegie Hall on February 11, 1993. If there were any doubt that Ross had achieved international stature as one of the media barons of our age, this event was designed to lay it to rest. Several thousand invitations had been sent (their envelopes addressed in calligraphy), and the orchestra section and the first tier were filled. The mistress of ceremonies was Beverly Sills. The speakers were the Reverend Jesse Jackson; former Governor Hugh Carey; Mayor David Dinkins; Pelé, the Brazilian soccer player who made the Cosmos famous; Liz Smith, gossip columnist; Steven Spielberg; Minoru Murofushi, from Itochu, formerly C. Itoh (one of the TWE partners); Gerald Levin, and three more Time Warner executives; Arthur Liman; Mark and Toni Ross; and Caroline Lang—who, as the program stated, was "speaking on behalf of her father Jack Lang, French Minister of Education and Culture." As Hilary Califano, the daughter of William Paley, was overheard murmuring to the person next to her, "Even Daddy didn't have something like this!"

The service had its moments, and they illustrated the old maxim that less is more (a very un-Ross-like maxim); for what was most affecting on this very elaborate occasion was the most simple and personal. "My father nearly burned the house down in what was a sincere and only attempt to fry an egg," Toni Ross recalled. "My father and I could dance up a storm together. My father still wanted me—at age thirty—to show off my swimming stroke to his friends; we had created it together."

Bob Daly, the chairman of Warner Bros., insisted that—notwithstanding all Ross's extraordinary talents and achievements—"what truly set him apart from others who accomplished greatness was his love and caring for people. . . . When Steve and I discussed Warner Bros., his prime concern was always about the people. What was on their minds? Were they happy? Did they need anything?

"On a personal note," Daly continued, "there was one way in which Steve knew he could always make me happy. Everyone who knew Steve well knew that his favorite food in the world was Entenmann's crumb cake. He could easily exist on a diet of Entenmann's crumb cake and coffee. When Steve found out that I shared his love for Entenmann's, he would offer it to me everytime we met, no matter what time of the day it was.

"Since Steve knew Entenmann's was not sold in L.A., he would go to any lengths to make sure that I never left New York without what he considered an ample supply to take home. Knowing Steve as you do, I'm sure you can imagine what he considered 'an ample supply.' I would find myself giving away boxes of it to anyone who crossed my path on the way to the airport. In addition, whenever anyone came out from New York for a meeting, Steve would make sure that they brought me a new supply. I was happy, but always somewhat embarrassed, to see top executives enter my office carrying grocery bags.

"It gave Steve such pleasure to give me those crumb cakes that it took me close to a year before I had the heart to tell him that Entenmann's had expanded its distribution to California and our favorite crumb cake could now be found at any local supermarket.

"I know that many of you are thinking of your own 'Steve Ross stories,'" Daly added, "and we all smile as we recall them. . . . It's really impossible to adequately describe this special quality. If you knew him, you just knew it."

Unlike Daly, however, many of the speakers missed the mark. Some of them—Dinkins, Lang, Smith, and Jackson—simply did not know Ross well enough to have any "Steve Ross stories" to tell. (Jackson, for one, spoke of "great Americans recently in transition: Arthur Ashe, Thurgood Marshall, Reginald Lewis—and Steve Ross.") These speakers had clearly been chosen not because of who they were in relation to Ross but, instead, who they were.

As carefully choreographed as Ross's funeral had been, it was slapdash compared to this memorial. Courtney Ross, who was once again in charge (the official producer was Lorne Michaels), seemed to have drawn certain lessons from the funeral. Mark Ross, who had spoken in a revealing way about the pain of his relationship with his father, was told that he was being allotted four minutes and he would speak third from last; he was, moreover, to be the sole family representative Mark had responded that he was going first, which he did (he was more reserved this time), and Toni (whose name did not appear on the program) went onstage with him.

Quincy Jones, who was closer than most to Ross but who had been rambling and somewhat inarticulate at the funeral, was told shortly before the service that—although he was its "musical director"—he would not be one of the speakers. This is said to have upset him very much. And Daly had been added to the list only after he protested that it was not right that he not speak on behalf of the studio. (One of the few from the company whom Courtney Ross did invite to speak was Bob Pittman, to the surprise of many. Explaining her decision, Pittman—who describes the Time Warner culture as "a culture of visionaries," Ross's legacy—said that Courtney Ross told him, "You're a dreamer.")

With all its meticulous orchestration and high-flown roster, the service was widely considered by Ross loyalists to have been a flop. It began at 11:00 A.M. and lasted nearly two and a half hours; after the first hour and a half, people began to drift out. The service was really more insult than tribute to the memory of someone who so prided himself on his talent as a showman. Its fatal conceptual error was that instead of trying to reflect the man—something which, if done well, could have held any crowd in thrall, let alone these masses of the faithful—it had strained to create an image of Ross as a historic world figure. Many in this audience would say later that they felt the memorial was more reflective of Courtney, her grandiosity, her ambition, than of Steve Ross. "She wanted to be Jackie Kennedy," one concluded.

On the morning of the service, a full-page ad had run in the *New York Times*, signed by "family, friends, and associates." (It was echoed, in a smaller version—in the programs distributed at the service.) In part, it featured the poem that Courtney Ross's sister, Lindsay Lonberg, had introduced at the funeral service, saying that Ross always carried it in his briefcase (a claim that raised eyebrows at the time). Above the poem was written: "In the words of the Emerson poem he carried as his talisman." This evoked much comment among his friends. As Beverly Sills had remarked at Ross's funeral, he was "a man without airs." And, while Ross was a gifted individual with a wide array of talents and proclivities, using words like "talisman" was not among them. (The poem, moreover, was not written by Emerson; it appears to have been written, rather, by Harry Emerson Fosdick, the early twentieth-century preacher known for his homiletic writing.)

Also on the day of the memorial, a letter from Courtney Ross was distributed throughout Time Warner, addressed: "Dear Member of the Time Warner Family." She thanked its recipients for the outpouring of letters, notes, and calls. "As part of our desire to honor his memory in the most fitting ways, and in ways Steve himself would have desired, we are seeking to gather written reflections and reminiscences about Steve from anyone who wishes to contribute," she wrote. "It doesn't matter if you met him only once *or not at all* [emphasis added]. We just would like to know what you felt about him in your heart."

It was almost as though Courtney Ross had contracted from Ross (and went on to reflect in her own style) the sense of insecurity that had dogged him always. It was unfortunate. There was no need to embellish, or to try to augment Ross's stature. For the "achievements" side of the ledger of Steve Ross's life demonstrated him to have been one of the most original entrepreneurs of his time.

His first twenty years in the business world were spent mainly in trial and error, but by the time he acquired Warner-Seven Arts he had begun to come into his own. He had by then the earmarks of a consummate dealmaker. He was unusually far-seeing: he recognized the potential of cable when few others did, and he was the only one among his peers in the movie business to do so. He saw software as a whole—movies, TV, music and cable programming; and he also grasped, early, that it was the development of programming that would spur the growth of cable. He viewed the entertainment business as a global business before most others did, and he set up a global distribution network that was the strongest in his industry.

As Ross would be the first to say, he did not accomplish these things alone. He had a knack for finding good people. And, with them, he had the attributes of an excellent teacher: he supported and empowered his divisional people—he was not threatened by them but knew that by giving them freedom they would do their best for him. He encouraged risk taking, and even made it his credo, but he did not do so blindly; for most of his years, his company grew on a sound, not leveraged, financial base.

He had really excelled only once he was in businesses about which he was passionate. Had Ross not acquired Warner-Seven Arts or some other entertainment company, it is unlikely that he would ever have come to the public's attention. He loved being associated with a creative enterprise, and much of what he did—the way he treated talent, and his operating heads, too—flowed from that. "Steve loved businesses that involved massaging human egos and he was extraordinarily good at it," commented Roger Smith.

Though the cable business was different (it was mainly a hardware business), Ross's enthusiasm for it had a similarly emotional source. Ross was a relentless, insatiable consumer, someone who liked having every imaginable service available to him at all times; so the idea of a universe of options, just a button's press away, held enormous appeal. His brief run at Sotheby's, in the early eighties, had been fuelled by that notion of yet another available consumer service. As Ross told me, what he envisioned—although the technology did not yet exist—was that "you would push a button and make a bid." For roughly twenty years, through setbacks and failures, the future possibilities of cable induced in him almost a froth of excitement.

There was, of course, much besides, less salutary. But these were the essential traits that enabled Ross to build WCI into the entertainment powerhouse it was at the moment it merged with Time Inc. Fairly or not, however, history will judge Steve Ross in large measure by the outcome of that merger. And whether it will ultimately be proved a success seems increasingly open to question—as Ross must have known at the time of his death.

The merger was bedevilled from the start, of course, by the debt incurred in its restructuring in response to Paramount's offer for Time. Before that—simply based on combining the two companies' cable interests, and ignoring any possibility of synergy—the merger probably made sense. After that, because of the debt burden that Ross abhorred, it probably did not.

Moreover, the ideas that Ross had so fervently embraced in the merger and its aftermath—globalization, particularly as expressed through his strategic alliances—seemed, shortly after his death, to have lost whatever currency they had had. Ross had argued, of course, that strategic alliances were so clearly the optimum means of gaining access to burgeoning foreign markets that bartering away major equity stakes in the company's prize assets was justified. By mid-1993, however, his argument seemed to have been proved wrong-headed on both counts. Access did not hinge on this form of alliance, as opposed to local joint ventures. And the equity stakes in Time Warner's entertainment properties that had been bartered for cash seemed so redolent with value, in this increasingly software-hungry world, that their trade was more suggestive of a desperate pawning of the family heirlooms than a sage corporate strategy.

At the time of Ross's death, Time Warner had been searching for a

European partner for TWE for three and a half years, without success. The absence of that partner, however, did not appear to be hampering the global reach of the company, which in 1992 had achieved record-breaking sales in worldwide theatrical distribution, worldwide home video, and international television syndication. The Warner Music Group —which is not part of TWE, but which nonetheless bills itself as "Time Warner's most global division"—also continued its dominance as the most profitable recorded music company in the world. And HBO was rapidly expanding into new global markets, through the establishing of local joint ventures.

Several months after Ross's death, when a new partner for TWE was finally announced, it was not a European company after all but U.S. West Inc., a regional Bell telephone company based near Denver. And Levin, in his interviews, made it plain that the buzzword which had provided the rationale both for the Time Warner merger and the notion of strategic alliances—"globalization"—was now yielding to something more contemporary: "technology."

This shift in emphasis had begun to emerge just weeks after Ross's death, when Levin had announced that Time Warner would be transforming part of its Orlando cable system into "the world's first full service network"—a two-way electronic superhighway that would provide video-on-demand, interactive games, interactive shopping, personal communication services, and long-distance telephone service, to begin service by early 1994. Interviewed by *Cable World,* Levin struck his usual lofty note: "It is a really profound aggregate of concepts. It's truly infinite. I would describe it as a perfect medium."

The U.S. West deal followed as a kind of corollary to the "superhighway" announcement, inasmuch as U.S. West would be helping to upgrade Time Warner's cable networks to carry interactive, data, and voice services. The deal augured a future of collaboration between cable and telephone companies, rather than the fierce competition that had been forecast. It was widely viewed, moreover, as a deal—Levin's—that enabled him to put his own stamp on the company, marking the start of a new, post-Ross era. (It was also a deal in which Ed Aboodi reaped the rewards of his long cultivation of, and allegiance to, Jerry Levin. He was said by some close to the transaction to have garnered a kingly fee of $30 million—if true, far better even than Aboodi had done under Ross.)

Had Ross lived, he would almost surely have approved this change in emphasis from globalization to technology—after all, this was the "frame-grabber," twenty years later, revivified! In the last speeches and interviews he gave, Ross had referred with some pride to the experiments with interactivity in the days of QUBE. And, in the keynote speech Ross delivered at the Edinburgh International Television Festival in August 1990—an occasion that marked his debut on the world stage, at a forum where Rupert Murdoch had been the keynote speaker the previous year—Ross had conjured up the near future:

> Twenty years ago, I dreamed that by now surely we would be viewing and ordering merchandise by cable television, from Marks & Spencer, Sears, Roebuck, or Galeries Lafayette, and our bank accounts would be directly charged . . . thus starting down the road toward a truly checkless society.
>
> Universities would be using interactive cable to teach students how to read Shakespeare, melding the printed word with live, interactive, electronic seminars.
>
> A doctor would be able to take a patient's electrocardiogram without either one leaving office or home.
>
> . . . I thought, too, that we'd be sending mail around the world electronically, over discrete cable channels, with a higher degree of security than the traditional postal service—and all in less than a few minutes.
>
> And certainly, people would be able to order up any movie or any record album ever produced and see it or hear it when they themselves wanted to; it would be delivered directly to their homes via their television sets.

"I was a little ahead of myself," Ross had added. "But not much, for these notions are already technically feasible, over interactive cable."

While Levin had changed the emphasis from globalization to technology, however, he had not changed the defining aspect of these strategic alliances, and that seemed more dubious than ever. U.S. West would be paying $2.5 billion for more than 25 percent of TWE ($1 billion would be put toward the new systems, $1.5 billion toward paring down Time Warner's $16 billion debt). That 25 percent ownership, combined with the Toshiba and Itochu stakes, would leave Time Warner owning just 63 percent of TWE—with its valuable Warner Bros., HBO, and cable assets, which together produce more than two thirds of the company's cash flow. Technological expertise could have been purchased outright; there was no intrinsic need to barter with the company's crown jewels. Indeed, as an article entitled "Fire Sale" by Sharon Moshavi in a November 1993 issue of *Forbes* would point out, Time Warner had sold interests in its prize assets for prices that averaged thirteen times cash flow—while, in the bidding war for Paramount Communications that was raging in the fall of 1993, offers had risen to twenty-one times cash flow and could well go higher. The analogy was not perfect, inasmuch as Time Warner had sold minority interests, not full ownership; still, Moshavi argued that Time Warner, in cutting its Toshiba-Itochu and U.S. West deals, might have left about $2 billion on the table. It may well be that Nick Nicholas over time will be proven to have been right when he charged that the Ross plan—one which Levin had now adapted and continued to implement—amounted to "selling the roses," while Nicholas had wanted to "sell the weeds."

And while the cost of the merger might prove ruinous if this strategy bleeds the company too badly, the merger's broad benefits had yet to materialize. Challenged as to those benefits, company executives would typically point to the outstanding performance of the company's operating units. That Time Warner represents one of the best collections of entertainment and media assets in the business is unarguable, but it is also beside the point. The operating units—mainly on the WCI side—are powerhouses, but they always were, and they would have continued to be, without the merger. The single clear benefit of the combination was the augmentation of the cable business, the idea that fired Ross initially (Time Warner is now the second largest in the country); but that alone, in the face of the debt and other continuing problems, is probably not enough on which to construct a case for a merger.

That no synergy has resulted from the merger should come as no surprise. One of the core precepts of WCI was the autonomy of its various operating units—a precept so honored in practice that the record companies, at times, competed outright with each other. Ross liked it that way. He believed in the benefits of freedom, and he also preferred a system in which he, alone, was the nexus; one in which, as Rafael de la Sierra had said, the right hand did not know what the left hand was doing—only Ross knew.

If there were sibling rivalries at WCI, Ross was always there as the father and arbiter; in the seventies, especially, the metaphor of the family was apt. But, as Felix Rohatyn had mentioned at Ross's funeral, the polar cultures of Time and Warner never melded. To the extent people refer to the "Time Warner family," it is a quaint anachronism. And, instead of the hoped-for synergy between various units, there is discord.

The most celebrated feud has been that between Robert Daly, at Warner Bros., and Michael Fuchs, at HBO. The seeds of it were sown, of course, at the time of the merger, when Daly and Semel stiff-armed Fuchs's desire for HBO to have a comedy label at the studio, and, eventually, to make movies for theatrical release. Since the merger, they have battled continually over how much HBO should pay for Warner Bros.

movies; and in June 1992, when HBO agreed to provide Savoy Pictures Entertainment, a new movie distributor, with as much as $500 million in capital in return for movie rights, Daly tried, unsuccessfully, to get Levin to intervene.

Antipathy has also existed between Robert Morgado, the former Carey assistant who became Ross's hatchet man in the early eighties and then was put in charge of the music business, and Mo Ostin, the long-time head of Warner Records, who built it up from a company with revenues of $100 million at the time of the Warner-Seven Arts acquisition to roughly $2 billion today. This, of course, has been a home-grown WCI feud, unrelated to the merger. But as long as Steve Ross was alive, it was manageable: Ostin simply bypassed Morgado and reported directly to Ross.

Once Ross was not there, however, the problem began to fester; and it was, presumably, exacerbated from Ostin's point of view by the fact that Morgado, an intensely political person, had been busily soldering his alliance with Jerry Levin for some time (perhaps, even, imagining himself as a prospective number two). In any event, there would no longer be any buffer between Ostin and Morgado. As a former executive who spent many years at WCI said of the situation, "Morgado doesn't give enough breathing room to the division heads. With Steve Ross, they felt like princes; with Morgado, they feel like employees."

What Levin must keep in mind, particularly with the studio and record heads, is that Ross not only treated them like princes but, ultimately, *made* them princes. Daly, for example, is said to have garnered about $70 million from the sale of his stock in the merger; he and the others are thus financially independent. As Daly said, "I've told Jerry—he's got the best employee in me, because I don't want his job—I just want to be left alone. If it changes—well, I'd hate not to come here. But I won't come in here one day unhappy." He also mentioned, in another conversation, that during the post-Atari cutbacks at WCI headquarters, the studio developed its own independent infrastructure. "Today, Warner Bros. is a self-contained company. If someone were to spin it off, all we would have to get is a new bank line," Daly remarked.

Time Inc., the publishing division—once proud flagship of the *old* Time Inc.—was from the start, and continues to be, such a stepchild in this "entertainment-oriented" merger that those in the more powerful Warner divisions regard it with either indifference or disdain. ("They're prima donnas," one such executive remarked. "I'm primo domo.") Nor was the latest emphasis upon technology as the company's raison d'être —and Levin's apostolic fervor about the electronic superhighway—at all heartening to those attempting to soldier on in print. According to a *BusinessWeek* article in May 1993, Time staffers said that Levin told them the magazines will still have a place in the multi-media world of Time Warner—as long as they remain editorially strong.

A rather qualified-sounding endorsement, but hardly surprising. Levin's roots at Time Inc. were, of course, on the video side, not print, and it is to those roots that he is returning. He is, moreover—despite his impassioned oratory at the time of Nicholas's firing—someone who has shown little respect for the magazines' integrity, treating them rather as something to be used for his ends. Particularly after the merger, he is said to have frequently intervened, scrutinizing and fine-tuning articles about the company. It had been much feared, when the merger was announced, that this was something Ross would do. In fact, that would have been out of character; even apart from the fact that he rarely read, he had had a long history of not interfering, generally, in WCI's creative processes. So, by all accounts, Ross did not interfere with the magazines; Levin did.

If his history is any guide, Levin will keep Time Inc. until it has served its purpose, and then, in all likelihood, he will dispose of it. (Thus, his assuming control of the board from the old WCI forces was not really the revenge of Time Inc.; it was only the victory of Gerald Levin.) The magazine division never really fit in the design of the merger; it was omitted from the initial joint-venture construct, and it has become only more extraneous over the years. Of course, that was almost surely Ross's long-term plan: the beauty of his scheme would have been—after having succeeded in selling his company and yet continuing to control it—to sell off the purported acquiror.

Once he became ill, however, nearly all his plans were short-circuited. One which he did carry out, which had been in gestation for months, was the firing of Nicholas. The reasons for doing so would have remained fairly constant, even after Ross knew that it was likely he would not survive long. Levin would not change the company's course *vis-à-vis* dealing with its debt, as Nicholas would have done; instead, he would do Ross's bidding, and continue to work with Aboodi on the strategic alliances Ross was so intent on. And—in the event that Ross, the luckiest man alive, somehow made it back—Levin would presumably continue to be as subservient, not to say obsequious, as he had always been.

That much is plain. But it is difficult to imagine that Ross, that almost clairvoyant judge of people, put Levin in Nicholas's place because he visualized Levin as a strong leader for his—Ross's—company, after his death. Levin was turned inward; he was opaque and he was unimposing.

He might be well suited to brewing transactions with Aboodi, and, especially, to immersing himself in the intricacies of the technological future. But he was altogether ill-equipped for the task of relating to the executives of Time Warner, with all their disparate and sometimes adversarial agendas, in ways that would inspire trust, loyalty, and a passion to follow his lead.

Only a couple of months after Ross's death, Seagram Co. quietly began accumulating Time Warner stock, eventually disclosing an intent to take its ownership up to 15 percent. While Seagram presented its move as a friendly one, it had not alerted Time Warner to its purchases until it passed the obligatory 5 percent mark—a suggestion, in itself, of an interest that was not friendly. Moreover, the move was said to have been fuelled by the avid interest of Seagram president Edgar Bronfman, Jr., in becoming actively involved in the entertainment business—and, perhaps, in seeing his friend Michael Ovitz replace Levin as chairman and CEO. "I see your fine Medici hand at work here," one knowing friend wrote in a note to Ovitz. Soon after Seagram's ownership was disclosed, Levin began discussing possible anti-takeover provisions with his advisers. And, by the late fall of 1993, after several months of quiescence, Seagram resumed its accumulating even though the stock was fully priced—lending credence to the idea that its intentions were indeed both serious and unfriendly.

That this threat of an eventual change in command would have displeased Ross is far from clear. He had so diligently promoted the ideology that the company and he were inseparable, joined in a kind of fixed symbiosis ("Steve Ross *is* WCI," Spielberg had declared), that it was difficult to imagine his really wanting anyone else to have it. Binding the company to him had always been his objective—more than ensuring its continuation without him. Whereas company founders intent on building an entity to outlast them regard the selection and grooming of a successor as one of their most important goals, Ross (alluding regretfully to Ken Rosen, when the subject of a successor arose) took care for decades to *avoid* any true contenders—and may well, in his view, have continued to do that to the very last. Levin had a capacious mind and a fascination with technology; that said, his persona—or lack of one—made him a most implausible successor to Ross, one almost certain to be dwarfed by Ross's shadow. Moreover, Ross's blessing of Levin was tentative, and limited (with fingers crossed?)—for, had he fully blessed Levin, there would have been an orderly and seemly transition, and Levin would not have felt impelled to seize control as he ultimately did.

At the time of the merger, some people, speculating that the merger itself reflected Ross's coming to terms with his mortality, had referred to its succession provisions as his "living will." But when I had mentioned this to Ross—who was so controlled that his countenance rarely divulged anything not intended—he started noticeably, and looked as though he'd been slapped. He forcefully denied that it was a "living will," and talked about how there was nothing like having a six-year-old to keep you going, and how he intended to be there for many years to come.

If he only had, Ross loyalists say, he, and he alone, might have made this unwieldy, fractious merger work. "Steve was the godfather," declared Ralph Peterson, of Warner Bros. "He would have brought Bob Daly and Michael Fuchs into a room together." Perhaps. In assessing the keys to his success, Ross tended to downplay the intricacies of his dealmaking, informed by his mathematical wizardry. In what proved to be our final interview, in September 1991, Ross had acknowledged that he could, indeed, multiply a three-digit number by another three-digit number in his head. "Numbers speak to me," he said. "But very little of this is about numbers. It's about people, really—realizing what they want."

He certainly excelled at that, I said. Whereupon he shot me a quick, faintly gimlet-eyed look, and added, "And that's not *bad* . . ."


Ross was intent on never being found out. Those who knew him well over many years, including family members, agreed that he rarely, if ever, let down the impenetrable facade; that he was frightened by the prospect of exposure; that it was therefore easier for him to have relationships with legions of his extended "family"—which involved, on his part, a great deal of *doing* and the receipt of an enormous and enormously needed amount of approbation but little genuine emotional contact—than with his real family; and that he was truly intimate with no one. It was a central paradox of Ross's life that the man with thousands of friends had none.

Many wondered what the specific secrets were that Ross was so eager to protect. While there was an abundance of secrets as the years wore on, his guardedness was so much his emotional style that one suspected, more, that it might have stemmed from a general discrepancy between the person he felt himself to be and the image he projected to the world. Whatever he did not want to reveal to others, it seemed he himself did not want to dwell on, either; family members emphasized the fact that he simply could not be alone; there was then no distraction from himself and, perhaps, no *sense* of himself, in the absence of others' responsiveness. His unease, in any event, was profound.

He was also someone who was continually creating and recreating himself; it emerged that at the very start he had cast aside family connections, much as he would later do with outworn sets of friends. His children, Mark and Toni, were amazed to discover after his death that he had had seven aunts and uncles whose existence he had never mentioned, even to their mother. When they questioned him about his family, he had always refused to discuss it. "I don't want to say my father 'abandoned' his family," Toni Ross said later, "but it is certainly true that he disconnected from them."

The old movies that Ross had loved so much when he was growing up, and that he watched so often in his later life, were of course redolent with old-fashioned values and virtues. "My father took me to see the John Wayne movie, *True Grit,* when I was nine; when I was twelve, he took me to meet John Wayne," Mark Ross recalled. "And my father was very John Wayne-like to me—he exemplified the themes in those movies, like supreme loyalty, and sacrificing yourself for someone else.

"He thought he could be everything to everybody," Ross continued. "He thought he could be Jimmy Stewart and John Wayne and Cary Grant to people."

No movie character so captured Steve Ross's imagination as George Bailey (played by Jimmy Stewart), the hero of *It's a Wonderful Life* "Steve Ross *was* George Bailey!" declared Spielberg, and he also said that Ross's "quest for the holy grail" was his perpetual search for a dinner guest who had never seen that movie; he would then screen it for the evening's entertainment. Family members agreed that Ross identified strongly with the character; indeed, when he checked into the hospital in Los Angeles where he was to undergo radical surgery, less than two months before he died, he signed in as "George Bailey."

Ross was not Bailey, of course. In fact, their lives—while starting out from a strikingly common point—diverged to the point of antithesis. The movie is a story about Bailey's yearning for escape, about being trapped, and about the price paid in relinquishing all grand ambitions. Perhaps it was that, as much as anything else, which drew Ross to this movie; perhaps it comforted him, in a sense, to dwell on the cost of such self-sacrifice. Ross had dreamed the same dreams of escape that Bailey did, but, unlike Bailey, he had realized them, and many, many more.

It seems, however, that he wanted, emotionally, to have it both ways. That had long been a characteristic trait. He wanted to reap the financial benefits of a founder, and he did, through his gargantuan contract and, ultimately, his payout in the merger; but he did not want to take the attendant risk, and so had not owned more than 1 or 2 percent of the stock. He wanted to best his opposite in every deal, reaping untold financial advantage, but he wanted to do it so cleverly that the person on the other side of the table left feeling that he had gotten what he wanted, and that Ross was exceedingly fair—a feat brilliantly exemplified in the deal with Time. He had wanted to escape "Bedford Falls" and achieve his dreams, but he also wanted to be seen as someone with the generosity, loyalty, and penchant for self-sacrifice of a George Bailey, or, as his son recalled, one of the characters played by John Wayne.

Ross defies facile, conclusive analysis. For example, to say that he was incessantly manipulating to project a certain image is not to suggest that his generosity was all sham. The limitless giving that became his hallmark in later years had started early, and in instances where it certainly had no public purpose. His daughter Toni recalled that when she was a little girl, Ross seemed "obsessed" with Christmas. "There were so many gifts, and you'd be opening and opening and opening presents, and you had to get them all opened before breakfast. And there were rules: certain ones had to be opened first, and then there were others, behind the tree, and you had to get to those last—it was exhausting!"

As she got older, Ross gave her "thousands and thousands and thousands of gifts." Finally, she had said, "No more." "He was a giving tree," she continued. "People needed things from him: that was his mind-set. He was stuck in that. That was the tragedy."

However murky the sources of some of Ross's behavior, this much is clear: he recreated himself in mythic proportions that were, by and large, untrue. The myth portrayed him as a man who was infinitely generous, loyal to the death, and who valued the well-being of his friends above his own—sacrificing himself for the good of others. But the truth was that his extraordinary generosity was funded to a great degree by the company; his loyalty, in many cases, endured as long as people were useful to him; and—driven by a compulsion to win—he tended to put his own interest ahead of others, in situations large and small.

Not only did Ross not sacrifice himself for the good of others, as did his putative soulmate, George Bailey, but the precise converse was true —even when it came to his best friend. He had, after all, sacrificed Jay Emmett to save himself.

# Epilogue

U pon hearing that Ross had checked into the hospital in Los Angeles as "George Bailey," one of his old friends exclaimed, "That was Steve's last deal. He figured he was probably going to die, and he wanted to try to convince God that he was George Bailey!" While it was unlikely that God would mistake the two, it was perhaps the ultimate success of Ross's success-filled life that after his death that is essentially how he was memorialized by so many people. Thus, in the end, he did have it both ways.

Roughly six weeks after the service in Carnegie Hall, another memorial was held at the Warner Brothers Studio in Los Angeles. As Quincy Jones would say, referring to the fact that this was the third Ross memorial, "It's because when we get hold of a good human being it's hard to let him go."

Certainly that was the way Bob Daly felt. Over the last decade, he had become strongly devoted to Ross. But when he first joined the company in late 1981, and for some time thereafter, Daly—who had come from CBS, an altogether different world—had not known exactly what to make of Ross and his profligate ways. Daly's bemusement, moreover, was shared by businessmen observing Ross from outside. As Marvin Davis, the former owner of Twentieth Century Fox, said, "His methods of business everybody thought were terrible. He was not cost-conscious. He gave out heavy rewards. We said, how can they possibly pay that? But, it was a love affair over there—people *loved* to work there—and they were successful." On being asked why he and others, seeing success, had not emulated Ross's ways, Davis replied, "I'm a businessman. A dollar's a dollar."

Daly said it took him two years to become comfortable with Ross's way of doing business. "I thought originally he was crazy. I'd say, wait a minute—why are we doing this? But I realized finally that what he was was a long-term thinker. There's a nice thing about being able to think long term and make people happy—and in the meantime build up an enormous amount of goodwill."

Now, Daly has appropriated Ross's approach. He said that after *Lethal Weapon* opened in the summer of 1992, he gave a lunch for seven people —several of the actors, the director, the head of production. "And after the lunch, I took out an envelope and poured seven keys onto the table. Out in front of our building were parked seven Range Rovers, in all different colors. They went out and chose the color they wanted.

"And the most amazing thing," Daly continued, "was when I looked at the expressions on the faces of our executives—they were as happy as the faces of the people getting the cars. Our people thought it was the greatest thing, and they were so proud to be working at this kind of a company."

Pointing to some of his competitors, including Disney and MCA, Daly added: "They all look at the return. They *see* the way we operate, but they can't do it. It's not in them. They want a return on their dollar today. Their attitude is, 'If I give you this, what do I get?'

"We never say that. We say, 'I'm giving you this because I like you. You're great. You don't have to give me anything.' That was Steve—and he taught us.

"Of course, if you think about this too much, and you don't go with the rush," Daly added, almost as an afterthought, "you could say to yourself, '*Seven* Range Rovers?' "

If Steve Ross had ever been on trial, Bob Daly—straightforward, decent, and honorable—would likely have been his best character witness. Unlike the stars and many others who readily endorsed the mythicized image that Ross projected, Daly did not idolize him. Theirs had, of course, been a relationship formed in business; Daly, therefore, was vouchsafed a view of him that those who knew him only socially did not have. And even Daly's view, like that of virtually everyone with whom Ross dealt, was partial and discrete. (Daly, for example, knew little or nothing of Ross's personal financial dealings, or the Westchester Premier

Theatre episode, or Caesar Kimmel and Warner Leisure, or, indeed, much of what went on back in New York.)

For all his affection, Daly acknowledged that Ross was "outrageous," and insisted that he did not "have him on a pedestal." "I fought harder with him than anyone in the company did," Daly said, "but it was with respect."

He pointed out that he had not been afraid to challenge Ross before his board; he had done so in the course of the Lorimar acquisition, when Ross wanted to go forward and Daly was convinced the price was too high. "After I got us out of the deal, he was mad at me," Daly said. "He said in a meeting that I'd played it too conservative. But then they came back." The deal was ultimately done, at a lower price. But it had often been a bone of contention: Ross thought Daly was too conservative.

He recalled that he also had had "a major fight" with Ross when Sony, in 1989, came to an agreement with producers Peter Guber and Jon Peters that they would run Columbia Pictures, which Sony was acquiring —despite the fact that Guber and Peters had recently signed a lucrative five-year deal with Warner Bros. Ross, expressing fury at the producers' not having first asked him to let them out of their contract, refused to do so; and, after a fierce battle with Sony, extracted a settlement valued at more than $750 million, in return for letting Guber and Peters go.

Daly and Aboodi attended the negotiating meetings with the Sony executives. "For twenty-one days, all I did was negotiate this deal, and it was all Steve wanted to talk about, night and day—it was beyond the pale, to the point where he was obsessed," Daly recalled. "He never came to the negotiations"—Daly agreed that that was Ross's custom so as to give himself more leeway—"but, of course, he wanted every word that was said. He was the total architect, totally on top of it—but he didn't go into the room."

These negotiations were taking place in September 1989, when the Time-Warner merger had finally cleared its court hurdles, and there was a get-together of Time and WCI executives at the traditional Time Inc. resort of Lyford Cay. "He had me captive there for four days," Daly recalled. "We were flying up to New York on the plane and he couldn't stop talking about it. He wanted to rehearse and rehearse and rehearse. Aboodi and I were going to go to the meeting with the Sony people the next day. He started to tell me what to say. You know, 'When they say this to you, then you say . . .'

"Finally, I said, 'Steve, you can tell me what to do, you can tell me what not to do. But you can't tell me what to say. I have a headache—I am not going to talk about this anymore.' I went to the sofa and fell asleep. And, later, we didn't talk about it. He understood." Daly added that he could never have gone back to New York to be Ross's number two, something Herb Siegel at one point had suggested; it would have driven him "crazy." "That's why Steve needed an Ed Aboodi—someone who would just sit there with him and work that way," Daly added.

Because he has spent his career working for two men, William Paley and Steve Ross, both of whom he considers "giants," Daly tends to compare them. And while Paley, in his view, had monumental strengths, he had none of Ross's almost compulsive humanity. "Steve was not perfect, but in the sense of being a chief executive, running a major corporation, the human part of Steve was as important as the dealmaking. The human part was enormous. It was so plain how he felt about the people here. He talked to every secretary. If he walked out without saying goodbye to Ann or Marisa [Daly's assistants], he'd say, 'Omygod! I didn't say goodbye,' and walk back in. And if Ann did anything for him while he was here, a dozen red roses would be on her desk the next day.

"I saw Paley walk through that CBS building for years," Daly added, "and he didn't talk to anyone but his own secretary." He added that, though he had worked for Paley for twenty-five years, he believed that Paley would not even have remembered if Daly had children.

In March 1993, at the Warner Brothers Studio, Daly produced for his friend a tribute, entitled *Celebration of a Life,* that would have made Ross, the showman, proud. In one sense, it was even an improvement over the East Hampton funeral: there were no family speeches, and so no exposure of that which was real, and lamentably wanting. It was an infinitely better event than the Carnegie Hall service, which Ross, in his lexicon, would surely have termed a "disaster." Rather than trying to make him into what he was not, this production stuck to his own version of who he was, adhering to the script that Ross had created for his life: a uniquely American parable of fantasy, escape, and enterprise. And, since three months had passed since his death, it was more festive than funereal— the perfect romantic ending to a romanticized life.

It was appropriate for Ross to be memorialized at the studio, for the studio had always been the favored child at WCI, its employees those on whom Ross lavished attention most copiously. It was home to the stars, whose egos he seemed never to tire of caressing. And although he was, quintessentially, a man of commerce, he liked to think of himself more as a nurturer of talent. Here in Hollywood, too, Ross did not need to feel insecure about his being relatively unschooled, and a non-reader, as he did in some circles in New York; in this street-smart culture, he was on even ground. What he *was* knowledgeable about, moreover, was old movies. He could match wits with anyone on stars and even supporting players in movies of the thirties, forties, and fifties (he was positively gleeful when he was able to stump his daughter Toni's film professor at Wesleyan University, Jeanine Basinger—"He had a fan's enthusiasm but a scholar's knowledge," she said). And, finally, this was a world of people whose metier was the creation of illusion. They made movies; Ross created his persona; the two were not altogether different. For some of them, at least, Ross exemplified a *lived* art.

Before the event began, several hundred guests mingled in a vast space, lined with blown-up photographs of Ross, at least three stories high. There were several of him and Courtney; others with Semel, with Daly, with his children, with Jerry Levin and Carmen Ferragano. Among the milling guests were most of Hollywood's elite, including even some who had not been part of Ross's circle of fans. Spielberg was absent; he was in Poland shooting *Schindler's List,* which he planned to dedicate to Ross. (Interestingly enough, Oskar Schindler, an intensely manipulative, luxury-loving German businessman who applied his wiles, ultimately, to saving Jews from the Nazis, and was ennobled by these acts of salvation, reminded Spielberg very much of Ross. He even had the actor who was to play Schindler study home movies of Ross.) In this setting, afterwards, guests would be offered a spread featuring Ross's favorite foods—caviar, Nathan's hot dogs, Häagen Dazs vanilla ice cream with hot fudge sauce, and, of course, Entenmann's crumb cake.

The evening's roster was rich with stars, but it also included, in addition to Daly and Semel, other executives who had worked with Ross for many years, such as Frank Wells, now president of Disney, and Mo Ostin —each of whom had "Steve Ross stories" to tell. Ostin, who generally avoids making speeches at all cost, agreed on this occasion. He recalled that he and his wife, celebrating their thirtieth anniversary in Paris, were having dinner at a restaurant and Ross was sitting with a group at another table. Suddenly, a thirty-piece string orchestra appeared and began playing "Our Love Is Here to Stay." "We couldn't believe it—that was Evelyn's and my favorite song when we were dating! And then we looked over at Steve Ross and saw that mischievous twinkle . . .'

". . . He *loved* people," Ostin concluded. "He wasn't the typical corporate head who only thought about the bottom line. He treated his executives like artists. . . ."

Quincy Jones, who referred to Ross as "Aces," for his card-counting talents, told the assembled crowd that he and his friend were sometimes on different wavelengths. He recalled one occasion a number of years ago when Ross, who had been deep in thought, suddenly emerged from his reverie and said, " 'Q, we've got to court the Baby Bells!'

"Well, you *know* I didn't know what he was talking about—I thought he meant those little cheeses—but if he said we had to court the cheese, hey, I was ready. His gig," Jones continued, "was the future."

Whoopi Goldberg, who said she had never got to know Ross that well, recalled that she first met him when they were filming *The Color Purple,* which Spielberg was directing and Jones producing, and Ross came to visit them on the set. "He was this sexy, good-looking guy, we were talking about movies, he knew all these things—so, after a while, I sashayed over to Q and said, 'Who *is* that guy?' And Q said, 'He owns Warner Bros.' I said, 'Oh!' I felt, you know, like I'd had a thought about a priest."

She recalled, too, that before she found out who Ross was, he had been counselling her—in what many in this crowd knew, first hand, was his trademark fashion. "He was saying, 'You have to *ask* for things.' "

"I said, 'Uh huh.' "

" 'You have to *ask* for the plane.' "

"I said, 'Uh huh, who do I ask?"

" 'Ask Q, ask Steven.' "

"I just knew him as a nice cat," she concluded, "who remembered me and would ask how I was and cared."

Warren Beatty had not known Ross that well either, but he had his own story to tell about the first time they met. It was in the mid-seventies, and he had had dinner with Ross in New York.

"After dinner we kept talking, we went for a walk around the East Side. It was midnight—then 1, 2, 3 A.M. We're talking, and walking. At 3:30 we sat on a park bench at Fifth Avenue and 76th Street. We talked about the demise of the liberal wing of the Democratic party—about the sadness of ex-athletes, how tough it was when you knew you weren't going to play football anymore—who we found attractive; who smart; who not smart—about the sexual revolution, the excitement of it, the dangers of it. We got around to his concern that I had not been married and he was afraid I was going to lose out on one of the great things in life. I remember walking back to the Carlyle with the sun coming up and thinking, 'Hey, it's the seventies! Maybe I could marry him!'

". . . He was a guy who inspired belief very quickly," Beatty continued. "That talent to inspire belief you can't overstate in a field as fragile as making movies. Steve made you feel you were part of his company even if you were making pictures at Disney, or Columbia, or wherever you might be."

Beatty recalled one of the studio's founders, Jack Warner, who had ruled it with an iron hand for many years. They had had a heated disagreement during the filming of *Bonnie and Clyde,* which culminated in Warner's telling him, " 'Look, kid, you're going to do the titles my way. Go outside and take a look at the water tower. Is that my name on the water tower or is it your name?'

"I started to go back to my office and I got a good look at the water tower—and I went running back. 'Jack! Jack! It's got my initials on it!'

"He said, 'You'll do it my way.'

"I couldn't help thinking how opposite Steve was," Beatty declared. He also said that Ross had called him when he heard that Beatty and Annette Bening were thinking of doing a remake of *An Affair to Remember,* and had said, " 'Promise me you won't make it with anybody but me.' " Beatty said he had thought for a few seconds, and assented. He is currently making the movie, at Warner Bros. "We'll think about him every day, making that picture," he concluded.

Streisand, for her part, announced that she was dedicating her next album to Ross. Declaring that "Steve loved making people happy," she went on to tell the following story. "I lost a piece of sculpture, I bid too low at auction. I came back to the country almost a year later, after shooting *Yentl*—I got off the plane, and I needed to see some art. I went to an art gallery, and there, on Madison Avenue, was the same piece— three times more expensive. Being a nice Jewish girl, I couldn't buy it.

"Months after that, Courtney and Steve gave a dinner party. And at the top of the stairs was *this* piece of sculpture! And I thought how glad I was that people I love had it. I told Steve the story, about losing it at auction. He said, 'Look at the card behind it.' It was a gift for me, for finishing *Yentl.* How he found it, how he traced it!"

However, she concluded, perhaps seeking to correct an impression to the contrary, "no gifts he gave could compare to his love and friendship."

The night before the memorial, when Clint Eastwood had accepted an Academy Award (his first) for Best Director for *Unforgiven,* he had dedicated it to Steve Ross. Now, he said that Ross had seen *Unforgiven* before he died, and had predicted that it would win an Academy Award. "Steve Ross passed away. Interest in the film in the press picked up. Maybe it's just irony—but if Steve Ross was indeed the spirit, then there was no way we would have lost last night."

All in all, in this production that glided so gracefully over the surface of Ross's life, there weren't many moments that revealed more than they were meant to. Ross, of course, had not "owned" Warner Bros., as Goldberg had put it—though the error was certainly understandable, since he had so much *acted* as if he did, spending shareholders' money as if it were his. And it was only appropriate for this impresario of largesse that planes and gifts should have emerged as one of the themes of the evening, but there was no examination of what a brilliant bartering ("peas for watermelons") it had been. The Streisand story did not exactly make sense—one had to ask how Ross knew that she had missed buying this piece of sculpture—until a friend of hers explained, later, that Streisand had lamented to Ross her having missed out on the chance to buy it. He, as one might have predicted, made it right.

But the fissures in the facade were few. And by the end of the event, when Terry Semel, who had been master of ceremonies, turned toward Ross's giant visage and declared, "You are still with us, you'll always be with us, and you were truly one of a kind," Ross's presence did seem almost palpable.

The tribute had been a smashing success. And the proof of its success was that it achieved, fleetingly, what Ross achieved when he was at his best: he made you want to believe. In order to really work his magic, he always had to be physically present and one-on-one; he was never quite as powerful in a small group, less powerful still in a large one, and robbed of his power altogether when he was reduced to print in deposition transcripts; reading those, the trace of the hustler rises unmistakably from the page.

He was, however, at his best a lot. Those people and things he set out to win, he generally did; as Ahmet Ertegun commented, "Steve Ross to me was the ultimate winner—that is, a person who really could not envision losing." It was as though he created a magnetic field: within its range were, mainly, his Warner family and those associated with it, who were powerfully drawn to him, many of whom loved him; and outside, his peers in the business community and in Hollywood, who generally regarded him with wariness, if not distrust.

This night, faced with his image and listening to his admirers invoke him, one could feel, again, the pull of that inexorable charm. The tension was between knowing and yet, for a moment, being tempted to forget so as to believe; almost, an *un*willing suspension of disbelief. For in order to believe, as Ross's more fervent adherents did, one would have to forget friends betrayed, an indictment eluded, company assets squandered, shareholders misled, dealmakers duped, that whole long history of chicanery that filled the *other* side of the ledger—across from the entries of his extraordinary talents, achievements, and (whatever his motivation) mountain of good deeds.

It was a formidably diverse and even cognitively dissonant whole to encompass; small wonder that Ross, who had always had to fuse the two, existed in such a state of perpetual unease. That the fusion worked so well for so long—even retaining a vestigial force after his death—probably says as much about us, his audience, as it does about Ross. For, just as he appeared to the Time dealmakers as the promise of rain after a long drought, causing them in their eagerness to forgo any real inquiry into his past, so innumerable others, too, chose to look away from what was troubling in order to relish the charge (as well as the favors) of his proximity. Some were drawn, in a straightforward way, by his talents; but it was the whole package, replete with self-mythicization, that had the widest popular appeal, striking a responsive, sentimental chord in so many, much as a highly romantic novel or movie might. As his son had said, he thought he could be Jimmy Stewart and John Wayne and Cary Grant, to people. To be with Ross (but only if you were a believer) was to escape the parameters of everyday life, which for him had always spelled ennui, and to enter *his* sphere—where experience (heavily orchestrated) was heightened, and fantasies routinely (at his bidding) came true.

In reality, of course, Ross was no heroic figure. More than anything else, he was a person who refused to acknowledge limits; it was this quality, in large part, that made him at once so magnetic and so flawed. Believing nothing was impossible (and being, in this sense, a throwback to an earlier, more adventurous time), he was daring and bold, and he saw with fresh eyes. But, feeling exempt from legal, ethical, and moral standards, he abrogated them at will. To violate all these standards, and never be publicly caught at it—more, to be perceived by thousands as the very exemplar of some of those standards—now *that,* for someone like Ross, was winning.

Even viewing him in this unforgiving light, however, did not rob him of his gifts—among which was a rare power to inspire and to lead. Here in Los Angeles, there was no mistaking that the company that *was* Ross was now bereft, and had no true leader. Earlier, Jerry Levin had mounted the stage and made some brief remarks; he had begun by saying, "Whoopi, just call Guy Salvadore—no problem with the planes!" and in closing, he had waved his hand in the direction of Ross's image, said, "Steve, here's looking at you, kid," and ambled off.

The void had never seemed so large. But one had to wonder, once again—wasn't that as planned?

# A Note on Sources

My reporting for this book began shortly after I finished my *New Yorker* piece on the Time-Warner merger, which appeared in January 1990. Steve Ross, whom I had interviewed for that piece, also agreed to cooperate with the book; he offered me lists of people whom I might interview, and generally urged them and others to do so if they wished. Consequently, I had access not only to Ross but to family members and a couple hundred of his friends and associates. When Ross became ill in the late fall of 1991, however, my interviews with him ended; and since we had been moving chronologically (and slowly), I never had a chance to discuss with him the darker episodes in his life, such as Westchester Premier Theatre and Atari.

Among those who provided me with vital interviews (for my *New Yorker* pieces and/or the book) were Robert Daly, Emanuel Gerard, David Horowitz, Connie Landis, Gerald Levin, Arthur Liman, Carol Maslow, Nicholas Nicholas, Cy O'Neil, Felix Rohatyn, Doris Rosenthal, Edward Rosenthal, Mark Ross, Toni Ross, Ellen Sarnoff, Terry Semel, Rafael de la Sierra, Roger Smith, and Steven Spielberg.

Among those who were helpful in providing context for the more central episodes in Ross's history were Joe Albritton, Ted Ashley, Jason Berman, Edward Bleier, Samuel Butler, John Calley, Alan Cohen, Gordon

Crawford, Alberto Cribiore, Michael Dann, Lou (Rosen) Davidson, Marvin Davis, Howard Dornbusch, Clint Eastwood, Allan Ecker, Ahmet Ertegun, Martin Fischer, George Freedman, Robert Friedman, Michael Fuchs, David Geffen, George Gould, Alan (Ace) Greenberg, Kitty Hart, Gus Hauser, John Heckler, Andrew Heiskell, Dustin Hoffman, Jac Holzman, Fred Isquith, Quincy Jones, Howard Kaminsky, Ray Kassar, Caesar Kimmel, Daniel Krasner, Arthur Krim, Jack Lang, Joe Lehman, Pierre Lescure, Sandy Lindenbaum, Dan Lufkin, Louis Marx, Michael Moone, Charles (Skip) Paul, Martin Payson, Ralph Peterson, Robert Pittman, Sandy Reisenbach, Judd Richheimer, Peter Rosenthal, John Rosenwald, Andre Rousselet, Mickey Rudin, Robert Ruttenberg, Norman Samnick, Albert Sarnoff, William Sarnoff, Harvey Schein, Allie Sherman, Abraham Silverstein, Joe Smith, Stanley Sporkin, Alfred Stern, Ray Troubh, William vanden Heuvel, Melvin Weiss, Frank Wells, Clay Whitehead, David Wolper, Vera Wyatt, and many others.

There were a number of people whom I have not listed because they spoke to me on the condition of confidentiality; however, their accounts have been supported by my interviews with others, or by documents.

While most of the information in this book was derived from interviews with roughly 250 people, whom I interviewed in person, and, in many instances, repeatedly over a period of a couple of years, I did gather some information from other sources. Certain documents were provided to me on the basis that I not reveal that I saw them—but, with those exceptions, the sources I drew on are the following.

In CHAPTERS ONE and TWO, which describe Ross's early years; FBI files, obtained through Freedom of Information Act requests; certificates of incorporation from the New Jersey Secretary of State; *Beat the Dealer* by Edward Thorp; *Gangster #2* by Mark Stuart; the *Newark Evening News; Life* magazine; Kinney's SEC filings, including prospectuses, annual reports, 10Ks, and proxies; *BusinessWeek.* CHAPTER THREE, Ross's rapid rise: SEC filings by Kinney and its successor companies; the *Wall Street Journal; Forbes; New York* magazine; *Indecent Exposure* by David McClintick; "Report to the President" by the Office of Telecommunications Policy; the *New York Times;* Ross's 1981 deposition in the litigation of shareholders' suits. CHAPTER FOUR, Westchester Premier Theatre: depositions of WCI employees—including Ross—taken in the course of the SEC investigation; trial transcripts and exhibits from *U.S.* v. *Weisman, et al ;* trial transcripts and exhibits from *U.S.* v. *Weiss; Vengeance Is Mine* by Jimmy Fratianno and Michael Zuckerman; *The American Lawyer* magazine; *The*

*Teamsters* by Steven Brill. CHAPTER FIVE, Atari: complaints and depositions —including Ross's—taken in the course of the WCI shareholder litigation; SEC filings by WCI; *BusinessWeek, Fortune,* the *Los Angeles Times, West; In Search of Excess* by Graef Crystal. CHAPTER SIX, the aftermath of Atari and Ross's struggle with Siegel: the *Wall Street Journal, New York* magazine, the *Los Angeles Times, Institutional Investor;* deposition of Rupert Murdoch in *News International* v. *Warner Communications, et al.* CHAPTER SEVEN, Kinney update: SEC filings by National Kinney; exhibits in *U.S.A.* v. *International Brotherhood of Teamsters, et al.,* and, specifically, *Investigations Officer* v. *Cirino Salerno* and *Investigations Officer* v. *William Cutolo* (including affidavits and statements by Vincent Cafaro); Cafaro's testimony before the Senate Permanent Subcommittee on Investigations, April 11, 1988; declarations by FBI agent R. Lindley Devecchio. CHAPTER EIGHT, the Time-Warner merger: documents from *Paramount Communications* v. *Time Inc. and Warner Communications Inc.; New York Observer* CHAPTER NINE, the firing of Nick Nicholas: the *New York Times;* documents filed with the FDIC and the New York State Banking Department. CHAPTER TEN: the *Wall Street Journal,* the *New York Times.*

# Acknowledgments

Trying to reflect accurately and fairly the life of someone as complex, shuttered, and compartmentalized (in that so many people knew him in one or another aspect of his life, but no one in the entirety) as Steve Ross was a formidable task. I do not claim to have completely achieved it; he remains somewhat enigmatic, and some—probably many—of his secrets remain undisturbed. But what I was able to accomplish would have been impossible had scores of people—his family, business associates, and friends—not been so generous in sharing their recollections, frank insights, and time with me. I am profoundly grateful to those named in my Note on Sources, and to those others who are unnamed. I know that quite a few of these people, particularly after his death, spoke to me out of their devotion to him; they wanted to do all they could to make sure that—whatever else I found—they had not failed to convey to me an understanding of his talents and his positive characteristics (what one old friend would often refer to as "the *good* Steve Ross"). I hope that they are not disappointed, for I have tried hard, on the positive side of the ledger, to give Ross his due.

I want to thank my editor, Alice Mayhew, for her continuing friendship, support, and judgment; she helped guide me through the progress of this book and treated the manuscript with superb, meticulous care. This is our second book together, and I am, as ever, in her debt. Elizabeth Stein, Alice Mayhew's assistant, not only shepherded this manuscript through with skill and diligence, but also thought of the long-sought title that, finally, pleased us all. Also at Simon & Schuster, I am grateful to Jennifer Weidman, whose acumen was invaluable. David Boies of Cravath, Swaine and Moore was there when I needed him, with the sagacity for which he is famous. Amanda Urban, my agent at International Creative Management, extended herself far beyond a business role, reading my pages as fast as I could turn them out and offering me sterling advice.

I also want to thank Robert Gottlieb, the former editor of *The New Yorker,* who insisted—despite my grousing that I didn't like writing stories about mergers—that the Time-Warner merger was too important to ignore. His instincts, as usual, were right. That merger piece and a later piece I wrote about Time Warner for *The New Yorker* in the summer of 1992 both benefitted in the editing process from his impeccable instincts —as well as those of my editors, John Bennet and Pat Crow (both of whom have saved me from myself on more than one occasion). Tina Brown, when she became editor of *The New Yorker,* was extremely generous in allowing me to take my leave to finish writing this book. I am grateful to her for that, and also for her enthusiastic, strong support of the final excerpt of this book, which appeared in *The New Yorker* in September 1993.

I want to thank, too, others at *The New Yorker* whose efforts went into the publication of sections of this book in the magazine: Harold Ambler, Ty Baldwin, Martin Baron, Virginia Cannon, Joe Cooper, Hal Espen, Eleanor Gould, Dan Henderson, Louisa Kamps, Katherine Kinast, Matthew Lane, Kris Maher, Pamela McCarthy, Terry McGarry, Elizabeth Pearson-Griffiths, Maurie Perl, Joselyn Simpson, Rob Spellman, and Eden Steinberg.

My researchers, Kerry Dolan and, later, Molly Moltedo, were excellent. I want to thank Hannah Hall, FOIA/Privacy Act Branch Chief at the SEC, and Joyce Morgison in the FBI FOIA/Privacy Office. I want to thank Ann Mintz for allowing me to use the *Forbes* library.

Last and most important, I am grateful beyond description to my son for his unending forbearance, as well as his quick humor, sensitivity, and all-around generosity of spirit, which brighten my life and also make me so proud; and to my mother—my wonderful, irrepressible, irreplaceable mother—to whom this book is dedicated. She has always been my most avid supporter, but in reading the manuscript pages of this book (which she often did before anyone else), she became a fan of Steve Ross's, too; I think it's fair to say that in some respects, Ross—or, at least, "the *good* Steve Ross"—was her kind of guy.

# Index

# PICTURE CREDITS

# FOR THE BEST IN PAPERBACKS, LOOK FOR THE 🐧

In every corner of the world, on every subject under the sun, Penguin represents quality and variety—the very best in publishing today.

For complete information about books available from Penguin—including Pelicans, Puffins, Peregrines, and Penguin Classics—and how to order them, write to us at the appropriate address below. Please note that for copyright reasons the selection of books varies from country to country.

**In the United Kingdom:** For a complete list of books available from Penguin in the U K , please write to *Dept E.P., Penguin Books Ltd, Harmondsworth, Middlesex, UB7 0DA*

**In the United States:** For a complete list of books available from Penguin in the U.S., please write to *Consumer Sales, Penguin USA, P.O. Box 999— Dept. 17109, Bergenfield, New Jersey 07621-0120* VISA and MasterCard holders call 1-800-253-6476 to order all Penguin titles.

**In Canada:** For a complete list of books available from Penguin in Canada, please write to *Penguin Books Canada Ltd, 10 Alcorn Avenue, Suite 300, Toronto, Ontario, Canada M4V 3B2.*

**In Australia:** For a complete list of books available from Penguin in Australia, please write to the *Marketing Department, Penguin Books Ltd, P O Box 257, Ringwood, Victoria 3134*

**In New Zealand:** For a complete list of books available from Penguin in New Zealand, please write to the *Marketing Department, Penguin Books (NZ) Ltd, Private Bag, Takapuna, Auckland 9*

**In India:** For a complete list of books available from Penguin, please write to *Penguin Overseas Ltd, 706 Eros Apartments, 56 Nehru Place, New Delhi, 110019*

**In Holland:** For a complete list of books available from Penguin in Holland, please write to *Penguin Books Nederland B.V , Postbus 195, NL-1380AD Weesp, Netherlands*

**In Germany:** For a complete list of books available from Penguin, please write to *Penguin Books Ltd, Friedrichstrasse 10-12, D-6000 Frankfurt Main 1, Federal Republic of Germany*

**In Spain:** For a complete list of books available from Penguin in Spain, please write to *Longman, Penguin España, Calle San Nicolas 15, E-28013 Madrid, Spain*

**In Japan:** For a complete list of books available from Penguin in Japan, please write to *Longman Penguin Japan Co Ltd, Yamaguchi Building, 2-12-9 Kanda Jimbocho, Chiyoda-Ku, Tokyo 101, Japan*